Public
Policy

CHATHAM HOUSE SERIES ON CHANGE IN AMERICAN POLITICS

edited by Aaron Wildavsky
University of California, Berkeley

Public Policy

Issues, Analysis, and Ideology

Edited by
ELLEN FRANKEL PAUL
Bowling Green State University
and
PHILIP A. RUSSO, JR.
Miami University, Oxford

CHATHAM HOUSE PUBLISHERS, INC.
Chatham, New Jersey

PUBLIC POLICY
Issues, Analysis, and Ideology

CHATHAM HOUSE PUBLISHERS, INC.
Post Office Box One
Chatham, New Jersey 07928

Publisher: Edward Artinian
Design: Pencils Portfolio, Inc.
Composition: Chatham Composer
Printing and Binding: Hamilton Printing Company

LIBRARY OF CONGRESS CATALOGING IN PUBLICATION DATA

Main entry under title:
Public Policy.

    (Chatham House series on change in American
politics)
    1. Policy sciences.   2. Public policy
(Law)--United States.   I. Paul, Ellen Frankel.
II. Russo, Philip A., 1951-   III. Series.
H97.P8   361'.973   81-10027
ISBN 0-934540-04-7   AACR2

MANUFACTURED IN THE UNITED STATES OF AMERICA

10 9 8 7 6 5 4 3 2 1

*This book is dedicated
to Mary and Philip Russo
and
to the memory of Louis Frankel*

Contents

1. Ellen Frankel Paul and Philip A. Russo, Jr.
PUBLIC POLICY AND VALUES   1

Part One: Energy and the Environment: The Big Tradeoff   11
  2. John H. Gibbons and William U. Chandler
A NATIONAL ENERGY CONSERVATION POLICY   13
  3. John V. Krutilla and R. Talbot Page
TOWARD A RESPONSIBLE ENERGY POLICY   21
  4. Samuel McCracken
THE WAR AGAINST THE ATOM   41
  5. Bruce L. Welch
THE REALITY OF SOLAR POWER   71

Part Two: Welfare Policy: Reforming the Mess   79
  6. John E. Tropman
AMERICAN WELFARE STRATEGIES:
THREE PROGRAMS UNDER THE SOCIAL SECURITY ACT   81
  7. Mark D. Worthington and Laurence E. Lynn, Jr.
INCREMENTAL WELFARE REFORM:
A STRATEGY WHOSE TIME HAS PASSED   98
  8. Nathan Glazer
REFORM WORK, NOT WELFARE   117
  9. Murray N. Rothbard
WELFARE AND THE WELFARE STATE   125

Part Three: In Search of a National Health Policy   141
  10. Theodore R. Marmor
THE POLITICS OF NATIONAL HEALTH INSURANCE:
ANALYSIS AND PRESCRIPTION   143
  11. Lawrence M. Mead
HEALTH POLICY: THE NEED FOR GOVERNANCE   165
  12. John Ehrenreich
TOWARD A HEALING SOCIETY   186

Part Four: Regulatory Policy: The Visible Hand   199
    13. Peter H. Schuck
PUBLIC INTEREST GROUPS AND THE POLICY PROCESS   201
    14. William Lilley III and James C. Miller III
THE NEW "SOCIAL REGULATION"   214
    15. Steven Kelman
REGULATION THAT WORKS   226
    16. Tibor R. Machan
DEREGULATION IS A MORAL ISSUE   234

Part Five: Equality and Social Justice: Affirmative Action   243
    17. Nathan Glazer
WHY *Bakke* WON'T END REVERSE DISCRIMINATION   245
    18. Ernest van den Haag
REVERSE DISCRIMINATION: A BRIEF AGAINST IT   256
    19. Thomas Sowell
ARE QUOTAS GOOD FOR BLACKS?   264
    20. Hardy Jones
FAIRNESS, MERITOCRACY, AND REVERSE DISCRIMINATION   274

Part Six: Politics of Planning   289
    21. Abba P. Lerner
STAGFLATION—ITS CAUSE AND CURE   291
    22. Initiative Committee for National Economic Planning
FOR A NATIONAL ECONOMIC PLANNING SYSTEM   299
    23. F. A. Hayek
THE NEW CONFUSION ABOUT "PLANNING"   304

About the Contributors   317

Acknowledgments

We wish to acknowledge the assistance of several colleagues at Miami University in preparing this volume. Dan Jacobs provided invaluable guidance into the intricacies of organizing and publishing an edited volume. Herb Waltzer, Paul Rejai, and Alan Engel offered their support and counsel. Reo Christenson read portions of the manuscript and made many useful recommendations on the introduction. Dotti Pierson, Jean West, Ken Nuger, and Bill Sommer contributed their typing and research skills to this effort. And, of course, Joanne and Jeffrey sustained us throughout.

We would also like to thank the following authors, periodicals, and publishers for their kind permission to reprint copyright materials:

John H. Gibbons and William U. Chandler, "A National Energy Conservation Policy," *Current History* 75, no. 438 (July/August 1978): 13-15 and 34.

John V. Krutilla and R. Talbot Page, "Toward a Responsible Energy Policy." Copyright © 1975 by The Regents of the University of California. Reprinted from *Policy Analysis* 1, no. 1 (Winter 1975): 77-100, by permission of The Regents.

Samuel McCracken, "The War Against the Atom." Reprinted from *Commentary*, September 1977, by permission; all rights reserved.

Bruce L. Welch, "The Reality of Solar Power," *The Nation* 226, no. 2 (January 1978): 44-48. Copyright 1978 The Nation Associates.

John E. Tropman, "American Welfare Strategies: Three Programs Under the Social Security Act," *Policy Sciences* 8 (1977): 33-47. Reprinted by permission of the author and Elsevier Scientific Publishing Company.

Mark D. Worthington and Laurence E. Lynn, Jr., "Incremental Welfare Reform: A Strategy Whose Time Has Passed," *Public Policy* 24, no. 1 (Winter 1977): 49-52 and 63-80. Copyright © 1977 by John Wiley & Sons, Inc.

Nathan Glazer, "Reform Work, Not Welfare." Reprinted with permission of the author from *The Public Interest*, no. 40 (Summer 1975): 3-10. Copyright © 1975 by National Affairs, Inc.

Murray N. Rothbard, "Welfare and the Welfare State," is reprinted with permission of Macmillan Publishing Co., Inc. from *For A New Liberty*, revised edition by Murray N. Rothbard. Copyright © 1973, 1978 by Murray N. Rothbard.

Abba P. Lerner, "Stagflation—Its Cause and Cure" is extracted from "From Pre-Keynes to Post-Keynes" which appeared in *Social Research* 4, no. 3 (Autumn 1977) and is reprinted by permission of the Graduate Faculty, The New School for Social Research, New York.

Initiative Committee for National Economic Planning, "For a National Economic Planning System," *Social Policy* 5, no. 6 (March/April 1975): 17-19. Reprinted by permission.

F.A. Hayek, "The New Confusion About 'Planning,' " *The Morgan Guaranty Survey,* January 1976.

Public Policy

Ellen Frankel Paul and
Philip A. Russo, Jr.

1. PUBLIC POLICY AND VALUES

In theory, public policy analysts propose solutions to identifiable social problems. By examining the relationships among policy goals, policy strategies, and policy outcomes, the policy analyst attempts to advise political decision makers on the allocation of societal resources, or Who gets What, When, Where, and How. The term "policy analyst" immediately conjures up images of a rather bland, faceless technician equipped with all the "right" tools of analysis, ranging from elaborate economic models to sophisticated decision-making techniques. We assume that the policy analyst is an impartial, objective adviser-technician who merely lays out alternative policy strategies to achieve specific policy objectives. Many analysts make the same assumption. This picture, although widely accepted, is somewhat distorted.

Is the analysis of public policy a neutral, objective enterprise? If so, one would suppose that every analyst, given the same data, would reach the same conclusion. But even if that were possible, what about the selection of ends to be sought? Is that a value-free choice? For example, is it self-evident to everyone that the public good demands greater material equality? Or that people will be made happier by pursuing the good life of pure contemplation? Or that the social good necessitates the supremacy of the German master race? Yet, politicians and philosophers have argued for these and other alternatives as ends to be sought by public policies. Surely, the selection of ends embodies an evaluative process, and there is no way to neutrally quantify such choices. The value-loaded context of public policy analysis is inevitable because it focuses upon something (policy) that is, by definition, purposive or value-loaded. It seems, then, that an analyst's values can influence the objective he seeks, as well as the choice of factors to be weighed in realizing that goal.

Nevertheless, values are not supposed to be a part of policy analysis. The analyst has a hard enough time mastering all the high-powered techniques of analysis without having to worry about values.[1] Values don't belong in policy analysis, anyway! Although some policy analysts would argue that values *do* belong in policy analysis, many more would admit only grudgingly that values play a part in analysis.

Can an analyst escape from the prison of his values? Values are the basis for judgments not only about political reality but also about the way political reality *ought* to be. Values shape the policy analyst's perception of problems to be solved, as well as his perception of the best strategies to pursue in the attempt to solve those problems. As one scholar observes:

> Values refer to ends or objectives, and to the legitimate means that inform public intervention. Values comprise the normative propositions that affirm what our social policy ought to be, and the normative and moral assumptions that underlie present practices.[2]

When these value judgments are integrated into an explanation of political life that specifies the relationships among policy goals, policy strategies, and policy outcomes, we can observe the rudiments of an ideology. An ideology is

> a value or belief system that is accepted as fact or truth by some group. It is composed of sets of attitudes toward the various institutions and processes of society. It provides the believer with a picture of the world both as it is and as it should be, and, in so doing, it organizes the tremendous complexity of the world into something fairly simple and understandable.[3]

Think about it, do policy analysts have an ideology?[4]

The following example will help illuminate this ideological, or value-laden, component of policy analysis. In California in recent years there was much controversy about protecting the natural beauty of the coastal areas. Environmentalists wanted to preserve the scenic vistas along Highway #1 from industrial development and new private home construction. Through "land use" legislation, this objective was accomplished.

How might three policy analysts evaluate this public policy? Clearly, an analyst sympathetic to the protection of natural beauty would approve of the end sought. When he evaluated the various costs and benefits of the legislation, he would rank very highly such factors as the enjoyment of travelers on the unspoiled highway and the advantage to future generations of preserving such terrain. The costs would be minimized in his estimation. Such factors as the loss of revenue to potential developers or the inability of present property owners to build on or to sell their land would be considered of less consequence than the social benefits to be received. Naturally he would endorse the policy.

Our second analyst may wish to employ the same cost-benefit tool. But suppose he greatly values industrialism and the growth of industries in California. In arriving at his cost-benefit analysis, he may downgrade the advantages of the enjoyment of travelers on the highway or the possible aesthetic value to generations yet unborn. The costs of such a policy may seem overwhelming to him. New shopping centers, factories, and power plants will not be constructed in the affected area; consequently, thousands of new jobs will not be created, and the products they would have manufactured may be irretrievably lost. His conclusion will be that the costs of such a "land use" policy clearly outweigh the benefits. The policy should be abandoned.

The third analyst presents an even thornier problem. His contention is that this "land use" policy cannot legitimately be evaluated on a cost-benefit criterion. Why? Because, he argues, it is an act of injustice to restrict the use of a person's property without his consent, and it is even more unjust to do so without offering any compensation. What our third analyst claims is that the desirability, or lack of it, of the end to be achieved — preserving the pristine beauty of the California coastline — is irrelevant. That is, he does not care about the disputed objectives employed by the first two analysts. For him, it is entirely a question of property rights. Justice alone determines his decision. Of course, to make matters even less objective or value-free, it is perfectly conceivable that other analysts, employing different theories of justice, may reach entirely different conclusions.

Where does this leave us? Is there no objective way to analyze public policy proposals? While it is undeniably true that the values held by any policy analyst will inevitably intrude upon his policy proposals, this should not be taken as a cause for despair. Even if we cannot demonstrate to the satisfaction of all people that some ultimate values are "right" and therefore ought to be pursued, perhaps we are not left in an amoral morass in which values arise only as the arbitrary whims of individuals. Such a relativistic or subjective attitude toward values leaves us in an untenable moral position when confronted with people who promulgate as ends to be sought values that most of us would acknowledge as morally reprehensible. Hitler in Germany and Pol Pot in Cambodia both sought to achieve their vision of the good society, the *end* of their policy, by the *means* of mass genocide. Confronted with these horrors, must we simply throw up our hands and concede that, philosophically, nothing can be declared absolutely "wrong" when it comes to the values individuals hold? Must we resort to nothing stronger than our whims in condemning such acts as atrocities?

Perhaps, to most of you, this does not seem to present any insurmountable problem. Genocide is wrong, and life-preserving values are right. But do you know this to be true by intuition, by a moral sense within you, or by deductive demonstration? Probing this question a bit deeper might lead you to speculate along the same lines as eighteenth-century Scottish philosopher David Hume, whose writings proved devastating to the last of these alternatives: the attempt to deduce from the facts of reality that some moral values are right and ought to be pursued, whereas other moral values are reprehensible and ought to be avoided. Hume argued that from the facts of reality, nothing can be concluded about what ends people ought to pursue. This contention has come to be known as the fact-value dichotomy, or the is-ought problem. For example, from the fact (the *is*) that the average woman is inferior to the average man in physical strength, does it follow that women either ought or ought not be excluded by law from becoming stevedores, truck drivers, and construction workers, or from pursuing other occupations that require physical prowess? Hume claims that *neither* conclusion can be reached by a logical deduction from what is. From the factual *is* of what exists in the world around us, no moral *ought* can be generated by the logical power of reason. This critique has, until very recently, been taken by philosophers as the definitive attack on all attempts to prove the validity of any specific values, or of any one moral system over another.

A few contemporary philosophers are currently working on theories that, if they succeed, will surmount this two-hundred-year-old philosophical dilemma. At this point, however, their work remains so highly speculative that it would afford little assistance to the policy analyst.

Barring a philosophical breakthrough that would surmount Hume's dichotomy, how should the policy analyst proceed? Perhaps the most that can be required of the analyst is an effort to make explicit the ends he desires to be achieved by his policy proposals. Let us emphasize, however, that this admonition to come "up front" with values definitely does not resolve the problem of relativism or subjectivism in the selection of values by individuals. It does not, in other words, allow us to condemn definitively Hitler's desire for a pure Aryan race as an end to be pursued by the means of eradicating supposedly inferior races. What it does allow us to do is (1) to pass personal judgments on the desirability of the ends a particular policy analyst advocates, and (2) to evaluate how effective or efficient the means proposed is to attain the policy objective.

Minimum-wage laws provide an excellent example of the need for specifying values on the part of policy proponents. If the advocates of minimum-wage laws were to come "up front" with their values, they might formulate their objectives in the following manner: "The value we wish to pursue by the advocacy of minimum-wage legislation is the increased monetary reward of those laborers at the bottom end of the economic scale. And we wish to improve their standard of living while promoting the additional end of full employment within the economy." Now that these objectives have been made explicit, we can move on to the task of evaluation. Among economists who have studied the effects of minimum-wage legislation as it has operated over the years, there is virtual unanimity in the conclusion that when Congress acts to increase the minimum wage, unemployment rises among precisely those groups that the advocates of such legislation intended to benefit, namely, the poor; uneducated, unskilled youths; and minority-group members. Thus, rather than furthering the stated objectives of increased well-being for the disadvantaged and full employment, the proposed solution—minimum-wage legislation—actually produces the opposite consequences.

In addition to this request for explicitness on the part of policy analysts, we would like to propose a taxonomy for organizing values. As indicated earlier, some values constitute the ultimate objectives a policy analyst seeks to further. These values we shall call *object values*. Other values serve as intermediaries to the pursuit of object values, and these shall be termed *instrumental values*. Furthermore, it might prove useful to classify values according to the degree of immediate self-interest that animates a policy analyst's object values. Thus, we might distinguish *egoistic values*, which look to the immediate satisfaction of the analyst's desires or the special interests he seeks to further, from *altruistic values,* which purport to seek the long-range good of society as a whole. But, again, we must emphasize that no resolution has been discovered to the problem of selecting between altruistic or egoistic values.

	Egoistic Value	Altruistic Value
Object Value	Improved medical, educational, and economic opportunities for veterans	Preserving quality of environment for present and future generations
Instrumental Value	Legislation to provide low-interest mortgages, college stipends, etc.	Legislation to control hazardous emissions, to designate protected lands, etc.

FIGURE 1.1. ORGANIZING VALUES

Figure 1.1 presents in matrix form a way of organizing values. The benefits to be derived from the typology include rendering explicit the valuations made by various analysts and laying open their instrumental means to achieving these values to future evaluation on the basis of effectiveness, efficiency, cost/benefit, Pareto optimality, and so forth. As you examine the figure, you should be able to classify the object values and instrumental values of egoistic veterans lobbies and altruistic conservationists.

Veterans lobbies, such as the Veterans of Foreign Wars, seek the egoistic object value of improving the medical, educational, and economic opportunities of their members. The means of achieving these ends are the instrumental values of such policy proposals for veterans benefits as low-interest mortgages, stipends for education, preferred hiring for civil service positions, and improved medical coverage. Once the objectives and means have been made explicit, one can appraise the utility of the means for achieving the stated goal and also evaluate the desirability of the object value.

Similarly, the objectives of a conservationist lobby such as the Sierra Club can be isolated. For environmentalists, the objective of retaining natural terrain in its pristine form for the enjoyment of present and future generations constitutes a supreme value. In order to achieve this objective, they advocate such instrumental values as legislation to regulate emission of hazardous chemicals from industrial plants, and to designate certain wilderness, wetlands, or coastlines as protected areas in which development will be controlled or banned.

What we have presented here must be viewed only as a method of identifying and differentiating the values that policy analysts either explicitly or tacitly advocate. We would urge all analysts to avoid the use of tacit or implicit values and clearly propound the object values they desire to further, so that others might evaluate the effectiveness of the instrumental values (policy proposals) they are offering in pursuit of their objectives.

Before moving on to the topical issues, let us pause for a moment to examine some basic evaluative concepts commonly employed in policy analysis and evident in the chapters of this book.

Rarely does one hear a political scientist or a politician discuss a policy proposal without invoking the hallowed dictum "Adopt my plan because it is in the *public interest.*" What does this mean? Surely the advocate intends to convey the impression that his favorite scheme will be good for society in general. But is society a collection of individuals with separate interests known only to themselves, or is society an interconnected "beehive" with an identifiable interest of its own separable from the individuals who compose it? On the first interpretation, it is not obvious that there is such a thing as the "public interest"; whereas on the second interpretation, such a concept may make sense. Even so, the interpretation of what constitutes the public interest and how one goes about determining it in a particular case is problematical. Do we determine the public interest by democratically counting noses for and against? Do we survey only those people directly affected by a policy proposal? Or do we ask experts to offer their evaluations of what is in the "public interest"?

A further complication arises. Is it the policy analyst's role to take for granted the public's conception of its own interest (presuming, of course, that such could be determined)? Or, rather, is the role of the analyst to help mold a more informed concept of the public interest? About the only thing that can be said concerning the "public interest" is that it is subject to a myriad of divergent interpretations, depending on the particular analyst's conception of society, of the means by which the public interest can be determined, and of the role of the analyst in shaping the public's view of its interest.

Economists have fastened upon the concept of *efficiency* in judging policy prescriptions. What they mean by this criterion is that a proposal must produce the most output for the least cost; that is, monetary expenditures must achieve the maximum output. Have we at last discovered an objective, value-free standard? Consider the following dilemma: A community hospital has been given a $100,000 bequest. They have two alternative programs presented to them for appropriating this money.

Proposal 1: $50,000 will be spent to provide life-sustaining equipment for a brain-damaged child who requires kidney dialysis, heart-monitoring equipment, and continuous use of an artificial respirator. The remaining $50,000 will be used to pay for kidney transplants for three critically ill patients.

Proposal 2: The entire $100,000 will be used to buy a sophisticated piece of diagnostic equipment called a CAT-scanner, which can give detailed pictures of slices of the brain and other parts of the body. This information is important in the early detection of tumors. It is estimated that 100 people will use this scanner each year for the life of the machine and that 10 of these individuals are statistically likely to have a detectable cancer. Their chances of survival will be greatly increased by this early detection device.

When we come to apply our efficiency criterion—"Most bang for the bucks"—where does this leave us? If proposal 1 is *not* chosen, four people will die; if it *is* chosen, three people will be able to lead normal lives and a child will be kept alive in a vegetative state. If proposal 2 is *not* chosen, one hundred people each year (for perhaps twenty-five years, the hypothetical life span of the equipment) will be denied its advantages and some will die because their cancer went undetected at an early stage; if it *is* chosen, some of the cancer victims will live. On an efficiency standard perhaps we ought to prefer proposal 2 because more people may potentially be saved. On the other hand, proposal 1 offers an immediate payoff in saving the lives of people who would die without the procedures. How are real individuals to be weighed against likely future patients? Even more troublesome is the whole notion of attempting to quantify in monetary terms the value of one human life against another. Ought we to save Dave, the kidney recipient, thus allowing Tom, the future cancer victim to die without diagnosis by the CAT-scanner? Is the value of a human life $100,000 but not $50,000? Should one kidney patient be traded off against ten cancer patients? The concept of efficiency is not as objective as it seemed originally.

Another evaluative tool often employed is the concept of *effectiveness*. Are the means chosen sufficient for the attainment of a stated policy goal? For example, proponents of increased welfare benefits contend that more expenditures for social programs will appreciably improve the standard of living of the poor.

Critics argue that providing more money (the means) will not automatically relieve the condition of poor people (the policy goal). Injections of money may drive fathers to desert their families or provide a disincentive for people to work by making welfare more attractive than a job. Either outcome would nullify the policy goal.

Perhaps the most puzzling evaluative concept is the idea of *justice*. It sounds simple enough, but again, different analysts mean different things by the term. Does justice mean treating similar categories of people the same way? Or does it entail treating dissimilar individuals differently? Aristotle, the classical Greek philosopher, invoked both theories, arguing that the first (or arithmetic) theory of justice was a lower conception than the second (distributive theory). The distributive theory means that those who serve the state the most should receive the greatest benefits. Today the question is still provocative. Is justice simply the recognition of historical property entitlements, as Robert Nozik, the Harvard philosopher, contends? To be just, then, would simply require that everyone "gets his own." Or is justice captured by "fairness," as Nozik's colleague, John Rawls, maintains? For him, justice means equality; and any departures from equality must be justified by their direct advantage to the least-well-off members of society. An analyst's theory of justice may often affect his policy judgments. An excellent example of this phenomenon can be found in the several chapters in part 5 on affirmative action.

Pareto optimality is another frequently employed concept. This idea originated with the Italian economist Vilfredo Pareto. Essentially what it means is that social benefits ought to be distributed up to the point at which future gains to some people will necessitate losses to others. For example: Ten of us discover $100 lying on the grass and decide to give each discoverer $10. Now, if we then decide to take $5 from five people and give it to the other five, Pareto optimality has been violated because some people have lost in order to achieve benefits for others. What Pareto optimality overlooks is whether all people place the same value on particular benefits. Let us say that the five individuals who would lose the money after the second distribution were independently wealthy, whereas the benefactors were starving. Obviously, $5 would mean something very different for the two groups: practically nothing for the wealthy, and perhaps the difference between life and death for the impoverished.

Perhaps the most prevalent evaluative tool employed by policy analysts is *cost/benefit*. This concept is descended from a school of nineteenth-century British political philosophy called Utilitarianism. What Utilitarians such as Jeremy Bentham claimed was that policy proposals ought to be judged by the extent to which happiness would be maximized and pain minimized. His famous aphorism, "the greatest happiness for the greatest number," succinctly captures this idea. Modern cost/benefit analysis attempts to quantify the benefits received by the recipients of a policy proposal against the costs incurred by those who would suffer from the policy. But this methodology raises serious questions. How do you take into account factors not easily quantifiable? For example, if two people would live if they received your kidneys, how do we run a cost/benefit analysis on such a proposal? Also, how do we determine exactly who will count as an affected party to any given policy? All policies have unknown secondary and tertiary effects, and how can these be determined?

Finally, policy analysts are confronted with another veritable "can of worms," *political feasibility.* What use is it to propose the perfect solution to a social problem (assuming that were possible) if the solution does not stand any chance of being adopted through our democratic political process? Such considerations often prompt analysts to take into account political realities before making policy recommendations. Again, this leaves considerable leeway for the imprint of a particular analyst's biases and perceptions of what is possible politically; indeed, what will "play in Peoria."

The ambiguities present in all these evaluative concepts ought to prick your critical faculties as you read and formulate your opinions on the issues presented in this volume. Remain alive to the tendency of an analyst's preconceptions and biases to shape the public policies he advocates. If the analysis of policy can never be value-free, this does not mean that values should remain hidden or obscure. Maybe the best that can be accomplished is for analysts to recognize their values, refine them, and then go on to make their analyses and policy conclusions. Selection, adoption, and support of public policy, as we have observed, is a normative enterprise—a judgment, yet ideally an informed judgment. Recognizing that values intrude on policy analysis, and that different values are manifested in the analysis of public policy, is an important dimension to making informed judgments.

The Organization and Objectives of This Volume

As you may have suspected, this volume will probably raise more questions than it will answer. What you will confront in the following chapters are diverse analyses of six policy issues that currently face our country. By providing a broad spectrum of analyses and prescriptions on each issue, we expose you to a wider range of policy alternatives than you probably envisioned. The selections in this volume are organized in a way that will aid you in assessing the extent to which an analyst values and ideological perspectives influence

1. The identification of the problem to be solved
2. The determination of the objective to be sought
3. The choice of criterion by which the proposed solution is evaluated

4. The evaluation of the various weights to be assigned those affected by the policy

Part 1 focuses on some of the public policy issues involving energy and the environment. The chapters address conservation strategies, the viability of alternative energy sources, and environmental consequences; they also raise questions about the future of America's energy and environmental concerns.

Part 2 deals with welfare reform. The chapters offer various analyses and prescriptions ranging from support for current welfare programs to a wholesale critique of the American welfare system.

Part 3 includes several divergent proposals "in search of a national health policy." The chapters address questions about the proper scope of public health policies, the promise and political feasibility of public health programs, and the nature and distribution of medical services in America.

Part 4 examines regulatory policies of the federal government in the light of their effects on consumers, the changes in the nature of the agencies in this decade, and the implications of governmental involvement in the marketplace.

Part 5 raises one of the most interesting policy questions that has arisen in America in the last decade: affirmative action. Have federal guidelines been effective in improving job prospects for minorities? And are these efforts just in their treatment of groups other than the disadvantaged?

The final part deals with the desirability of governmental planning as a cure for the nation's economic ills. Stagflation—the simultaneous appearance of inflation and high unemployment—is the focus of discussion, and the solutions offered range from advocacy of central planning, to an incomes policy, and finally to a free-market resolution.

The sometimes extreme divergence of opinion on a single issue in the following chapters is exciting and thought-provoking and the observation that values and ideology may influence the outcomes of policy analysis should enable you to form more critical judgments about the policy proposals of your political representatives, professors, and the media.

NOTES

1. Ralph E. Strauch, " 'Squishy' Problems and Quantitative Methods," *Policy Sciences,* Fall 1975, pp. 175-84, discusses some of the problems inherent in the employment of various quantitative decision models. He points out that analysts must recognize that these models are only "perspectives," not "surrogates," for explaining real-world phenomenon.
2. M. Rein, *Social Science and Public Policy* (New York: Penguin, 1976), p. 38.
3. Lyman T. Sargent, *Contemporary Political Ideologies* (Homewood, Ill.: Dorsey, 1972), p. 1.
4. For an in-depth discussion of this problem, see Lawrence Tribe, "Policy Science: Analysis or Ideology," *Philosophy and Public Affairs,* Fall 1972.

PART ONE

Energy and the Environment:
The Big Tradeoff

In the 1970s environmental protection came to the forefront as a policy issue. Environmentalists discovered the "ecosystem," and pointing to the disruptive nature of industrial enterprises within it, pressured government to adopt certain environmental conservation policies such as controls on strip mining and offshore drilling. In 1973, at the height of the environmental movement, many Arab countries put an embargo on the sale of crude oil to the United States. Enter the "energy crisis." With the drain on U.S. crude oil reserves reaching a critical stage, many individuals and groups called upon the government to reevaluate its environmental controls in an attempt to come up with an effective energy policy. The stage was set for the policy dispute. It would be a tradeoff: energy or the environment.

One underlying theme has emerged in the energy versus environment policy dispute: The problems facing America's energy needs and environmental concerns are technical. That is, to solve the problems of energy and the environment, we have only to apply the appropriate technology. For example, to ensure that the ozone layer in our atmosphere is not depleted, we merely prohibit the use of fluorocarbons in the manufacture of aerosols. Or, to reduce our dependency on foreign crude oil, and thus solve our energy problems, we should look to the sun and harness solar power. Simple; just a technical problem. Or is it? Political decisions (public policies) must be made prior to committing societal resources to any particular technical strategy. Just as a political decision was made to prohibit the use of fluorocarbons in aerosols, so society must make political decisions and adopt policies that favor the application of one technology over another. As a result, some values are ranked higher than other values. That's politics and policy making.

The chapters in this part address the policy problems of America's energy needs and environmental concerns. Each author analyzes the problem and offers a policy response. As you will see, their prescriptions vary widely.

Gibbons and Chandler consider the prospect of a national energy conservation policy and attempt to dispel the "negative myths" of conservation. Observing that an energy conservation policy requires substituting new technology for old technology and changing our energy-using behavior, the authors briefly assess the political and economic implications of energy conservation. They conclude that a national energy policy could be efficient, effective, and politically feasible and that "the economic well-being of the United States can be maintained while energy growth is diminished."

Krutilla and Page review various energy "technologies" including nuclear reactors, fossil fuels, geothermal sources, and solar power. The authors argue that whatever energy policy we adopt, the analysis of it must incorporate "ethical criteria" (values) that focus on environmental consequences and intergenerational equity. McCracken's analysis does this while echoing the concern that we must leave future generations some sort of viable energy resource and technology; he advocates that we embrace nuclear power as the cornerstone of our present energy policy. On the other hand, Bruce Welch, analyzing the costs and benefits of nuclear versus solar energy, concludes that "you can't hold back the dawn" and that many of our energy and environmental tradeoffs can be resolved by formulating a national energy policy that facilitates the development and application of solar power.

John H. Gibbons and William U. Chandler

2. A NATIONAL ENERGY CONSERVATION POLICY

Energy conservation became necessary during the oil embargo of 1973-74 because of shortages and sharply rising prices; consequently, most people have come to associate energy conservation almost exclusively with curtailment. In contrast to curtailment (heroic measures to reduce consumption quickly by whatever means are least costly), conservation is the economic response to total energy cost. It means changing technology and procedures to reduce the demand for energy (or for specific scarce fuels) without corresponding reductions in living standards. Conservation can be regarded as a means of enhancing our economic welfare, leaving society materially better off. Thus, conservation is an act of enlightened self-interest.

When the price of energy was much lower, uses that are now economically wasteful were economically rational. The manufacture and use of automobiles that provide only 10 miles per gallon is a good example. Waste, in this sense, is not a vice in and of itself; it is an economic term. Some may object that unless the costs of energy are carefully and broadly defined, this definition of waste does not properly take into consideration the external costs of energy use (e.g., air pollution from automobiles). This objection is appropriate. The failure to internalize all the costs of energy production and consumption has created many of our most serious environmental problems and social inequities. Legislation like the Federal Clean Air and Water Acts, the Coal Surface Mining Control and Reclamation Act, and the Federal Mine Health and Safety Act has now brought us closer to internalizing the cost of energy use, as well as the use of most goods and services.

The implementation of a comprehensive National Energy Policy must incorporate total social costs of energy. Attention must also be paid to fuel switching (as a means of conserving scarce fuel or avoiding the use of particularly obnoxious fuel forms), which, with conservation and curtailment, completes the list of means of reducing energy use.

The implementation of an energy conservation policy has been hampered by the following misconceptions regarding the meaning and practice of conservation:

Energy and the production of goods and services are intimately and inextricably linked; energy is a relatively fixed factor in the gross national product.

Energy consumption and jobs are inextricably tied together. More energy consumption means more jobs, and vice versa.

Higher illumination levels generally help productivity; low illumination is injurious to the eyes.

Reducing the growth of energy consumption implies the replacement of machines (e.g., bulldozers) with manual labor (e.g., men and women wielding picks and shovels to build interstate highways).

Turning down the thermostat at night is counterproductive—the energy used in heating up the house in the morning more than offsets any savings.

Recent energy conservation research dispels these misconceptions and aids in understanding the potential of conservation over the next thirty years or so.

There are basically two types of responses to energy price increases and other indications of increasing scarcity: behavioral changes, and changes in existing as well as new energy-consuming equipment.

Behavioral changes include many of the actions we take under emergency conditions, like curtailing the use of automobiles, using energy-consuming equipment less, taking shorter showers, and so forth. These are short-term changes that can be made quickly and at little or no cost. Other changes, like lowering thermostat settings, are important and yield benefits in health and comfort (many buildings are not only overlighted but also overheated in winter and overcooled in summer).

Over the mid- and long term, modifications in energy-consuming equipment can yield substantial savings in energy and money, because energy use in the United States is far from efficient. The inefficiency of a typical gas-heated home is an excellent example. In combustion as much as 25 percent of the energy in the gas goes uselessly up the stack. The pilot light can consume 10 percent of the gas used in a home. Losses through poorly insulated heating ducts can amount to 40 percent. Altogether, from 35 to 55 percent of the useful energy in the natural gas can be wasted in a typical gas furnace system. The situation is similar in homes heated by oil and electricity. In addition to the inefficiency of delivery of heat into the residence, there are two other major sources of loss. First, the thermal shell of the residence is often very transparent to heat and cold, and thus loses energy. Second, the "availability" of heat from these furnaces (typically more than 1000°F) is inherently vastly greater than required—thereby incurring further losses.

The possibility for conservation in industry can amaze even the proponents of conservation. A recent *Wall Street Journal*[1] article reported the following vignettes of energy savings investments in industry:

> One company invested $30,000 in boiler controls: savings from this investment equal $60,000 per year, a 200 percent annual rate of return.
>
> A tire manufacturer spent $40,000 to insulate steam valves: savings amount to $80,000 per year, another 200 percent per year rate of return.
>
> General Electric invested $13,000 at one of its plants to shut down certain equipment automatically: annual savings are $51,000.

These are easy and obvious efforts; however, the number of conservation actions are apparently very large.

Incorporation of energy efficiency into new energy consuming products, like new houses, can yield very large benefits. In fact, careful design and construction can do more than conserve energy. Double-paned glass, thicker insulation, and other energy-conserving investments in buildings may decrease the total investment in the structure, for example, by decreasing the size of the air conditioner or furnace that must be provided. Due to this offsetting effect, large improvements in energy efficiency can be obtained with small net changes in total investment.

A prudent consumer would measure the benefit of his expenditure on various energy-saving options and decide which would yield the highest value to him. Educational programs modeled after the highly successful Agricultural Extension Service to give the consumer helpful information about intelligent investments in energy-intensive products are being tested in ten states.

Industry can respond to increasing energy prices in a variety of ways; thus industrial response requires detailed examination. Aluminum production, for example, can be reduced in energy intensity by nearly 40 percent, while chemical production may be able to manage only a 20 percent reduction. Uranium enrichment, the process by which nuclear reactor fuel and weapons material for the military is made and which consumes 4 percent of all the electric power in the United States, can be reduced in energy intensity by 90 percent. These improvements can come only over a time span corresponding to the replacement of existing production plants, and as a response to increases in energy prices.[2]

Another example that highlights the potential for conservation in new equipment and illustrates the problem of achieving such savings is what we may call "the paradox of the automobile." To increase gas mileage while retaining a certain amenity level, that is, interior space, safety, and other essential features, we must pay the price of adding improved design and high-technology features like micro-processors (mini-computers) for fuel combustion control and more expensive but lighter-weight materials like aluminum, or other innovations. Thus, there is a tradeoff between fuel and nonfuel costs. The dilemma consists of choosing the right point between the two extremes of fuel and nonfuel costs. The total cost of owning and operating an automobile (the sum of fuel and non-fuel costs) is remarkably insensitive to fuel economy over the broad range of performance from 15 miles to nearly 35 miles per gallon. In other words, it makes little economic difference to the buyer to choose a 35-mile-per-gallon car instead of a 15-mile-per-gallon car. But one can argue that it is in the national interest to choose the more efficient car and to build a more sophisticated domestic car. Though not in the purest sense a paradox, it is puzzling that a choice so profoundly important on the social level is of such little consequence on the individual level. Clearly, the market process does not enable consumers to discern the most efficient choice in terms of merged national and individual self-interest.

Are there many such market distortions? In energy, the answer unfortunately is yes. In the past, the government instituted many regulations and incentives that still provide major subsidies to energy production and use in the U.S. economy. These include natural gas price controls, tax incentives, and loan subsidies for energy production. New federal regulations and incentives and federal oil policy can alter this situation. For example, Congress has mandated minimum automobile average gas mileage (under the Energy Policy and Conservation Act of 1975, 1985 cars must obtain an average of 27 miles per gallon). Tax rebates and low-cost loans can be provided for homeowners who insulate their homes. New construction standards for improved energy efficiency are being promulgated. But perhaps more important, subsidies, like the subsidies for the transport of foreign oil to the United States, should be stripped away from general tax revenue. Only when all the costs of energy production are included in the price of energy (that is, internalized) will price signals indicate the need to induce high energy efficiency utilization.

Implications for Economic Growth, Employment, and Technology

One way to try to understand the impact energy conservation may have on the critical national issues of economic growth, employment, and the future of technology is through the "scenario." Scenario analysis has been widely used to assess the impacts of certain policy choices on our energy future. One such effort[3] constructed a series of scenarios of different energy use levels in the

United States to the year 2010, using a combination of econometric and engineering analysis techniques. In one low-energy growth scenario, total energy consumption in the United States is projected to be about 30 percent higher in 2010 than it is now. This glimpse of an imaginary but plausible future assumes that

> Real income doubles by 2010, a growth significantly lower than obtained in 1950-75.
>
> Real energy prices steadily increase and double by the year 2010, corresponding to an average 2 percent increase per year. State and federal policy strongly supports actions to increase the efficiency of energy use.
>
> Population increases by about one third (Bureau of Census Series II projections).

Results of the analysis indicate that an economically rational response to these conditions could result in the following possibilities:

> Energy use in buildings could decline at an annual rate of .6 percent, compared to an annual rate of increase of 3 percent currently (in part due to tough building codes and appliance efficiency standards).
>
> Electricity could account for 30 to 50 percent of U.S. energy consumption in 2010, compared with 28 percent today, depending on policy actions and the relative prices of other forms of energy.
>
> Natural gas could supply 11 percent of total demand, compared with 24 percent now.
>
> Auto efficiency doubles, in part due to regulations.
>
> Energy consumed per unit output of industry in 2010 is 35 percent lower than in 1975.

In other words, energy utilization efficiencies are made possible by the intelligent response of advanced technology to high and rising energy prices.

Perhaps the single most important conclusion of this study is the statement that the economic well-being of the United States can be maintained while energy growth is diminished. In this projection, gross national product grows at a longer-term average annual real rate of about 2 percent (higher in the near term and lower in the long term). This rate reflects the expected slowdown in the growth of the labor force, because of the decreasing birthrate, and the continued long-term shift in the economy to service-oriented activity. If GNP grows faster, then more energy will be required (e.g., an average 3 percent annual GNP growth will require about 35 percent more energy than an average 2 percent annual growth).

As for employment, the study indicated no major difference in the demand for workers between the lowest and the highest energy demand projection considered.[4] Moreover, energy conservation does not imply the substitution of manual labor for energy, since 20 cents worth of energy will buy the equivalent of a day's work of one laborer at a wheelbarrow. It therefore does not seem likely that we will opt for a return to wheelbarrows, picks, and shovels! Instead, highly technical skills, those of electronics technicians, skilled construction workers, engineers, and others who can provide ingenuity in place of the brute force consumption of energy and other resources, will be required.

Consideration of a national energy conservation policy begins with a definition of conservation, including three kinds of conservation: curtailment, fuel switching, and what we call conservation itself. Curtailment involves heroic measures to reduce energy consumption quickly by the cheapest means available. Fuel switching is a method of conserving specific fuels and can be an important complement of conservation. Conservation is the term we reserve for the policy of substituting new technology or different procedures for energy without reducing the amenities we enjoy. Conservation in this sense—an economic sense—is a means of leaving society better off than it would be without it, and is thus an act of enlightened self-interest.

Changing our energy-using behavior can be accomplished much more quickly than can the substitution of new and more efficient energy-consuming equipment. Lowering thermostat settings is a behavioral change that can yield large savings. With the exception of modifications or retrofits to existing property, the replacement of a more energy-efficient house or car must await the end of the useful life of the house or car. The rate of capital equipment turnover, therefore, controls to a large extent the rate at which conservation can be implemented. As a means of dealing with near-term shortages, policy makers can focus on behavioral changes or curtailments, but they must view the retrofit deficit, strengthen the United States dollar overseas, and slow inflation at home. These economic benefits would offset the cost of the rationing program.

A crucial subsidiary advantage of gasoline rationing would be the protection of existing jobs and the creation of new jobs. In his November 8, 1977, address to the nation on energy problems, President Carter noted that "every $5 billion increase in oil imports costs us 200,000 American jobs. It costs us business investments. Vast amounts of American wealth no longer stay in the United States to build our factories and to give us a better life." Mandatory gasoline rationing would undoubtedly create still more thousands of new jobs because domestic purchasing power will be diverted from foreign petroleum sellers—and highly automated U.S. and overseas oil refineries—toward more labor-intensive goods and services produced at home.

As the Department of Energy's Contingency Rationing Plan now stands — and in this regard it resembles the Office of Price Administration's World War II rationing program — all licensed drivers would receive the same periodic entitlement to gasoline supplies.

The national security (both economic and physical) and the international prestige of the United States are now at risk to feed its petroleum habit; thus it is only equitable that every adult member of the society should receive a fair stake in petroleum allocation. Furthermore, the nation's entire energy enterprise is now increasingly dependent on social, taxpayer-supported investments and billions of dollars of tax subsidies to producers for exploration, construction, and research and development.

Rationing was used successfully during World War II to equitably distribute reduced supplies of gasoline and other strategic materials desperately needed by the armed forces of the United States and its allies. The wartime gasoline rationing system met basic civilian needs for motoring fuel, was flexibly managed at the local level by neighborhood rationing boards, and came to be appreciated by the driving public, who felt it guaranteed them their fair share of dwindling supplies at a price they could afford.

Black marketeering and counterfeiting did not become serious until later in the war, when stepped-up German submarine attacks on Allied shipping and the start of the great Allied counteroffensives increased the military's need for U.S. oil supplies, a need that was met by sharply reducing the civilian population's monthly rations. Since wartime motorists were not encouraged to buy and sell rationing coupons on a "white market" as they are in contemporary rationing systems, the black market flourished.

Petroleum price controls went hand-in-glove with rationing during World War II, and they are also central to today's Contingency Rationing Plan. Price controls must accompany any oil rationing program. Petroleum prices are at the heart of the equity issue because if some form of price ceiling were not imposed the system would soon degenerate to de facto "rationing-by-price" and price gouging (the free market's equivalent of black marketeering).

Petroleum rationing's final advantage, apart from the fact that it would enable the federal government to consolidate its multiple regulatory strategies for conserving oil, is that it will forcefully educate the American people to the seriousness of the nation's energy problem — which the administration and Congress have failed to do. In addition, the very fact that a petroleum rationing program is impending, let alone in operation, should enormously stimulate the privately financed search for inexhaustible power sources like solar energy, wind, and biomass, which will usher in the sustainable energy era.

NOTES

1. *Wall Street Journal,* 9 February 1978.
2. J. H. Gibbons et al., "U.S. Energy Demand: Some Low Energy Futures," *Science 200* 142 (1978). These estimates are based on the assumption that real energy prices will double by the year 2010.
3. Ibid.
4. Ibid.

John V. Krutilla and
R. Talbot Page

3. TOWARD A RESPONSIBLE ENERGY POLICY

Our energy problems have been developing for many years, deepened by our own past actions. National policy has long followed the assumption that the more we extract and use our natural resources, the faster we build up the economy. The larger the volume of materials we process, the richer and more secure we become—and coal, oil, and gas are the largest material flows, in terms of value. By extracting "dormant" resources today, so the idea goes, we can turn them into productive assets, promising future generations a higher level of well-being than they would enjoy if we were to let the resources lie fallow in the ground. This idea was applied not only to energy materials but to all our natural resources. For two centuries we favored mineral extraction on our national lands, codifying the practice in the 1872 Mining Law. We lowered the price of energy by subsidizing it with depletion deductions and other tax preferences; we further encouraged energy consumption by establishing a promotional price system with volume discounts for larger consumption. We reduced the ostensible cost of energy and materials by ignoring the environmental costs associated with extracting and processing them.

This exploitative policy toward natural resources does not appear to have been entirely intentional. Nor has it been completely uniform. Large areas of land have been preserved from development. The control of gas prices by federal regulation has discouraged exploration and development. Yet the bias in policy toward development and exploitation is pronounced. In the past this policy may have made sense: resources appeared limitless; pollution and other environmental costs associated with their extraction were relatively small and localized; and our comparative advantage vis-à-vis other countries lay in our abundance of natural resources.

Over the years our pro-exploitation policy has had an effect on the economy. As energy became cheaper in this country than in many others, we came to use it more and more intensively, ultimately becoming dependent upon large energy flows. Now that conditions are changing, we are caught in a pattern of our own making. Whatever our stated policy, we will be forced to rely on new domestic sources and to pay higher prices for energy in the years to come. And as we adjust to a less energy-intensive economy implied by the higher prices, the amount and pain of adjustment will be increased by our previous policy encouraging exploitation.

In our shift from coal to oil and gas, we moved from an abundant energy resource—but one with health costs—to two relatively scarce ones. Concurrently, nuclear energy was confidently expected to become a major source of supply. But the predictions about nuclear power turned out to be overoptimistic. Thus, with the switch from coal to oil and with the shortfall in nuclear power, we became increasingly dependent on imported oil—on the same sources sought by most other industrial countries to serve their own growing needs. And now, compounding this tightness in supply, people—and not just those associated with environmental organizations—are increasingly resistant to having a coal or a nuclear electric plant built in their locality.

We cannot fall back on the once comforting assertions that we have hundreds of years' supply of coal and shale oil: in many cases the environmental costs of developing these resources are so high that much of the material may best be left in place. Suddenly we find ourselves in short supply of energy commodities.

For the short run, at least, we are "locked in" from both sides. Short-term adjustments in demand for energy will be painful, and many of the supply options will take years to develop. At first, as last winter's experience demonstrated, it is demand that will have to give way the most. As we look farther ahead, energy conservation would appear to be a more fundamental and far-reaching response, and at the same time, hopefully, more supply options will open up. But balanced against these possibilities is the juggernaut of geometric growth. Pushed by a rise in both population and GNP, the growth in energy demand has and will continue to have considerable momentum. While mathematically this growth cannot continue indefinitely or even for many more doubling periods, how and when best to mitigate it is a very open question.

In the following pages we discuss some of the options and considerations we believe should go into the formulation of a new energy policy. This policy should be a balance of more conservation and new supplies; it should be chosen with the proper concern for associated environmental and private costs, and for the timing and uncertainty of the various options; and it should demonstrate a proper regard for intergenerational equity.[1]

Criteria

How are we to decide on the amount and type of conservation to pursue and how are we to decide on which new sources to develop under what timing and on what scale? So far, many of these decisions have been left to the marketplace. The desirability of the market decision in the case of energy development and consumption depends upon three conditions: (1) the competitiveness of the energy industries, (2) the nature and size of environmental costs, and (3) the degree to which those affected by today's market decisions are fairly represented in today's market.

A discussion of the nature of competition and its imperfections in the energy industries would lead us far afield and, perhaps irretrievably, into bogs of controversy. Suffice it for us to mention that conventional economic theory predicts that monopolistic industries will restrict output compared with the competitive norm. But, on the other side, electric and gas utilities, being natural monopolies, have the incentive to discriminate between more and less elastic customers, and in fact there does exist a declining block rate structure which promotes the consumption of energy through volume discounts to larger (more elastic) customers; the oil and gas industry has been remarkably successful in achieving low effective income tax rates, often in the neighborhood of 2 or 3 percent; and it has sometimes been alleged that, through joint ventures, the rather small number of major oil companies have colluded to pick up lease contracts at bargain prices. To the extent that there are imperfections in the competitiveness of the energy industries, these are grounds to believe that promotion and consumption of energy will be favored over conservation.

While the nature and implications of market imperfections in the energy industries appear to be perennial and unanswered questions in economics, at the present time—when policy is being formulated in response to potential shortages and dislocations—we can sidestep most of the controversial questions to pose in a practical way a criterion for energy conservation: We should work for more conservation up to the point where the costs of pushing further exceed the benefits. In the short run, the costs of conservation are the costs associated with adjusting to a lower rate of energy consumption. For example, we will conserve more energy by moving toward an inverted electric rate structure, but the amount of energy conserved in the short term should be balanced against the dislocations and adjustment costs associated with the shift. Such costs of conserving a million Btu's are not worth bearing if new supplies of the same amount of energy can be obtained at less cost. This comparison is a useful rule of thumb in a shortage or short-term crisis. In the long run, the conventional rule of thumb is that if energy is priced "correctly," the right amount of conservation will follow automatically. As is mentioned below, complications arise because of environmental costs, uncertainty, and questions concerning the intertemporal distribution of welfare, but here, as in the short run, the general idea is that energy saved through conservation should be balanced against energy obtained through new sources.

When the decision of which new supplies to develop and under what schedule is left to the marketplace, it is made upon the test of profitability. It is sometimes thought that by leaving these decisions to the market, economic efficiency will automatically be achieved. But in the market, the only costs and benefits considered are private ones, those borne by the firms making the decisions. Environmental costs are excluded from the analysis except as the firms are forced to bear them by rules of liability, government regulation, or pollution taxes. (It is important to point out that the failure to include environmental costs is not unique to decision making by the marketplace: in choosing and developing new sources of supply, government agencies, too, have often neglected environmental costs.) By the test of private market profitability, new sources will be scheduled in order of their private costs, from lowest to highest. Because of the neglect of environmental costs, as we shall affirm in a moment, not only will the order of introduction probably be wrong, but too much energy will be developed at any given time.

Largely in reaction to this neglect, environmentalists have stressed the importance of considering the environmental costs in choosing and developing new sources of supply. Occasionally they go so far as to advocate the selection of new sources on the basis of environmental costs alone. By this criterion, new sources would be scheduled from those lowest to highest in environmental costs, regardless of the private costs.

Ever since the time of Pigou, in the early twentieth century, economists have pointed out that such decisions should be made on the basis of both private and environmental costs. Certainly both types of costs should be taken into account, but while this position has made fine reading in textbooks, it has not prevailed in practice. The environmentalists' criterion—which is conceptually just as inefficient as the private-market solution and symmetrically opposite to it— does serve a useful purpose in this regard: it nudges us away from the prevailing concentration on private costs and toward a consideration of total social costs.

All this may seem simple and obvious, but there are pitfalls for the unwary practitioner. For example, it is sometimes suggested that environmental costs should be considered along with private costs in deciding upon a set of admissible projects, but that once this set is chosen, environmental costs need play no further role, leaving the selection and scheduling of projects from the admissible set to be made on the basis of private costs alone. Such a procedure would be efficient only if the ratio of private to environmental costs were constant over all the projects in the admissible set.

A deeper problem surfaces when we consider how to count costs and benefits (whether private or environmental) distributed over time. By standard practice, future costs and benefits are discounted, but discounted at what rate?

Here, again, we run into an unresolved controversy. It has been argued that when a proposed project carries with it the risk of irreversible costs, or when a project's stream of net costs are growing, the project should be discounted at a higher than normal rate. And in response to the Atomic Energy Commission's cost-benefit study of the breeder reactor, the National Resources Defense Council goes further to argue that for projects imposing the risk of very large future costs, one necessary, *but by no means sufficient,* test should be that the project have a favorable cost-benefit ratio under a wide range of discount rates, including the highest (before tax) rates found in the private economy. A project like the breeder, with potentially catastrophic future costs, should be "an investment at least as productive as the industries it draws resources away from."[2] Another test is one of fairness.

However, when there are uncertainties, irreversibilities, and potentially catastrophic consequences, the matter is both more fundamental and broader than somehow choosing a discount rate. Basically, the problem is one of intergenerational equity. In the example of the breeder reactor, the present generation receives the electricity while future generations are burdened with perpetual care of plutonium, which is both extremely toxic and a prime weapon material. Generally, markets are considered fair only if all those affected by the outcomes are present in the market (without externalities) and the distribution of market power is considered fair. In the case of deciding which new supplies to develop, the distribution of market power is indeed uneven: the present generation controls the total stock of resources, leaving future generations with no voice in today's decisions. Another way of describing the situation is to say that the present generation may undertake projects to its own benefit yet at the same time regard these projects as leading to an unfair redistribution of welfare. One can be a beneficiary of an outcome and still feel that others are victimized by one's own good fortune—and so it may be between generations.

So far our decision-making institutions have not systematically resolved the question of intergenerational equity. Yet as our means of transferring costs from the present to the future increase—for example, by generating long-lived pollutants—the need to bring intergenerational fairness into the decision-making process becomes more compelling. This is especially the case with projects carrying small and largely unknown probabilities of future catastrophes.

How should institutions for this type of decision making function, and what form should they take? These questions are difficult to answer, but it seems clear at least that since the future cannot represent itself, there should be broad opportunity for different groups to bring the charge of unfairness. The decision of what is fair intertemporally is too important to be left to small elite groups of decision makers, especially when there are vested interests at stake.

The institutions should function in such a way that the larger the potential adverse effect and the more uncertain the probability of its occurrence, the more cautious and thorough the decision-making procedure should be and the more information should be generated by the procedure itself. Projects with greater risk of future catastrophe should pass stricter tests. There should be some way of setting up barriers against possible redistributions of welfare.

One such barrier would be to subject a potentially risky project to a "penalty" charge at its inception. Presumably, the charge would increase with the size and uncertainty of the risk and would be determined by a decision-making process involving opponents and advocates. For a once-only charge, this scheme appears equivalent to subjecting the more risky project to a higher effective discount rate. But if the charge were to be more flexible—levied over several years, from the beginning of the project, in response to what is learned about the project's consequences—the scheme is no longer equivalent to a single adjustment in the discount rate.

Beyond this conceptual difference, a charge explicitly levied and collected would have an important practical effect. We commonly, and often appropriately, subsidize projects with large risks of not attaining good outcomes. Frequently, however, these projects are mixed affairs involving some risk of very *bad* outcomes, so that the government inadvertently finds itself underwriting programs with potentially catastrophic effects. A charge scheme would tend to reverse this, making it possible to discriminate between risks of adverse as contrasted with beneficial outcomes.

In the following sections we mention some of the important costs and benefits associated with various options, along with some of the redistributional possibilities. The latter can be safely ignored in the case of projects with little distributional impact, applying standard cost-benefit analysis and scheduling such projects in the order of their total (private plus environmental) costs. One beneficial result is that less promising projects may be avoided entirely and ones with high environmental costs may be delayed sufficiently until such time as technological advances provide us with acceptable defensive strategies for their use. But the greater the distributional potential, the more these projects should be subjected to explicit social choice concerning their intergenerational fairness. We wish to stress that the equity considerations cannot be resolved by a mechanical cost-benefit analysis. The question of intertemporal fairness logically precedes the typical efficiency questions posed by economists. A full and open debate must attend projects in proportion to the potential size and relative uncertainty of their redistributional effects. Only in this way will sufficient knowledge be generated to make sensible decisions, ones we can live with. Setting up institutions whereby this can be done is of primary importance.

Options for Energy Conservation: Prospects and Limitations

If the environmental standards mandated by the Clean Air Act are to be substantially honored, and the limited supplies of oil and gas are to be husbanded so as to ensure that the basic functions of the economy will not be disrupted, there appears to be no alternative in the short run to widespread, makeshift, energy conservation measures. The combination of such conservation measures with one of the mildest winters on record was enough to enable the country to survive last year's critical period without economic dislocations. We need to recognize, however, how crucial the bonus of good weather was. Limited refinery capacity will still affect the supply of gasoline, and gasoline stringencies may occur during the more extensive summer driving season for a number of years. But as enough time elapses to permit normal economic adjustments—for example, improved commuter facilities promoting the use of more energy-efficient mass transportation and a shift in our stock of automobiles toward smaller, more energy-efficient, vehicles—substantially more significant economies in the energy budget may be achieved. In the longer run, commuters faced with higher travel costs are likely to move closer to their work, and this relocation can decrease the amount of cross-commuting.

Estimates of the energy savings that can be achieved through conservation have been made by a number of sources. The Office of Emergency Preparedness, for example, estimated that anywhere from 15 to 17 quadrillion Btu's—more than 20 percent of expected consumption—might be saved through conservation practices implemented over the period from 1972 through 1975. Over a longer period (say, 1980 and beyond), still an intermediate time frame but one which would permit some of the adjustments to take place, possible annual savings were set as high as 36 quadrillion Btu's—something like 30 percent of the consumption expected in the absence of conservation measures.[3]

An economic study of the adjustments that would be indicated in response to rising relative prices of energy commodities was undertaken recently by members of the staff of the Environmental Protection Agency (EPA).[4] The estimate of relative reduction in annual demand, resulting largely through substituting capital for energy in response to a 25 percent rise in the relative price of energy commodities, was put at 41 quadrillion Btu's by the end of a twenty-year adjustment period, 1970-90. This represents an annual saving of about 30 percent of the energy that would have been consumed in the absence of the change in the relative price of energy commodities. The EPA study provides a systematic review of the several sectors accounting for the consumption of energy and an evaluation of the substitutions and reductions based on price elasticities, given sufficient time to allow economic adjustment processes to work themselves out.

While the study reflects the extent to which demands for energy may presently be excessive because of the inefficient pricing policies pursued heretofore, a number of observations seem warranted. It is likely that the relative rise of fuel prices will exceed the 25 percent postulated, but it is not clear that increasing relative costs and prices will be accompanied by an equivalent additional relative reduction in the demand for energy. It will depend in part on what additional areas will permit capital substitution for energy as the relative prices of energy commodities rise. Since the substitution implicit in this economic adjustment process is largely (but not entirely) capital for energy, substantial demands are going to be made for investment funds to develop supply options as well as to finance the massive conversion implicit in the substitution of new plant and equipment in response to the rise in energy prices. Thus, the change in relative prices of energy and capital, rather than of energy and of commodities in general, is relevant. Unless there is also an increase in the propensity to save, capital as well as energy may be in short supply, and the possibilities for substitution may not be as extensive as suggested.

There are nonpricing policies that can be pursued in addition to eliminating preferential tax treatment for oil and gas and subsidizing federal hydroelectric plants (and transmission facilities). For example, we might consider the appropriate taxation of commodities whose prices do not otherwise reflect the external or environmental costs of their production, distribution, and consumption; we might undertake initial public assistance to reduce risk in establishing enterprises requiring a minimum scale of operation for the competitive provision of energy-conserving facilities, for example, solar residential heating (reported to be economically competitive provided units are made and distributed in sufficient volume to achieve scale economies); and, of course, we could mount a discriminating and adequately programmed research and development effort to advance the technology of energy conservation and production over the long run.

Despite the prospects for energy conservation, *none of the studies we have cited lead to the conclusion that energy demands will not continue to grow.* A reduction in the rate of growth of about 50 percent over a twenty-year adjustment period, implicit in the EPA study, would still require an annual provision of additional energy in an amount roughly equivalent to the projected savings. But even if it were possible to achieve a negligible-to-zero growth in energy demand, an unrealistic prospect for the time frame relevant to our present concerns, additional sources of energy would be required to replace current sources which would be depleted with time. The important consideration is that while energy conservation is an indispensable objective for both the short and long run, it will not by itself suffice to solve either the short- or long-run energy problem facing the country. *In addition to pursuing the energy-conservation strategy, attention must be given to various energy supply options relevant to each time period.*

A Promised Nonfossil-Fuel Option

Part of the present short-term problem relates to the incrimination of coal as a source of unacceptable air pollution when used for the production of electrical energy in steam electric power stations. The substitution of gas and oil for coal, and the limitation on the supplies of these energy commodities, resulted in last winter's concern about sufficient fuel for transportation and industrial processes, electric power production, and commercial and home heating, and the concern may continue to be warranted for a number of years. Granted that we appear to require petroleum products for transportation purposes, is there an alternative to low sulfur oil and natural gas for electric power production that does not involve coal?

At one time there was considerable hope that nuclear power would displace fossil fuel as the source of energy in thermal electric power production. The at-site environmental effects of nuclear power plant operation, assuming present light water reactor (LWR) technology, are alleged to be less damaging than the products of fossil fuel combustion. There appear to be two serious difficulties with the nuclear energy option, however. The first is that for a number of reasons—and these are largely unrelated to opposition to nuclear power on other environmental grounds—the development of nuclear plants has been substantially retarded. Technical, personnel, and other factors have intervened to such an extent that actual nuclear power capacity in 1985 is expected to fall short by some 100,000 to 250,000 megawatts of previously projected capacity.[5] There is no way in the short run in which nuclear capacity can substitute for fossil-fuel-burning plants to meet the indicated demand for electrical energy so as to permit our diverting liquid and gaseous hydrocarbon supplies to transportation and residential heating uses while remaining free from dependence on coal.

The second difficulty with nuclear energy concerns its ultimate desirability in any event. While the at-site environmental effects may be less from nuclear reaction than from fossil-fuel combustion, nuclear energy poses a very serious long-run problem of waste disposal. The radioactive products of fission are highly toxic and have half-lives extending to thousands of years—which means that they must be contained safely for tens of thousands of years before decay ultimately dissipates their toxicity. At present we have no satisfactory (i.e., fail-safe) method of storage. Radioactive waste generation imposes at least two burdens on society: first, to provide a fail-safe method of storage in perpetuity, which requires methods not yet known; and second, to develop a social discipline and stability never attained by previous societies. It also raises critical implications about the kind of society that would emerge in response to the need to deal with such a serious and growing safety problem. This poses the moral question of whether the present generation should saddle future generations forever with the burden of safeguarding our toxic nuclear wastes.

This ethical question has already been largely decided by default: There are nuclear plants already on line, and with those on order, nearly 200,000 megawatts are scheduled to be operating within ten years or so. And, as Kneese has said, if such plants operate for only a decade or two, they will have imposed a burden on society in perpetuity.[6] Once the toxic materials are introduced and are susceptible of being released into the environment, the burden is virtually irreversible in terms of a time frame relevant to human societies.

Nevertheless, for years to come we will still be faced with making decisions about the scale and character of the burden. Far-reaching choices are yet to be made regarding the second-generation nuclear technologies involving the so-called breeder reactors. While we have several possible breeder-reactor designs as potential contenders, the liquid metal-cooled fast breeder reactor (LMFBR) is receiving the bulk of the research and development effort, both in the United States and abroad.[7] The breeder technology is more complex than that of the LWR and may pose somewhat higher probabilities of accidental failure. Liquid sodium, used as a coolant in the favored design, is highly reactive with air and water and, becoming radioactive, must be kept extremely free from impurities that would cause it to become corrosive and possibly lead to leaks in the intricate plumbing. Using plutonium as the fuel, which is extremely toxic[8] and has a half-life of 24,400 years, a major accident could result in virtually permanent contamination of an area. Consequently, much effort has been expended to develop reliable components for handling the highly reactive sodium—but with reliability, costs mount to the extent that some critics of the LMFBR consider the design to be ultimately uneconomical.[9]

In addition to the nonzero probability of accidental failures, some of major proportions, the vulnerability of power and processing plants to sabotage poses a serious problem. Moreover, the value of plutonium will make it a target for diversion to unauthorized purposes, whether for pecuniary or more malicious reasons.[10] If the LMFBR were to be widely deployed, substantial quantities of plutonium would be in transit, and while conceivably the problem of fail-safe security could be solved within the United States (and this is by no means a certainty), that might not be the case elsewhere. For this reason, we would be wise to undertake a more careful investigation of alternatives to the LMFBR.

One such alternative, which would involve a longer developmental horizon, involves a thermal breeder fueled with molten uranium salts. Because the fuel is molten, continuous on-line reprocessing would be possible.[11] While the technology is not as far advanced as that of the LMFBR, and at present is not receiving much official attention, its capability of confining power generation and fuel reprocessing to one location has substantial security and environmental advantages.

Given our own and other countries' past commitment to one or another of the fission technologies, and given the existing stock of nuclear weapons, it may be that we have lost the option of keeping the environment permanently uncontaminated with highly toxic products of fission. And with the continuing pursuit of fission technology in other countries, it may be that our own persistence in that direction will not add significantly to the problem of developing viable security measures for containing virulent substances in perpetuity. On the other hand, if alternative strategies offer some possibility of releasing fewer such materials into the environment and appreciably reducing their impact, we have an obligation to review them conscientiously.

For example, given other countries' attention to the breeder reactor, the availability of energy from this source would not be affected by the failure of the United States to develop its own breeder technology. The industrial world's potential dependence on breeder technology to meet its energy needs after fossil-fuel sources have been exhausted does not depend in any essential respect on the U.S. breeder development program. Moreover, if the resources devoted to the development of the breeder in the United States were redirected toward alternative, environmentally more acceptable, energy supply options, it is conceivable that the development of the "ultimate" source of clean, inexhaustible energy could be advanced sufficiently to reduce appreciably the problem associated with the storage of highly toxic products of fission. It should be noted that the problem concerns not merely the mounting of solar, fusion, and perhaps geothermal research and development efforts but also the decision to support larger, more aggressive, research and development programs in these areas by diverting the resources currently allocated to the breeder reactor program. These are significant policy issues on which the public generally, as well as the technical experts, must be heard. The outcomes are sufficiently important to require testing through public debate and evaluation.

To summarize briefly, one advantage of using nuclear reaction as a source of energy for the production of electricity is that the environmental problems arising from routine operation of the light water reactor are somewhat less severe than those associated with the combustion of fossil fuels, especially the higher sulfur fuels. Moreover, the additional supplies of fissionable materials, particularly if the breeder technology is developed and deployed, would greatly lessen our dependence on fossil fuels in the long run. This latter advantage, of course, could be achieved alternatively by a fusion technology not involving plutonium.[12] The disadvantages are, first, the short-run impossibility of attaining sufficient nuclear reactor production to displace fossil fuel widely enough to solve current needs and, second, the critical long-term hazards of transporting and storing extremely long-lived and toxic products of fission.

Fossil-Fuel Options

If, as appears likely, we cannot rely solely on conservation strategies to meet our short-term and intermediate-term energy needs, and we choose to defer a heavy dependence on nuclear fission on basic ethical, if not other, grounds, where does this leave us? Several possibilities are considered below.

Just as the rise in price is expected to have an impact on the quantity demanded, so it is likely to stimulate some response in fossil-fuel supplies. A doubling of the price of crude oil, which has taken place for new sources, will make some deposits that were marginal to uneconomic at the earlier price now economically recoverable. The amount of this crude oil that would be available from onshore sources bears investigation. Since most of the new production has been offshore in recent times, it is likely that the offshore sources will remain the most attractive from the standpoint of private resource costs. As the environmental impacts of these offshore operations are still under investigation, we do not yet have a means of determining whether the total (environmental as well as resource) costs affect the relative attractiveness of the offshore compared with onshore sources—nor the extent to which the environmental costs are likely to differ, say, between Atlantic and Gulf Outer Continental Shelf operations.[13] These important matters must be studied so that discriminating attention may be given to the scheduling of expanded production in order to minimize the total social costs of such oil extraction and transportation. *Information on these questions should be obtained before any further leasing of public lands for oil exploitation.*

Rising prices of petroleum products have implications also for the commercial feasibility of extracting oil from shale. A rough estimate has put shale oil reserves at 168 trillion barrels,[14] with reserves in the richest zones of the Green River Formation of Colorado, Utah, and Wyoming, yielding upwards of 25 gallons per ton, set at nearly 600 billion barrels.[15] If only private resource costs of extraction and transportation are considered, these higher-grade oil shale occurrences are commercially attractive at current high prices.

The environmental costs of exploiting these deposits, however, are formidable. The deer herd and related wildlife in the Piceance Creek Basin in Colorado are unusually valuable—yet their destruction probably represents the least significant of the environmental impacts that extraction would have on the region. The mind-boggling volume of spoils,[16] the attendant risk of disposal-pile failure, the environmental implications of dewatering the mines, and related water-quality problems raise very serious questions at this stage regarding the total social costs associated with using these shale oil reserves.[17] Conceivably, environmentally nondegrading processes might be developed that would eliminate a large share of the expected social cost.[18] Work currently in progress may eventually make it possible to evaluate carefully the social costs of environmental degradation inherent in the extraction of oil from shale. At the moment, however, because of the expected environmental component of total cost, shale oil does not appear to be a strong candidate for the lowest total cost position among the energy supply options.

An alternative option for obtaining petroleum for transportation, and possibly for residential heating, would be to return to coal to generate electricity. In 1973, approximately 1.5 million barrels of petroleum were used daily by the electric utility industry. The amount projected for 1985 runs to 2.67 million barrels a day. The 1973 consumption for electric generating plants is roughly equivalent to 120 million tons of coal, and this volume will almost double to 226 million tons by 1985.

If a nonfission energy option is chosen, however, the amount of coal required for electric generating plants will increase very substantially. If only half of the 300,000 to 400,000 megawatts of nuclear power projected for 1985 were required under a low-growth energy conservation regime, an additional 400 million to 550 million tons of coal would still be needed annually to fuel the electric utility industry. Combined electric utility requirements alone would indicate a need for coal production to more than double between the present and 1985.

Initially, coal from low sulfur deposits could be substituted for low sulfur petroleum. Given time and a vigorous research and development program to produce an effective sulfur and particulate emission-control technology, more extensive sources of coal could be drawn upon to provide the needed fuel. But the environmental impact of returning to coal will be felt at the extraction stage as well as during conversion. The deep mining of coal may be the most hazardous occupation in America—it averages 100 fatalities and 10,000 nonfatal casualties annually, quite apart from damage done to the miners' health from long exposure to airborne particulates. Advances in underground mining technology and their more widespread deployment, of course, could reduce the number of miners exposed for any given volume of coal mined. Surface mining is not as hazardous, but it has long-run landscape and related aesthetic costs. Where seams are thin and in areas of steep slopes, contour mining is particularly damaging to the landscape. In certain regions of the West—the Northern Great Plains, for example—where coal seams are exceptionally thick and the amount of surface area disturbed per unit of coal extracted is small (11 acres per million tons of coal, assuming an average 50-foot seam), the relation between volume of coal taken and surface disturbance is much smaller. Where annual precipitation is favorable, it appears feasible to restore the strip-mined areas if this is done with appropriate safeguards and attention to rehabilitation.[19]

The sources of the required coal are a matter of interest. Unpublished preliminary estimates (not for attribution) suggest that deep-mined western coal is available at prices equivalent to those of strip-mined eastern coal, and that deep-mined western coal, while involving higher transportation costs, imposes no rehabilitation costs. The costs of western surface-mined coal, including estimated costs for rehabilitation,[20] appear to be lower than those of deep-mined coal. Unfortunately, the estimates are highly aggregated and no distinction is made regarding the sulfur content of the coal at each location.

Nonfission sources of fuel are abundant and therefore very attractive if environmental costs are ignored. But even when these costs are taken into account, their environmental implications appear to be less awesome than those posed by the nuclear fission technology. Yet since the fossil-fuel options are likely to vary in total social costs, it is urgent that we evaluate the environmental implications of each to ensure that we do not draw on those of higher social cost while not exploiting others to their fullest capacity.

Possible Nonfossil-Fuel, Nonnuclear Options

Most of the serious attention given to the displacement of petroleum in non-transportation energy demands has focused on coal and nuclear materials as substitutes. Yet solar sources of energy appear to be worth considering for our residential heating needs over the intermediate term, and geothermal sources seem capable of meeting part of our electrical generating requirements, even over the short run.

A distinction should be made between the uses of solar energy at lower and higher temperatures. Solar energy is basically a diffuse source of heat. The technology for its application in low-temperature uses such as space heating is simple and proven. In much of the country, it has been competitive with other sources of energy for supplementary residential heating for some time, even at the former lower fuel prices. With the rising cost of fossil fuel, substantial displacement by solar energy could be accomplished with known technology in residential heating and possibly cooling. Of course, there would have to be a re-designing or replacement of existing residential structures that were built without features essential to the efficient interception and utilization of the sun's rays. Replacement of the present housing stock would undoubtedly take a long time, and it is not clear how much of the present housing stock could be renovated to use solar energy.

Because of the high capital cost of setting up a supplementary solar collector, it would take a decade or two for the lower operating cost to result in a saving on the total cost of production. The reluctance of builders to substitute higher capital costs (more visible to buyers) for lower operating costs appears to be one of the main obstacles to the introduction of solar collectors for space heating and cooling.

The use of solar energy directly in high-temperature applications, on the other hand, does not appear to be immediately so promising. Because solar energy is so diffuse a heat source, the investment in collectors to concentrate heat sufficiently to produce temperatures required in conventional steam-cycle central-station electrical generating plants will be some multiple of the investment for fossil-fuel and nuclear stations. Accordingly, it seems doubtful that either land or capital will be used extensively for the higher-temperature applications using direct insolation as an energy source.

More sophisticated technologies such as the photovoltaic cell, capable of directly converting solar to electrical energy, are still further from commercial feasibility. While the technology of the photovoltaic cell is known, present economic efficiencies are so low that this energy source is used only for space exploration and similar highly specialized purposes where the cost per unit of electricity is an incidental consideration. Advances that would permit us to produce moderately economical electricity from solar radiation cannot realistically be expected within the near future.

Another possible partial substitute for nuclear or fossil fuel in the production of electricity is geothermal energy. Heat sources in the earth's crust exist in the form of dry steam, hot water, and hot dry rock. The Geysers field in northern California, one of the country's large dry steam fields, has been regarded with interest by the Pacific Gas and Electric Company. The steam it produces is of low pressure and temperature when compared with pressures and temperatures in modern steam electric plants, but there are indications that, with appropriate plant design, energy can be generated economically depending upon various factors, the life of the field being one. The potential of dry steam sources in the United States has been estimated at 100,000 megawatts over a twenty-year production cycle.[21]

Dry steam wells produce steam unaccompanied by liquid water, which makes power generation both more simple and more economical. Geothermal wells more commonly produce a mixture of steam and water, and in the conventional process the water must be separated from the steam before the latter can be used in power production. Where the water has a high salinity content, disposal can create difficulties if the saline water cannot be reinjected into the system after the steam has been extracted. Alternatively, the hot water itself can be used in power production, serving as a heat-exchange medium to transfer heat to a secondary fluid having a lower boiling point, and this secondary fluid, in turn, can be used to drive turbines. There is some loss of heat in the transfer, but less so than in extracting the usable steam from the hot water. At present we do not have enough experience with the secondary fluid technology to evaluate its commercial feasibility, yet under favorable conditions it is expected to produce electricity at prices comparable to those of fossil-fuel plants.[22]

Until now, geothermal technology has concentrated on dry steam and hot water systems. But the preponderant source of geothermal heat in the earth's interior is contained in dry rock. While the thermal content of dry rock is much greater than that of dry steam and hot water systems, it is more difficult to exploit for the production of electricity. Plans to tap this source of energy involve the creation of artificial fractures in the rock occurring below the surface at substantial depth and circulation of water through the area to extract the heat from the rock. Research in this area is being conducted by a group at the Los Alamos Scientific Laboratories, but there is still little empirical, as contrasted with theoretical, information on which to base judgments regarding the comparative economics of the technology. Were it to be found economical, the dry rock sources would represent a reservoir of heat substantially greater than the dry steam or hot water sources combined.

Although geothermal energy is now considered a significant potential source, it is clear that much research and development will be needed for its efficient exploitation. Moreover, the by-products of geothermal technology pose potential environmental problems: Because of their mineralized nature, the water and even residues in the dry steam will require disposal. Where they can be reinjected into the reservoirs conveniently, they may present no environmental difficulties and indeed may serve to prevent the problem of land subsidence that can occur with the withdrawal of steam and water. Reinjection will be difficult in some cases, however, and these will demand attention.

Air pollution can also be a threat. Noxious gases are often a by-product of geothermal reservoirs, and while some gases can readily be separated from the steam, hydrogen sulfide cannot. It has been suggested that the amount of sulfur that escapes into the atmosphere from the Geysers operation is comparable to that emitted from the burning of low sulfur oil in conventional fossil-fuel plants.[23]

Like solar energy, geothermal energy merits far more intensive investigation than the meager efforts accorded it so far. The possibilities for exploiting geothermal energy can be realized only by mounting a considerable developmental effort to verify the most likely sources for the short run and to provide the defensive strategies essential for dealing with the noxious substances associated with some of the sources. While geothermal energy, like solar energy, is not likely to displace other sources entirely, it holds promise of becoming a significant supplement, whether or not the deployment of fission technology is deferred indefinitely. It could be relatively inexpensive as well when the total cost, including environmental cost, is considered. More important, neither the solar nor geothermal technologies involve the problem of intertemporal equity that plagues the nuclear fission option.

Summary and Conclusions

We have attempted to identify a few of the more important issues and options that need to be considered in providing energy for the American economy. The short-run "crisis" may well have been simply the first act of a longer serial that will involve working through fundamental adjustments to our way of thinking and the way we organize our lives over the next several decades. We have argued for energy conservation. Not only would this be part of a program to develop a larger measure of independence from unstable foreign sources of supply, but it might prove necessary in order to bring the consumption of energy into alignment with its total real (resource and environmental) costs.

However, conservation alone will not be able to deal with the problem entirely over the next quarter of a century. One reason, of course, is that in the long run the maintenance of our industrial society will depend on advances in technology that will release us from dependence upon the finite sources of conventional energy. To increase the probability of success in this regard, we shall need a well-functioning industrial economy capable of supporting the kind of research and development effort required. This will doubtless call for some growth in energy consumption. Thus, if we can achieve only partially our objectives through the more efficient use of energy, new sources will be required over the next five, ten, and twenty-five years, and we need to be apprised of the relative total costs of these new supply options.

The problem of determining the optimal schedule of supply is complicated both by the environmental costs suffered currently and by those which will have their greatest cumulative impact in the future, causing intertemporal equity problems. This aspect of the energy supply problem has grown enormously in the past few decades for several reasons: (1) we are beginning to experience a diminishing environmental assimilative capacity as we overload our pollutable reservoirs; (2) we are generating new types of wastes, ones which the environment seems less able, or unable, to assimilate; and (3) geometric growth in the demand for energy and materials generally, along with leaner deposits, promises to result in disturbances of land surfaces of magnitudes far beyond our previous experience. These factors lead to large-scale environmental costs affecting people in the present and spilling over into the future— and as our technological ability advances, so, it appears, does our power to impose even greater burdens and hazards upon generations to come. The enormity of the potential costs demands that they be dealt with in the decision-making process. It carries the matter beyond the point where it can be handled by conventional admonitions for benefit-cost analysis to include externalities or by pleas for generalized "effluent" taxes to perfect the market. The potential redistributions of economic well-being are so great that the problem has become fundamentally an ethical one.

The possibility of shifting increased costs associated with some technological resource options lends importance to the matter of scheduling and timing. Those options that carry the highest risks of serious long-run adverse welfare effects might well receive explicit consideration for deferral in the hope that more benign alternatives can be developed in the interim or at least that defensive strategies can be worked out to cope more adequately with the adverse side effects of their deployment.

So far the decision-making process has lagged in this respect. The satisfactory integration of economic and ethical considerations has not been adequately achieved. It appears, however, that changes are beginning to occur in response to the growing gravity of the problem. The decision-making process is becoming somewhat more broadly based through public hearings and the mechanism of adversary proceedings, so that decisions that have been reached on narrow technical grounds are becoming more open to challenge. But these avenues of public participation need to be increased and the process accelerated.

What if the issues surrounding energy supply (and conservation) do in fact become more susceptible to public participation and there is more responsiveness to considerations of environmental costs and intertemporal equity? In what direction are things likely to go? A more critical view of such options as the fission technologies might emerge, and more interest might be shown in potentially less hazardous sources such as the solar, geothermal, and fusion technologies. Conservation programs might appear more attractive than before, when only private resource costs were considered. In the process, more explicit consideration would be given to intertemporal welfare distribution than has been true in the past.

NOTES

1. This article draws heavily on, among other sources, discussions with many individuals—indeed, too many to mention separately. We have benefited greatly from discussions with present and former colleagues at Resources for the Future and with members of the staffs of the Ford Energy Policy Project, the Center for Advanced Computation at the University of Illinois, the Department of the Interior, and the Federal Energy Administration. Helpful also have been the reviews and comments from members of the Environmental Defense Fund, the Natural Resources Defense Council, the Sierra Club, and the Wilderness Society. While there is doubtless something in the paper with which all of these contributors will agree, it is unlikely that any will subscribe to all of our viewpoints and conclusions. Accordingly, while the assistance we have received from others is great indeed, we alone assume responsibility for the positions taken and for any inadvertent errors of analysis or fact that may remain.
2. Thomas B. Cochran and Arthur R. Tamplin, "Comments" on WASH 1536 (The AEC Draft Environmental Statement, Liquid Metal Fast Breeder Reactor Program) (Washington, D.C.: Natural Resources Defense Council, 1974), pp. 4-7. Xeroxed.
3. Office of Emergency Preparedness, *Energy Conservation: A Staff Study Prepared for the Energy Subcommittee of the Domestic Council* (Washington, D.C., July 1972).
4. Marquis R. Seidel, Steven E. Plotkin, and Robert O. Reck, *Energy Conservation Strategies* (Washington, D.C.: Office of Research and Monitoring, U.S. Environmental Protection Agency, July 1973).
5. National Petroleum Council, *U.S. Energy Outlook: Nuclear Energy Availability* (Washington, D.C., 1973); cf. "Industry Report 1973-74," *Nuclear News,* mid-February 1974.
6. Allen V. Kneese, "The Faustian Bargain," *Resources* (Washington, D.C.: Resources for the Future, Inc., September 1973).
7. The United Kingdom, France, and the Soviet Union all have LMFBRs in operation.
8. The toxicity of plutonium has been likened to that of botulism. See Peter H. Metzger, *The Atomic Establishment* (New York: Simon and Schuster, 1972), p. 145, n. 225.
9. Allen L. Hammond, William D. Metz, and Thomas H. Maugh II, *Energy and the Future* (Washington, D.C.: American Association for the Advancement of Science, 1973).
10. See U.S. Senate, "The Threat of Nuclear Theft and Sabotage," 93d Congress, 2d sess., *Congressional Record* 120, no. 59, 30 April 1974.
11. Hammond, Metz, and Maugh, *Energy and the Future.*
12. Lawrence Lessing, "Lasers Blast Shortcut to the Ultimate Energy Solution," *Fortune,* May 1974.

13. A beginning in this direction has been made by the Council on Environmental Quality. See the Council's *OCS Oil and Gas—An Environmental Assessment,* a report to the President (Washington, D.C., April 1974).

14. Donald Duncan and Vernon Swanson, *Organic-Rich Shale of the United States and World Land Areas,* U.S. Geological Survey Circular 523 (Washington, D.C.: Government Printing Office, 1965), p. 9.

15. U.S. Department of the Interior, *Prospects for Oil Shale Development—Colorado, Utah, Wyoming* (Washington, D.C., May 1968), pp. 11-12. For comparison, the consumption of oil in the United States in 1974 was approximately 6 billion barrels.

16. At 25 gallons to the ton, about 10 billion tons of spoil materials would be generated annually to produce oil at the rate of the 1974 U.S. consumption.

17. Cf. U.S. Department of the Interior, *Final Environmental Statement for the Prototype Oil Shale Leasing Program,* vol. 1, *Regional Impacts of Oil Shale* (Washington, D.C.: Government Printing Office, 1973).

18. For an interesting possibility in this connection, see, for example, Ben Weichman, "Energy and Environmental Impact from the Development of Oil Shale and Associated Minerals" (paper presented at the 65th annual meeting of the American Institute of Chemical Engineers, November 1972, revised 1974).

19. National Academy of Sciences, *Rehabilitation Potential of Western Coal Lands,* a report to the Energy Policy Project of the Ford Foundation (Cambridge, Mass.: Ballinger, 1974).

20. Ibid.

21. U.S. Senate, Committee on Interior and Insular Affairs, "Geothermal Energy in the United States," in Committee Print, 92d Congress, 2d sess., May 1972, pp. 112-16.

22. Hammond, Metz, and Maugh, *Energy and the Future,* p. 57.

23. Ibid., p. 60.

Samuel McCracken

4. THE WAR AGAINST THE ATOM

Most discussions of nuclear power are conducted in a haze of misinformation; there are few areas of public controversy where so much of what everyone "knows" is not really so. Let us begin with a discussion of a few of the least controversial facts about the processes by which nuclear power is generated. These are neither many nor complicated, but it is essential they be understood as a basis for discussing the somewhat complicated issues that grow out of them.

I

The promises and problems of nuclear energy rest on the fact that the atoms of some forms of each element are inherently unstable. Each atomic nucleus (except the common form of hydrogen) contains two sorts of particles: protons and neutrons. Protons have a positive electrical charge, and neutrons have no charge. In a stable form of an element, the protons and neutrons stay closely bound together in the nucleus. Such forms will remain as they are forever, and are not radioactive. In an unstable form, or isotope, neutrons escape from the nucleus, with two important consequences. The first is that the atom is no longer what it was: it has become a different substance. The second is that the departing neutrons may hit something, with a variety of results. The result that is of interest in the present case is that when a neutron strikes a nucleus of the class called "fissionable" (those of uranium and plutonium are the best known), it may enter the nucleus and cause it to split.

There are three consequences of that split: the atom breaks down into two lighter atoms, known as fission products, typically highly unstable and therefore highly radioactive; other neutrons escape from the nucleus; and there is a release of energy. The other escaping neutrons may strike other nuclei, and these too will split; if enough fissionable material is present, there will be a self-sustaining chain reaction, releasing great amounts of energy. If the mass of fissionable material is great enough, such a chain reaction can, with considerable difficulty, be contained so as to produce an explosion.

A nuclear power plant of the type now being built or scheduled to be built through this century uses the chain reaction as a source of heat to make steam to operate turbines which spin generators. Apart from the reactor itself, a nuclear power plant is much like a coal- or oil-fired one.

The fissionable material in most common use is an isotope of uranium: U-235. (The number denotes the total protons and neutrons in the nucleus.) Only .7 percent of all uranium is of this type; the overwhelming proportion of all uranium in nature is a nonfissionable isotope, U-238. In order to use natural uranium as a fuel, it is necessary to raise the proportion of U-235 in it by a process known as enrichment. Uranium for bombs must be enriched to nearly 90 percent U-235. In the power reactors used in this country, 3 percent will do. The enrichment process is extremely complicated and expensive, consuming vast amounts of capital to build and vast amounts of electricity to operate. It also leaves large amounts of nonfissionable U-238 for which there is at present no use.

Among other fissionable elements are thorium, which is more plentiful in nature than uranium, and plutonium, which does not occur in nature except in traces, but which is easily produced in reactors as a by-product. All uranium-burning reactors produce some plutonium incidentally, and plutonium breeder reactors produce it in large quantities deliberately.

There is a considerable variety of possible reactor designs, and the choice among them has become a major issue of public policy. Most of the nuclear reactors in the world today (and, with one exception, all those producing power in the United States) are light-water reactors. In these, ordinary water is circulated around the reactor core and heated by the nuclear reaction, thus serving to cool the core. In one type of light-water reactor, the cooling water is allowed to boil into steam, which is piped directly to the generating turbines. This is known as the boiling-water reactor. In another type, the cooling water is kept under pressure, preventing it from boiling, and is piped to a separate steam generator. This is known as the pressurized-water reactor. Water also serves the necessary purpose of slowing down the neutrons flowing through the reactor core so that they will be able to split nuclei. For this purpose, the water is called a "moderator," and its presence is no less essential to a chain reaction than the fuel itself. At present, light-water reactors are fueled with U-235, although they can also use plutonium or a mix of plutonium and uranium.

Getting the fuel for a light-water reactor is complicated. Uranium ore must be first processed to produce uranium oxide, known as "yellowcake." This is then converted to uranium hexafluoride, a gaseous form essential to the enrichment process. After enrichment, the uranium hexafluoride is converted to uranium dioxide, and this is fabricated into fuel rods. This series of processes makes up the so-called front end of the cycle—that is, before the reactor. Each of these steps in the front end is, with present technology, mandatory for light-water reactors.

After an optimum period in the reactor, spent fuel is ready to be either discarded or reprocessed. It contains, in addition to wastes, unburned uranium and plutonium. In a complete "back end," the uranium and plutonium would be separated from the wastes and fabricated into new fuel that could be used in several ways. The wastes proper would then be disposed of. Currently, however, no fuel is being reprocessed, and it is the position of the Carter administration that none shall be. So the back end of the cycle consists now simply of disposal, and this process is currently being held to its first stage, in which the spent fuel rods are maintained in pools of cooling water at the reactor site.

The light-water reactor is the basis of the U.S. commercial nuclear power industry; it is also now the most common form in use worldwide. But the first experimental reactors used to generate power were breeders. In a plutonium breeder reactor, the fuel can be either U-235 or Pu-239, used to produce a chain reaction just as in the light-water reactor. But the core of a breeder reactor is surrounded by a "blanket" composed of U-238. Because it can be transmuted by neutron bombardment into plutonium, U-238 is called a "fertile" material. Neutrons escaping from the chain reaction are absorbed by U-238 nuclei, transmuting them first into a highly unstable isotope of uranium, U-239. Almost immediately this decays into a much more long-lived and fissionable isotope of plutonium, Pu-239. This substance is as useful for reactor fuel as U-235.

A plutonium breeder reactor is sometimes said to create more fuel than it uses, something which it of course cannot do without violating physical laws. What it can do is to produce more plutonium from U-238 than it burns. And this has made it both enemies and friends. There are other types of breeder reactors of which the most developed uses the common element thorium to breed the fissionable isotope U-233.

II

Beyond these facts, we enter the world of controversy. The opponents of nuclear power are more or less agreed as to what is wrong with it, and their charges are quickly summarized. These charges have been specified at impressive length in many sources, but as yet there has been no single influential exposition of the case against nuclear power as successful as, say, Paul Ehrlich's *The Population Bomb*. Ralph Nader's definitive statement, *The Menace of Atomic Energy*,[1] has been published. It is a thorough summary of the case *contra*, and Nader's name on the spine will no doubt assure it a prominent place on the antinuclear bookshelf. It is an extraordinarily tendentious work (the "suggestions for further reading" list only firmly antinuclear authorities) and I will have something to say about its specific faults later. There is a good deal of useful information along with some dubious analysis in a recent Ford Foundation-sponsored work, *Nuclear Power: Issues and Choices*.[2] This work appears to underlie most of the Carter administration's nuclear policy. An organization active in opposing nuclear power nationwide has been the Union of Concerned Scientists, based largely at MIT, which, despite its name, does not require one to be a scientist to join and does not record how many of its members are in fact scientists. A Ralph Nader organization called Critical Mass, the Sierra Club, the Friends of the Earth, and the *Bulletin of the Atomic Scientists* have also all been active in opposition. The summary that follows is assembled from these and other sources, since most versions of the critique are interchangeable.[3]

The routine operation of power reactors and their fuel cycle is said to be dangerous because such reactors release small amounts of radioactive material into the atmosphere, and it is said that there is unacceptable danger to humans from any amount of radiation, no matter how small.

It was once alleged falsely that nuclear plants posed the additional danger of accidentally exploding like an atomic bomb, but this charge is now rarely heard, although it is sometimes implied on the jackets of antinuclear books. Instead, the most common risk talked about with regard to light-water reactors is that of "meltdown," an accident which may be initiated if the water cooling the reactor core stops flowing. In such an accident, the loss of water removes the moderator and stops the chain reaction itself, but the inherent heat of the radioactive fuel and fission products, if not cooled by water, will cause an inexorable rise in temperature that will eventually melt the fuel and everything beneath it, possibly leading to a serious release of radioactive materials into the atmosphere. In 1965, an Atomic Energy Commission report estimated that the worst possible meltdown accident would kill 27,000 people, injure 73,000, and cause $17 billion in property damage. It is often said that in 1966 the Enrico Fermi reactor near Detroit went into a "partial meltdown" and that in 1975 a fire at the Browns Ferry plant in Alabama came very close to causing a meltdown.*

Plutonium breeder reactors, besides producing plutonium, a fuel alleged to be too dangerous to permit in society, are also said to impose a risk of nuclear explosion.

It is pointed out that homeowners' insurance policies exclude nuclear accidents, and it is claimed that the risk of such accidents is so great that no company will insure against them.

---

*In 1979, America was once again witness to the spectre of a possible meltdown. The nuclear accident at Three Mile Island, Pennsylvania, resulted in evacuation of an entire community and an investigation into the licensing practices of the Nuclear Regulatory Commission. — *Ed.*

Waste disposal sometimes appears even to those who consider nuclear power safe in every other respect to be not only an insoluble problem but so dangerous as to be a sufficient cause for the abolition of nuclear power. The perilousness of nuclear wastes is widely asserted: The fission products of a nuclear reactor are said, besides being uniquely dangerous, to be "the longest-lived" substances known to man, and plutonium, not technically a fission product, has been called "toxic beyond human experience." It is often pointed out that there have been leaks of wastes from the government storage facility at Hanford, Washington, and it is widely contended that there now exists no technology to deal with the wastes that will remain dangerous for hundreds of thousands of years, and that none is now foreseeable. Barry Commoner has spoken of the need for a "nuclear priesthood," dedicated to the safeguarding of nuclear wastes into the infinite future.

Critics of nuclear power say that nuclear plants are guilty of "thermal pollution," that is, they can raise the temperature of the cooling water they discharge into lakes, rivers, and oceans by many degrees, with catastrophic consequences for aquatic life.

Critics of nuclear power widely allege that nuclear power is uneconomical, partially because its routine costs are believed to much higher than for other forms of power generation, and partially because nuclear plants are supposedly much less reliable than other types.

Nuclear critics claim also that plutonium is a potential boon for terrorists in two ways: first of all, as a poison (a few kilos of plutonium, properly dispersed, could allegedly kill everyone in the world). Second, it is often said that a dedicated band of terrorists could acquire enough plutonium to construct their own atomic bomb, with predictably horrific results. To thwart both these dangers, it is maintained that it will be necessary to construct security systems that will amount to a garrison state.

Finally, it is said that a nuclear power industry is inextricably tied up with nuclear weapons proliferation because nations that do not currently have a nuclear weapons capability will be able to attain one by using plutonium-reactor fuel to make plutonium bombs. The best-known advocate of this view is the person best situated to build it into policy: the President of the United States.

These charges against nuclear power would be terrifying if true. Indeed, were no more than half of them true—or even plausible—nuclear power would almost certainly be too dangerous not only to be a solution to the energy crisis but also too dangerous to be allowed to continue at the present level. If these charges were true, there might even be some sense to the idiotic slogan "Split wood, not atoms." But they are not true.

III

The belief that a functioning nuclear reactor and its fuel cycle pose a radiation threat illustrates a common habit among the antinuclear lobby: holding nuclear reactors to a standard of safety that, if generalized, would forbid not only all other forms of power generation but also most of the things man makes or finds in nature.

The standard measure of the biological effect of radiation upon humans is the "roentgen equivalent man," abbreviated rem. The most commonly used subunit is the millirem, abbreviated mrem. The International Commission on Radiological Protection's limit for annual exposure per person is 500 mrem a year. This is a conservative limit, and there are areas in the world where people are naturally exposed to as much as 1,500 mrem a year without apparent damage.

The first thing to understand is that exposure to radiation is an inescapable consequence of living on the earth: we are all exposed to "background radiation" from natural sources, including radioactive minerals such as uranium, and cosmic rays. In the United States this exposure ranges from as high as 175 mrem a year to as little as 50, depending on location. The U.S. average is 130 mrem. Radioactive materials such as granite, which is — in these exquisitely sensitive contexts — highly radioactive, add 10 mrem or so a year. Petr Beckmann of the University of Colorado[4] has pointed out that if Grand Central Station were to be held to the Nuclear Regulatory Commission standards for reactors, it could not be licensed. There is, additionally, approximately 120 mrem a year more in man-made radiation. Most of this comes from X rays and other medical sources. Fallout accounts for 4 mrem a year, and color television for about 1 mrem. Nuclear plants add, in the United States, approximately .003 mrem a year. Without nuclear plants, the average American absorbs 250 mrem a year; with nuclear plants, he absorbs 250.003 mrem.

It is often argued by nuclear critics that radiation is so dangerous that *no* addition to the natural background is tolerable. If this be so, then it is a little hard to know why the critics are concentrating on nuclear plants. If one lives next to the property line of a nuclear reactor, the NRC permits an added exposure of 5 mrem a year. The added risk of cancer is equal to that imposed by smoking one cigarette a year.

These doses are perhaps put in perspective by the fact that a single chest X ray adds some 50 mrem, and simply flying from New York to Los Angeles 5 mrem. Worse still, if one moves from Dallas to Denver, the additional annual exposure is nearly 100 mrem: that is, twenty times the radiation permitted to the neighbor of an operating nuclear plant. This is simply the consequence of Denver's altitude. The practical effect of all this extra radiation is perhaps to be noted in the fact that Colorado's cancer incidence is *lower* than the national average.

Bernard Cohen of the University of Pittsburgh[5] has provided a neat illustration of the real risk from the emissions of a nuclear reactor. If one lives at its property line, and wishes to move away in order to escape the risks of the 5-mrem-a-year which is the maximum emission permitted — in practice, no reactor comes near the permitted maximum — one must take care not to move to a house more than 500 feet farther away from one's place of work. If one does, the increased risk from auto accident will outweigh the decreased risk from radiation.

Although the opponents of nuclear power talk as if it were generally accepted that minute amounts of radiation result in genetic damage to human beings, it is not generally realized that this assumption rests on laboratory results with animals that appear to be contradicted by actual experience with humans. At Hiroshima and Nagasaki, thousands of humans were exposed to levels of radiation that not even the harshest critic of nuclear power believes can come from a reactor. Thirty years later, there has been no detectable increase in genetic damage among the offspring of this population.

There are undoubtedly risks of cancer from exposure to radiation. That they are in any event tiny is evident from the fact that any number of highly radioactive (but nonindustrialized) sections of the country combine high background radiation with low cancer rates. The important point is that nuclear reactors, routinely operated, are among the most negligible emitters of radiation, and thus among the most negligible causes of cancer from radiation.

The truth is that cigarette smokers pose a greater risk of cancer to their neighbors than all the nuclear plants in the country; and any smoker who opposes nuclear power on the grounds that it is carcinogenic lives in the grip of a potentially explosive contradiction.

So much for the dangers posed by routine operation of a nuclear reactor and the fuel cycle; those posed by accidents are a more complicated matter. By far the most serious accident possible in a light-water reactor is the so-called meltdown. A meltdown would begin with a break in one of the pipes carrying heated water or steam from the reactor core to a heat exchanger or a turbine. All reactors have redundant systems to supply emergency cooling water, but if all these were to fail, even though the lack of a moderator would shut down the chain reaction, the heat growing out of the fission products contained in the core would no longer be carried away, and the fuel would begin to melt. The stainless-steel pressure vessel, covering the reactor proper, is designed to contain the effects of this, but if it should fail, the domed containment structure is made to hold in the various radioactive products dispersed within it. Only if this containment structure fails — and it is designed to withstand the impact from a crashing jetliner—would there be a release of radioactive material into the atmosphere. What would happen next depends on the location of the reactor and on the weather. The consequences would range from none to very serious ones indeed. There would be none if a minimum of radioactivity were released and it were widely dispersed over sparsely populated areas. And there would be very serious results if a great deal of radioactivity were emitted and it were dispersed in a concentrated fashion over densely populated areas.

Now, although there is some disagreement as to the precise magnitude of casualties in the worst possible meltdown disaster, all parties agree that the worst possible meltdown disaster would be a major one. The real disagreement comes on probabilities, which are essential to understanding the real risk of anything. In general, the worse the accident, the less the probability. The worst possible airline accident, for example, would be something like a fully loaded 747 crashing into the Rose Bowl on New Year Day, an event which might kill perhaps 30,000 people. The worst possible electric-power generation accident would be not a nuclear meltdown but the failure of a hydroelectric dam at the head of a heavily populated valley. This might kill as many as a quarter of a million people and destroy many billions of dollars' worth of property. If such an accident were very much less probable than a meltdown, we might discount the fact that it threatens a much higher death toll. As it happens, the dam accident is substantially *more* likely than a major meltdown accident.

In 1975, the Atomic Energy Commission published a study that attempted to calculate the risks of a meltdown, the Reactor Safety Study (RSS), known as the Rasmussen report from its director, Norman Rasmussen of MIT. The RSS concludes that the maximum credible light-water reactor accident would result in 3,300 deaths immediately, with 45,000 deaths from cancer over a period of thirty years, and $14 billion in property damage. It also concludes that the chance of such an accident is vanishingly remote, perhaps 10,000 times smaller than similar death tolls from such disasters as dam failures and tropical storms. The probability that, with 100 reactors operating, 1,000 people would be killed in a single accident is the same as for 1,000 people being killed by a single meteorite—once very billion years.

The RSS has been subjected to very severe criticism from both the American Physical Society and the Union of Concerned Scientists. Among the most telling claims made against it are that the system of analysis it uses was developed to predict relative, but not absolute, safety, and that the report pays inadequate regard to the possibility that failure in one component may lead to failure in another, as when water spilling from a broken pipe disables a safety device. It is not necessary to accept all the criticisms made of the report (for instance, that it ignores sabotage) to see that its critics have raised substantial questions about the validity of its predictions.

If the probabilities predicted by the RSS were not themselves so remote, however—that with 100 reactors operating, one person would be killed by them once every two centuries—the criticism would be more disturbing. As it stands, there is much sense in the conclusion reached by the Ford Foundation report, which is that although the risks of a meltdown may be greater than indicated in the RSS, they are still very remote. Moreover, they are not greater in likelihood and intensity than risks society already accepts and has learned to live with. In this century, the Ford Foundation report notes, the United States has already seen two hurricanes that have taken over a thousand lives each and resulted in billions of dollars of property damage.

Still, it should be obvious that we need a reactor-safety study in whose judgments there will be widespread confidence. Such a study, moreover, should compare the relative risks of light-water reactors to other types. If whatever risks inhere in the light-water reactor turn out to be substantially idiosyncratic to it, rather than typical of nuclear power, we need to know that.

The plutonium breeder is alleged to present even more serious safety problems than the light-water reactor. The principal allegation about the operation of the reactor itself is that should it suffer a meltdown, it is possible for the melted plutonium fuel to reassemble itself in such a way as to achieve critical mass and undergo a nuclear explosion. The technical community is divided on this issue, and it would be foolish in the face of such division for a layman to maintain that it could not happen. But it is important to understand what it would involve and how unlikely it is.

There is as yet no body of data on operating plutonium breeders that would allow any hard assessment of the risks of a meltdown. But the design of such reactors makes it very unlikely. The liquid sodium coolant is circulated at very low pressure which makes a pipe rupture less probable in prospect and less serious in actuality. So a loss-of-coolant accident is very unlikely, as is the prospect that all emergency systems would fail. Even if they did, it is not certain that the fuel would reassemble so as to form a critical mass, and any explosion that did occur would be of a different order from a bomb explosion. Reactor-grade plutonium is heavily contaminated with Pu-240, which makes it a bad weapons material. (Nuclear critics consistently mislabel reactor plutonium as "weapons grade." While it can be used to make bombs, they are highly inefficient and likely to explode prematurely. There is a weapons-grade plutonium, but it is pure Pu-239, and it is not produced in power reactors.) Further, since much of the art of making an atomic bomb lies in the elaborate mechanisms to contain the explosion long enough for it to build up, an accidental reassembly would lead to a fizzle rather than a real explosion. It is probable that such an "explosion" would be held within a containment structure. The risk of such an explosion occurring and releasing radiation must be akin to that of being hit by a meteorite.

An overheating incident in 1966 at the Fermi breeder plant near Detroit has been the subject of John G. Fuller's extremely ignorant and sensational book, *We Almost Lost Detroit*.[6] Space and life are too short to catalog the errors of this work, but it is perhaps sufficient to note that Fuller regularly characterizes the liquid sodium coolant, actually less viscous than water, as "syrup-like," and he paints a picture of the site of the plant, eight years after the accident, still contaminated by radioactive sodium. In fact, the preponderant and most dangerous isotope created in a breeder's coolant, Na-24, has a half-life of fifteen hours. It was effectively nonexistent a month after the reactor shut down. Even the much less dangerous Na-22, produced in far smaller quantities, has a half-life of only thirty months and was thus greatly reduced in amount after eight years had passed. Others have followed and expanded upon Fuller's errors in this work. One is often told that the accident nearly involved a meltdown, although the plant did not yet contain enough fission products for this, and that it is now inoperative, without being told that it was an experimental reactor closed only after having been successfully repaired and restarted.

The tale of the Fermi reactor is the tale of a major reactor that suffered a very serious accident without a single human injury, much less a death. Citing it as proof that nuclear energy is too dangerous is like trying to prove that cars are too dangerous by citing examples of safety belts working.

But the case for the breeder is more than a negation of the case against it. The true potential of the breeder is almost never conceded by nuclear critics. For it could do more than allow us to outlast the present supply of uranium in the ground. Since it allows the conversion of our presently useless stock of already mined U-238, it would allow us to generate electricity for several hundred years without mining another ounce of fuel. This is what an all-breeder generating capacity would mean—true energy independence for the United States and the saving of thousands of lives in the mines.

The principle of the half-truth is nowhere better illustrated than in the antinuclear movement's discussion of insurance. It is true that homeowners' insurance policies exclude damage because of nuclear accidents. But this is because nuclear accidents are separately covered under insurance set up by the Price-Anderson Act. Under the act, a coverage is established of $560 million per accident. A portion of this—currently $140 million—is covered by insurance purchased from private insurance companies. The balance is covered by insurance purchased from the federal government. By 1980, the private companies will have gradually taken over the entire coverage, and as new plants are built, the limit will be raised. And should an accident occur, all operating plants will be assessed a retrospective charge of $5 million.

The critics' perennial question—"If a major accident that would cost $17 billion is so extraordinarily remote, why won't the insurance companies sell insurance for it?"—is easily answered. Although the extreme case is highly unlikely over any span of years, it could—however unlikely this may be—occur tomorrow. Although no premium would have been paid remotely covering the cost, the cost would have to be paid. And because a major nuclear accident would make the death of the whole industry a high probability, there would be little chance of recovering the cost out of future premiums. A similar principle applies to the insuring of fireworks displays: the premium drops proportional to the experience and future stability of the firm lighting the fuse.

Should a nuclear accident occur beyond the insured limits, it seems very likely that the Congress would provide retrospective compensation. It must also be noted that Price-Anderson insurance is superior to other insurance in two respects: for the great majority of likely accidents, it would pay full compensation to the victims, and unlike all other disaster insurance, the premium is paid not by the beneficiary but by a third party.

It is evident that the single most frightening charge made against nuclear energy is that it produces extraordinarily dangerous wastes that must be guarded for millions of years. The antinuclear lobby calls on us to remember our obligations to our descendants, and regularly tells us that we have as yet devised no means to deal with the waste problem. No part of the antinuclear dogma is more suffused with ignorance, sensationalism, and downright dishonesty than this charge.

To begin with, the actual danger posed by these wastes is grossly exaggerated. The wastes are of two general types. Fission products, elements lighter than uranium and highly radioactive, are the debris of the split nuclei and have comparatively short half-lives. These are also called "high-level wastes." Transuranics, elements heavier than uranium, are caused by its irradiation and have long half-lives. These are also called "low-level wastes."

The best-known of the transuranics is plutonium, and it is also the most sensationalized. It is said to have been named for "Pluto, the god of hell," a statement which is erroneous as to fact (it was named by astronomical analogy as the element beyond Neptunium) and ignorant of the Greco-Roman notion of Hades. It is regularly said to be the most toxic substance known to man, and sometimes even to be toxic beyond human experience. It is hard to disagree with Petr Beckmann's characterization of such statements as "melodramatic piffle."

It should be first observed that plutonium is a waste substance only if it is not used as a fuel. If it be a waste substance requiring long-term storage it is only because we make it so. Plutonium is of course a very toxic substance, but it is not uniquely so. Bernard Cohen has estimated that if the entire electric-power industry of the United States operated with fast breeder reactors, the annual production of plutonium would, if dispersed with maximum efficiency and then inhaled, be sufficient to cause 1 trillion deaths. This indeed sounds terrifying. But two things must be remembered. First, the annual production of plutonium could not possibly be dispersed with such efficiency. Second, we routinely handle far more dangerous substances: our present annual production of hydrogen cyanide, if similarly dispersed and inhaled, would cause 6 trillion deaths; our annual production of ammonia, 8 trillion; our annual production of phosgene, 18 trillion; and our annual production of chlorine, no fewer than 400 trillion deaths.

Cohen also points out that there is more danger to us from the radium deposited in the earth's crust than from prospective plutonium production. Specifically, if all the present generating capacity were fired by fast breeder reactors producing as much plutonium as they consumed, the total amount of plutonium in existence would be no more radioactive than the radium that already exists in a little over half a foot of the earth's crust. Even this comparison overstates the danger from plutonium. When ingested, naturally occurring radium is forty times as toxic as plutonium, and it is a source of the dangerous radioactive gas, radon. If we correct for this, we will see that all the plutonium produced by an all-breeder power system would, if dispersed throughout the earth's crust, be no more dangerous than the radium occurring naturally in 4 *mm* of that crust. It should hardly need pointing out that this plutonium would not be dispersed throughout the environment, but would be in reactors and processing plants.

Nor, in looking for things that are more poisonous than plutonium, need one confine oneself to naturally occurring radioactive substances. Arsenic trioxide when ingested is fifty times more toxic than plutonium, and we import this insecticide in quantities that would exceed the wastes from an all-nuclear economy. And we spray it about very nearly at random and have no plans whatsoever for disposing of it in any manner.

Plutonium is, additionally, often characterized by such terms as "searingly radioactive," a phrase recently applied to it by *Time*. This is exceptionally ignorant and misleading. Plutonium radiation consists of alpha particles, and these are stopped by a sheet of paper or a few inches of air. Indeed, they are stopped by the epidermis, and pose a threat to humans only when ingested or inhaled. Their principal threat is as a carcinogen, and there is general agreement that in this regard plutonium is extremely potent. The depth of the extremity is a matter for debate, but no one regards the problem as something to be ignored. For a society that tolerates cigarettes to use this hazard as an excuse for rejecting the extraordinary benefits of plutonium is lunatic.

Further, a great deal is made of plutonium's half-life of 24,000 years. (This is the half-life of its most common isotope, Pu-239. Its other isotopes have half-lives ranging from less than a second to 80 million years.) It is, on this basis, frequently called "one of the longest-lived substances known to man." This characterization is particularly idiotic. For one thing, it obscures the fact that the longer-lived a radioactive substance is, the less dangerous its radiation is—for it emits radiation at a lower rate. Fission products—high-level wastes—have comparatively short half-lives because they decay at so furious a rate. But the characterization obscures something even more important: radioactive poisons are the only poisons that have half-lives as *short* as 24,000, or even 80 million, years. Stable isotopes are eternal and have *infinite* half-lives. A gram of plutonium will eventually end up as slightly less than a gram of lead. A gram of arsenic will always be a gram of arsenic.

The Union of Concerned Scientists has issued a brochure which describes the alleged qualities of certain high-level wastes, and then cites, as if it applied to these same wastes, a government estimate for a very large amount of nuclear wastes to be created by the year 2000. But the UCS suppresses the fact that the government's estimate applies not to high-level wastes, but to *low-level* wastes, which are so feeble in radiation that they can be buried in trenches.

But these confusions and misstatements pale beside those made about the state of waste-disposal technology. A principal stock-in-trade of the antinuclear lobby is a series of leaks of high-level wastes from storage tanks at the government's Hanford, Washington, facility. These leaks, deplorable enough in themselves, are regularly cited as representative of the risks in current techniques. One is never told that the tanks in question are of early postwar design, and have long since been superseded. It is as if the safety record of the railroads in 1845, when accidents were very common, had been used in 1925 to justify closing them down.

The most common assertion one hears in this area, however, is the flat statement that we do not now know how to dispose of high-level wastes, which must be isolated from contact with the biosphere for many thousands of years. This challenge has already been met, and the endlessly repeated statement that it has not is the nearest equivalent in the debate over nuclear power to a classic Big Lie.

The technology for disposal, which has been demonstrated in a pilot project at Hanford, and actually used in Europe, involves first "calcining" the waste to a sandlike substance of greatly reduced bulk, and then using this "sand" as a component to make glass. The resulting glass is radioactive but chemically inert. It can then be buried deep in geologically stable salt formations, where no water has flowed for millions of years. It will require no surveillance, let alone a "nuclear priesthood." If there were an immediate need for such storage, it would no doubt have already been implemented. But the fact is that there are not now enough wastes in inventory to make such a process economical, and there will not be for some years. It thus makes good sense to keep existing wastes in temporary storage and to hold up on final disposal while an already adequate technology is improved.

Most antinuclear prophets simply ignore this process or lump it together with a number of purely speculative suggestions, such as launching wastes by rocket into the sun. Nader and Abbotts ignore it except to quote an outdated press release of the Energy Research and Development Administration noting that it will not work for ERDA's inventory of weapons waste. The problem has now been corrected by a new process developed at Hanford. But in any event, Nader and Abbotts conveniently omit to note that this problem was never applicable to existing or prospective wastes from power reactors. And although they cite the problem as an example of ERDA's inability to manage "its own" wastes, they do not note that the neutralization of military wastes that led to the problem was carried out long before there was an ERDA. It is this sort of thing which raises grave doubts about Ralph Nader's secular sanctity. The best that can be said for such tactics is that they belong to an advocate whose concern is not with truth but propaganda.

Elsewhere in their discussion of waste disposal, Nader and Abbotts make the claim that technology cannot guarantee geologically stable areas in which to deposit wastes. This is true but irrelevant. Nature provides such areas and technology can locate them. Nader and Abbotts misleadingly suggest that a false start at finding such an area in Kansas means that none exists. Had Nader been operating in the early nineteenth century, the railways would have had a very hard time getting started.

It is not surprising that antinuclear advocates should wish to perpetuate the lie that wastes are an insoluble problem. As they themselves often note, the issue is perhaps the strongest they have going for them, and it must be a terrible thought that some interfering scientist somewhere may have gone and solved it.

The "thermal pollution" charge laid at the door of nuclear power plants is a mixture of half-truth, exaggeration, and gross sentimentality. First of all, the root phenomenon is not peculiar to nuclear plants. All thermal-power plants waste a great deal of heat and must dispose of it, generally into bodies of water or through cooling towers into the atmosphere. Light-water reactors have a slightly lower thermal efficiency than fossil-fuel plants, and therefore discharge more heat, but breeder reactors are at least as efficient as fossil-fueled plants. If "thermal pollution" is really an argument for rejecting nuclear energy, it is also an argument for rejecting most of our electricity.

The most commonly attacked "thermal pollution" involves the discharge of waste heat into bodies of water. The critics are fond of citing the temperature rise at the discharge exit, which may be as high as 70 degrees. They are less fond of citing the temperature rise over a few hundred square feet, which will be only a degree or two.

But even this slight change will have an effect on the aquatic life near a reactor, as it makes the water an unsuitable environment for some species. In doing so, however, it makes it more suitable for other species. Lobsters, for example, thrive in the slightly warmed water near a reactor.

When a reactor shuts down, as for refueling, a species that has moved into warm water may have difficulty in surviving a temporary cooling of the water. Much has been made of the fact that menhaden, fish important in fertilizer and pet food are enticed into the slightly warmed waters near reactors located on the Atlantic and then killed off when the water cools during a shutdown. A not dissimilar phenomenon occurs when the elderly of the species *homo* die of cold during a natural-gas shortage, but of this we hear little. If we had no need of energy, it would perhaps be possible to let our hearts bleed for the menhaden, who no doubt prefer ending up as fertilizer or cat food to death by thermal pollution. But the fact is that our need for safe energy is crucial, and it is only those who have never known what it is like to be without energy who can seriously contemplate a brutal policy of sacrificing human interests to those of fish. In a related piece of folly, the opponents of the Seabrook plant in New Hampshire have opposed its cooling system on the grounds that it would inhale and destroy a certain diet of aquatic life each day. The amount involved is about what three or four whales consume, but one does not hear the same people urging a moratorium on the existence of whales.

"Thermal pollution," in short, is a bugbear invented to cover for the embarrassing fact that nuclear power plants do not assault the environment with the same ferocity as such putatively safe energy sources as coal. "Thermal pollution" is common to all thermal plants; it can be taken seriously only by indulging a studied contempt for human welfare in the interests, real or otherwise, of marine life.

The economic argument against nuclear power is made in multifarious ways. Sometimes it appears to grow out of simple ignorance, as when the utilities are alleged to prefer expensive nuclear plants because with great capital investment higher rates can be charged, quite as if that capital did not have to be recovered out of income. Sometimes it is based on the implied assumption that the government ought never to subsidize the development of a new technology, as when it is objected that the government does not make a profit on its fuel-enrichment operation. Those who make this charge have not been heard to object to the government subsidy of mass transport through Amtrak and the Urban Mass Transit Administration. Sometimes it is based on manipulation of the facts, as when figures for western low-sulfur coal burned near the mine in comparatively cheap power plants are misapplied to plants burning high-sulfur coal in very expensive scrubber-equipped plants. And sometimes it is based on the lurid charge that the total energy needed to build and operate a nuclear plant is greater than what it produces — that the nuclear industry has made no net addition to the nation's energy supply. In fact, building and operating a light-water plant, including the enrichment of its fuel, uses 6 percent of its lifetime output. A coal-fired plant uses between 6.7 and 7.8 percent, depending on whether it burns surface or deep-mined coal. There is hardly a better example of the disparity that exists between the antinuclear gospel and simple reality.

But the most reprehensible form of the argument is that nuclear plants are less reliable than other types. Part of this charge is based on a half-truth, namely, that stringent safety standards require these plants to be shut down for comparatively trivial reasons, and that the discovery of a problem in one plant may lead to a temporary shutdown in all plants of the same general type. Such incidents are sometimes badly misreported; thus, when a hairline crack, releasing no water or radioactivity, was discovered in a standby cooling pipe at the Commonwealth Edison Dresden plant near Chicago, 23 plants with similar standby systems were ordered to close down for inspection. No cracks were found in any of them, but the incident was reported widely as one in which 23 plants had been shut down because of cracks in their cooling systems. Less widely reported is the fact that Commonwealth Edison's nuclear plants have proved just as reliable as its coal plants.

Still more dubious is the practice of stating reliability factors for nuclear plants in isolation, without comparing them to other types, and comparing them to much smaller conventional plants.

The fact is that over the nation, nuclear reactors are about as reliable as fossil plants of equivalent size. There are two basic measures of reliability: the availability factor, which measures the proportion of the time a generator is actually ready to generate electricity, and the capacity factor, which measures the proportion of capacity actually used. It is the capacity factor that is significant for the economics of power generation. In 1975 and 1976, nuclear plants used to generate base loads attained a higher capacity than either coal or oil plants used for the same purpose. In the same years, the nuclear plants attained availability factors a few percentage points less than coal and oil. And if fossil-fuel plants were held to safety standards as rigorous as nuclear plants, they would post a still lower availability factor. Indeed, as still unreliable scrubbers become more common on coal-fired plants, this is just what will happen.

In their summation of the economic issues, Nader and Abbotts maintain that a definitive statement on nuclear economics is the number of plants that have been canceled or deferred. By November 1975, 130,000 megawatts-electric had been canceled or deferred, representing over two-thirds of all cancellations or deferrals of power plants within the industry.

This is statistical demagoguery; such figures are meaningless except in context. First of all, when a utility defers a nuclear plant, it does so because it plans to delay the adding of new capacity that had already been planned for. Recently such deferrals have occurred because the rate of growth in demand has finally slowed and we are not going to need capacity that before the energy crisis it seemed reasonable to plan for. But a deferral is not a vote of no-confidence in nuclear power: to the contrary, it is a statement that when there is adequate demand to employ a new plant, it will be nuclear rather than otherwise. Nader and Abbotts thus make an especially perverse use of the fact that nuclear plants have been deferred. And although utilities cancel power plants for a variety of reasons, most do so because of reduced demand projections. Had the electric industry, in the days when it was placing orders for future demand, regarded nuclear power as the *only* form worth ordering, it would have placed even more orders for nuclear plants, and would now be canceling even more nuclear capacity. But the fact that "100 percent of all capacity deferred or canceled has been nuclear" would then derive from the industry's confidence in nuclear power as opposed to other forms, not its mistrust of nuclear economics.

The statistics that really would be indicative of such mistrust would be the megawattage of nuclear capacity canceled *and replaced by some other form of generation.* We should not hold our breath waiting for Nader to publish this figure. The Nuclear Regulatory Commission reports that no utility, having applied for a permit to build a nuclear reactor, has ever canceled the nuclear plant in favor of a fossil-fuel plant. That is the measure of the industry's confidence in nuclear power.

Nor should we expect Nader to publish an accounting of the net cost to householders of "environmentalist" delaying tactics. Each stage in the approval and construction of a nuclear plant is now routinely opposed by organizations of nuclear critics. The heavy legal fees thus incurred by the utilities end up on the electric bill. Still worse is the inflationary cost exacted by delay. Almost as sure as death and taxes is the continuing rise in construction costs. The antinuclear lobby delights in quoting cost overruns, but rarely notes the influence on these of the delays which they work to cause. These costs too are borne by consumers and are cruelly regressive upon the poor, a bit of brutal condescension from the middle classes where antinuclear sentiment is strongest.

The antinuclear lobby works to ban plutonium—that substance which contains more energy for its volume than any other—on the spurious ground that it will inevitably be stolen and used by terrorists. Plutonium is alleged to be a ready tool for these gentry in two forms: as a poison and as bomb material. The difficulties in acquiring a stock of the substance are the same in either case.

They are immense. The only time plutonium is vulnerable is after it has been separated in a reprocessing plant and before it is loaded into a reactor. At any other time, it is so poisoned by fission products as to be both dangerous and useless. It would be practically impossible to smuggle plutonium out of a facility in little bits. Because it is radioactive, plutonium on the person is detectable in amounts as small as a gram. In order to extract the minimum ten kilograms needed for a bomb, a smuggler would neeed to execute at least 10,000 separate thefts.

A recent demonstration in which an army assault team using mortars and high explosives required fourteen hours to get into a plutonium depository suggests the unlikelihood of covert theft from stationary deposits. This means that the plutonium would have to be hijacked from a convoy. The difficulties here are extraordinary. Hijacking a shipment of plutonium on the way to a reactor would, oxymoronically, have to be a covert semimilitary operation. Plutonium has long been shipped in this country as part of weapons production, and formidable precautions have been developed. These include radio tracking of the trucks, devices that disable the trucks if hijacked, and escort vehicles carrying armed guards. A group of terrorists equipped to overwhelm such a convoy would be better advised to steal a tactical nuclear warhead ready-made. They would be mad to expend their energies on stealing unsatisfactory material for a bomb design that might not work and that might well explode prematurely and blow them up.

For it is essential to realize that building a plutonium bomb is a feat that has to date been accomplished by only a handful of nation-states. It ought to be readily apparent that there is very little likelihood of a small band of terrorists accomplishing what India accomplished only with difficulty.

As a matter of fact, building a bomb from plutonium-reactor fuel is a task even more difficult than that accomplished by the Indians. For reactor-grade plutonium, although primarily composed of Pu-239, is heavily contaminated with Pu-240, which can cause a bomb to explode prematurely and fizzle. The original discovery of Pu-240 very nearly ended the Manhattan Project.

One disturbing fact is that it probably will not matter whether plutonium *is* an ideal substance for terrorism as long as enough people *think* it is. If most people in New York City can be persuaded to believe that a few kilograms of plutonium can be so distributed as to kill them all, it will be appreciably harder for any government to resist demands made by terrorists allegedly wielding substantial amounts of plutonium. It can be seen that prospective terrorists are getting a good deal of help from those who go about spreading lurid falsehoods about the toxicity of plutonium and the ease with which the plutonium in reactors can be made into bombs.

A related fright widely merchandised is that safeguarding plutonium from terrorists requires a police state that will inevitably destroy our civil liberties. This view ignores the fact that we are already shipping plutonium around the country in substantial quantities for military purposes, that it is not hijacked, and that we have had to establish no repressive mechanism to achieve this result. It is possible that establishing a system to track down terrorists who make sensational but false claims involving plutonium as a poison or a bomb might require such a mechanism, but that problem will exist whether terrorists acquire plutonium or not, and is in any event largely the creature of the antinuclear movement.

Nuclear proliferation is, of course, an excellent thing to be against because so few people are for it. The problem is that it is very doubtful that U.S. energy policy can have any effect whatever on the course of nuclear proliferation. The most obvious reason for this is that those countries that lack a backstop of coal and oil — France first among them — will develop breeder technology for their own needs whether we do so or not, and will finance that development by exporting breeder technology. There is simply no possibility that the United States can prohibit the world wide production of plutonium by sitting on the breeder reactor. Indeed, it cannot sit on the breeder because the French, with the Superphénix, are rushing to commercialize it.

Moreover, diverting plutonium from a power reactor is a highly inefficient way of making plutonium suitable for weapons. It is far more efficient to use a research reactor for the purpose, and as a matter of fact that is precisely how the Indians appear to have made the plutonium for their bomb: in a research — not a power — reactor supplied them by Canada. This fact is obscured by constant misstatements to the contrary by people who should know better, including the *New Republic's* TRB. And the United States, having no monopoly on research reactors, is just as powerless to prevent nuclear proliferation by putting an embargo on them.

The prevention of nuclear proliferation is a very serious problem, but it must be solved on its own terms if it is to be solved at all. It cannot be solved by false nostrums that require the adoption of a suicidal energy policy. It *might* be solved, though, by the adoption of reactor systems that do not lend themselves at all to bomb production. One of these, the gas-fueled reactor, is fueled only with nonfissionable material, and never has more than a few kilograms of fissionable uranium in its core at one time. This is still in the design stages, but there is another reactor design that is not only very hard to adapt for bombs but is actually now in use and development: the Canadian heavy-water reactor known as the CANDU. This reactor has a form of water as coolant and moderator that contains deuterium, a heavy isotope of hydrogen, rather than normal hydrogen. The superior moderating abilities of heavy water permit the employment of natural unenriched uranium, useless as bomb material, as the fuel, and such a reactor needs no expensive and complicated enrichment plant. Because it uses pressure tubes in its boiler rather than the teakettle design common to light-water reactors, even the theoretical likelihood of a loss-of-coolant accident is tiny, and its possible consequences far smaller. The CANDU core design also enables it to be refueled without being shut down, thus allowing a theoretical availability of 100 percent. There are a number of CANDU reactors generating power in Canada at extraordinary proportions of capacity.

The CANDU design is adaptable to a number of fuel cycles. The Canadian nuclear industry is now turning its attention to modifying the CANDU to operate on the thorium-uranium cycle. In this cycle, the plentiful fertile thorium is bred to the fissile uranium which is then burned as fuel without being removed from the reactor. Such a CANDU reactor could gain the advantages of the plutonium breeder while avoiding even the residual dangers of plutonium.

If the antinuclear lobby were genuinely and intelligently interested in safer energy sources that do not raise even hypothetical problems of nuclear proliferation, it would be urging ERDA to acquire a CANDU reactor for demonstration-and-development purposes.

If the risks of nuclear energy are very much less than its critics allege, they are still not negligible, and indeed would be sufficient ground for its rejection if there were a workable technology with fewer risks. But it is in comparison with the alternative that nuclear energy really begins to shine. Far from being our most dangerous source of energy, nuclear energy is our safest.

The widely held impression to the contrary depends on a habit of forgetting the actual deaths caused by existing technologies, and comparing the void thereby created with hypothetical deaths caused by nuclear energy. As we have seen, the hypothetical deaths of nuclear energy are still no more than that. But the actual deaths caused by other technologies are countable and many.

We can begin with coal. Coal-fired electricity now costs a great many lives each year, a figure, even on the most conservative estimate, well into the thousands nationally. The electricity generated by a 1000 mwh coal-fired generator carries two price tags, one in dollars and one in lives. D. J. Rose and colleagues at MIT have calculated this second price tag. If we add up the number of coal miners killed in accidents, coal miners killed by "black lung" disease, and workers killed in transporting coal from the mine to the power plant, we see that each such plant kills at least 11 people a year. One can imagine how quickly the nuclear industry would be shut down if a single plant killed 11 people a year. Furthermore, if we add in the people killed by pollution from the plant, the exact number of which is a matter of controversy, we see that the price tag will list between 20 and 100 more human lives. This, it must be remembered, is the cost per year of *one* large coal-fired plant: between 31 and 111 lives a year. These deaths, it also must be remembered, are of actual people who die every year in order that coal-fired plants may be operated. In contrast, when we calculate all the deaths caused by a 1000 mwh light-water reactor—including all those killed by the fuel cycle, by the operation of the reactor, and by waste disposal, we arrive at a total of one-half a death a year. This half-death, by the way, is still largely hypothetical, since it includes amortized figures for a number of accidents that have not yet happened. While a few uranium miners are killed each year, *no one* has ever been killed by a commercial power reactor.

The death ratio between the two systems of power generation is thus seen to be between 60 and 225 to 1, favor nuclear. It is not surprising, given such figures, that nuclear critics rarely dwell on the dangers of coal. Nader and Abbotts engage in a particularly neat bit of footwork, in which an attempt to conceal the truth is paraded as an attempt at candor:

> It should be pointed out that, compared to workers in other energy industries, particularly those in the coal fuel cycle, the numbers of workers injured by the atomic industry are smaller. But it should also be recognized that nuclear power produces much less of the nation's energy than coal power. Moreover, because the occupational dangers of nuclear power include cancers which will not become evident for several years, the full toll of the atomic industry can only be estimated.

This sleazy evasion suggests that the numbers of workers killed in the coal cycle are approximately in proportion to the amount of energy produced from coal, and that the occupational hazards of coal mining are limited to those killed in accidents. The facts are quite otherwise, and the fact that Ralph Nader could put his name to this scandalous paragraph suggests that his admirers overrate either his intelligence or his integrity.

It is one of life's little ironies that coal contains small amounts of radioactive elements, mostly radium and thorium, and that the typical coal-fired plant has a level of radioactive emission *greater* than that allowed for a nuclear plant. If the NRC had responsibility for regulating our coal-fired plants, they would have to be shut down.

The antinuclear lobby implies that waste disposal is a problem uniquely of nuclear power. The fact is that coal-fired plants solve part of this problem by disposing of their wastes into the air and thence into our lungs, and the rest by dumping. The amount disposed of into the atmosphere comes to some thirty pounds a year for each American. The solid wastes carted away to the dump from coal-fired plants total tens of millions of tons a year: some 36,500 truck-loads a year for a 1000 megawatt plant. These contain not only such nonradio-active poisons as mercury, selenium, vanadium, and benzopyrene, but radioac-tive materials such as uranium and thorium in amounts that would be imper-missible for emission from a nuclear plant.

It has been misleadingly suggested that the airborne disposal of coal wastes can be prevented in a benign fashion by the use of "scrubbers," expensive and unreliable devices that remove pollutants from smokestack effluents and trap them in millions of tons of sludge, itself a major form of pollution. This is the sort of "solved" waste-disposal problem that the antinuclear lobby wishes to saddle us with.

A massive commitment to coal would raise yet another problem, the possi-bility that a substantial increase in atmospheric carbon dioxide would lead to a long-term warming of the earth—the so-called greenhouse effect. A recent re-port by a blue-ribbon panel of the National Academy of Scientists under the chairmanship of Roger Revelle estimates that the worldwide temperature might, within two hundred years, be raised as much as 11 degrees by this effect. The possible results for agriculture and for marine life thoroughly justify the panel's conclusion that the consequences of increased coal use would be "highly adverse." There is a pathetic irony in the sight of self-proclaimed "environmen-talists" proposing to tamper with the earth's climate in this fashion.

Compared to coal, almost any technology looks safe, including oil. But even if political and other considerations made oil a reasonable source for gen-erating power, it would pose terrible dangers. High-sulfur oil is environmental-ly far from benign, and when stored in large tanks, all oil poses a very serious hazard. The Bayonne fire of 1973, in which tankers and shore tanks caught fire, produced clouds of smoke that, had the wind carried them over Manhattan, and had there been an inversion, would have made the London "killer smog" of 1952, with its nearly 4,000 deaths, seem tame. The same can be said for the Brooklyn fire of 1976.

While natural gas produces minimal pollution, its potential for explosion is very considerable and has killed people in the hundreds. There is considerable evidence that we are learning to handle natural gas safely, but had uranium built up a record similar to that of natural gas, we would never have gotten the chance to learn how to live with it.

Even hydropower, which is environmentally pretty benign as long as ev-erything goes right, has great potential for catastrophic accident. The Vaiont disaster in 1963 killed 2,000 people, and a University of California study has identified a number of dams the failure of which would cause tens of thousands of deaths. One of these is estimated to have a potential of 260,000 deaths. This is in fact a larger death toll than anyone has ever suggested might result from a nuclear reactor accident, and its probability is substantially greater than the most serious nuclear accidents.

Sometimes nuclear critics, conceding that existing nonnuclear sources of energy are unsatisfactory, propose certain innovative technologies. Although all of these are safer than coal, and some even rival nuclear power in this respect, all have the disadvantage of being unworkable.

Solar and wind power are the most commonly promoted of these. Both have a place in a rational energy plan, but neither can fulfill the claims made for it by less critical supporters.[7]

Solar power is most useful for heating hot water and, in the proper climates, providing heat for houses. At present this use of solar power is so expensive as to be competitive only with electric heat. When it comes to providing electricity itself, cautious optimism suggests that solar power may one day be an option for individual homes—exploiting the one great advantage of the sun as an energy provider, that it is delivered to the doorstep—but the technology for such individual systems is now prohibitively expensive.

Solar power is less promising as a means of central generation. Solar energy for this purpose can be captured in two ways: by mirror systems that boil water to spin conventional turbogenerators, and by photovoltaic cells that produce electricity directly. Both types are at present too expensive to contemplate. Additionally, the photovoltaic system requires very large land areas. With luck, a 1000-megawatt plant (comparable to a large nuclear installation in capacity) would occupy 50 square miles.

Although wind power has real promise for very small demands at exotic locations, such as mountain-top weather stations, it too has been overtouted by nuclear critics. ERDA is sponsoring the construction of a very large wind-rotor that will produce all of 1.5 megawatts and cost $7 million. Producing as much electricity as a conventional nuclear plant would require 666 150-foot high towers costing nearly $5 billion and completely dependent upon the weather. Only fantasists imagine such a technology as a significant source of energy.

The most promising source of energy under development is the fusion process. In fusion, the energy release occurs when two light atoms are fused together to make one. Because the fusion requires an immense amount of energy simply to maintain itself, any defect in a fusion reactor shuts it down; moreover, the basic fuel is almost limitlessly available in seawater. The disadvantage is that we do not yet know how to make the process work. Researchers now work with microscopic reactors that have only recently begun to generate more energy than is needed to sustain them. It is clear that commercial use of the fusion process at best is very distant, and there are those who doubt that it will ever pan out.

The fact is that for the foreseeable future our choice is between nuclear fission and coal. All our choices should be so easy.

IV

The antinuclear movement has mounted campaigns to abolish nuclear power in seven states, and has failed in each case. Probably because polls indicate that the majority of Americans favor the development of nuclear power, none of the referenda was candidly drawn or promoted as a ban on it. Rather, each was drawn and promoted as a nuclear-safeguards proposal which would make nuclear energy safer rather than nonexistent. And each was loaded with standards which no nuclear reactor, present or projected, could ever hope to meet. The effect of these referenda would have been to stop the development of nuclear power in six of the states and to close the industry down entirely in a seventh.

One provision in the California referendum hypocritically required that all reactor-safety systems, including the emergency core-cooling system, undergo tests on an operating reactor. That is, it would have been necessary to initiate a loss-of-coolant accident in an operating reactor, an accident which the proponents of the referendum tell us is too dangerous ever to risk. Another section of the California referendum (substantially duplicated in the other states) required that the legislature certify that no radiation from waste escape with harmful effect into the atmosphere or the land. No coal-fired facility could meet an analogous requirement that no sulfur dioxide escape into the atmosphere. Indeed, no coal plant could meet a requirement forbidding it to emit radiation.

In the seven states, 20 percent of the population of the country had a chance to vote on nuclear power. But in discussing the rejections of these referenda, Nader and Abbotts treat them as victories rather than as defeats, and adopt the cynical explanation that the opponents outspent the proponents. That is, the people really are too dumb to be trusted with such decisions.

These referenda have in the long run probably done actual harm to the cause of nuclear safety. An intelligent California referendum need have done little more than propose some new teeth for present federal regulations, such as fines so great for noncompliance with safety regulations that utilities would find compliance cheaper than defiance. There is of course no excuse for $10,000 fines for noncompliances that save $200,000. As it stands, such referenda have been given a bad name as disguised moratoria, and it is likely that their failure will make development of genuine safeguards legislation and referenda more difficult. It is the old story of the mindless extreme destroying the sensible middle.

Far from being cast down by its failures in these referenda, the antinuclear movement appears to be metastasizing. The spring of 1977 saw the sudden development of a new direction to the nuclear debate, the birth of a movement dedicated to stopping nuclear power through the tactics of civil disobedience.

By April 1977, the proposed nuclear plant at Seabrook, New Hampshire was already in trouble as the result of environmentalist suits and Environmental Protection Agency rulings on its cooling system, which was alleged to be harmful to clams;[8] on April 30, it became the target of a group of activists under the name of the Clamshell Alliance. Several thousand of these occupied the construction site, and when about 1,400 refused to move along, they were arrested for trespass. These the State of New Hampshire foolishly refused to release before trial on their own recognizance, but held them at various locations where before they were finally released there assuredly occurred much effective organization of the antinuclear movement.

The Boston "alternative" press reported on the incident with immense relish, announcing that the activism of the 60s had returned and that nuclear energy was going to become a domestic Vietnam. It could hardly have been happier news had the United States gotten involved in a new war in Southeast Asia.

The infant direct-action movement is patently and passionately antidemocratic. The construction of the Seabrook reactor is already regulated by laws passed by democratically elected legislatures and signed into law by democratically elected executives. These laws have been administered by constitutionally appointed officials and judges. The whole process has been a model of democracy and reflects the fact that a majority of Americans favor the development of nuclear power. But with the Clamshell Alliance and its like, the bottom line is that democracy has come up with the wrong answer, and so much the worse for democracy. The issue must therefore be decided not through democracy but through the physical actions of an elitist and highly organized minority that takes over for the degenerate and plutocratic state. Sam Lovejoy, the leading spirit of the alliance, has been quoted as putting it neatly: "No law ever closed down a nuke." What Lovejoy wants, he must have, whatever the law says. The legal arm of the movement, however, is nearly as peremptory; its flavor is admirably conveyed in a quotation attributed to an "environmentalist" lawyer: "It's about time we put the Seabrook reactor out of its misery."

Judged in the light of the *Zeitgeist*, nuclear power is the perfect demon. Kick it and you kick large corporations, the government, and technology, all with one blow of the foot. Since almost no one yet understands that his welfare depends on nuclear power—even though the welfare of many already does— moral indignation against it comes unusually cheap. The movement is also rather callous, as evidenced by its calm willingness to sacrifice the lives of coal miners—that is, the actual lives of the actual coal miners who are killed over the decades in their thousands—to prevent the hypothetical deaths of hypothetical people from nuclear power. Endangered individuals, especially if they are mere humans, appear to be much less worthy of protection than endangered species. The Seabrook reactor may fall victim to the interests of the clam, and the Dickey-Lincoln hydroelectric project in Maine has been stymied to save a few specimens of an otherwise extinct plant called the furbish lousewort, which appears to be, not to put too fine a point on it, a noxious weed having nothing to recommend it but its name.

The antinuclear movement combines a number of strands that have come to the fore in the last decade or so. One of these is the Manicheanism that can see technological development only as a choice between savage despoiling of the earth and apocalyptic risk on the one hand and a concern for "the environment" that puts clams before people on the other. Because we are in the early stages of the environmentalism fueled by this Manicheanism, none of those now calling the dance has to pay the piper, and indeed many may be able to escape altogether, leaving the problems they have created to their descendants.

Another is a kind of fashionable semi-Luddite fear of the unknown that fixes on certain new examples of industrial society as horrid and to be dispensed with while silently embracing all the others. This is entirely consistent with the history of Luddism, which has been by and large a conservative movement that seeks fresh targets when familiarity has put to rest its fear of the new and unknown over old ones.

Uneasiness with affluence has also bred a smilarly selective asceticism that has become a commonplace perhaps best exemplified in communards who take their stereo sets—and hence a considerable proportion of modern technology—into the hills with them. This makes it easy for well-heeled suburbanites to preach a more restrained use of energy when all it means to them is giving up their electric can openers. Such people in effect tell the billions in the undeveloped world who have only begun to sight liberation by the industrial revolution that they must give up cake.

Critics of nuclear power generally set great store by conservation as a means of reducing demand and thereby the need for new nuclear capacity. The first problem with this position is that it is not in any event desirable to generate all our power with fossil fuels. That is, over the long run, nuclear power is needed not only to add to the present capacity, but to replace it. The second problem is that all too often among the critics of the atom "conservation" is a euphemism for "de-development."

There is no way to argue against genuine conservation. Waste—that is, the *unnecessary* expenditure of anything—must be one of the most indefensible of all categories, and there clearly are a number of ways in which the United States could engage in genuine conservation, i.e., the elimination of true waste. But much of the waste alleged by the antinuclear lobby is in fact simply expenditure on ends they do not approve (like air conditioning).

One chestnut beloved by the lobby is that the Swiss and the Swedes maintain our standard of living but use only half as much energy as we do. Ergo, half our consumption must be waste. The short answer to this is that in common with the rest of the industrialized world, the United States has an extremely low energy consumption for its GNP, and our use in fact lies on the curve of lowest consumption. A somewhat longer answer has been given by Beckmann, who points out that we could get by with less energy if we had no energy-intensive industry and instead made watches and wrote insurance, imported most of our food, and arranged to acquire a new topography that would allow us to generate most of our electricity with falling water. Like so much of the economics of the critics, the thought of Scandinavianization turns out to be a romantic fantasy.

The critics of nuclear power have concentrated on alleging that it is unsafe. Although no large-scale energy conversion can ever be totally safe, we have seen that on the critics' own criterion, nuclear power is to be preferred to the available alternatives.

But safety is not the only grounds for preferring nuclear energy to other forms. One reason is of course political. A nuclear economy based on breeder reactors, whether on the plutonium or thorium cycle, would make the United States forever safe from energy blackmail. Thorium is one of the most abundant elements in nature, and the existing U-238 supply already mined would feed an all-breeder economy for several hundred years.

Furthermore, *pace* the antinuclear lobby, nuclear power is especially desirable if we mean to fulfill our obligations to our descendants. That movement is informed with a very tender concern for generations yet unborn, and regularly asserts that our obligation to these generations prohibits us from leaving them with an insoluble waste-disposal problem. This is true but irrelevant; as we have already seen, we are not leaving them any such problem. But we are leaving them a negative legacy much more serious. For we are consuming vast amounts of petrochemical feedstocks—coal, oil, and gas—as fuel. It happens that it has been our good fortune to find a substitute for these materials used as fuel. For their use in the fabrication of much of our world, we have developed no replacement, and if we go on using coal, oil, and gas as fuel we shall ensure that at some point in the future our descendants will run out of petrochemicals. Had we any real sense of responsibility in these matters, we would be working to make the term "fossil fuel" seem ludicrous. Our present behavior will very probably force our descendants to return to the industrial economy of the early nineteenth century. Our waste of their heritage is the more scandalous because it is unnecessary.

Recently a funny thing happened at the National Council of Churches, a division of which has declared plutonium morally dubious and called for a moratorium on its use. Defenders of this bizarre intrusion of theology into science, which awoke echoes of Galileo's encounter with the Inquisition, explained that because the scientific community was split down the middle on plutonium, the theological community ought to have a deciding vote. Plutonium, they said, was not a technical or scientific issue, but a moral one.

It is of course always very much easier to argue for or against anything in the soft morasses of "moral issues," and one can hardly blame the plutonophobes for trying to get the discussion into this marsh. The problem is that the alleged split within the scientific community finds, almost without exception, all those with the relevant expertness—the specialists in nuclear physics, health physics, and radiation medicine—for, and scientists from almost every field that does not bear on the problem, against. This is as true for nuclear energy in general as for the carefully controlled use of plutonium.

The real importance of the National Council's nuclear ukase, however, is to recall that some years back it had actually endorsed nuclear energy as a gift from God. And so it seemed then, and so it would still seem had our society not long since learned to believe that such gifts must be unambiguously delightful, harmless, and without serious inconvenience or challenge.

The fact is that historically such gifts take considerable courage on the part of mankind if they are to be grasped and used for benefit. We remember with amusement those who opposed the railroad because it would stop the cows from giving milk and because the human constitution could not endure speeds as great as 30 miles an hour. Our amusement will be no more than condescension, however, if we think that we are safe from similar attacks of ignorant terror. If we are lucky, our descendants will be no more than amused by the nuclear Luddism of our time.

NOTES

1. With John Abbotts (Norton).
2. Ballinger.
3. The nuclear bookshelf is growing wider. Among works not mentioned elsewhere in this chapter, the most noteworthy—sometimes for useful information, sometimes as specimens of pathology—are Sheldon Novick's *The Electric War* (Sierra Club), a very highly undisciplined work whose publisher seems to regard editing as anti-ecological; Jacqui Srouji's *Critical*

Mass (Aurora), a mixture of good sense, extreme naivete, and courage, but as undisciplined and unedited on the pro-side as Novick on the anti-; John J. Berger's *Nuclear Power: The Unviable Option* (Ramparts), a canonical brief work against nuclear power; *The Fight Over Nuclear Power* by Fred H. Schmidt and David Bodansky (Albion), a highly informative and lucid work by two distinguished physicists; Peter Faulkner's *The Silent Bomb* (Vintage/Friends of the Earth), an anthology of snippets, not very clearly identified as such, from other antinuclear old reliables, plus connecting material by Faulkner with some curious scientific errors, a preface by Paul R. Ehrlich which is itself a syllabus of antinuclear errors, and a very useful and fair-minded list of the sources of information.

4. Beckmann publishes *Access to Energy,* a witty and profoundly informative newsletter on the nuclear debate and new energy technologies. His book, *The Health Hazards of NOT Going Nuclear* (Golem Press), combines vigorous polemic and a wealth of information. Both the newsletter and the book are available from Box 2298-H, Boulder, Colorado 80302.

5. It is symptomatic of the situation that Cohen is not a better-known figure outside his professional field. A distinguished physicist who has been president of the nuclear division of the American Physical Society and who is also a graceful, lucid, and thoughtful writer, Cohen has published a number of devastatingly thorough analyses of nuclear safety. These have attracted much less popular attention than routine yelps of hysteria from scientific illiterates. It is especially regrettable that Cohen's *Nuclear Science and Society* (Anchor, 1974), an admirable introduction to the subject, should have gone out of print.

Curiously, some nuclear opponents make a virtue of ignorance, maintaining that experts in the nuclear area have a commitment that prevents objectivity, and that experts in nuclear industry should stay out of the debate because of conflict of interest. This attempt to exclude the opposition conveniently overlooks the fact that many leading opponents of nuclear energy themselves earn their living by opposing it. Although a nuclear engineer will not advance his career by becoming a nuclear critic, he need not become a nuclear publicist in order to draw paychecks. A professional critic, by contrast, lives quite directly by opposing nuclear energy. He is like a public-relations officer in the nuclear industry, and one ought to apply some skepticism to his alleged disinterestedness, as well as to that of "environmental" lawyers. One should be especially skeptical of antinuclear "martyrs": speaking of three General Electric engineers who resigned over the issue of nuclear safety, Paul Ehrlich praises their "sacrifices." He does not note that when they resigned they had become members of a parareligious organization that guarantees them an income should antinuclear activities prove insufficiently lucrative. They are also reported to be continuing their participation in the General Electric profit-sharing plan.

6. Ballantine.

7. The same can be said, *mutatis mutandis,* for even more exotic forms such as geothermal power and wave power.

8. The EPA has recently reversed its regional administrator and approved the cooling system, a decision that has been appealed by the Friends of the Clam. In a related action, some of them went to the site and deposited thereon a quantity of dead fish and clams, who no doubt were glad to die that others might live. It was a scene anticipated a century ago by Lewis Carroll: "I like the Walrus best," said Alice, "because he was a *little* sorry for the poor oysters." "He ate more than the Carpenter, though," said Tweedledee.

Bruce L. Welch

5. THE REALITY OF SOLAR POWER

*It is no longer resources that limit decisions. It is the deci-
sion that makes the resources. That is the fundamental
revolutionary change—perhaps the most revolutionary
that mankind has ever known.* —U Thant

There is no shortage of energy, only a shortage of initiative for making energy
accessible in usable form. We are still in a position to choose our future energy
sources and, hence, to shape other important characteristics of society that depend upon them. The process of making that choice and the forces that shape it
are of major public concern. . . .

Quietly, as inexorably as the sun rises, a solar electric age is being born.
Acting against the major thrust of administrative policy and the inadequate advice of "prestigious" scientific committees, the Congress is paving the way.

In congressional committee, the ERDA (Energy Research and Development Administration) Authorization Act for fiscal 1978 was amended to provide $13 million for the purchase of flat-plate solar cell arrays to generate elec-
tricity, and $6 million for research and development related to their automated
production. Appropriation of these funds seems assured.

In addition, funds for the Department of Defense to buy solar cell systems,
staggered over three years commencing in fiscal 1979, were included in both the
House ($39 million) and the Senate ($98 million) versions of the National Energy Act. A conference committee on October 27 decided to provide $98 million
for this purpose, of which $53 million will be for the purchase of silicon solar
cell arrays and the remainder for supporting services and equipment. Congress
expects that these purchases will save the Department of Defense $328 million
net, in 1975 dollars, over a twenty-five-year period and make solar cell systems
competitive in conventional energy markets by 1983. The production of this
equipment for the Defense Department is expected to lower the open market
price of the arrays by 1983 to a point where large sustaining markets (e.g., residential power) will develop, possibly at prices as low as $750 per peak kilowatt.
Additional purchases from other quarters may well cause even greater price reductions within this period of time.

While the cost of nuclear power has climbed over the past two decades at about twice the general rate of inflation, the cost of generating electricity from sunlight—even uncorrected for inflation—has sharply and consistently declined. In 1955, an assembly of solar cells capable of generating a kilowatt of electric power in full sunlight (a "peak" kilowatt) cost about $600,000. Today, such units can be bought in modest quantities for less than $10,000 per peak kilowatt. These remarkable savings have occurred despite the facts that solar manufacturing plants are not yet automated and that the total U.S. production, while steadily increasing, was only 330 to 350 kilowatts in 1976.

Moreover, a Federal Energy Administration report of July 1977 demonstrated that, if a purchase contract for 152 megawatts of flat-plate silicon solar cell arrays were staggered over three years, a first buy of 32 megawatts in 1978 to be followed by buys of 50 megawatts and 70 megawatts at one-year intervals, the last delivery to be made in fiscal 1983 (purchases customarily call for delivery dates in future years), the total cost of the 152-megawatt purchase would be $240 million, an average of $1,570 per kilowatt; and that the open market price could be driven as low as $500 per kilowatt in constant 1975 dollars for the last solar cells delivered in fiscal 1983. These projections are fully consistent with historical experience for other semiconductor products. Moreover, they are based upon actual estimates obtained from three leading manufacturers. The FEA circulated these projections widely to industry and government in draft form before releasing its report, and they were judged to be attainable. A market impact analysis released by the BDM Corporation of McLean, Virginia last October estimated that such a purchase might drive array prices as low as $440 per peak kilowatt by 1983.

The total cost of installing the 152 megawatts of flat-plate solar cell arrays in the illustrative case, including the solar cell arrays, power conditioning equipment, support structures and storage batteries, would be about $450 million. If, for example, the Department of Defense were to make a purchase of that size, it could replace 20 percent of its gasoline-powered generators with solar cells at a net savings, in 1975 dollars, of $1.5 billion over twenty-five years from reduced operating, maintenance and fuel costs. These are conservative estimates, because purchase costs of gasoline generators and their fuel tanks, installation costs and the expense of training mechanics were not included.

The staggered purchase of the relatively modest quantity of 152 megawatts of peak solar cell electrical generating capacity would justify the capital investment to automate three to five companies in this fledgling industry, and the consequent reduction in the price of solar cells would open vast new markets and thereby drive prices even lower. The FEA has estimated that potential annual markets for public lighting and for driving small electrical motors and water pumps could alone reach 7,900 peak megawatts—an annual market which, incidentally, is about three times the current annual sales of nuclear generating capacity in the United States. Moreover, prices that would tap a 13,000-megawatt per annum market for the on-site solar generation of residential electricity may then be expected to come rapidly into range.

A contract just awarded for solar cells capable of delivering 362 peak kilowatts of electricity to meet all the power needs of Mississippi County Community College in Blytheville, Arkansas, was signed at a price of $3,026 per peak kilowatt of capacity, about half what informed observers had expected the contract to command. This development suggests that the FEA's estimates of the price-lowering effect of orders more than 420 times that large were greatly understated.

The installation cost, in comparable 1975 dollars, of some nuclear plants now under construction, and which will come on line in the early to mid-1980s, is about $1,000 per kilowatt of electrical generating capacity (later construction will probably cost more). But this figure does not include the first fuel loading of a plant, which will add 15 to 20 percent to capital costs. Nor does it include such extras as design for added resistance to earthquake, flood or aircraft impact; the purchase of more than 3 square miles of land, at a minimum, for siting; the cost of power lines and other distributing equipment, operating and maintenance expenses, security, decommissioning, waste storage and disposal; or the cost of government assistance, regulation, subsidy, insurance and emergency services. Moreover, large nuclear plants have been found to operate only about 50 percent of the time at their installed capacity rating, and up to 20 percent of the power that they do generate is lost internally and in transmission.

Solar cells, because of variations in sunlight, have an average capacity of only about 25 percent, and about 30 percent of the power generated is lost if cycled through storage batteries. Yet, solar cells installed on one's own roof to power direct current appliances at a cost of about $500 per peak kilowatt of generating capacity may seem an attractive alternative to nuclear power in some locations, even considering the appreciable added cost of a power storage system. Most authorities anticipate that, in addition to economies from increased production, substantially lower costs will be brought about through technical advances now in sight. This means that within a decade electricity from solar cells could actually become much cheaper than nuclear power for consumers in many areas of the United States. The equation will be affected by the relative lifetime of solar arrays and nuclear plants, a comparison that cannot yet be made because of insufficient experience with either system. However, solar cells should last as long as their encapsulation maintains its integrity to protect them from weather. Compared to nuclear power plants, they are extremely simple devices. For the former, we lack even such important information as the pattern of aging-associated neutron bombardment embrittlement of metal in reactor pressure vessel walls. Claims that large nuclear power plants will have a forty-year life are wholly conjectural; indeed, it has not yet been determined that they can function safely and reliably for a single decade.

A solar electric age is coming no matter what the federal administration does. The government can merely speed or slow its coming. If we wish it to be so, solar cells for generating electricity can become cost-competitive with nuclear fission in widespread applications within little more than half the time that it takes to build a new nuclear power plant. The nation has the realistic option to meet much of its need for further expansion of electrical generating capacity with autonomous solar cell arrays powered by the sun.

For this to happen, large amounts of government money are not required. Indeed, considering the promise that the solar electric age offers for bringing needed diversity and competition into world energy markets, it is regrettable, in a way, that it is to be born of government funds. The absurdity is that government spending is required to offset the inhibitory effects of other government spending.[1]

Solar cell electricity would have come into widespread use spontaneously, and much sooner, had it not been for the false promise of economic competitiveness given nuclear fission by more than a quarter century of indulgent government support of the nuclear industry, support that continues and is even growing. Solar technologies would develop rapidly if the government would simply withdraw all support from the nuclear industry. The $450 million that the FEA estimated would be required to lower the price of solar cells to $500 per peak kilowatt or less, with a resulting savings of about $1.5 billion to the Department of Defense, is considerably less than one third the amount provided in the fiscal 1978 budget for continued research, development and demonstration related to nuclear power.

Why, then, does the Carter administration press so obdurately for rapid expansion of nuclear power? Why does it so resist a major solar initiative? One reason is that nuclear interests have pervasive influence among the small "elite" corps of scientists who provide technical advice on such subjects at the top echelon of government. Solar energy interests have almost no voice at all. True, scientists are supposed to be totally objective, to seek persistently and weigh all relevant information. But, sadly that ideal is not always achieved. All too often the authority and credibility of reports from major scientific study groups or committees, and hence the justification for using them to guide public policy, is assumed from the prestige of the study's sponsors and participants. This is commonly true even when the panel participants are obviously not qualified in, and have not carefully considered, all important areas of science that their advice appears to weigh. The study report, *Nuclear Power, Issues and Choices,* is a case in point.

Its prestigious backing with a $500,000 Ford Foundation grant administered by the Mitre Corporation and its stellar cast of panelists[2] would guarantee it high visibility under any conditions. The facts that it appeared while President Carter was formulating his energy program and that two members of the study group were given key positions in his new administration could only enhance its chance to influence national policy. A copy of the report was hand-delivered to the new President by his science adviser. On the day that the report was released, the study group was called to the White House to brief the President in person. In the ensuing months, the President's energy program and his acts and comments on energy issues have been in remarkable accord with the recommendations of the Ford-Mitre report. Bias and inadequacies in the structure and conduct of this study are therefore of major consequence and of public interest.

With regard to alternative energy sources, the report acknowledged that, "An assessment of the need for nuclear power should consider potential alternatives that might be economically competitive or might avoid specific serious problems associated with nuclear power and fossil fuels." However, it stated that the "goal" should be to have supplies of energy available at moderate cost when present resources are "gone"; that solar energy in general, and solar cells for generating electricity in particular, will be too expensive to compete with coal and nuclear power through the next three decades; that there is "little value in demonstrating clearly noncompetitive technology," and that it would be "inefficient and unnecessarily limiting" to try to make alternative energy sources available "prematurely."

While the panel's remarkable assurance about the appropriate timing for transition to alternative fuels may not be reflected in the President's thinking, there is every indication that its recommendations are reflected in the administrative policy of the new Department of Energy in ways that could cause the deployment of solar energy technologies to be drastically delayed. This is regrettable, because the panel's judgment that the solar technologies could not be competitive are unduly pessimistic and are not based upon a careful analysis of the relevant available information.

To focus on but one crucial error: in summarily dismissing solar cells, the Ford-Mitre report said that "current collector costs are about $200,000 per kilowatt of peak electrical capacity." In fact, that price—which was not a misprint (I confirmed this with the author of that section of the report)—was almost twenty years out of date. Solar cells cost $200,000 per peak kilowatt in

1959; in September 1976, eight months before the Ford-Mitre report was released, ERDA purchased solar cell arrays for less than 8 percent of the price quoted by the Ford-Mitre study group—$15,500 per peak kilowatt in quantities as small as 130 kilowatts. The price had been $21,000 per peak kilowatt six months earlier, and $31,000 per peak kilowatt in March 1975, which was about the time the Ford-Mitre study group was assembled.

Superficiality, inaccuracy, and lack of percipience were not confined to the panel's treatment of solar cells; they characterized their comments on other "solar" technologies as well. These deficiencies may be understood in terms of the relative vacuum in which the analysis of solar energy technologies evolved. The sections of the report on solar energy were the primary responsibility of an experimental physicist who for more than twenty years has had active professional interests in nuclear energy; he is currently involved in laser separation techniques for uranium enrichment. He has never been directly involved in any aspect of solar energy research or application, although, in 1975, he was chairman of a National Research Council committee formed to explore the optimal role and organizational characteristics of the then prospective Solar Energy Research Institute. And he is the only member of the Ford-Mitre study panel who had had prior professional experience in any way related to solar energy. The chairman of the panel lists his professional interest in *American Men and Women of Science* as "military and civilian applications of nuclear energy."

The Mitre Corporation, where the Ford-Mitre study was actually conducted, has been a major center of activity for quality research and systems analysis in solar energy technology for more than five years. Yet, the Ford-Mitre study group worked in total isolation from the solar energy experts who were under the same roof. I heard this first from a member of the Mitre solar energy group, and later confirmed it with the author of the solar energy section of the Ford-Mitre report. In our conversation, he justified not seeking and evaluating ideas and information from people in the solar energy field by classifying them collectively as "enthusiast nuts." (The accuracy of this label must be weighed against the historical facts that the price of nuclear power has consistently outstripped the enthusiastic projections of its advocates, whereas the cost of solar energy has consistently declined more rapidly than the relatively conservative predictions of professionals in that field.)

When a prestigious panel makes recommendations on an important public issue, it implies that those recommendations are based upon a thorough and balanced weighing of all relevant information. When that is not the case, and the deficiencies are not clearly stated, their recommendations comprise at best an irresponsible disservice to the scientific community, the government and the public at large.

For years after penicillin was developed it was so expensive that physicians took care to collect urine from the few favored patients who received it so that the penicillin could be recycled. Today, thanks to the economies of a large market and mass production, penicillin is available in every physician's office at an almost trivial price.

Similarly, solar cells will soon be cheap enough to generate electricty in widespread applications. It has been estimated that the basic electrical power requirements of a village of 250 people in Iran could be met by 20 peak kilowatts of solar cells. Such a need can reasonably be expected to be met for about $10,000 within little more than five years. Similar needs exist in innumerable villages throughout the world, and it will soon be possible for such needs to be profitably met.

The rate at which solar cells will actually spread throughout this and other industrialized countries will depend upon the development of adequate low-cost ways to store the electrical energy. It is in the administration's tepid encouragement of new storage technologies that its reluctance to promote solar energy really shows. The budget authority for fiscal 1978 provides only $48.4 million for all aspects of energy storage research, development and demonstration— less than 3 percent of the amount provided for nuclear fission. Almost four times as much is being spent by the federal government for research, development, and demonstration related to the storage of commercial nuclear waste. Although hydrogen is a strong bet to be the major energy storage medium of the future, the fiscal 1978 budget provides only $6 million toward that goal. It is no exaggeration to say that the Department of Energy has not set up a crash program to find better ways to store electrical power. For nuclear power, storage of electrical energy is not particularly important; for distributed solar systems it is crucial.

The federal government should withdraw its multifarious supports from the nuclear power industry and remove remaining institutional obstacles to the rapid development of distributed solar energy systems. If this were done, electrical power production would gradually return to the private sector, the economy would be stimulated dramatically, and the nation would develop a safer, less wasteful and more resilient electric power base.

Finally, and viewing all areas of the nation's continued welfare, it is imperative that we evolve a more reliable science advisory system. To its credit, the Congress has shown that it knows that the recommendations of "prestigious" scientific committees cannot be taken as gospel. It is increasingly essential, for the shaping of national policy, to have scientific advice that can be relied upon to be comprehensive, competent, and unbiased.

NOTES

1. See Welch: "Nuclear Energy on the Dole," *The Nation,* 26 February 1977.
2. Spurgeon M. Keeney, Jr., Chairman; Seymour Abrahamson, Kenneth J. Arrow, Harold Brown, Albert Carnesale, Abram Chayes, Hollis B. Chenery, Paul Doty, Philip J. Farley, Richard L. Garwin, Marvin L. Goldberger, Carl Kaysen, Hans H. Landsberg, Gordon J. MacDonald, Joseph S. Nye, Wolfgang K. H. Panofsky, Howard Raiffa, George W. Rathjens, John C. Sawhill, Thomas C. Schelling, and Arthur Upton.

PART TWO

Welfare Policy:
Reforming the Mess

Of all America's domestic policies, welfare programs are the most disputed. Policy analysts from a wide spectrum of political perspectives have long argued about the costs, benefits, and objectives of various welfare programs. Welfare reform policies have been hotly debated by conservatives and liberals in Congress, as well as by the bureaucrats who administer the programs. Although these groups disagree as to the proper policies to adopt, they all agree that we are in a "welfare mess."

What makes welfare policy so controversial? Proponents of social welfare programs acknowledge government's social obligation to care for those who have been unable (through no fault of their own) to pull themselves up by their bootstraps, yet consider many welfare programs dehumanizing and demeaning. Opponents of welfare feel that the idea of welfare is anathema to fundamental values held by the American public; consequently, many individuals and groups view welfare as "creeping socialism." The point is, welfare policy can be reduced to bedrock values and ideological perspectives that posit certain assumptions about human nature, political relationships, economic conditions, and societal obligations.

How did we get into the "welfare mess"? Present welfare policies are the result of almost fifty years of governmental responses to domestic problems that include unemployment, poverty, the elderly, and the disabled. In chapter 6, John Tropman reviews the evolution of various welfare policies starting with the Social Security Act of 1935, which was America's first undertaking in the welfare business. Tropman points out how changing attitudes about the idea of welfare, welfare rights, and welfare coverage have influenced the nature and direction of welfare programs. He illustrates that any analysis of welfare policy must take into account that present welfare policies are the result of historical perceptions of domestic problems and political compromises in responding to those perceptions.

Worthington and Lynn observe that the traditional incremental strategies of welfare reform must be abandoned. They review the underlying assumptions of "incremental" and "comprehensive" welfare reform policies, and illustrate how the two approaches differ in their subjective judgments about poverty and the poor. According to the authors, the piecemeal approach to welfare reform has resulted in programs that are "expensive, inefficient, inequitable, and confusing," and it is time for a comprehensive welfare reform package including an integrated tax and transfer system based on the notion of a negative income tax. In contrast, Nathan Glazer claims that we are focusing on the wrong target; we should make work, particularly low-income jobs that individuals turn from in favor of the welfare rolls, more attractive through better on-the-job health programs, government subsidies to workers based on family size, and financial transfer programs such as the negative income tax. Glazer concludes that we need no new studies of welfare reform but instead need a "commission on low-income and low-benefit jobs."

In the final chapter in this part Murray Rothbard argues for the abolition of government welfare programs. Rothbard observes that public welfare programs do not effectively discriminate between the deserving and the nondeserving poor. In addition, he claims that being poor and on welfare is not a temporary or accidental circumstance, but is the result of both an individual's conscious and calculated choice and incentives provided by government to make welfare more attractive than work. Rothbard criticizes the idea of a negative income tax and advocates a welfare system of private charity for the deserving poor, much like that utilized by the Mormon Church.

John E. Tropman

6. AMERICAN WELFARE STRATEGIES: THREE PROGRAMS UNDER THE SOCIAL SECURITY ACT

Paradoxical as it may seem, many people in the American and international communities are not aware that the American national welfare structure is basically derived from programs made possible through a single piece of legislation, the act popularly known as the Social Security Act, and its amendments. One of the reasons this fact is not well known lies in the rather diverse nature of the programs, and the different political and programmatic evolution which has shaped them since their passage. This situation provides the policy and administrative scholar an opportunity to look at different approaches to providing social welfare benefits, and, in a global way, assess some of the differences in outcomes. One of the purposes of this paper is to undertake just such an analysis and assessment.

A second purpose, and one as important as the initial one, rests in an attempt to link the development of the different program modalities with different elements in the value structure of the social system in which they operate. Programs and policies do not spring fully developed from some policy-making Zeus. Rather, they are the result of elements contesting in the social and political structure. Numerous studies link policy and administrative outcomes to rather specific near-term causes (Minister X hates Minister Y, etc.). Yet too often administrative and policy scenarios are repeated with a completely different cast of characters, leading one to think that sets of predisposing causes are at least as operative as precipitating ones. And although we are using the area of income security and poverty relief specifically here, such an approach would be helpful in many different policy areas. Consider our national schizophrenia on the issue of alcohol problems, for example, which has led to two constitutional amendments. Understanding the cultural matrix is crucial for policy analysis.

A Social-Historical Overview

A detailed social historical account of poverty relief remains to be written. But it is possible to outline some of the key elements in the political culture which any income relief or assistance program would have to take into account.

Three Hundred Years of Hostility

Perhaps most salient here is the fact that the poor have been the object of unremitting hostility for several hundred years. In England, getting the poor to work was a central policy concern. Work, good for both society and the soul, was a central feature of hatred of the poor. Somehow, it was felt that they were lazy and would not work. In the United States, one of the first instructions of the Massachusetts Bay Company (1629) was:

> Noe idle drone bee permitted to live amongst us, which if you take care of now at the first to establish, will be an undoubted meanes, through God's Assistance, to prevent a world of disorders and many grevious sins and sinners.

The English Poor Law Reform of 1834 did nothing to change this attitude. Generally viewed as a repressive law, it established the principle of "less eligibility," which specifies that any person ·receiving assistance "shall not be made really or apparently so eligible as the situation (i.e., position or station) of the independent laborer of the lowest class." In practice, this has come to mean that any money grant has to be below the lowest wage. At that time, the poor were sent to workhouses. Though old, the issue is not dead. A recent study shows that less eligibility still operates here in the United States. The reform also argued that not only poverty was bad but pauperism, or the taking of help for being poor, was also bad. The poor were thus doubly disliked, for being poor and for receiving help.

The importance of work seems to be crucial. It appears that the only government aid program which engenders acid hostility is public assistance—where people do not work or have some excuse (illness, for example) which is acceptable. A Report of the Illinois legislature says: "The cold, hard fact of life is that man works out of necessity. Man does not work because he likes to work but because he has to work. . . . If the government is going to feed, clothe, provide a home and fire without the necessity of work, many people won't work. It's that simple."

THE PIERCE VETO

In England, the central government had taken some responsibility for the provision of relief, but in America, under the federal system, this responsibility was left to the states. There was a strong feeling that what little relief would be given should be completely a local responsibility. The reluctance to have any responsibility for social welfare's devolution upon the federal government became clear to Dorothea Dix in 1854. She had successfully convinced many state legislatures to make state provisions for the mentally ill. On the crest of this success, she almost singlehandedly convinced the Congress of the United States to pass such a bill. This bill provided land which could be used to build mental hospitals. In a famous veto, President Franklin Pierce commented:

> It cannot be questioned that if Congress have the power to make provision for the indigent insane without the limits of this District, it has the same power to make provision for the indigent who are not insane; and thus to transfer to the Federal Government the charge of all the poor in the States.

The federal government would not in fact enter the social welfare field until the 1930s. It is a credit to the prescience, if not the judgment, of President Pierce, however, that he correctly foresaw the route events would take.

Thus, in the eighteenth and nineteenth centuries the climate toward the poor was not sympathetic; it was harsh and judgmental. Titmuss has referred to this attitude as "metaphysical individualism." White and Fine have referred to the prominence of the "laissez faire" concept. To be in need was the individual's own fault; society would help only in the most extreme cases.

PRIVATE CHARITY

To suggest that there was a generally hostile attitude is not to imply that nothing was being done to help. The predominant norm prevented government from taking much responsibility; and certainly anything more than minimal was too much. This situation pushed development of relief programs into the private sector. Thus, special agencies for the poor developed in the private rather than the public arena. With this location of help, there also developed a group of people helping the poor; friendly visitors who saw themselves as having a vocation rather than being government employees. Both factors have had a lasting impact on social welfare. It set the precedent that the poor need individual attention from individual persons, as well as money, and became the tradition out of which one of the Social Security Act programs—public assistance—justified its concept of caseload. In the United States, the private sector had, until the Depression, the primary responsibility for programs of poverty relief.[1]

THE DEPRESSION

During the 1930s, the Depression put such stress on private agencies' resources that there came to be a general feeling that something else should be done for those in need. The federal government, under President Roosevelt, was receptive. Politically, however, several developing strains of thought had to be harmonized in any legislation. First, there was the notion that specific groups of people were "deserving" of aid. Second, there was the idea that it might be possible to "insure" against such disasters like losing one's job, or that one could insure against poverty in old age by paying in a little over a lifetime, like an annuity. Third, there was the group of charitable workers who had been heavily responsible for poverty relief since the late 1800s. Their concepts of the causes and consequences of poverty, and the appropriate structure of relief, could not be ignored. As it turned out, it appears their ideal was to create, through governmental action, a sort of giant private social agency, which would operate much like the social agencies of that time but with vastly augmented resources. And finally, there was the federal system itself. Somehow, an accommodation had to be made between state and federal interests.

The Social Security Programs

In this nexus of pressures, then, the Social Security Act was passed (P.L. 271, 74th Congress; approved 8-14-35; 49 Stat. 620). With its passage the federal government took on the responsibility of providing security against economic hardship for some designated groups of Americans. Such security was not to be provided in a single program, however. The climate of American opinion surrounding poverty, especially the federal government's responsibility concerning poverty, was too unfavorable to permit the "family allowance" plan being considered as in other countries. There was not the deep concern for social factors producing poverty which was to find its expression (and a set of proposed solutions) in the Beveridge report in England. The American strategy was to make the poor "eligible" by categories. The strategy of the category system was to designate certain groups of needy for special legislative attention.

In the act three basic programs were developed to meet the need for help and economic security.[2] The first two programs are "insurance" programs, for which a special tax is levied. The third program is a collection of various "assistances"—called the Public Assistance Titles. As we shall see, even the name makes a difference in the legitimacy.

SOCIAL SECURITY

The Social Security Program (OASDHI) is one which provides a fixed money payment for Old Age, Survivors, and Dependents of the Insured person, and also provides medical care for older people and in some instances for others. The locus of administrative control in the Social Security program is in Washington. It is a federally administered program, and payments are made by federal employees of the Social Security Administration.

The Social Security Administration is decentralized by region, by districts within each region, and through the use of field offices within these areas. While the Social Security Administration employee is a federal employee, it seems that an organizationally localized professionalism has developed, similar to what happened in the Tennessee Valley Authority and the Forest Service. The growth of organization-specific techniques has been generated through in-service training, and is discussed in print.

Over the years, social security has secured a place on the American scene for itself. It has not been under the same attack which has plagued the administration of public assistance, although recently, questions about its fiscal base have been raised. One reason for this relative freedom is, of course, its high-quality administration. Policies are clear and are enforced across the board. A person is eligible for social security whatever his geographical location; there is no "residence requirement" as there was in the Public Assistance Program. The fact that it is a totally federal program simplifies and consolidates the administration. Three other factors are important. First, everyone who is insured gets social security, regardless of his financial need. This provision has removed much of social security from the class of "aid to the needy" programs. A second and related feature of the program, which helps in the public relations, is that benefits have been determined on the basis of wage rate and on the number of quarters in which one was working under an insured occupational category. Thus, the benefits are tied directly to work. Finally, there is a special tax which Americans pay for social security, which is plainly marked on every pay voucher. This tax money goes into the Social Security Trust Fund, from which current benefits are paid. This trust fund supports the "insurance" concept and creates the image that "I have paid in, and I deserve to get it back." The aspect of insurance — indeed, the very name "insurance" — lends a legitimacy and aura of public acceptance to the Social Security Program.

However, in 1974, three programs previously thought of as "welfare programs, Old Age Assistance, Aid to the Blind, and Aid to the Permanently and Totally Disabled (OAA, AB, and APTD) were transferred to the Social Security Administration and are now administered there, under the title of Supplemental Security Income (SSI). This transfer represents the first time that the Social Security Administration has administered a "means tested" program, and it has created some implications which can be considered later. Suffice it to say now that the program is federally financed (as opposed to grants-in-aid to the states under the Public Assistance Administration) but the grants may be supplemented by the states either through the State Departments of Welfare or through the Social Security Administration itself. In the case of state supplementation, and many states have chosen to supplement, the amount is purely a state decision.

UNEMPLOYMENT COMPENSATION

The program of unemployment compensation is administratively unique. Under Title III of the Social Security Act, the federal government collects a tax (3.2 percent on the first $4,200 of workers wages) based on the employers' "experience" with unemployment — the more a particular employer "contributes" to unemployment (i.e., creates unemployment), the more tax he has to pay. Unemployment Compensation is not, however, a federal program. The law provides that if the state has an Unemployment Compensation Program, then it can secure a credit of up to 90 percent of the federal tax. In effect, the law allows for a Federal Unemployment Compensation Program only if the state does not have one. The locus of control in the Unemployment Compensation Program is fundamentally in the states, with loose federal supervision. The federal law, administered by the Bureau of Employment Security in the Department of Labor, sets up certain requirements which the states must meet if they are going to receive their rebate. These requirements are essentially

(1) The payment of benefits through a public employment office
(2) The deposit of state funds in an unemployment insurance fund managed by the federal treasury
(3) The right of unemployed workers to refuse jobs which do not meet prescribed standards without having the benefits withheld
(4) The right of an unemployed worker to a hearing before an impartial tribunal if his claim for benefits is denied.

These requirements are broad ones, they permit some considerable difference between the states. Although benefits are supposed to be "adequate" for "a limited period," there is wide latitude in interpretation of these terms. This situation arises because each state has had to pass its own unemployment compensation law, and thus there is ample room for the play of state interests. Under Title IX of the Social Security Act, the Social Security Administration makes grants to the states for 100 percent of the administration of the program. Both the state administration, and the federal responsibility for paying for state administration, create potential loci of friction between the federal and the state levels.

While the specific titles of the Social Security Act make provision only for unemployment insurance, the program as it evolved has links with employment services. Haber and Murray note: "When the Social Security Act was passed in 1935, the desirability of coordination of unemployment insurance and the public employment service was taken for granted and made a condition for states receiving Title III grants." Thus at the state level, two services are provided, employment counseling as well as an unemployment benefit. Thus state employment service workers, like public assistance workers, have a counseling job to do, but they have, like Social Security Administration workers, an insurance program to administer. They have not developed the bureau professionalism of the Social Security Administration, nor the identification with an outside profession (social work) of the public assistance workers.

THE PUBLIC ASSISTANCE

The third set of programs funded under the Social Security Act is that called Public Assistance. Initially, there were three programs—Old Age Assistance (OAA), Aid to the Blind (AB), and Aid to (Families With) Dependent Children (AFDC). In 1950, an amendment was passed which made provision for Aid to Permanently and Totally Disabled (APTD). The act provides that out of general revenue funds the federal government will make public assistance grants-in-aid to the states designed to help with the kinds of problems suggested here. It is a mutually contributory program; the states make only small contributions to each program, and the federal government is footing much of the bill. Since these categorical programs do not cover the many situations which can place persons in financial need, there is a program of General Assistance funded out of state and local funds to fill the gaps.[3] To qualify for aid, each state must submit a "state plan" as provided for in the Social Security Act to the Social and Rehabilitation Service, Department of Health, Education, and Welfare. The plan must be in conformity with the act and subsequent interpretations at the federal level. Remuneration is made to the states in two parts. One type of rebate is for the actual grants made to clients. A second rebate reimburses the state for personnel costs, since certain types of personnel, and certain client/personnel ratios are encouraged or required.

If the state plan, or state action as it turns out, is not in conformity with federal law and interpretation, then the grant-in-aid funds may be withheld by the federal government. This step is a serious one, and has only occurred in a few instances. In at least one case (the "Jenner Amendment" controversy) the law was changed to permit a state to do what it wished.

Just as for the Unemployment Compensation Program, there are sizable state administrations for public assistance, since the federal government itself does not make any payments directly to individual citizens. Basically, two forms of assistance administration are used. In one method the state is the actual agent, and sets up field offices around the state. In the other method, the county acts as the agent, under supervision by the state.

As in the Unemployment Compensation Program, two services are given—financial help in the form of grants, and "services" in the form of personal counseling. In the Unemployment Compensation Program the counseling usually takes the form of assistance in seeking and securing a job. In the Public Assistance Program, there is an attempt to make the services "professional" in a social work sense, and counseling may range over a broad variety of personal topics. Every "client" is assigned to a caseworker. However, the concept of services and payments, developed recently, divided workers into "service" and "assistance payment" workers.

The arrangements of these programs have now changed. Under recent revisions, the Blind, Disabled, and Aged Programs have been moved over to the Social Security Administration, leaving Aid to Families with Dependent Children as the single public assistance.[4]

Policy Problems in Income Relief Programs

As might be expected, each of the programs has a set of policy problems unique to it. Basically, in each case, these problems have to do with coverage, and benefit levels. However, the Public Assistance Program is somewhat unique in this regard because it suffers from a crucial lack of public confidence and from a public hatred of its personnel, which undermines its own efforts.

Social Security Policy

The first questions of policy which are involved in the administration of social security are of two kinds: (1) what shall be included within the scope of the program, and (2) how shall internal administrative arrangements be set up. Regarding the latter, perhaps the more minor issue, the questions about the proper mechanisms to maintain uniformity through the field offices are prominent. These have been solved, to a degree, through multiple supervision and functional decentralization.

The more serious policy issue relates to the kind of programs and the kinds of people involved in social security. Social security coverage has been continually broadened. The occupations covered have also broadened. The important question is, "Should everyone be covered, and, if not, where should we stop." The coverage has now become quite broad. It is perhaps a measure of the progress of the Social Security Program that a new set of of crucial policy issues confronts it now. Basically, these new issues are (1) a crisis in confidence about its fiscal integrity; and (2) the administration of a means-tested program.

In recent years, the social security payroll tax, which used to be quite minor, has climbed to a total of 11.7 percent of salary, half paid by the employer and half paid by the employee, to a limit of $15,300.* These amounts are definitely not trivial, and have brought increased scrutiny to the Social Security Program.

The potentially onerous level of the current tax is brought into sharper relief by the discovery that the Social Security Trust Fund will have more claims

---

*In 1979, the social security tax was 12.2 percent of salary to a limit of $22,900 and remained at that level in 1980. However, in 1981 the social security was increased to 13.3 percent of salary to a limit of $29,700. In all cases, half of the tax is paid by the employee, and half by the employer. — Ed.

than funds if current rates of expenditure are maintained with no increase in income. This "cash flow" problem results from both increased benefits packages and increased numbers of claimants. Either the tax rate will have to be raised, or the upper limit on income taxed will have to be raised, or the federal Congress will have to supply some General Revenue Funds or some combination of the above alternatives will have to be developed to take up the slack. Whatever the alternatives chosen, social security will be more criticized and investigated than ever before.

The addition of the SSI program (paid for by General Revenue) has created a different type of crisis. While the fiscal crisis was external, the SSI crisis is internal, internal in the sense of staff. The social security staff hitherto have never administered a means-tested program. It has proceeded smoothly in Michigan, but has tested a staff basically trained in an orientation which is not one of meeting "need."

And the "need-based" addition to the social security system may, in time, become an external matter if it erodes the omnibus image that the country holds of the program.

Employment Compensation Policy

Policy issues in the Unemployment Compensation Program are also complex in nature. Essentially they relate to the level of payment and the nature of the experience rating. Many people believe the levels of payment should be raised. William Haber concluded that only federal legislation will help.

> And it is clear, after many years of exhorting the states to increase their maximums, that no amount of urging by high officials of the federal government or anyone else is going to raise maximum benefits. . . . it is clear that the maximums will be raised to adequate levels only if a minimum federal standard is enacted.

A second issue relates to the "experience ratings" provision, in which an employer is charged a tax on the basis of the amount he "contributes" to unemployment. Since this amount is determined by the number of people (his ex-employees) who are drawing unemployment compensation, there is much to be gained by a challenge. It would probably pay a large corporation to have lawyers challenge claims to unemployment compensation. Any claim which is disallowed is thus a reduction in the employer's "contributions" to unemployment (experience rating) and, hence, to this tax. The "experience rating" structure which was set up under some kind of "fair share" idea, has resulted in continual challenge by some employers to the claimant, independent of the claimant's particular justification. And while this procedure may be judicially a fair one, it is also a time-consuming and expensive one for both employer and employee.

And because of different employment patterns in different industries, there is a question raised about the experience rating concept itself.

These issues are not the only ones. There are questions about the level of tax, the base which is taxed, the length of time benefits should be given, the relationship between employment counseling roles and unemployment compensation roles within the state Employment Security Commissions, to mention a few. Yet overall, it appears fair to conclude that the program has more support than the Public Assistance Program.

Public Assistance Policy

Public assistance policy represents perhaps the most complex area of the three programs. Much of the onus distilled from the historical climate devolves on this program and the administrators must cope with not only the usual run of administrative problems, but also with the extra and special problem of public hostility and distrust. This negative public attitude not only augments the usual difficulties but creates special and unique ones.

STATE PLAN

Routinely, the public assistance administration has state issues to consider. As an intergovernmental program, issues of intergovernmental relations are always present. State and federal governments do not agree, and this is often reflected in controversy around the approval of the state plan. And since the state has to make a regular appropriation to cover its share of the assistance budget, the assistance program comes in for regular review in each state legislature. This review would be pro forma or minimal in many cases, but in the case of assistance, the undercurrent of public distrust and hostility has this regular opportunity to surface.

STAFF

Another regular source of difficulty lies in the staff area: who are appropriate staff, and what is their role. These questions involve issues of professionals versus nonprofessionals. Assistance operates, as was mentioned, on a caseload concept. It was assumed, and was encouraged, that the caseworkers be people with MSW degrees. However, the arithmetic is such that there can never be sufficient MSW persons to handle the public assistance caseload. Many of the personnel are nonprofessionals.

> In 1965 there were 35,000 public welfare workers. Of this number, 1,500 have professional degrees and are members of the professional association. While this is a minority estimate because there are likely persons who are trained but not members of the professional association, it nevertheless presents a picture of the general relation.

Indeed, the problem of sufficient "professional staff" is as old as the profession. Lewis reports in the *Encyclopedia of Social Work* that in 1893 only in Boston, Baltimore, and Brooklyn, Charity Organization Societies were able to assign friendly visitors to a significant proportion of cases.

Social workers also have clung tenaciously to the belief that more MSW workers would help reduce the rolls. There is not only no evidence on this point but, as it turned out, the assistance rolls were so far below poverty levels that increases were almost inevitable. In any event, having made the claim, social workers were not able to "deliver" lower rolls, and are now regarded suspiciously by state and federal legislators.

SERVICE VS. PAYMENT

The professional-nonprofessional issue is linked to another policy issue: the nature of the service required for assistance recipients. Social workers generally were identified with a "service" view of assistance, in which the primary goal was personal counseling, and financial assistance was a "means to an end." Nonprofessionals were identified with the posture that money payment was all that was necessary, and one became involved in personal problems and difficulties only if absolutely necessary. However valuable and important the distinctions here, neither group fell fully within those limits. However, the identifications stuck in the public mind, and legislators are now saying that "high cost" professionals are not needed to give "service" of an amorphous sort to a continually changing group of clients. Influenced perhaps by the style of administration in social security and unemployment compensation, Congress has moved to separate income support from "service," to separate income support services from counseling services. However, it appears that the problems do not fall into easily separable categories, and tension has been created between "payments" employees (who tend to regard themselves as somewhat lower on the organizational status ladder) and "social services" employees.

CHEATING

These regular administrative problems have an overlay within the system resulting from negative public attitudes. People in general appear to be convinced that those who receive aid are cheating. Overall, the level of cheating is about 4 percent. Williamson, in his study of attitudes toward the poor, found that his respondents believe that 41 percent of the recipients lie. In state after state, investigation after investigation goes on to find and reduce the number of people who are receiving public aid illegally. Things reached a low point in the "midnight search" program in California, which created a public furor. Investigators were sent out in the middle of the night to inspect the homes of Californians who were receiving AFDC, to search for men.

RISE IN RATES

During the period of the 60s, rates of welfare use rose dramatically. Between 1966 and 1971, the cases per 100 families rose from 2.4 to 5.6 percent, an increase of 133 percent. The caseload rise led to increased criticism of the welfare system, and at least one major interpretation of the function of welfare as responsive to the urban riots. Welfare, Piven and Cloward argue, serves to keep the urban masses from full revolt. However, in all the discussion about the rise in rates, two points are usually overlooked. First, there has always been a substantial gap between the program enrollees and the total number of people who might be eligible. One of the reasons that rolls can grow so rapidly is that persons who would be entitled to benefits, but have not applied for them, have begun making application. Second, while costs have indeed increased, the "value" of the average grant, taken as proportion of the per capita income in the state in that year, has decreased.

WELFARE RIGHTS

One feature which accounts for the apparent increased willingness to apply, and has been an important psychological as well as political factor, is the development of a welfare rights organization. Welfare benefits have been one of the few areas of our society in which the actual beneficiaries are not organized to press for more and better benefits. Given that American society is almost characterized by such "interest groups," this omission is of interest. But in "the egalitarian decade" of the 60s, the rights of many groups who suffered from discrimination of one sort or another were pressed. In the welfare case, the group support for application, the sense that one was simply exercising a right rather than abusing society's generous impulses, was surely an important factor. And for the first time, a group of welfare users (the clients) was available to make policy inputs along with the traditional group of purveyors (social workers, the American Public Welfare Association).

Three Incidents in Assistance Administration

It might be useful to describe some of the special problems in the administration of assistance through some incidents which have brought the federal government into conflict with a state administration. Three cases will be illustrative — the so-called Jenner amendment case, the "suitable homes" provisions, and Title XX.

Jenner Amendment

In the Jenner amendment controversy, the central issue was whether or not a state could publish the names of the people receiving relief. Such a publication had been against the law since the 1939 amendments to the Social Security Act (p. 1, 379, 76th Congress). The legislature of the state of Indiana passed an act which allowed this to be done, and hence did not conform to the federal statute. Funds were withheld from Indiana. While Indiana passed the bill, other states had not been idle, though they did not go as far. The state legislatures of Georgia, Illinois, Florida, Oklahoma, and Alabama urged Congress to repeal the section of the Social Security Act which forbade the publication of names. Several bills were introduced to this effect, including one by Representative Reed of New York state and one by Representative Harrison of Virginia. They did not pass. Senator Jenner attached a rider to the appropriations bill for the Federal Security Administration (the early name for the Department of Health, Education, and Welfare) but it did not pass. Finally, a 1951 conference committee included the amendment on a minor tax bill. All it said was that a state should not be refused money for making public the names of relief recipients. The federal government had lost.

Several of the public attitudes mentioned are active here. The basic public attitude which permitted the federal Congress and the various state legislatures to act as they did must be noted. Apparently it was an attempt to shame the recipients of relief into getting off the rolls. Again we see the public and the legislative bodies making the assumption that people are cheating, and that unless they are exposed to public shame, they will not get off the rolls. The federal administration took the view that the names of recipients should not be revealed — a position in accord with social workers' views of the matter — but lost.

This incident points out the difficulties in the federal enforcement of standards in the states. If the states feel strongly enough, it is probable that the enabling legislation will be changed to the detriment of federal standards. Of course, this kind of problem can come up only when there are specific federal standards to meet, as in the case of grants-in-aid for public assistance. The standards in unemployment compensation, for example, are too broad and diffuse to permit much federal enforcement. I know of no case where funds for unemployment compensation have been withheld.

It should be noted, however, that this conflict was not one of federal government versus state government, as such. The state administrators in Indiana were not particularly happy about the turn of events. They themselves were not in favor of opening the lists to public inspection. What actually is involved here is a "government versus the public" controversy, which results in part from the "bad press" public assistance has. From this point of view, the administrators are very vulnerable to public attack. For example, Senator Harry Byrd (D-Va.), "shocked" to hear about a number of persons on public aid in Washington, D.C., who were not technically "eligible," instituted a "crackdown." Children in families which were refused grants wound up in an overcrowded home for children.

Suitable Homes

These cases were not the only ones to come up. There is the "suitable homes" case in Louisiana. A state law was passed providing that any woman who had an illegitimate child while on relief (AFDC) must prove that she was maintaining a "suitable home" to remain eligible. Grants to such women were terminated and they had to reapply. Although this provision received unfavorable editorial comment from the *New York Times,* and the *Chicago Sun-Times,* the Secretary of Health, Education, and Welfare did not find the state law incongruent with the federal requirements. At one point, up to 2,200 children were affected.

The fear that there are "men in the house" of women on relief breaks out in another case—the California inspection case. In California, midnight and early-morning raids had been ordered on the homes of ADC recipients, to ascertain whether or not a man was in the household. Social workers covered the front and back doors of the dwelling, to prevent the man from escaping, should one be present. This procedure brought a rash of protests and resignations. One scholar adjuged it to be unconstitutional. Although the raids are in abeyance, the issue of the right to engage in such activity has never been settled.

Finally, there are the myriad of local cases in assistance which become grist for the local press. One stalwart in Illinois recommended that the poor in Chicago be sent downstate to farms owned by the state, where they could grow their own food and learn to spin their own yarn for clothes. This plan does not seem to be much of an improvement over the Nichols plan, advocated in 1932, under which restaurants would dump uneaten food into five-gallon containers, for which the poor would be eligible by chopping wood donated by farmers.

Title XX

Some of the problems in federal-state relations were thought to be solved as well as some loopholes in the federal law plugged by the most recent addition to the Social Security Act, Title XX. This title provides money to the states for services. States must provide a plan for such social services, but the plan is not reviewed for content by the federal government; it is only viewed with respect to its conformity to certain present categories (so much service must go to people receiving welfare payments, for example). Further, and unlike the provision in the 1962 amendments to the Social Security Act, it sets a total national maximum ($2.5 billion) for social services spending, and sets a share for each state according to its percentage of the national population. Previously, federal reimbursement had been open-ended, in the sense that the federal government was required to match what each state spent in this area according to federal formula(s), but the definition of what constituted services was very broad. In at least one way, this new title seeks to reduce federal-state conflict and limit spending (through the national ceilings) without the federal government becoming deeply involved in arguments with the states over what constitutes "service" to clients.

Policy Issues and Implications

Considering the three programs individually and within the historical context makes possible a greater understanding of some of the problems and difficulties faced by these programs. It is immediately clear that, for historical and socio-political reasons, the insurance concept is much more acceptable, and its administration much more tranquil, than the concept of "public assistance" and its administration. This conclusion does not rest on an analysis of these three programs alone. Other programs for the "poor" have suffered much the same difficulty as the Public Assistance Program. An early version of the Office of Economic Opportunity Program ("the poverty program") was developed in the 1930s and has now virtually gone out of existence. And the modern "poverty program" rose and fell within four years. Hence, successful policy in the area of income and poverty relief must take these events into account. If not, it is likely that future programs to aid the poor in the United States will suffer the same fate as the predecessor programs. It is not, however, exactly clear what "taking these events into account" would entail. Certainly we would be on relatively safe ground concluding that the insurance approach has more general public support. However, second thoughts indicate that the "insurance" approach also contains, and not by necessity, a benefit and allocations pattern which does not respond to the level of individual need. If one is eligible for OASDHI, one's benefit amount is determined not by need, but by whatever category of eligibility is appropriate. The same is true for unemployment compensation. We might, therefore, tentatively note the possibility that it is nearly universal coverage which is the important element, along with the insurance feature. It may be that the only way middle-class antagonism toward the poor can be muted is to include both groups in a benefit package in such a way that reduction of the benefits to the poor reduces benefits to the middle class as well. Additional explorations of the source of middle-class hostility, historically and contemporaneously, toward the poor may suggest more sophisticated alternatives.

In terms of policy making, then, how does the government proceed? The answer to this question depends in part on the point of view. One sanguine opinion points to two ways in which the Social Security Board has proceeded to make policy. Hale argues that the board had three principles:

(1) That states should actually be involved in building federal policy
(2) That policy must be based upon "facts"
(3) That policy decisions must be made known to all concerned

He further argues that the Social Security Board uses either a "common law" approach, or a "case approach" in coming to a decision. The implication of the presentation is that the policy-making approach is decidedly a nonpolitical one, with the "facts showing clearly what decision should be made."

Such a placid approach is not the only characterization available, however. Leon Lefson talks about the development of the Aid to the Permanently and Totally Disabled in California in decidedly political terms. He feels that four factors influence the administration of a new law:

(1) The political climate when the law was passed
(2) The way the administration (both state and local) interprets that climate
(3) The nature of the relationship between the administration and the policy-making board
(4) And, for states which use the county form of assistance administration, the strength of the county supervisors.

I would tend to agree with Lefson. While I would not wish to discount the importance of the attempts to keep the administration nonpolitical, it is my conclusion that a political calculus always enters into the administrative calculus. An administrator cannot go ahead and develop policy with no regard for its political implications; he may soon find himself without funds. Especially in the administration of public assistance, the political aspects of the administration come to the fore because of the relative lack of public sympathy for program goals.

In this paper, then, we have attempted to suggest three very different types of administration which have developed to administer the programs under the Social Security Act. Each has its problems and its advantages, but we have emphasized how the grant-in-aid program makes control by the federal level difficult, and often tenuous. The differences in administration have in part been explained by the different political climates surrounding the programs, and by the differing degrees of public acceptance and support which they enjoy. Other differences in professional staffing and interrelationships were suggested. Perhaps the most important conclusion one could draw from this comparative approach, for welfare administration as well as for other forms of administration, is that there are many ways to organize a program, and that an important part of the ultimate success of the program will depend upon these initial organizational forms. However, from the point of view of policy formation, the question of how the organization should be set up is often a difficult one, with important political overtones. One ignores these overtones at his peril.

NOTES

1. By responsibility I do not mean that they were the only group providing money. The government was providing cash. In 1890, the social welfare expenditures were 2.4 percent of the gross national product ($318 million of expenditures). By 1969-70 this proportion had risen to 15 percent. Rather, the private agencies were dominant in their conceptions of poverty causes and cures, and in the public eye (*Social Security Bulletin,* December 1970, p. 4).
2. There is a provision in the act for a grant-in-aid program for child welfare purposes. We will not discuss that program here. An interesting study, done at the time of passage by an academic who later had important policy roles is *Social Security in the United States* by Paul Douglas (1936).
3. It should be emphasized that "General Assistance" is *not* a federal program, nor does it receive any assistance from the federal government.
4. There is not, however, completely firm agreement on the programs to which "assistance" refers. I am using it to refer to the program with that title. Others, however, would argue that SSI is a public assistance, even though it is now within the administration of the Social Security Program. I am not including other types of payments, such as medical payments here either.

Mark D. Worthington and Laurence E. Lynn, Jr.

7. INCREMENTAL WELFARE REFORM: A STRATEGY WHOSE TIME HAS PASSED

Over the last decade a broad consensus has emerged that our current public programs that supplement individual and family incomes need to be reformed. These programs are expensive, inefficient, inequitable, and confusing. They are resented by taxpayers and transfer recipients alike. Because of this widespread dissatisfaction, the President and the Congress are almost certain to use the momentum of a new presidential term to make some fundamental changes in income assistance policies and programs.*

But what form will these changes take? Virtually every major study of income assistance programs has recommended thorough overhaul of existing programs, that is, the replacement of many, and possibly most, of the existing categorical cash and in-kind income assistance programs with a relatively simple and uniformly administered cash assistance program.[1] Moreover, the arguments for comprehensive reform that these studies have put forth grow stronger with each passing year. Yet a small but growing number of experts are now advocating incremental, piecemeal changes in income assistance programs as the preferred approach to welfare reform. To be sure, there have always been "incrementalists," including Gilbert Steiner of the Brookings Institution and Alvin Schorr of the Community Service Society, who believe that the poor do better under a system of many categorical cash and in-kind assistance programs, each providing specialized benefits, than they would do under a single, unified cash assistance program.[2] Recently, however, the ranks of the incrementalists have been growing, and they now include several former advocates of comprehensive reform, among them Richard Nathan of the Brookings Institution, who, though influential in the design and sponsorship of President Richard M. Nixon's Family Assistance Plan, has become the most vocal of the new incrementalists.[3]

History is unquestionably on the side of those advocating piecemeal reform. Nixon's Family Assistance Plan, a proposal for comprehensive reform,

---

*The authors refer to the early years of Jimmy Carter's Presidency. — Ed.

98

was never enacted by the Congress, whereas many important incremental reforms, including the 1970 Food Stamp reforms, the Supplemental Security Income (SSI) program, and the Earned Income Tax Credit, were enacted without significant controversy. The conclusion is inescapable: Incremental reforms are much more likely to be implemented by our pluralistic political processes than comprehensive reforms.

Beyond this single argument, however, the allure of piecemeal welfare reform is, in our view, quite misleading. Incremental reforms are touted as less expensive and therefore more affordable when resources are limited. In fact, they are more expensive in the long run. Incremental reforms are justified as making it easier to maintain desirable behavioral incentives, primarily incentives to work, among recipients. In fact, they perpetuate the categorical distinctions among people and needs that make efficient program administration impossible and that create disincentives to work and to live as families. Incremental reforms are described as permitting a more flexible adaptation of programs to specific, differentiable policy objectives. On the contrary, the present categorical system is relatively rigid; comprehensive reform would increase, not decrease, policy flexibility.

But these contrasts oversimplify the issues; our thesis is more complex. Incremental reforms are being oversold as a strategy to provide for the consumption needs of the low-income population. While many incremental measures will improve the adequacy and equity of existing programs—we cite several of our preferences below—piecemeal reform will leave unsolved most of the problems associated with "the welfare mess." Indeed, some incremental reforms will make matters considerably worse. At the same time, both the relative economy of a comprehensive cash assistance program and its adaptability to multiple goals have not been sufficiently appreciated. We believe that a careful exposition of the issues raised by the advocates of piecemeal welfare reform will make the case for a comprehensive overhaul of our income assistance programs even more convincing.

Our motivation for advancing this thesis at this time is clear. Historically, the issue of welfare reform receives priority attention during the first two years of a President's term of office, then fades with the approach of the next election. If this pattern is repeated, the events of 1977 and 1978 will probably shape the directions of federal income maintenance for the next decade. It is important, therefore, that the public understand the nature and implications of the alternatives to be considered during the next two years. In particular, it is essential that the proposals of the new incrementalists be carefully analyzed lest they be chosen for the wrong reasons and the nation miss a major opportunity for comprehensive reform.

In the next section of this chapter we review the coverage and characteristics of existing income assistance programs and evaluate the major proposals for incremental reform of these programs. The following section reanalyzes the subject in terms of issues rather than specific proposals in an effort to clarify areas of agreement and disagreement between proponents of different strategies for welfare reform. Finally, in the light of this analysis, we restate the case for comprehensive reform of income assistance programs.

What Do Incrementalists Want?

Incrementalists comprise a loose coalition of individuals and organizations who view the income transfer system from different perspectives and who advocate a diverse assortment of proposals.[4] They are united only in their pragmatic opposition or indifference to comprehensive reform schemes such as a negative income tax. For the most part, their proposals have not been subjected to the rigorous analysis that comprehensive proposals have received. As a result, they tend to be vague and general, often changing in shape as they are debated, and rarely appearing in print.

Nevertheless, it seems fair to say that most incrementalists would agree with Richard Nathan, who recently wrote:

> . . . because income security programs have developed and grown so much in the past decade, the idea of a comprehensive replacement strategy has been passed over by events. The need now is to fill in the gaps by dealing with deficiencies and by taking steps, some of them quite important, to improve and rationalize existing programs. This position rests on two essential points: (1) the idea of multiple goals requiring multiple programs; and (2) a diagnosis that challenges the conventional wisdom that existing programs are such a "mess" that total replacement is the only answer.[5]

Following Nathan's reasoning, the basic premises of an incremental welfare reform strategy can be described as follows:

A transfer system should achieve many goals, and multiple goals require multiple programs.

The existing categorical welfare programs are essentially sound.

Incremental legislative changes can "fill in the gaps" by increasing and extending benefits.

Incremental administrative changes can improve efficiency of operation.

Comprehensive welfare reform would be costly, disruptive, and unnecessary—if not undesirable. . . .

A Critical Look at Incremental Reform

Because incremental reform proposals do not often come in tightly coordinated packages, but instead are offered by their various sponsors as specific solutions to specific problems, it is perhaps best to assess them individually, on their own terms. The major proposals for change in existing programs and some of the alternative proposals for new programs will be reexamined and evaluated as incremental reforms, taking into consideration the problems and issues that are not addressed, as well as those that are addressed.

AFDC

The minimum-benefit proposal for AFDC is intended to alleviate two problems: the inadequacy of flow benefits in some states and the inequity of widely different benefits among states. Under an incremental reform proposal, either the federal government would require states to meet certain benefit standards, with no change in the current format of the program, or else it would alter the matching formula, perhaps even fully financing the minimum benefit, in order to induce states to meet those standards. It seems unlikely that the federal government could induce states to raise benefits sufficiently by simply raising the matching rate. For example, Mississippi, the state with the lowest payment standard ($60 per month for a family of four), now pays only 17 percent of its AFDC costs; further increases in the federal share could not induce the benefit increase that is needed. The only ways to assure an adequate AFDC minimum benefit in all states are to mandate national standards as a condition for receiving federal funds, or to pay the full minimum benefit out of the federal budget.

Regardless of the variant adopted, however, any proposal that retains the basic format of the AFDC program will necessarily perpetuate two severe weaknesses of that approach. The first is the strained relationship between the states and the federal government. Under the current program, each level of government exercises unnecessary and undesirable control over the budget and operations of the other. Because AFDC is an open-ended matching grant program, states have a blank check from the federal government. They also determine, in essence, which of their citizens will receive federal assistance and in what amounts. On the other hand, state expenditures under AFDC are regulated by the federal government. The frustration of governors and state legislatures is well known, and a minimum-benefit provision would further strain relations. The second fundamental weakness is the inequitable treatment of recipients by the federal government. Currently, for example, the federal share of basic AFDC payments to a four-person family with no other income varied from $50 per month in Mississippi to $256 per month in Vermont. Thus, for two families who were identical save for state of residence, the federal contribution towards subsistence varied by a factor of five. A minimum-benefit provision would alleviate this inequity, but it could not eliminate it.

An incremental alternative superior to the minimum-benefit proposal could be designed following the precedent of the adult categorical programs, which were replaced by SSI. AFDC could be converted from the present federal-state matching grant program to a simplified federal minimum/state supplement program. The federal government would fully finance a nationwide minimum-benefit structure, designed to replace the federal share of benefits in the state with the highest payment standard. (Currently, that amount is about $3,100 per year, $3,900 if the food stamp bonus were "cashed out.") With the funds they now spend as their current share of AFDC financing, states could supplement the benefits of recipients within their borders.[6] Administration could be federal, as with SSI, or state and local, as with food stamps. This alternative proposal would accomplish the same objectives as the AFDC minimum benefit: it would increase assistance to recipients in low benefit states, and it would reduce the disparity in benefits among states. In addition, however, the federal minimum/state supplement option would restructure antagonistic intergovernmental relations and assure an equitable distribution of federal benefits.

It is instructive to note the sharp contrast between the vigorous debate over the desirability of "federalizing welfare" (i.e., adopting federal standards or administration for the AFDC program) and the virtual absence of debate when welfare for the adult categories was federalized (i.e., when the SSI program was passed). The SSI program is smaller, less expensive, and more stable, and for these reasons it raises fewer issues. Of greater significance, however, is that the SSI population is universally believed to be deserving of generous public assistance. The AFDC population, on the other hand, is the very symbol of "the welfare mess." Any proposal involving AFDC raises a hue and cry over work incentives, desertion, and illegitimacy, and the merits of using working people's taxes to support those who "could" work but do not. Perhaps the greatest source of complexity and confusion in the welfare reform debate is the political necessity of continuing to stigmatize AFDC adults in the name of the work ethic.

Unemployment Insurance

The Seidman proposal, which would provide special UI payments to regular UI exhaustees and to new entrants and reentrants to the labor force, is an extreme example of how our social insurance programs can be stretched badly out of shape in order to meet welfare objectives. The UI system was designed to provide short-term income support during a temporary spell of unemployment.

Moreover, as a social insurance program it was intended to serve as a wage replacement during periods when earnings are disrupted involuntarily, with benefits directly related to past wage history. The Seidman proposal is not consistent with these principles. It would provide uniform weekly payments to recipients who, for the most part, have no recent employment experience. The proposal is intended to assure a source of respectable, employment-related income to every family with an employable worker. The underlying concern, we assume, is to help families that have little other source of support because of unfavorable economic conditions. But if the target is the low income population, UI is a costly and highly inefficient delivery mechanism. According to an estimate prepared for the Ford Foundation's Welfare Study Project, as many as 26 million people could become eligible for a special UI program such as the one proposed by Seidman and Lesser.[7] Regular UI beneficiaries now total less than 7 million. Most of the new beneficiaries would be teenagers and middle-aged women in multiple-earner, middle- and upper-income families. These two populations have special employment needs worthy of concern, but those needs are not primarily income needs and they should not be met with special UI entitlements. Regular UI exhaustees, as well as new entrants and reentrants to the labor force, are typically members of nonpoor families.[8] In fact, less than 30 percent of regular UI beneficiaries can be considered poor when family income is considered on an annual basis.[9] This is not to say that UI is a bad program, but rather that it is a highly inefficient way to help low-income families. The most efficient way to help low-income families is to relate benefits to income, not to employment status.

Food Stamps
In contrast to UI, the Food Stamp Program is a relatively efficient transfer mechanism. Nevertheless, it could be significantly improved. The reforms pending in Congress would make the program more equitable and less complex. Further, the proposal to eliminate the purchase requirement is a step in the right direction. Studies have consistently shown that the purchase requirement is a major barrier to the participation of many eligible households; removal of that barrier would make the program more accessible and therefore more equitable. Elimination of the purchase requirement would also have another, less obvious, benefit: It would eliminate the spending constraint for most households. That is, food stamp benefits for most households would be no more restrictive than cash. Under the current rules, a low-income household must allocate a significant amount (20 to 25 percent) of its income to purchase food stamps, and the entire coupon allotment (now $166 per month for a family of four) must be used to purchase food. This is an unnecessary and paternalistic burden for many

households with other important spending needs. If the purchase requirement is eliminated, however, only the bonus value would be transferred in coupons. The family would have to spend only the amount of the actual transfer, usually much smaller than the full allotment, on food.

Housing Allowances

Although in our opinion the housing allowance concept is superior to public housing and other production-oriented subsidy programs that are intended to assist the low-income population in meeting its housing needs, it is subject to the same criticism as a Food Stamp Program with no purchase requirement: a housing allowance is a disguised cash assistance program. Since the "earmark" would be applied only to the amount of the allowance (comparable to the food stamp bonus value), only the poorest recipients would find the transfer restrictive. This raises the question why, other than on grounds of political expediency, another separate program should be established to provide disguised cash assistance. If there is more money available for income assistance to this population, why not fold it in with a cashed-out Food Stamp Program? The result would be somewhat higher benefits ($3,000 to $4,000) and a somewhat higher reduction rate (about 50 percent). This cashed-out version of the "in-kind strategy" would cover the same population, provide the same level of benefits, and maintain work incentives. Because it would require a simpler administrative and delivery structure, however, the cash strategy would be far more economical.

Earnings Supplements and Wage Rate Subsidies

These two work-conditioned transfers are intended to help those who are able and willing to work—including those already working—but who cannot earn an adequate income. The major weakness of this approach, crucial in a time of 7 percent unemployment, is that it does not help those who are able and willing to work but who cannot find employment. Thus, an earnings supplement program or a wage subsidy program alone cannot adequately provide necessary assistance to the employable category of the low-income population.

There are other weaknesses. A wage rate subsidy is intended to help low-income workers; instead, it would assist low-wage workers. The difference is significant; a census survey shows that less than 20 percent of those who earned less than the minimum wage were members of poor families.[10] An earnings supplement, which would be related to total income as well as to earnings, would be more efficient. But in order to relate benefits to income, an earnings supplement must have a benefit reduction range similar to other assistance programs. Moreover, no evidence exists that a modest earnings supplement would provide a significant inducement to increase work effort—especially when other assistance (e.g., food stamps) is available. We prefer an income-assistance program that relates benefits strictly to the need for assistance. Adequate work incentives can be maintained by a relatively low benefit reduction rate and a work registration requirement.

Incremental reforms of the Food Stamp and AFDC programs would unquestionably improve the current welfare system. Nevertheless, even the adoption of the most ambitious incremental reforms would leave significant problems and issues unaddressed. The low-income population would continue to be categorized and segmented, with common income needs treated in very different ways. A complex assortment of cash and in-kind assistance programs would continue to coexist, needlessly and inefficiently, with overlapping coverage and cumulating work disincentives. Income-transfer programs would continue to be financed and administered in a highly fragmented manner, with authority spread among at lest twenty-one committees within the Congress, seven departments and three independent agencies within the federal executive, fifty governors and state legislatures, fifty-four state and territorial welfare departments, and countless local welfare agencies. Social insurance programs would continue to be stretched in dubious and grossly inefficient attempts to meet welfare objectives. Taxes would continue to be collected from low-income families to support nonworking families with higher total incomes. The government would have no deliberate income-assistance policy and inadequate fiscal and policy control over welfare programs. Neither welfare and social insurance programs nor tax and transfer programs would be satisfactorily integrated. The roles and responsiblities of different levels of government would be inconsistently defined.

In short, the "welfare mess" would remain.

What Are the Important Issues?

More is at issue with the income-transfer system than can be captured in the terms "incremental reform" and "comprehensive reform." Strictly speaking, these terms denote strategic approaches to a set of common goals. The tendency, however, is to use the two terms to describe opposing positions on a cluster of issues. For some purposes this may be a useful shorthand, since most incrementalists and most advocates of comprehensive reform tend to agree among themselves on several general principles of welfare reform. Most incrementalists for example tend to favor categorical distinctions among classes of recipients; most advocates of comprehensive reform favor more universal and uniform standards of eligibility for assistance. Most incrementalists tend to favor multiple programs that provide benefits both in cash and in kind, while most advocates of comprehensive reform prefer a single, consolidated, cash-assistance program to meet the regular income needs of the poor. Most incrementalists favor an adaptive strategy of using whatever welfare program, social insurance program, or tax provision will improve benefit adequacy or help fill a gap in coverage; on the other hand, most advocates of comprehensive reform have a less flexible view of transfer policy and favor more strictly defined roles for welfare and social insurance programs and a more deliberate integration of the tax and transfer systems. Nevertheless, these tendencies are neither exhaustive nor definitive. One does not have to be an incrementalist to favor some categorical distinctions, nor an advocate of comprehensive reform to favor a more coherent welfare system. The major welfare reform issues that may have been lost or confused in the midst of debate should be considered explicitly. These are the issues that must be resolved in the design of any system of income assistance.

Categorization vs. Universality
Are certain categories of the low-income population more deserving or more in need than others? Or is need determined only by income and family size? At present, this seems to be the most divisive issue. Those who advocate categorization of the poor usually draw a distinction between those who are dependent for reasons beyond their control, such as the aged, blind, and disabled and some single-parent families, and those who might be economically independent but are not, such as able-bodied individuals, nonaged childless couples, and two-parent families. Because they may have no access to other income, the former groups should be provided at least a minimally adequate level of benefits. However, because they are not expected to work, these groups might reasonably be subjected to relatively high benefit reduction rates for other income. Households with employable members, according to this view, do not need and should not be provided benefits that assure adequate income. These households should derive their primary support from earnings. Low-benefit supplements to earnings, with low reduction rates to preserve work incentives, are more appropriate for this category.

Those who generally oppose categorization argue that the need for income assistance, regardless of the physical capability of the family head, should be assessed solely on the basis of income and family size. Especially in a time when at least 7 million workers are unemployed, it seems unfair to draw distinctions that imply that some of the poor are deserving while others are not. Concern that assistance not go to the shiftless and the lazy would be more appropriately directed to the design of work incentives — even to a strictly enforced work test — and the maintenance of a full-employment economy — than to differential levels of assistance that deal a double penalty to the families of the unemployed and underemployed.

Moreover, many critics of categorized assistance to the low-income population believe that the differential treatment of one-parent and two-parent families has contributed to the dramatic increase in divorce, desertion, and illegitimacy that took place in the 1960s. Because AFDC provides a more reliable source of income support than employment in the secondary labor market, it has been argued that the stability of low-income families is undermined. Many fathers choose to leave their homes so that their families can qualify for welfare; many mothers choose to remain unmarried in order to protect their one sure source of income for their children. For many low-income families that stay together, recognition that the family can obtain more reliable income support from the welfare department than it can from its primary earner is a constant source of tension. Critics maintain that a welfare system that is built on unfair distinctions among low-income families necessarily creates inequities and perverse behavioral incentives. Only an income-assistance system that provides support solely on the basis of income and family size, they argue, can avoid this problem.

Finally, opponents of categorization point out the impracticality of dividing the low-income population into distinct and separate groups. Determinations of employability, and even disability, are complex and necessarily subjective, varying among caseworkers and according to labor market conditions. Administrative problems are compounded because the system has to cope with the large numbers of people who move into and out of poverty from year to year because family circumstances change. (Over a period of several years, twice as many people are apt to experience poverty as are poor at any one time, in significant part because of such changes.) Consequently, categorization is often arbitrary and unfair, and is the primary cause of the bad reputation acquired by the welfare bureaucracy.

Neither incrementalists nor comprehensive reformers are rigid on this issue. Many incrementalists, while accepting the categorical distinctions of the present programs, propose changes (such as special UI and housing allowances) that would tend to equalize assistance to the two nonaged categories. Most proponents of comprehensive reform, while generally preferring uniform treatment of the low-income population, nevertheless build into their systems more generous treatment of the aged, blind, and disabled.

In-Kind vs. Cash

Do special needs require special benefits? Or are all income needs best fulfilled with cash assistance? Some advocates of in-kind transfers assert that low-income families have many different needs and that, consequently, benefits should be provided in many different ways. Other advocates of in-kind assistance argue that, because of the nature of the markets for some goods and services (such as housing), public intervention is necessary to obtain an increase in the supply available to low-income consumers. Some point out that public provision of certain services (such as education or medical care) may be appropriate if there is a special concern for assuring equality of opportunity or equality of access among all citizens, rich and poor. Others argue that it is desirable to constrain the consumption of welfare recipients—through the use of earmarked cash assistance (as with housing allowance) or vouchers (as with food stamps) or through direct provision of goods and services (as with medical insurance)—in order to assure that recipients utilize their resources in an approved manner. Finally, some who would prefer straight cash assistance nevertheless often advocate in-kind assistance because, they maintain, the Congress and the public are more likely to provide higher benefits of this type than they would if benefits were paid in cash.

Proponents of cash assistance counter that cash is more helpful to low-income families and less expensive to the taxpayer. Low-income families have subnutritional diets and substandard housing, they argue, primarily because these families have inadequate incomes. Cash assistance allows them to meet their individual needs in the most flexible manner, and it places on them the responsibility to determine the best use of available resources. Critics of in-kind assistance also argue that it is futile to attempt to constrain the use of transfers; most recipients are able to shift resources, which in the absence of the transfer would have been used for the approved expenditures (for example, on food), in order to increase expenditures on some other goods or services (for example, on housing). Moreover, it is not even necessary to constrain the use of transfers, since low-income families spend almost all their incomes on basic necessities anyway. Finally, cash assistance requires much lower overhead expense, so that more of the welfare budget ends up in the hands of those it is intended to help.

Again, there is no fixed division on this issue. While virtually all advocates of comprehensive reform support reliance on cash assistance to provide for regular and predictable income needs, most also propose to establish a separate health insurance program to provide for irregular and unpredictable medical expenses.[11] On the other side, incrementalists are more and more advocating steps toward conversion to a mostly cash system (for example, by eliminating the food stamp purchase requirement).

Discretion vs. Standardization

An issue related to the cash vs. in-kind controversy is the extent of variation in the treatment of similar families within the same program. Many who believe that different categories of people require different levels of assistance, and that different kinds of needs require different kinds of benefits, also argue that an assistance program should maintain the flexibility to adjust further the level or the nature of benefits to account for specific circumstances. This position is reflected in most welfare programs. AFDC benefits, for example, originally were derived from individual caseworker assessments of family budget needs, and the AFDC and Food Stamp programs still allow the deduction from "countable" income of many specific expenditures, such as work-related day-care expenses and relatively high housing payments.

Advocates of standardization decry the discretion left to welfare caseworkers, which they say results in serious, though unintended, inequities in the treatment of recipients. A thousand caseworkers each pursuing equitable entitlements can create a notably inequitable result. Further, discretionary deductions from income allow participation of many recipients with relatively high incomes, and thus are a primary source of dissatisfaction with existing welfare programs. Moreover, such discretion is a major cause of fraud, error, and abuse. Income is the best indicator of the need for assistance; special and discretionary provisions necessarily lead to inequity and inefficiency.

Advocates of comprehensive reform generally insist on uniformity of treatment among recipients. Many, however, favor the continuation of several itemized deductions such as those for day-care expenses, and most recognize the need for a separate and more discretionary program for emergency assistance administered at the state and local level. On the other hand, many incrementalists advocate standardization of treatment within broad categories of recipients. Existing programs are moving increasingly to uniform benefit levels and assessments of need. The federal SSI program has no discretionary variations, and both the AFDC and Food Stamp programs are incrementally losing their discretionary features.

Multi-Program vs. Single-Program System

Categorization of people and needs seems to lead to the creation of categorical programs. Do multiple goals require multiple programs? Many analysts claim they do. If different classes of people are to be treated in different ways, they argue, separate programs should deal with each class; if different kinds of needs are to be adequately fulfilled, separate programs should deal with each need. Others counter that this is faulty analysis. Even multiple objectives, they point out, very often can be achieved through variations in treatment within the same program. For example, it is unnecessary to operate three separate cash-assistance programs in order to provide differential benefits to the three major categorical populations. One program can adequately serve the same function. Moreover, a consolidated cash-assistance program, whether benefits are uniform or categorical, would be far simpler and more efficient to administer.

Once again, incrementalists and advocates of comprehensive reform cannot be strictly separated. No seriously considered reform proposal to date has suggested wholesale elimination of the existing system and replacement with a single, consolidated cash-assistance program. While most would replace the three major assistance programs (SSI, AFDC, and Food Stamps), none has yet tackled total elimination of others such as public housing and veterans assistance.

The Roles of Welfare and Social Insurance

Social insurance programs, as well as welfare programs, are a major source of income support to the poor. Indeed, many believe that social security and unemployment insurance benefits should be increased and extended to provide as much assistance as possible to the low-income population. Some argue that this is an appropriate role for social insurance; others feel that it is the only form of assistance that is respectable in the eyes of the public.

Critics of these arguments point out that, since most social insurance beneficiaries are not poor, increasing the benefits of these programs is a costly and inefficient way to provide aid to the low-income population. Unless resources are unconstrained, increased benefits should be provided through an income-tested assistance program. To be sure, social insurance programs have a very important place in the income transfer system. But programs such as unemployment insurance and social security should serve a strict wage replacement function, with benefits related to past earnings that have been disrupted by unemployment, disability, retirement, or death. It should be the role of an income-tested assistance program, not a social insurance program, to assure a minimum level of income support.

On this issue, as with others, no fixed distinctions can be discerned. Although incrementalists tend to be flexible in the use of social insurance to meet welfare goals and comprehensive reformers tend to favor a stricter delineation of role, divergent views can be found within both groups.

The Integration of Tax and Transfer Systems

The relationships between taxes and transfers are becoming more widely understood. A reduction in taxes is as helpful to a low-income family that pays taxes as an increase in assistance payments. The tax-exempt income level, which is defined by the sum of personal exemptions and the minimum standard deduction, has been raised several times in recent years in order to reduce the income tax burden on low- and middle-income families. Moreover, the Earned Income Tax Credit has set a precedent as the first tax provision to be "refundable" even to families that have no tax liability. These tax provisions underline the interdependence of taxes and transfers.

Some advocates of comprehensive reform have gone beyond the bounds of the welfare and social insurance programs to propose an explicit integration of tax and transfer systems. The same standards that are used to measure ability to pay personal income taxes, they argue, should logically be extended as the measure of need for income assistance. It makes little sense to collect income taxes from families poor enough to receive public assistance. Only a conscious integration of both systems can eliminate this anomaly. Proposals for a "negative income tax," for example, would establish a common standard for taxation and assistance. Families with income above that standard would be liable to pay taxes; families with income below that standard would be eligible to receive assistance benefits. Such coordination of tax and transfer policy would substantially reduce the inequity of the present situation.

Intergovernmental Relations

The general issue of the roles, responsibilities, and interrelations of the various levels of government involved in existing transfer programs is a matter of increasing concern to advocates of welfare reform. At present, intergovernmental roles are notably inconsistent. The federal and state governments, for example, each serve a different role in each of the three major assistance programs and in the two major social insurance programs. Many who are involved with these programs argue that the multiple problems of concern to reformers cannot be adequately addressed without the establishment of a more rigid definition of responsibilities within the income transfer system. Only then can the confusion and tension that characterizes the relations among public welfare institutions be significantly improved. This issue concerns many incrementalists, as well as most proponents of comprehensive reform.

It's Time for Comprehensive Reform

If existing programs came anywhere close to meeting the basic goals of an income-transfer system[12] — adequacy of benefits, horizontal and vertical equity, target effectiveness, administrative efficiency, coherency, and fiscal and policy control — or even if incremental changes could offer hope of substantial improvement toward most of these goals, it would be tempting to continue on the path of incrementalism. It appears to be the path of least political resistance. Unfortunately, while past incremental reforms have improved the adequacy of benefits and filled some of the gaps in coverage, they have exacerbated the problems of inequity and inefficiency. They have increased the number of people receiving varying benefits from more than one program and facing work disincentives associated with cumulating benefit reduction rates. Moreover, incremental reforms offer no hope for improving the coherency and control of the growing number of welfare and social insurance programs, no hope for facilitating the rational integration of tax and transfer policies, and no hope for repairing the fractured state of intergovernmental relations.

For these reasons, we favor the replacement of the existing welfare programs with a fully integrated tax and transfer system. The model we suggest is the Friedman negative income tax.[13] The idea is not new, but it is hard to improve upon. The concept is simple. The tax-exempt income level would be raised to provide a common standard for taxation and assistance. We would recommend a standard of $8,000 for a household of four. Those with income above that standard would have positive taxable income: They would pay taxes. Those with income below that standard would have unused personal exemptions and deductions, or "negative taxable income"; they would be eligible to receive an income supplement equal to a portion of that amount. We recommend a supplement rate of 50 percent. Thus, a family of four with no other income would receive a basic benefit of $4,000. Most families have some other income and would receive a lower benefit payment, reduced by one half of income up to $8,000, where the family would break even. Since benefits would be reduced by only one half of earned income, those who work would always be better off than those who do not.[14] Consistent with the present tax law, aged and blind persons would receive an extra personal exemption; we also recommend extending this treatment to disabled persons. The benefits to the aged, blind, or disabled poor thus would be correspondingly higher.[15]

Any assistance from programs not eliminated (perhaps, for example, public housing because of long-term legal commitments) would be offset by reductions in payments to negative income tax recipients. In this manner, duplication of benefits would be avoided and horizontal equity assured. The proposal would also provide substantial tax relief to the middle-income population as a direct result of the meshing of tax and transfer systems and would assure vertical equity (i.e., that people with higher earnings would receive higher total income). Further, the consolidation of cash-assistance programs would allow greater fiscal and policy control over the transfer system, and integration with the tax system would facilitate coordination of tax and transfer policies.

In addition, with a unified income-assistance program, other national policies could be determined without the often distorting consideration of the potential impact on the low-income population. The long-term financial crisis of the social security system, for example, could be more easily addressed if its programs did not include such welfare-oriented features as the minimum benefit and the dependents' allowance. The seemingly interminable extensions of unemployment insurance might not appear necessary if an adequate income were assured even to the families of employable workers. The debate over consumer cost-sharing in national health insurance could center more on efficient utililization of medical care resources if the burden on low-income consumers were significantly lessened by a negative income tax. Even the consideration of such apparently remote issues as energy and environmental protection have been significantly restricted by distributional concerns. Again and again, we find the lack of an explicit and efficient mechanism for income maintenance to be an unnecessary barrier to good public policy in other areas. Thus the advantages of an integrated tax and transfer system extend far beyond the problems of our current welfare programs.

While we prefer the suggested uniform treatment of the low-income population, we feel it is important to point out that the negative income tax could provide categorical cash assistance instead. Differentiation of supplement rates would be the simplest way of accomplishing this objective. The aged, blind, and disabled population and single-parent families might receive, for example, 67 percent of the gap between household income and the tax and transfer income standard. Thus, using the standard we suggested, a single-parent family of four with no other income would receive a basic benefit of $5,333, and benefits would be reduced by two thirds of any other income. Households in the employable category, however, might receive a lower supplement, say 33 percent. This would be $2,667 for a family of four, reduced by only one third of other income. The parameters are not crucial, but the central point is: A categorical but consolidated negative income tax can accomplish the objectives of the three clusters of assistance programs described earlier and it can accomplish these objectives in a manner that is more equitable, more efficient, and more coherent. Multiple objectives do not require multiple programs.

To repeat, we endorse a universal negative income tax that does not distinguish among categories of the low-income population. Such distinctions, we believe, are unfair and unwise. Nevertheless, it is important to emphasize that the essential issues of welfare reform cannot be separated into mutually exclusive packages of incremental and comprehensive reform. This point has too long been lost in the midst of competing strategies. The central question is how to achieve an optimal income-assistance system. We believe the answer is clear, and it is comprehensive reform.

Is It Feasible?

Incrementalists are fond of telling us that comprehensive reform would be too costly. To do it right, they say, would be enormously expensive. But that misses the crucial point: To do it any other way would be even more expensive. For any given benefit levels, for any given benefit reduction rates, for any given categorical distinctions, or for any given total amount of money—for any specification of income transfer parameters—a consolidated approach is superior. It puts money in the hands of the target population at less expense to the taxpayer. Comprehensive reform can come in many sizes. The package we propose would increase net transfer costs by about $5 billion, and it would not extend eligibility beyond the scope of the present income-assistance programs. Parameters easily could be changed to fit a more generous or a more restrictive budget. But whatever the price tag, the same issues must be faced and the same conclusion must be reached. Comprehensive reform is the answer.

Incrementalists also like to tell us that comprehensive reform is politically infeasible, that neither the Congress nor the public would support such a drastic solution. We think they're wrong. The Family Assistance Plan, the first significant attempt at comprehensive welfare reform, was passed by the House of Representatives in two consecutive Congresses. The last two Republican Presidents and the last two Democratic presidential nominees have supported comprehensive reform. Virtually every major government study of the welfare system has concluded with a recommendation for consolidated cash assistance—the Heineman Commission, the Moynihan Urban Affairs Council, the Carlucci Task Force, the Griffiths Subcommittee. Organizations of state and local officials (such as the Governors' Conference, the Conference of Mayors, and the National Association of Counties), national business organizations (such as the Conference Board and the Chamber of Commerce), public interest groups (such as the Urban League and Common Cause), and religious organizations (such as the National Council of Churches, the U.S. Catholic Conference, and the Synagogue Council of America)—all these organizations have at some time come to the same conclusion. All have advocated comprehensive welfare reform.

According to a recent Harris poll, 94 percent of the American public feel that "it is not right to let people who need welfare go hungry." At the same time, 80 percent think that the welfare problem is serious and merits reform. The American people are generous in support of those who need assistance. But they are tired of paying for welfare programs that seem to grow out of control; they are resentful of a system that stifles work effort and appears to treat those who do not work better than those who do; and they are disgusted with a system that invites fraud, abuse, and error.

The time has passed for tireless tinkering with welfare programs. The time is right for comprehensive reform.

NOTES

1. The following groups have come to the same general conclusion that the welfare system needs comprehensive reform: the Presidential Commission on Income Maintenance, established by President Johnson and chaired by Ben Heineman (1969); the Urban Affairs Council, established by President Nixon and directed by Daniel P. Moynihan (1969); the House Ways and Means Committee, chaired by Rep. Wilbur Mills (1970 and 1971); the interagency Welfare Reform Task Force, established by HEW Secretary Caspar Weinberger and chaired by Under Secretary Frank Carlucci (1973-74); the Joint Economic Committee's Subcommittee on Fiscal Policy, chaired by Rep. Martha Griffiths (1974). In addition, many public interest groups have studied the welfare system and reached the same conclusion.

2. See, for example, Gilbert Y. Steiner, "Reform Follows Reality: The Growth of Welfare," *The Public Interest*, no. 34 (Winter 1974): 47-65.

3. Richard P. Nathan, "Alternatives for Federal Income Security Policy," in *Qualities of Life: Critical Choices for Americans*, vol. 7 (Lexington, Mass.: Lexington Books, 1976).

4. For a review of the incrementalism vs. overhaul debate, see Laurence E. Lynn, Jr., "A Decade of Developments in the Income Maintenance System," in *A Decade of Federal Anti-Poverty Policy: Achievements, Failures and Lessons,* ed. Robert H. Haveman (New York: Academic, 1979).

5. Richard P. Nathan, "Food Stamps and Welfare Reform," *Policy Analysis* 2, no. 1 (Winter 1976): 63.

6. In fact, under this proposal, all states could supplement up to current AFDC levels and still realize at least some measure of net fiscal relief.

7. This figure represents the number of noninstitutionalized, nondisabled persons between the ages of 18 and 64 who are not employed and not receiving regular UI benefits and who are not heads of single-parent families with preschool children.

8. Mathematical Policy Research, "A Longitudinal Study of Unemployment Insurance Exhaustees" (Princeton, N.J., January 1976).

9. Martin Feldstein, "Unemployment Compensation: Adverse Incentives and Distributional Anomalies" (Harvard Institute for Economic Research, Discussion Paper 317, 1973).

10. This figure was taken from special tabulations of the 1967 Survey of Economic Opportunity, which was carried out by the Census Bureau for the Office of Economic Opportunity. See also Michael Barth, "Universal Wage-Rate Subsidy: Benefits and Effects," in *The Economics of Federal Subsidy Programs, Part 4, Higher Education and Manpower Subsidies,* U.S. Congress, Joint Economic Committee (Washington, D.C.: U.S. Government Printing Office, 1972).

11. Since any program of compulsory health insurance would make medical expenses regular and predictable, regardless of who provides the insurance, a

legitimate question can be raised as to why the direct provision of health insurance, rather than just the general requirement that there be coverage, should be the responsibility of government.

12. For further discussion of policy goals, see Michael C. Barth, George J. Carcagno, and John L. Palmer, *Toward an Effective Income Support System: Problems, Prospects and Choices* (Madison, Wisc.: Institute for Research on Poverty, 1974).

13. Milton Friedman, "The Case for the Negative Income Tax," in *The Republican Papers* (New York: Doubleday, 1968).

14. Thus, a four-person family with employment income from a full-time job at the minimum wage ($4,784) would be eligible to receive a supplemental benefit equal to $1,608. The shorthand discussion of welfare benefits for a family of four sometimes obscured important differences in coverage and benefit levels. Under this proposal, low-income individuals and childless couples also would be eligible for assistance. A single individual with no other income would be eligible to receive a basic benefit of $1,400 and would have a break-even income level of $2,800. For a childless couple, these figures would be $2,400 and $4,800 respectively.

15. This proposal is similar to the Income Supplement Plan prepared by HEW staff under the direction of former Secretary Caspar Weinberger. That proposal has been published and can be obtained from the Office of Income Security Policy, Office of the Assistant Secretary for Planning and Evaluation.

Nathan Glazer

8. Reform Work, Not Welfare

We are not thinking about welfare much these days. With a high and rising rate of unemployment, the key issue is clearly what to do about putting men and women back to work. But the welfare issue is always lurking in the wings, and while we await the next bout of reform, some analysis of how we might go about dealing with the unpleasant reality of our very large population of welfare families is surely in order.

Discussions of welfare by those who politically are in the center or on the left generally take it as a cardinal principle that there is not and cannot be a relationship between work and welfare. The welfare client is by definition a person who cannot work: Even if the old and the disabled and the blind have now been removed from welfare, the remaining element is not considered capable of work, since it consists, overwhelmingly, of young children and of women taking care of children. Further, since the political right is always protesting that the burden of welfare is too great, those concerned for the unfortunates on welfare try to make their case for what is after all the descendent of public charity as strong as possible. One way of making it strong is to argue that people on welfare cannot work and should not be expected to work. By now, however, the effort to set up an impenetrable barrier between work and welfare—part of the design of the original system—has clearly broken down.

Initially, the barrier seemed to stand firm. On the one side, according to the social security design of the 1930s, were those whose entitlement to an adequate income in the absence of work was based on contributions made while they had worked: Thus workers would receive social security when they retired, their wives and children would receive social security if they died or became disabled, and they were to receive unemployment insurance when they became unemployed. Welfare was to be a residual system, one that would decline over time as individuals gained access to work-related insurance. As we know, though, it didn't happen that way.

At the time the welfare system was first set up, the barrier may not have been considered a crucial feature, for it was not likely that welfare would be considered more desirable than work if such a choice existed. But as welfare benefits in large northern states began to rise, welfare became an attractive alternative to work. Thus, the *Boston Globe* of March 30 has a long story about a family on welfare in Boston, whose point is to show neither the worst nor the best of welfare, but rather to demonstrate that Governor Dukakis' resistance to an increase in benefits is unfair. The article is titled "Welfare: A Treadmill, Not a Free Ride." There are pictures of an attractive looking family—a mother and six children ranging in age from 17 to 4—living in East Cambridge. The mother is well-organized. She buys food stamps twice a month, refuses to live in a housing project, is a member of a community women's group at Catholic charities, and is studying for her high school diploma. Her monthly cash grant is $466, she gets a flat grant every three months of $142, and her monthly savings from food stamps amount to $86. Her cash income may be given as $599 monthly, or $7,188 a year. If she and her family spent the average amount paid personally for health care in this country (and the mother gets some psychiatric care), this would amount at full costs to an additional $1,750 in health care expenses. Since there are no financial restrictions for this family on the use of health care, and the mother is intelligent and knowledgeable, one may assume that full use of this opportunity is taken. The three older children go free of charge to an alternative school which costs paying pupils $2,000 a year, and another child goes to a day-care center whose cost for a paying child would be $1,000 a year. Cash income and free health and educational services to this family thus amount to $15,938. The older children work summers, and I will not cost that out. The family pays no taxes, and need put nothing aside for savings, as the welfare department is committed to meeting its needs. A working head of a family would have to earn at least $20,000 to match this standard of living.

This example should give us a sense of the situation in those states, such as Massachusetts, whose welfare benefits are at the upper end of the scale for generosity. (Actually, five states in July 1974 provided higher average cash grants per family than Massachusetts, and New York provided, surprisingly, 16.6 percent more.)

I should make it clear that this example was published by a very liberal newspaper, not a conservative one. It was intended to arouse sympathy for people on welfare, and support for a scheduled inflation-related increase in welfare benefits that an economy-minded governor was resisting. Hence, unless the *Boston Globe* made a grave tactical error in selecting this case, it is not an exceptional one.

It is true that a working head of family would have to make $20,000 a year to afford this pattern of expenditures. However, a working head of family with an income of $20,000 a year and six children probably would not even dream of spending $4,000 a year for education, and would not make so much use of health care facilities that were not covered by insurance (e.g., psychiatric care).

There is a real dilemma here: The costing out of welfare benefits amounts to a great deal in public funds, but the satisfactions given by this sum to the welfare recipient do not match the satisfactions given by an income of the same size that could be freely spent. Thus we have a classic "no-win" situation, in which the welfare recipient feels she is not getting much, and the public feels it is paying out too much. But leaving this issue aside, the fact is that a welfare recipient would have to earn a substantial income to match what welfare gives.

The first problem, then, with the design of the impenetrable barrier is that the attraction on the welfare side began to build up in the northern and western states, threatening an influx from the work-supported side.

The second problem was that the social distinction between those who should work and those who shouldn't began to break down. Women with young children were once not expected to work. This was not true in the South, where black women were expected to work whether they were mothers or not, and whether they had preschool children or not, and their scanty welfare grants recognized that they would be supplementing their income through work. But in the North, a universalistic ethic and expectation prevailed, covering both black and white women: Mothers of young children should stay home to take care of them. We are all aware of the breakdown of this expectation. In 1972, 39.4 percent of children under 18 had mothers in the working force, and even 29.1 percent of children under six had mothers in the labor force.* More striking is what has happened to families headed by women: 51.0 percent of children under 18 in such families have mothers in the labor force, 38.9 percent of children under six. The distinction between black and white women has— fortunately—now broken down. Indeed, a higher proportion of white children in female-headed families now have mothers in the labor force than black children (for children under 18, white 55.2 percent, black 43.6 percent; for children under six, 41.1 percent to 35.6 percent)(*Children of Working Mothers*, March 1972, Special Labor Force Report 154, Department of Labor, Bureau of Labor Statistics, 1973).

The third problem that developed is that the number of welfare families without male earners began to grow rapidly in the northern and western states in a time of relatively full employment and job availability, and this led to great

---

*As we move into the 1980s, approximately 48 percent of all children below the age of 18 have mothers who are either employed or seeking employment. Of these children, approximately 6.5 million are below the age of 6. In families headed by women, approximately 59 percent of the children under 18 in such families have mothers in the workforce, 46 percent of children under 6. A higher proportion of white children in female-headed families have mothers in the labor force than black children—for children under 18, white approximately 63 percent, black 51 percent; for children under the age of 6, 50 percent white and 40 percent black.—Ed.

concern that the welfare system was leading to the breakup of families. We now know more about this matter than when it first became a serious issue in the later 1960s, but we still do not know—I believe—how to account for the great increase in the number of female-headed families among blacks, and the great increase generally in such families on welfare. We cannot ignore the likelihood of a dynamic interplay between welfare availability and attractiveness and family breakup. (Welfare did become more attractive as rights to welfare and of welfare receivers were strengthened by the public legal advocates of the late 1960s.) Undoubtedly the welfare system does in some respects lead to the breakup of families, if we take the term "breakup" literally. Mothers with children are able to find support from welfare if they find their husbands insupportable, and thus will leave them or eject them more freely. Young women living with their families who have given birth out of wedlock may now set up their own households. The actual abandonment of wives and children by nonworking or low-earning husbands to make their families eligible for welfare must be infrequent in the generous northern and western states, since it is usually not necessary: The presence of a husband, working or not, is not a bar to welfare in many of these states. On the other hand, Blanche Bernstein and others have been concerned with what they call "income maximization"—feigned family breakup, in order to gain access to the benefits of welfare without being required to report husbands' earnings. (A report by Blanche Bernstein and William Meezan, "The Impact of Welfare on Family Stability," March 1975, Center for New York City Affairs, New School for Social Research, throws light on this issue.) Family breakup affects the barrier between work and welfare in a significant way. The decision whether to work or spend full time raising her children is considered by welfare authorities to be the prerogative of the mother, and the pressure on welfare mothers to work is not great, despite the rising number of working mothers in the population as a whole. But what of the men who were the fathers of these children, who may leave or are thrown out *because* of welfare? Should not the monetary returns from *their* labor support their children?

Thus the distinction between those who could not work and those who could, which the social security design of the 1940s had assumed was neatly drawn, has become complex and obscure, confusing and confounding all efforts to reform the welfare system.

For if there is a close interrelationship between work and welfare, to improve the conditions of those on welfare—and in many states and in many respects one can make a very good case for improving their conditions—means to increase the incentives for crossing from the work side to the welfare side. The reform design involved in the Family Assistance Plan (FAP) and its descendants was intended to take into account the new reality that mothers could, did, and often wanted to work. But the extensive congressional hearings and studies occasioned by FAP and by welfare generally broadcast the news that there was no way of making work, for those mothers without advanced education and valuable skills, a real competitor to welfare. Our efforts to make work attractive to those on welfare were frustrated by the fact that—as we have seen from the Boston case—it is a rare job in the real world that gives anything like the benefits of welfare to most mothers on welfare. The key issue, as we learned again and again, was that to reduce income-tested benefits as returns from work rose meant in effect to tax returns from work so heavily as to make it economically unattractive. And we could no longer, by the late 1960s, count on traditional social or cultural pressures to make work more attractive than welfare. In the later 1960s, lawyers, poverty workers, intellectuals, and others undertook an enormous effort designed to give welfare as much dignity, as much worth and virtue, as work. Fortunately, the commitment of the ordinary person to work is so intense that even this enormous wave of propaganda has not yet converted most poor people, as we can see from studies of the poor which ask for their attitudes to work and welfare. But it has had some effect. And the logic of income-tested benefits declining as income from work rose did the rest: There was no way of reforming welfare by linking it to work. And indeed the effort has been abandoned.

As a result, we in the United States are unique among developed nations for the enormous number of mothers and children that we support on welfare, that is, on a system of grants based on need and not linked to work or work effort. This is an unpleasant situation to be in. What, then, can we do about it?

I would like to suggest a line of thought which creates far more difficulty than reforming welfare, but which offers far more promise: Let us leave welfare where it is, and try to make work—the kind of work that people on welfare, or the fathers of children on welfare, might take—more attractive.

It is well known that we have in this country a dual labor market, one in which there are good jobs and poor jobs, and the differences between them are striking. One kind of job will earn high wages, under union or civil service protection, with health insurance, supplementation to unemployment insurance, vacations with pay, pension benefits to supplement social security, and perhaps other fringe benefits. The second kind of job provides the minimum wage, with little security, with no paid vacations, with no health insurance, with no supplementation to unemployment insurance and social security, and with no fringe benefits. We may expand this well-known notion of a dual labor market to describe a triple system of support for people in this country. One kind is the regular, good job. A second is the poor job with no benefits. A third is welfare, which gives all the benefits of the good job: full health insurance, insurance against unexpected disasters, insurance against the costs of a growing family, and — while this may not in fact be an attraction for most people on welfare — leisure, far beyond that given by the vacation with pay. Good jobs can compete with welfare; poor jobs cannot. The task of reform should be not to make welfare better (in the generous states it is good enough); it should be to make the poor jobs more attractive.

Economists point out that there are great difficulties in the way of making poor jobs more attractive, because their returns are set by a market mechanism which in itself is efficient and which we do not want unduly to disturb. Obviously, to improve such jobs is a difficult enterprise. It is not, I believe, impossible.

Thus, one benefit that comes with welfare is free health care. We have recently been faced with the ironic problem of those who, in losing their jobs, have also lost their health insurance. The problem of instituting universal health insurance so that in this respect work becomes as attractive as welfare is no simple one. Enormous as the problem is, we cannot ignore the fact that it has been solved — at least in its large dimensions — in most other developed countries, and in this respect every worker in those countries, no matter how humble, is not at a disadvantage compared to those who live on welfare or its equivalent.

A second approach to making work competitive to welfare would be to introduce in compensation for work a component related to the number of children. We do not want to confuse the workings of the market by saddling employers with the need to compensate workers with more children better than workers with none or fewer children. But most other developed nations have dealt with this problem by attaching to compensation for work a children's supplement or allowance that comes from national insurance funds. These have different origins — the desire to increase population, to make life for large families better, to redistribute income — but they are now to be found in all the countries of the European community. The family allowance (for three children) as a percentage of average industrial earnings is 21 percent in Belgium, 20 percent in France, 14 percent in the Netherlands, 11 percent in Italy, 8 percent in Denmark, 5 percent in Germany and the United Kingdom (*The Economist*, 12 April 1975, p. 35). Some of these allowances are granted to working heads of families; some are given generally to all families. In this country we are unique in giving the benefits of children's allowances only to those who do *not* work — aside from the very modest assistance given by dependents' allowances on the income tax, which benefit those with good jobs more than those with poor jobs. Children's allowances raise fewer problems than health insurance. No great interests are involved that might oppose one scheme or another. The effect on increasing the birth rate — which would offend many — seems likely to be minimal.

We could relate children's allowances directly to wages—more than one earner in a family could divide the allowance for dependent children—or we could make them available to any head of family, whether he or she worked or not. I would much prefer relating them to wages, so that wages would reflect family needs in the same way that take-home pay is now affected by number of dependents through the withholding of income tax. The aim would be not only to provide assistance to those with larger families, but to give value and meaning to work, because it is through work that this assistance comes.

These are perhaps the two clearest means by which the second-rate job can be made closer in worth to the first-rate job. For other possibilities the answers are less clear. Can we provide unemployment insurance for every job, even casual labor? Could we provide a one-month vacation for all such jobs, so that some of the leisure that comes with welfare could be attached to work? Could the regularity of return offered by welfare be ensured for jobs that are casual and insecure? Just as we must look to Europe for examples of how different universal health insurance systems and children's allowance systems might work, we should look to Europe—and Japan—to find out why in these countries so much more work is much more regular.

Martin Feldstein has pointed out that "changes in aggregate demand have a substantially smaller impact on employment in Britain than they do in the United States . . . a one percent change in industrial production has about twice as big an effect on the unemployment rate in the United States as it does in Britain." He believes the reasons for this are not clear, and suggests they may include differences in "seniority arrangements and unemployment insurance provisions . . . differences in industrial structure, in the competitiveness of product markets, and in long-established national attitudes about the proper relation between employers and employees. . . ." As an economist, he points out that advantages in income maintenance and job security may be paid for with lower productivity. But on the other hand, there are general social costs that must be paid for our more volatile unemployment.

Similarly, he points out, seasonal unemployment is much higher in this country than in England, and one wonders why this should be, and what measures might be introduced to modify our wide seasonal sweeps in unemployment (Martin Feldstein, "The Economics of the New Unemployment," *The Public Interest,* Fall 1973, pp. 19-21).

This is not a complete program to make poor jobs more competitive with welfare. These suggestions—universal job-linked health insurance, job-linked children's allowances, making jobs more secure and steady—are only meant to begin discussion, and to turn around our way of thinking about these problems. We have concentrated too much on improving or reforming welfare or on simply redistributing income without relating it to work. These have not proved very attractive approaches. The American electorate did not take kindly to George McGovern's proposal of the "demogrant," payable to all, independent of any relationship to work. We have recently seen a sign of what I believe is a better approach—the rebate to all earners of low incomes of a proportion of their earnings, to be taken from income tax if they pay it, and from the Treasury if their income tax is not large enough. This is the kind of approach to income redistribution we should find attractive. It goes to the poor, it is related to work, there is no incentive in it of any kind to prefer welfare to work, and there is a positive incentive in it to find work more attractive, for you are getting more than your wages if they are very low. Leslie Lenkowsky also points out that, as against other income maintenance schemes which try to supplement low wages, there is no incentive here for worker and employer to agree to defraud the government through reporting lower wages, for the return goes directly from the government to the worker. Presumably our ingenious economists will find some drawbacks in this scheme, but Congress' move to rebate some part of earnings and taxes for low-income earners is a step in the right direction.

The improvement of low-paid work is an enterprise that is not utopian. We can see many of the mechanisms in operation in other capitalist or free enterprise countries. What is likely to be its effect on welfare? If one reason for welfare is the abandoning of families by men who cannot get steady jobs, or whose jobs simply do not provide enough for themselves and their family, an effort to improve poor jobs will have an effect. If another reason for welfare is the unattractiveness to many mothers of the jobs they could get, this approach will also have an effect. Even if its effect on welfare is modest, its effect on income redistribution may be substantial. And in any case, it has two great virtues over schemes designed to reform welfare and redistribute income: It requires no measure of compulsion to get people to work, and it adds to the attractiveness and, we might say, the dignity of work.

Perhaps the time has come when, instead of new studies of welfare reform, we should have a commission on low-income and low-benefit jobs, and consider how we may upgrade them.

Murray N. Rothbard

9. WELFARE AND THE WELFARE STATE

Why the Welfare Crisis?

Almost everyone, regardless of ideology, agrees that there is something terribly wrong with the accelerating, runaway welfare system in the United States, a system in which an ever-increasing proportion of the population lives as idle, compulsory claimants on the production of the rest of society. A few figures and comparisons will sketch in some of the dimensions of this galloping problem. In 1934, in the middle of the greatest depression in American history, at a nadir of our economic life, total government social welfare expenditures were $5.8 billion, of which direct welfare payments ("public aid") amounted to $2.5 billion. In 1976, after four decades of the greatest boom in American history, at a time when we had reached the status of having the highest standard of living in the history of the world with a relatively low level of unemployment, government social welfare expenditures totaled $331.4 billion, of which direct welfare amounted to $48.9 billion. In short, total social welfare spending rose by the enormous sum of 5614 percent in these four decades, and direct welfare aid increased by 1856 percent. Or, put another way, social welfare spending increased by an average of 133.7 percent per year during this 1934-76 period, while direct welfare aid increased by 44.2 percent per annum.

If we concentrate further on direct welfare, we find that spending stayed about the same from 1934 to 1950, and then took off into the stratosphere along with the post-World War II boom. In the years from 1950 to 1976, in fact, welfare aid increased by the huge sum of 84.4 percent per year. . . .

Most people think of being on welfare as a process external to the welfare clients themselves, as almost a natural disaster (like a tidal wave or volcanic eruption) that occurs beyond and despite the will of the people on welfare. The usual dictum is that "poverty" is the cause of individuals or families being on welfare. But on whatever criterion one wants to define poverty, on the basis of any chosen income level, it is undeniable that the number of people or families below that "poverty line" has been steadily *decreasing* since the 1930s, not vice versa. Thus, the extent of poverty can scarcely account for the spectacular growth in the welfare clientele.

The solution to the puzzle becomes clear once one realizes that the number of welfare recipients has what is called in economics a "positive supply function"; in other words, that when the *incentives* to go on welfare rise, the welfare rolls will lengthen, and that a similar result will occur if the *disincentives* to go on welfare become weaker. Oddly enough, nobody challenges this finding in any *other* area of the economy. Suppose, for example, that someone (whether the government or a dotty billionaire is not important here) offers an extra $10,000 to everyone who will work in a shoe factory. Clearly, the supply of eager workers in the shoe business will multiply. The same will happen when *dis*incentives are reduced (e.g., if the government promises to relieve every shoe worker from paying income taxes). If we begin to apply the same analysis to welfare clientele as to all other areas of economic life, the answer to the welfare puzzle becomes crystal-clear.

What, then, are the important incentives/disincentives for going on welfare, and how have they been changing? Clearly, an extremely important factor is the relation between the income to be gained on welfare, *as compared with* the income to be earned from productive work. Suppose, to put it simply, that the "average," or going wage (very roughly, the wage open to an "average" worker), in a certain area is $7,000 a year. Suppose, also, that the income to be obtained from welfare is $3,000 a year. This means that the average net gain to be made from working (before taxes) is $4,000 a year. Suppose now that the welfare payments go up to $5,000 (or, alternatively, that the average wage is reduced to $5,000). The differential—the *net* gain to be made from working—has now been cut in half, reduced from $4,000 to $2,000 a year. It stands to reason that the result will be an enormous increase in the welfare rolls (which will increase still more when we consider that the $7,000 workers will have to pay higher taxes in order to support a swollen and virtually nontaxpaying welfare clientele). We would then expect that if—as, of course, has been the case—welfare payment levels have been rising faster than average wages, an increasing number of people will flock to the welfare rolls. This effect will be still greater if we consider that, of course, not everyone earns the "average"; it will be the "marginal" workers, the ones earning below the average, who will flock to the welfare rolls. In our example, if the welfare payment rises to $5,000 a year, what can we expect to happen to the workers making $4,000? $5,000? or even $6,000? The $5,000-a-year man who previously earned a net of $2,000 higher than the welfare client now finds that his differential has been reduced to zero, that he is making no more—even *less* after taxes!—than the welfare client kept in idleness by the state. Is it any wonder that he will begin to flock to the welfare bonanza?

Specifically, during the period between 1952 and 1970, when the welfare rolls quintupled from 2 to 10 million, the average monthly benefit of a welfare family more than doubled, from $82 to $187, an increase of almost 130 percent at a time when consumer prices were rising by only 50 percent. Furthermore, in 1968, the Citizens Budget Commission of New York City compared the ten states in the union having the fastest rise in welfare rolls with the ten states enjoying the lowest rate of growth. The commission found that the average monthly welfare benefit in the ten fastest-growing states was twice as high as in the ten slowest states. (Monthly welfare payments per person averaged $177 in the former group of states, and only $88 in the latter.)[1]

Another example of the impact of high welfare payments and of their relation to wages available from working was cited by the McCone Commission investigating the Watts riot of 1965. The commission found that a job at the minimum wage paid about $220 a month, out of which had to come such work-related expenses as clothing and transportation. In contrast, the average welfare family in the area received from $177 to $238 a month, out of which no work-related expenses had to be deducted.[2]

Another powerful factor in swelling the welfare rolls is the increasing disappearance of the various sturdy disincentives for going on welfare. The leading disincentive has always been the stigma that every person on the welfare dole used to feel, the stigma of being parasitic and living off production instead of contributing to production. This stigma has been socially removed by the permeating values of modern liberalism; furthermore, the government agencies and social workers themselves have increasingly rolled out the red carpet to welcome and even urge people to get on welfare as quickly as possible. The "classical" view of the social worker was to help people to help themselves, to aid people in achieving and maintaining their independence and to stand on their own feet. For welfare clients, the aim of social workers used to be to help them get *off* the welfare rolls as quickly as possible. But now social workers have the opposite aim: to try to get as many people *on* welfare as possible, to advertise and proclaim their "rights." The result has been a continuing easing of eligibility requirements, a reduction in red tape, and the withering away of the enforcing of residency, work, or even income requirements for being on the dole. Anyone who suggests, however faintly, that welfare recipients should be required to accept employment and get off the dole is considered a reactionary moral leper. And with the old stigma increasingly removed, people now tend more and more to move rapidly toward welfare instead of shrinking from it. Irving Kristol has trenchantly written of the "welfare explosion" of the 1960s:

> This "explosion" was created—in part intentionally, in larger part unwittingly by public officials and public employees who were executing public policies as part of a "War on Poverty." And these policies had been advocated and enacted by many of the same people who were subsequently so bewildered by the "welfare explosion." Not surprisingly it took them a

while to realize that the problem they were trying to solve was the problem they were creating.

Here . . . are the reasons behind the "welfare explosion" of the 1960s:

(1) The number of poor people who are eligible for welfare will increase as one elevates the official definitions of "poverty" and "need." The War on Poverty elevated these official definitions; therefore, an increase in the number of "eligibles" automatically followed.

(2) The number of eligible poor who actually apply for welfare will increase as welfare benefits go up—as they did throughout the 1960s. When welfare payments (and associated benefits, such as Medicaid and food stamps) compete with low wages, many poor people will rationally prefer welfare. In New York City today, as in many other large cities, welfare benefits not only compete with low wages; they outstrip them.

(3) The reluctance of people actually eligible for welfare to apply for it—a reluctance based on pride or ignorance or fear—will diminish if any organized campaign is instituted to "sign them up." Such a campaign was successfully launched in the 1960s by (a) various community organizations sponsored and financed by the Office of Economic Opportunity; (b) the Welfare Rights Movement; and (c) the social work profession, which was now populated by college graduates who thought it their moral duty to help people get on welfare—instead of, as used to be the case, helping them get off welfare. In addition, the courts cooperated by striking down various legal obstacles (for example, residence requirements). . . .

Somehow, the fact that more poor people are on welfare, receiving more generous payments, does not seem to have made this country a nice place to live—not even for the poor on welfare, whose condition seems not noticeably better than when they were poor and off welfare. Something appears to have gone wrong; a liberal and compassionate social policy has bred all sorts of unanticipated and perverse consequences.[3]

The spirit that used to animate the social work profession was a far different—and a libertarian—one. There were two basic principles: (a) that all relief and welfare payments should be voluntary, by private agencies, rather than by the coercive levy of government; and (b) that the object of giving should be to help the recipient become independent and productive as soon as possible. Of course, in ultimate logic, (b) follows from (a), since no private agency is able to tap the virtually unlimited funds that can be mulcted from the long-suffering taxpayer. Since private aid funds are strictly limited, there is therefore no room for the idea of welfare "rights" as an unlimited and permanent claim on the production of others. As a further corollary of the limitation on funds, the social workers also realized that there was no room for aid to malingerers, those who refused to work, or who used the aid as a racket; hence came the concept of the "deserving" as against the "undeserving" poor. Thus, the nineteenth-century laissez-faire English agency, the Charity Organisation Society, included among the undeserving poor ineligible for aid those who did not need relief, impostors, and the man whose "condition is due to improvidence or thriftlessness, and there is no hope of being able to make him independent of charitable . . . assistance in the future."[4]

English laissez-faire liberalism, even though it generally accepted "Poor Law" governmental welfare, insisted that there be a strong disincentive effect: not only strict eligibility rules for assistance, but also making the workhouse conditions unpleasant enough to insure that workhouse relief would be a strong deterrent rather than an attractive opportunity. For the "undeserving poor," those responsible for their own fate, abuse of the relief system could only be curbed by "making it as distasteful as possible to the applicants; that is, by insisting (as a general rule) on a labour test or residence in a workhouse."[5]

While a strict deterrent is far better than an open welcome and a preachment about the recipients' "rights," the libertarian position calls for the complete abolition of governmental welfare and reliance on private charitable aid, based as it necessarily will be on helping the "deserving poor" on the road to independence as rapidly as possible. There was, after all, little or no governmental welfare in the United States until the Depression of the 1930s, and yet—in an era of a far lower general standard of living—there was no mass starvation in the streets. A highly successful private welfare program in the present-day is the one conducted by the three-million-member Mormon Church. This remarkable people, hounded by poverty and persecution, emigrated to Utah and nearby states in the nineteenth century, and by thrift and hard work raised themselves to a general level of prosperity and affluence. Very few Mormons are on welfare; Mormons are taught to be independent, self-reliant, and to shun the public dole. Mormons are devout believers and have therefore successfully internalized these admirable values. Furthermore, the Mormon Church operates an extensive private welfare plan for its members—based, again, on the principle of helping their members toward independence as rapidly as possible.

Note, for example, the following principles from the "Welfare Plan" of the Mormon Church. "Ever since its organization in 1830, the Church has encouraged its members to establish and maintain their economic independence; it has encouraged thrift and fostered the establishment of employment-creating industries; it has stood ready at all times to help needy faithful members." In 1936, the Mormon Church developed a "Church Welfare Plan, . . . a system under which the curse of idleness would be done away with, the evils of a dole abolished, and independence, industry, thrift and self-respect be once more established amongst our people. The aim of the Church is to help the people to help themselves. Work is to be enthroned as the ruling principle of the lives of our Church membership."[6] Mormon social workers in the program are instructed to act accordingly: "Faithful to this principle, welfare workers will earnestly teach and urge Church members to be self-sustaining to the full extent of their powers. No true Latter-Day Saint will, while physically able, voluntarily shift from himself the burden of his own support. So long as he can, under the inspiration of the Almighty and with his own labors, he will supply himself with the necessities of life."[7] The immediate objectives of the welfare program are to: "(1) Place in gainful employment those who are able to work. (2) Provide employment within the Welfare Program, in so far as possible, for those who cannot be placed in gainful employment. (3) Acquire the means with which to supply the needy, for whom the Church assumes responsibility, with the necessities of life."[8] Insofar as possible, this program is carried on in small, decentralized, grass-roots groups: "Families, neighbors, quorums and wards and other Church organizational units may find it wise and desirable to form small groups for extending mutual help one to the other. Such groups may plant and harvest crops, process foods, store food, clothing and fuel, and carry out other projects for their mutual benefit."[9]

Specifically, the Mormon bishops and priesthood quorums are enjoined to aid their brethren to self-help: "In his temporal administrations the bishop looks at every able-bodied needy person as a purely temporary problem, caring for him until he can help himself. The priesthood quorum must look at its needy member as a continuing problem until not alone his temporal needs are met but his spiritual ones also. As a concrete example— a bishop extends help while the artisan or craftsman is out of work and in want; a priesthood quorum assists in establishing him in work and tries to see that he becomes fully self-supporting and active in his priesthood duties." Concrete rehabilitation activities for needy members enjoined upon the priesthood quorums include: "(1) Placing quorum members and members of their families in permanent jobs. In some instances through trade school training, apprenticeships, and in other ways, quorums have assisted their quorum members to qualify themselves for better jobs. (2) Assisting quorum members and their families to get established in businesses of their own. . . ."[10]

The prime objective of the Mormon Church is to find jobs for their needy. To this end, "The finding of suitable jobs, under the Welfare Program, is a major responsibility of priesthood quorum members. They and members of the

Relief Society should be constantly on the alert for employment opportunities. If every member of the ward welfare committee does well his or her work in this respect, most of the unemployed will be placed in gainful employment at the group or ward level."[11] Other members are rehabilitated as self-employed, the church may aid with a small loan, and the member's priesthood quorum may guarantee repayment from its funds. Those Mormons who cannot be placed in jobs or rehabilitated as self-employed "are to be given, in so far as possible, work at productive labor on Church properties. . . ." The Church is insistent on work by the recipient as far as possible: "It is imperative that people being sustained through the bishops storehouse program work to the extent of their ability, thus earning what they receive. . . . Work of an individual on welfare projects should be considered as temporary rather than permanent employment. It should nevertheless continue so long as assistance is rendered to the individual through the bishops storehouse program. In this way the spiritual welfare of people will be served as their temporal needs are supplied. Feelings of diffidence will be removed. . . ."[12] Failing other work, the bishop may assign welfare recipients to aid individual members who are in need of help, the aided members reimbursing the Church at prevailing wage rates. In general, in return for their assistance, the welfare recipients are expected to make whatever contributions they can to the Church welfare program, either in funds, produce, or by their labor.[13]

Complementary to this comprehensive system of private aid on the principle of fostering independence, the Mormon Church sternly discourages its members from going on public welfare. "It is requested that local Church officers stress the importance of each individual, each family and each Church community becoming self-sustaining and independent of public relief." And: "To seek and accept direct public relief all too often invites the curse of idleness and fosters the other evils of dole. It destroys one's independence, industry, thrift and self-respect."[14]

There is no finer model than the Mormon Church for a private, voluntary, rational, individualistic welfare program. Let government welfare be abolished, and one would expect that numerous such programs for rational mutual aid would spring up throughout the country. . . .

What Can Government Do?

What, then, *can* the government do to help the poor? The only correct answer is also the libertarian answer: Get out of the way. Let the government get out of the way of the productive energies of all groups in the population, rich, middle class, and poor alike, and the result will be an enormous increase in the welfare and the standard of living of everyone, and most particularly of the poor who are the ones supposedly helped by the miscalled "welfare state."

There are four major ways in which the government can get out of the way of the American people. First, it can abolish—or at the very least drastically reduce—the level of all taxation, taxation which cripples productive energies, savings, investment, and technological advance. In fact, the creation of jobs and increase of wage rates resulting from abolishing these taxes would benefit the lower-income groups *more* than anyone else. As Professer Brozen points out: "With less attempt to use state power to compress the inequality in the distribution of income, inequality would diminish more rapidly. Low wage rates would rise more rapidly with a higher rate of saving and capital formation, and inequality would diminish with the rise in income of wage earners."[15] The best way to help the poor is to slash taxes and allow savings, investment, and creation of jobs to proceed unhampered. As Dr. F. A. Harper pointed out years ago, productive investment is the "greatest economic charity." Wrote Harper:

> According to one view, sharing a crust of bread is advocated as the method of charity. The other advocates savings and tools for the production of additional loaves of bread, which is the greatest economic charity.
> The two views are in conflict because the two methods are mutually exclusive in absorbing one's time and means in all the choices he makes day by day. . . .
> The reason for the difference in view really stems from different concepts about the nature of the economic world. The former view stems from the belief that the total of economic goods is a constant. The latter view is built on the belief that expansion in production is possible without any necessary limit.
> The difference between the two views is like the difference between a two- and three-dimensional perspective of production. The two-dimensional size is fixed at any instant of time, but the third dimension and therefore the size of the total is expandable without limit by savings and tools.
> All the history of mankind denies that there is a fixed total of economic goods. History further reveals that savings and expansion of tools constitute the only way to any appreciable increase.[16]

The libertarian writer Isabel Paterson put the case eloquently:

> As between the private philanthropist and the private capitalist acting as such, take the case of the truly needy man, who is not incapacitated, and suppose that the philanthropist gives him food and clothes and shelter—when he has used them, he is just where he was before, except that he may have acquired the habit of dependence. But suppose someone with no benevolent motive whatever, simply wanting work done for his own reasons, should hire the needy man for a wage. The employer has not done a good deed. Yet the condition of the employed man has actually changed. What is the vital difference between the two actions?

It is that the unphilanthropic employer has brought the man he employed *back into the production line,* on the great circuit of energy; whereas the philanthropist can only divert energy in such manner that there can be no return into production, and therefore less likelihood of the object of his benefaction finding employment. . . .

If the full role of *sincere* philanthropists were called, from the beginning of time, it would be found that all of them together by their strictly philanthropic activities have never conferred upon humanity one-tenth of the benefit derived from the normally self-interested efforts of Thomas Alva Edison, to say nothing of the greater minds who worked out the scientific principles which Edison applied. Innumerable speculative thinkers, inventors, and organizers, have contributed to the comfort, health, and happiness of their fellow men — because that was not their objective.[17]

Second, and as a corollary to a drastic reduction or abolition of taxation, would come an equivalent reduction in government expenditures. No longer would scarce economic resources be siphoned off into wasteful and unproductive expenditures: into the multibillion dollar space program, public works, the military-industrial complex, or whatever. Instead, these resources would be available to produce goods and services desired by the mass of the consuming population. The outpouring of goods and services would provide new and better goods to the consumers at far lower prices. No longer would we suffer the inefficiencies and the injury to productivity of government subsidies and contracts. Furthermore, the diversion of most of the nation's scientists and engineers to wasteful military and other governmental research and expenditure would be released for peaceful and productive activities and inventions benefitting the nation's consumers.[18]

Third, if the government also cut out the numerous ways in which it taxes the poorer to subsidize the wealthier, such as we have named above (higher education, farm subsidies, irrigation, Lockheed, etc.), this in itself would stop the government's deliberate exactions upon the poor. By ceasing to tax the poorer in order to subsidize the richer, the government would aid the poor by removing its burdens from their productive activity.

Finally, one of the most significant ways in which the government could aid the poor is by removing its own direct roadblocks from their productive energies. Thus, minimum wage laws disemploy the poorest and least productive members of the population. Government privileges to trade unions enable them to keep the poorer and minority-group workers from productive and high-wage employment. And licensing laws, the outlawing of gambling, and other government restrictions prevent the poor from starting small businesses and creating jobs on their own. Thus, the government has everywhere clamped onerous restrictions on peddling, ranging from outright prohibition to heavy license fees. Peddling was the classic path by which immigrants, poor and lacking capital, were able to become entrepreneurs and eventually to become big businessmen. But now this route has been cut off—largely to confer monopoly privileges on each city's retail stores, who fear that they would lose profits if faced with the highly mobile competition of street peddlers.

Typical of how government has frustrated the productive activities of the poor is the case of the neurosurgeon Dr. Thomas Matthew, founder of the black self-help organization NEGRO, which floats bonds to finance its operations. In the mid-1960s, Dr. Matthew, over the opposition of the New York City government, established a successful interracial hospital in the black section of Jamaica, Queens. He soon found, however, that public transportation in Jamaica was so abysmal that transportation service was totally inadequate for the hospital's patients and staff. Finding bus service inadequate, Dr. Matthew purchased a few buses and established a regular bus service in Jamaica, service that was regular, efficient, and successful. The problem was that Dr. Matthew did not have a city license to operate a bus line—that privilege is reserved to inefficient but protected monopolies. The ingenious Dr. Matthew, discovering that the city did not allow any unlicensed buses to charge fares, made his bus service free, except that any riders who wished could buy a 25-cent company bond instead whenever they rode the buses.

So successful was the Matthew bus service that he proceeded to establish another bus line in Harlem; but it was at this point, in early 1968, that the New York City government took fright and cracked down. The government went to court and put both lines out of business for operating without licenses.

A few years later, Dr. Matthew and his colleagues seized an unused building in Harlem owned by the city government. (The New York City government is the city's biggest "slumlord," owning as it does a vast amount of useful buildings abandoned because of nonpayment of high property taxes and rotting away, rendered useless and uninhabitable.) In this building, Dr. Matthew established a low-cost hospital—at a time of soaring hospital costs and scarcity of hospital space. The city finally succeeded in putting this hospital, too, out of business, claiming "fire violations." Again and again, in area after area, the role of government has been to thwart the economic activities of the poor. It is no wonder that when Dr. Matthew was asked by a white official of the New York City government how it could best aid Negro self-help projects, Matthew replied: "Get out of our way, and let us try something."

Another example of how government functions occurred a few years ago, when the federal and New York City governments loudly proclaimed that they would rehabilitate a group of thirty-seven buildings in Harlem. But instead of following the usual practice of private industry and awarding rehabilitation contracts on each house individually, the government instead awarded one contract on the entire thirty-seven building package. By doing so, the government made sure that small black-owned construction firms would not be able to bid, and so the prize contract naturally went to a large white-owned company. Still another example: In 1966, the federal Small Business Administration proudly proclaimed a program for encouraging new black-owned small business. But the government put certain key restrictions on its loans. First, it decided that any borrower must be "at the poverty level." Now since the very poor are not apt to be setting up their own businesses, this restriction ruled out many small businesses, by owners with moderately small incomes—just the ones likely to be small entrepreneurs. To top this, the New York SBA added a further restriction: All blacks seeking such loans must "prove a real need in their community" for filling a recognizable "economic void"—the need and the void to be proved to the satisfaction of remote bureaucrats far from the actual economic scene.[19]

A fascinating gauge of whether or to what extent government is helping or hurting the poor in the "welfare state" is provided by an unpublished study by the Institute for Policy Studies of Washington, D.C. An inquiry was made on the estimated flow of government money (federal and district) *into* the low-income Negro ghetto of Shaw-Cardozo in Washington, D.C., as compared to the *outflow* that the area pays in taxes to the government. In fiscal 1967, the Shaw-Cardozo area had a population of 84,000 (of whom 79,000 were black) with a median family income of $5,600 per year. Total earned personal income for the residents of the area for that year amounted to $126.5 million. The value of total government benefits flowing into the district (ranging from welfare payments to the estimated expenditure on public schools) during fical 1967 was estimated at $45.7 million. A generous subsidy, amounting to almost 40 percent of total Shaw-Cardozo income? Perhaps, but against this we have to offset the total outflow of taxes from Shaw-Cardozo, best estimated at $50.0 million—a net *outflow* from this low-income ghetto of $4.3 million! Can it still be maintained that abolition of the entire massive, unproductive welfare state structure would hurt the poor.[20]

Government could then best help the poor—and the rest of society—by getting out of the way: by removing its vast and crippling network of taxes, subsidies, inefficiencies, and monopoly privileges. As Professor Brozen summed up his analysis of the "welfare state":

> The state has typically been a device for producing affluence for a few at the expense of many. The market has produced affluence for many with little cost even to a few. The state has not changed its ways since Roman days of bread and circuses for the masses, even though it now pretends to provide education and medicine as well as free milk and performing arts. It still is the source of monopoly privilege and power for the few behind its facade

of providing welfare for the many—welfare which would be more abundant if politicians would not expropriate the means they use to provide the illusion that they care about their constituents.[21]

The Negative Income Tax

Unfortunately, the recent trend—embraced by a wide spectrum of advocates (with unimportant modifications) from President Nixon to Milton Friedman on the right to a large number on the left—is to abolish the current welfare system *not* in the direction of freedom but toward its very opposite. This new trend is the "guaranteed annual income" or "negative income tax," or President Nixon's "Family Assistance Plan." Citing the inefficiencies, inequities, and red tape of the present system, the guaranteed annual income would make the dole easy, "efficient," and automatic: The income tax authorities will pay money each year to families earning below a certain base income—this automatic dole to be financed, of course, by taxing working families making *more* than the base amount. Estimated costs of this seemingly neat and simple scheme are supposed to be only a few billion dollars per year.

But there is an extremely important catch: the costs are estimated *on the assumption* that everyone—the people on the universal dole as well as those financing it—will continue to work to the same extent as before. But this assumption begs the question. For the chief problem is the enormously crippling disincentive effect the guaranteed annual income will have on taxpayer and recipient alike.

The one element that saves the present welfare system from being an utter disaster is precisely the red tape and the stigma involved in going on welfare. The welfare recipient still bears a psychic stigma, even though weakened in recent years, and he still has to face a typically inefficient, impersonal, and tangled bureaucracy. But the guaranteed annual income, *precisely* by making the dole efficient, easy, and automatic, will remove the major obstacles, the major disincentives, to the "supply function" for welfare, and will lead to a massive flocking to the guaranteed dole. Moreover, everyone will now consider the new dole as an automatic "right" rather than as a privilege or gift, and all stigma will be removed.

Suppose, for example, that $4,000 per year is declared the "poverty line," and that everyone earning income below that line receives the difference from Uncle Sam automatically as a result of filling out his income tax return. Those making zero income will receive $4,000 from the government, those making $3,000 will get $1,000, and so on. It seems clear that there will be no real reason for *anyone* making less than $4,000 a year to keep on working. Why should he, when his nonworking neighbor will wind up with the same income as himself? In short, the net income from working will then be zero, and the entire working population below the magic $4,000 line will quit work and flock to its "rightful" dole.

But this is not all; what of the people making either $4,000, or slightly or even moderately above that line? The man making $4,500 a year will soon find that the lazy slob next door who refuses to work will be getting his $4,000 a year from the federal government; his own *net* income from forty hours a week of hard work will be only $500 a year. So he will quit work and go on the negative-tax dole. The same will undoubtedly hold true for those making $5,000 a year, etc.

The baleful process is not over. As all the people making below $4,000 and even considerably above $4,000 leave work and go on the dole, the total dole payments will skyrocket enormously, and they can only be financed by taxing *more* heavily the higher income folk who will continue to work. But then *their* net, after-tax incomes will fall sharply, until many of *them* will quit work and go on the dole too. Let us contemplate the man making $6,000 a year. He is, at the outset, faced with a net income from working of only $2,000, and if he has to pay, let us say, $500 a year to finance the dole of the nonworkers, his net after-tax income will be only $1,500 a year. If he then has to pay *another* $1,000 to finance the rapid expansion of others on the dole, his net income will fall to $500 and he will go on the dole. Thus, the logical conclusion of the guaranteed annual income will be a vicious spiral into disaster, heading toward the logical and impossible goal of virtually no one working, and everyone on the dole.

In addition to all this, there are some important extra considerations. In practice, of course, the dole, once set at $4,000, will not remain there; irresistible pressure by welfare clients and other pressure goups will inexorably raise the base level every year, thereby bringing the vicious spiral and economic disaster that much closer. In practice, too, the guaranteed annual income will *not,* as in the hopes of its conservative advocates, *replace* the existing patchwork welfare system; it will simply be added *on top of* the existing programs. This, for example, is precisely what happened to the states' old-age relief programs. The major talking point of the New Deal's federal Social Security program was that it would efficiently *replace* the then existing patchwork old-age relief programs of the states. In practice, of course, it did no such thing, and old-age relief is far higher now than it was in the 1930s. An ever-rising Social Security structure was simply placed on top of existing programs. In practice, finally, President Nixon's sop to conservatives that able-bodied recipients of the new dole would be forced to work is a patent phony. They would, for one thing, only have to find "suitable" work, and it is the universal experience of state unemployment relief agencies that almost no "suitable" jobs are ever found.[22]

The various schemes for a guaranteed annual income are no genuine replacement for the universally acknowledged evils of the welfare system; they would only plunge us still more deeply into those evils. The only workable solution is the libertarian one: the abolition of the welfare dole in favor of freedom and voluntary action for all persons, rich and poor alike.

NOTES

1. See Roger A. Freeman, "The Wayward Welfare State," *Modern Age*, Fall 1971, pp. 401-2. In a detailed state-by-state study, Professors Brehm and Saving estimated that over 60 percent of the number of welfare clients in each state in 1951 could be accounted for by the level of welfare payments in that state; by the end of the '50s, the percentage had increased to over 80 percent. C. T. Brehm and T. R. Saving, "The Demand for General Assistance Payments," *American Economic Review*, December 1964, pp. 1002-18.
2. Governor's Commission on the Los Angeles Riots, *Violence in the City—An End or a Beginning?* 2 December 1965, p. 72; quoted in Edward C. Banfield, *The Unheavenly City* (Boston: Little, Brown, 1970), p. 288.
3. Irving Kristol, "Welfare: The best of intentions, the worst of results," *Atlantic Monthly*, August 1971, p. 47.
4. Charity Organisation Society, *15th Annual Report*, 1883, p. 54; quoted in Charles L. Mowat, *The Charity Organisation Society, 1869-1913* (London: Methuen, 1961), p. 35.
5. Charity Organisation Society, *2nd Annual Report, 1870*, p. 5; quoted in ibid., p. 36.
6. *Welfare Plan of the Church of Jesus Christ of Latter-Day Saints* (The General Church Welfare Committee, 1960), p. 1.
7. Ibid., p. 4.
8. Ibid.
9. Ibid., p. 5.
10. Ibid., p. 19.
11. Ibid., p. 22.
12. Ibid., p. 25.
13. Ibid., pp. 25, 46.
14. Ibid., pp. 46, 48.
15. Yale Brozen, "Welfare Without the Welfare State," *The Freeman*, December 1966, p. 47.
16. F.A. Harper, "The Greatest Economic Charity," in *On Freedom and Free Enterprise*, ed. M. Sennholz (Princeton, N.J.: Van Nostrand, 1956), p. 106.
17. Isabel Paterson, *The God of the Machine* (New York: Putnam's, 1943), pp. 248-50.
18. On the massive diversion of scientists and engineers to government in recent years, see H. L. Nieburg, *In the Name of Science* (Chicago: Quadrangle,

1966); on the inefficiencies and misallocations of the military-industrial complex, see Seymour Melman, ed., *The War Economy of the United States* (New York: St. Martin's, 1971).

19. On the Matthew and Small Business Administration cases, see Jane Jacobs, *The Economy of Cities* (New York: Random House, 1969), pp. 225-28.

20. Data adapted from an unpublished study by Earl F. Mellor, "Public Goods and Services: Costs and Benefits, A Study of the Shaw-Cardozo Area of Washington, D.C.," (presented to the Institute for Policy Studies, Washington, D.C., 31 October 1969).

21. Brozen, "Welfare Without the Welfare State," p. 52.

22. For a brilliant theoretical critique of the guaranteed annual income, negative income tax, and Nixon schemes, see Henry Hazlitt, *Man vs. Welfare State,* (New Rochelle, N.Y.: Arlington House, 1969), pp. 62-100. For a definitive and up-to-date empirical critique of all guaranteed annual income plans and experiments, including President Carter's welfare reform scheme, see Martin Anderson, *Welfare: the Political Economy of Welfare Reform in the United States* (Stanford, Calif.: Hoover Institution, 1978).

PART THREE

In Search of
A National Health Policy

In recent years, many policy makers have become increasingly concerned about the quality of health care provided in America. They argue that all Americans, regardless of their socioeconomic status, deserve a life free from debilitating diseases, catastrophic illness, and an environment hazardous to our health. Many groups observe that thousands of Americans are deprived of this advantage annually because of their inability to obtain quality health care.

The rapid increase in the cost of medical services in the last decade has resulted in many governmental efforts to extend health care benefits to an ever increasing percentage of the public. Recently, Congress has considered a number of policy proposals ranging from extending Medicare and Medicaid coverage to legislation that would limit the cost of hospital care and to various national health insurance programs.

The policy debate on health care involves more than just the cost of medical services. It raises policy questions about the nature and quality of health care and the manner in which medical services should be delivered to the American public. In chapter 10, Theodore Marmor briefly reviews the problems of American medicine. He then assesses the various national health insurance proposals and prescribes a two-pronged health policy: national health insurance for preschool children "kiddie care" and a universal tax-credit catastrophic insurance plan.

Lawrence Mead, in "Health Policy: The Need for Governance," maintains that a national health policy is one way of controlling the health sector and ensuring the delivery of health services to the American public. He reviews the alternatives, including professional health organizations, a free-market resolution, and public policy controls. Although Mead advocates public policy controls on the health sector, he observes that a national health policy may not be the solution because "any attempt to administer an entire national health system would create insufferable planning and coordination problems." Mead concludes his analysis with the reflection that the political process, as it operates in America today, is well suited for expressing and ranking health policy preferences; yet "any realistic approach to public control must accept wrestling with governance and eschew unpolitical solutions."

John Ehrenreich undertakes a radical critique of America's health system, arguing that the United States is a "sick society." Ehrenreich observes that analyses of health policy wrongly focus on the inequitable distribution of health services, and argues that we must recognize that the "doctor-patient relationship and the entire structure of medical services reproduce the exploitative relations of the larger society."

Theodore R. Marmor

10. The Politics of National Health Insurance: Analysis and Prescription

Most Americans, the polls tell us, are alarmed by a "medical care crisis." Yet most are also satisfied with their own medical treatment. This paradox suggests that the admittedly serious problems of American medicine—its cost, availability, and quality—are compounded by rhetorical exaggeration and by our unrealistic expectations for the national health insurance (NHI) proposals before us. Any sensible NHI plan must balance conflicting purposes. It has to be fiscally possible, administratively manageable, politically feasible, and likely to improve the health of Americans without accelerating the rate of medical inflation (14 percent in 1975).[1] Many NHI proponents suggest that problems of cost, access, and quality can be simultaneously relieved; few realistically show how this can be done.

This chapter[2] represents an effort to chart a course between the rhetoric of crisis and smug complacency. The first section outlines the substance of the current problem and of the prominent competing NHI plans. The second section proposes a staged, rational health insurance plan—national child health insurance and a tax credit plan for catastrophic medical expenses—that is within our fiscal, political, and administrative capacity.

The Problem and the Proposals

Crisis?

Americans are assaulted by cries of alarm from their leaders and the media. Medicine's rising costs, maldistributed services, inefficient organization, and poor quality of care have been cited by people as disparate as Richard Nixon and Edward Kennedy. Even the sober editors of *Fortune* have placed American medicine "on the brink of chaos."[3]

But what the opinion surveys of the early 1970s suggested was that a large majority of Americans agreed there was a medical crisis but did not regard it as their own. Three quarters to four fifths of the population, depending on the survey and the questions asked, were satisfied with their doctors and medical care yet had misgivings about the "system" that produced it all. Fewer than 10 percent were dissatisfied with their health care, although nearly 40 percent worried about medical care's high cost and perceived inaccessibility. The intensity of this concern about American medicine has, it appears, increased since the early 1970s.[4]

Perhaps people are merely echoing the doomsday cries of the vocal elite. The specific complaints of Americans probably depend in part on class position. The rich do not like waiting, and they pay to avoid it. The poor do not like high costs, and they wait. The middle class dislike both the waiting and the cost. All would like easier access to a personal physician in time of need. But few would advocate wholesale organizational change to satisfy their specific complaints.[5]

Why do our politicians magnify these admittedly serious medical concerns into a picture of impending collapse? Do post-New Deal reformers assume that only warnings of disaster can spur public action? In the effort to awaken interest in certain problems, have they misled us into regarding American medicine as worsening on all fronts? The typical exaggeration in movements for political reform is surely partly to blame: the "issue attention" cycle starts with doomsaying.[6] Whatever the origins, the rhetoric of crisis hinders realistic appraisal.

The Problems of American Medicine

Concern about the cost, access, and quality of medical care is certainly warranted. Cost heads the list: The more than $118 billion that Americans spent on medical care in 1975 — averaging $558 per person, compared with $485 in 1974 — amounts to 8.3 percent of the gross national product, up from 4.6 percent two decades ago.[7]

But to talk about total national expenditures is to use the language of statisticians. What *citizens* worry about are their out-of-pocket costs. And they worry about insurance benefits expiring just when they are essential — to meet the rare financial catastrophe.[8] Governments likewise worry more about *their* costs than about total health expenditures. The public sector has become the largest payer for health care. In 1965, the federal budget for Medicare and Medicaid was $5.9 billion; in 1975 it was $25 billion.[9] So there are three cost problems, not one: cost to the society, to individuals, and to government programs. Even though government costs have sky-rocketed, the needs of clientele have increased as economic conditions have worsened: the real per capita value of Medicaid benefits — taking inflation into account — has recently declined despite the annual dollar increases in program expenditures.

American medical care is also attacked as disorganized, badly distributed, fragmented, and losing patients "between the units." There are serious shortages of doctors in the rural areas and inner cities, and complaints abound about the scarcity of the traditional family doctor.[10]

The quality of medical care comes to public attention through malpractice suits and accounts of the high cost of malpractice insurance. But errors of medical competence may be rarer and may do less social harm than *questionable* and *inefficient* practices. Questionable practice risks injury to patients for insufficient medical benefits (e.g., by overprescribing drugs or performing unnecessary surgery). Inefficient practice opts for the needlessly expensive or diverts medical resources from cost-effective uses (such as immunizations and prenatal checkups) to very expensive care.

From criticism of the questionable and inefficient, it is a short step to skepticism about all sophisticated medical care. Thus, some people are talking about iatrogenic (physician-caused) disorders. And many are calling for environmental reform, antismoking campaigns, and highway safety programs, arguing that these and not national health insurance are the appropriate focus. Indeed, for some NHI is a "giant step sideways."[11] Some observers worry that we will put scarce public resources into traditional and costly medical care at the very time that other ways to improve our health are available.[12]

Many of these criticisms have merit. All lend plausibility to the fear of breakdown. However, the foregoing litany of problems implies more agreement among critics than exists. The proposals for national health insurance reveal conflicting standards for assessing American medicine and genuine disputes about how to deal with the competing demands for greater access, improved quality, and less rapid increases in cost. In fact, cost is the only agreed-upon issue of alarm. The various other "problems" are just that, defects that any sensible analyst would recognize but that are not uniformly worsening so as to justify a fear of disaster. This is particularly true about access, where the gap between rich and poor adults has been substantially reduced in the past decade (see table 10.1), but where worn-out calls about crisis will give hope of rapid progress that the prolonged political struggle over NHI will surely frustrate.

Competing Proposals for NHI

All sides agree on at least one thing: the need for a larger governmental role in financing medical care. Some groups—most notably the American Medical Association—have concentrated on financial accessibility to care. The AMA Medicredit proposal was designed as a federal subsidy of health insurance premiums in hope of stimulating broader insurance coverage for the population. It would have replaced the present tax deduction for medical care expenditures with a tax *credit* to offset in whole or in part the premiums of (qualified) insurance policies. The amount of the credit would have varied by income tax bracket: the higher the taxable income, the lower the tax credit.

TABLE 10.1. PHYSICIAN VISITS PER CAPITA BY AGE AND FAMILY INCOME GROUP,
FISCAL YEARS 1964, 1967, AND CALENDAR YEAR 1969

Age and Income Group*	1964	1967	1969
All ages	4.5	4.3	4.3
Low income	4.3	4.3	4.6
Middle income	4.5	4.2	4.0
High income	5.1	4.6	4.3
Ratio, high income to low income	1.19	1.07	.93
Under 15 years			
Low income	2.7	2.8	2.8
Middle income	2.8	3.9	3.6
High income	4.5	4.4	4.3
Ratio, high income to low income	1.67	1.57	1.54
15 to 64 years			
Low income	4.4	4.6	4.8
Middle income	4.7	4.1	4.1
High income	4.9	4.6	4.2
Ratio, high income to low income	1.11	1.00	.88
65 years and older			
Low income	6.3	5.8	6.1
Middle income	7.0	6.7	5.8
High income	7.3	6.5	7.5
Ratio, high income to low income	1.16	1.12	1.23

*Low income: under $4,000 in 1964; under $5,000 in 1967 and 1969. Middle income:
$4,000 to $6,999 in 1964; $5,000 to $9,999 in 1967 and 1969. High income: $7,000
and above in 1964; $10,000 and above in 1967 and 1969.

SOURCE: Spyros Andreopoulos, ed., *Primary Care: Where Medicine Fails* (New
York: Wiley, 1974), p. 163.

Compared with Medicredit, the major proposals presently before the Congress all call for more government intervention. The most ambitious, the Kennedy-Corman bill, proposes a government monopoly of the health insurance business. To insure that "money would no longer be a consideration for a patient seeking any health service," it would establish a program with universal eligibility and unusually broad coverage of service, financed jointly by payroll taxes and general revenues. There would be no cost sharing by patients: medical care would be "free" at the point of service, with the federal government paying providers directly. Cost escalation would be addressed by limiting the total budget for medical care; distribution, by creating incentives for the establishment of comprehensive health service organizations and for the location of health personnel in underserved areas; and quality, by policing the standard of care.[13]

Politically fashionable are plans that would provide protection only against financially catastrophic expenses, leaving other problems to different governmental programs and to private health insurance. The catastrophic portion of the Long-Ribicoff bill covers hospitalization beyond 60 days and annual medical expenditures of more than $2,000.[14] Martin Feldstein's major risk insurance proposal (MRI) would protect against financial disaster while requiring the patient to pay directly for most medical expenses, thereby, it is hoped, reducing the rate of medical inflation. MRI is a comprehensive universal health insurance policy with a very high deductible—it would pay all medical bills that exceed 10 percent of annual income.[15] Quite similar, though administered by the IRS as a tax credit scheme for large medical expenses, is the bill sponsored by Senator William Brock of Tennessee.[16]

Catastrophic insurance is effective and cheap—typical predictions place the federal cost at less than $5 billion—because its objective is limited: it focuses on financial catastrophe, not on reorganization of the health sector. Long-Ribicoff, for example, leaves almost intact the present subcatastrophic system. Feldstein's MRI appears to do so, but with a major qualification. In removing current tax incentives for insurance, and in using a deductible high in relation to average yearly medical expenditures but short of catastrophic, MRI attempts to shift the burden of medical-financial decisions from physician to more cost-conscious patient, combating medical inflation with consumer restraint. But these policies, if fully implemented, would reintroduce the financial barriers to care that many NHI advocates see as the access problem in the first place.

Finally, there are mixed strategies that call for increased government regulation and partial federal subsidy of the present system. The leading hybrid is the Ford administration's Comprehensive Health Insurance Plan (CHIP), a potpourri of efforts to expand insurance (through mandated coverage by employers), to rationalize Medicaid (through larger contributions by patients as the incomes of welfare families rise), and to control costs (through state regulation and the encouragement of prepaid group practice).

The mandated employer plans provide a way of insuring vast numbers of families with minimum impact on the federal budget. Employers under CHIP would be required to offer policies with broad benefits and to pay three quarters of the premium, with the employee paying one quarter of the premium and responsible for substantial sharing of costs at the time of use. More modest payment scales would obtain for families in lower income categories. Whatever the specific features, such plans distribute current health expenditures among patients, employers, and the government; they do not lower health costs unless they result in less care. They *appear* to reduce costs, because the federal price tag is so much lower than under other proposals (e.g., Kennedy-Corman). But saying that CHIP costs $45 billion and Kennedy-Corman $100 billion is misleading. It would be accurate if, and only if, unions dropped their present benefits and accepted the cost sharing of CHIP. More likely under CHIP would be employer supplementation of the federally mandated plan, in which case total health expenditures would not be radically different from those under Kennedy-Corman.

Very similar to CHIP in benefit structure and out-of-pocket payments is the Kennedy-Mills proposal, which, though half a Kennedy-Corman loaf, represented a more politically acceptable alternative in the fiscally constrained bargaining environment of 1974. It is in financing that Kennedy-Mills differs most sharply from CHIP. It would be run by the Social Security Administration, as Medicare is, using the insurance industry as fiscal intermediary. It would be financed by a 4 percent payroll tax (up to $20,000), with the employer nominally paying 3 percent and the employee not more than 1 percent. In addition, there would be a 2.5 percent tax on self-employment and unearned income up to $20,000, a 1 percent tax on family welfare payments, and miscellaneous state and federal contributions.[17] The estimated *federal* cost of Kennedy-Mills ($77 billion) vastly exceeds that of CHIP ($43 billion), but both are lower than Kennedy-Corman's $103 billion (1974 estimates by the secretary of HEW).

What is striking is how the political debate over these alternatives—so relatively close in substance—distorts their differences. The influence of ideology on the shape of the various bills makes comparison of proposals difficult. No one bill, no matter what its proponents claim, can possibly solve all the shortcomings of the health industry. Solutions to one problem conflict with solutions to another. As the AMA puts it, improving "any system of medical care depends basically on balancing three strong and competing dynamics: the desire to make medical care available to all, the desire to control cost, and the desire for high quality care."[18] Any two of these goals works against the third.

The important question, then, is how each of the various plans would affect the cost, quality, organization, and distribution of medical care. One has to judge proposals not by their legal form but by their probable results, as revealed by experience in other countries. Would any current plan reduce the more than $10 billion annual increase in the national health care bill? Probably not. In Canada and Sweden, large-scale government financing has not reversed the upward spiral, especially since financing is dispersed among different units of government.[19] There is evidence that, where financing is concentrated at one governmental level and service providers are directly budgeted (rather than reimbursed by insurance), expenditures and the rate of medical inflation are lower. With its National Health Service, England in the last fifteen years—compared with Canada, Sweden, and the United States—has spent a third less of its resources on medical care and has experienced roughly a third the rate of inflation.[20] To the 16 percent of Americans who favor putting doctors on salary in an English-style system, this will be a welcome argument.[21] But even to others, Britain's financing concentration seems desirable to emulate. Thus, the "conservative" emphasis on controlling inflation may best be accomplished by a greater degree of governmental centralization than even many "liberals" favor.

Of the leading U.S. plans, Kennedy-Corman — with its concentrated federal financing[22] — affords the best theoretical prospects for curbing inflation. To be effective, however, it must be fully implemented, which is at present unlikely. The Feldstein plan is runner-up, placing financial responsibility on patients in order to restrain inflation. But to work, such a plan must bar supplementary insurance — a daunting political task.[23] Hence, the most promising antiinflation proposals are politically the least likely to pass.

The more likely to win out is CHIP or some other mixed plan that would offer more business and further subsidies to health care insurers and providers without imposing strict central budgetary control. Such a fiscally decentralized plan would be inflationary yet still leave major gaps in coverage: the worst of both worlds.

NHI will probably be more successful in improving access than in containing costs. But financial barriers are only part of the access problem. Equally serious, as noted earlier, is unavailability of care in major areas and specialties.[24] No attempted remedy has worked well — neither educational loan forgiveness for service in underdoctored areas, nor substitution of rural or ghetto medical service for physicians' military obligations, nor subsidies for medical centers in underserved locales. Other Western democracies have learned that poor distribution persists after the medical purchasing powers of poor city neighborhoods and remote rural areas are improved.[25] Only draconian assignment to regions and specialties would work, for young doctors have good professional and social reasons for establishing specialty practices in affluent suburban neighborhoods.

Whether fiscally centralized or decentralized, NHI probably will do little to improve the quality of care. It may provide incentives for preventive care;[26] but it cannot check malpractice or doubtful practice much better than present institutions do, and it may actually stimulate the demand for costly and inefficient procedures. The quality of medical care depends much more on professional self-regulation and consumer awareness than on any conceivable health insurance plan's regulations. Adequate financing alone cannot ensure good care.

This sober assessment of NHI's capacities is no excuse for inaction. The major task of insurance is to calm fears of financial disaster. Quality, prevention, and reorganization are peripheral issues. The argument that more medical care of the traditional sort will not markedly improve our health is beside the point when one is concerned with the fair distribution of expenses. Some have argued that NHI without incentives for prevention of illness and improvement of health is not worth having. But would anyone seriously argue that automobile insurance is not worth having if it doesn't prevent accidents and improve the quality of automobiles?

Recognizing the conflicting objectives of the various proposals is the beginning of prudent choice. Should we spend a larger share of the nation's resources on medical care services, through the federal government or otherwise? Should medical care be more accessible (and perhaps less fancy)? Should it be of substantially higher quality (and therefore more expensive), and should it be delivered more humanely (to the objection of some currently satisfied providers)? Should its use be independent of ability to pay (and therefore likely to be more costly in the aggregate)?

These questions will not be asked if post-New Deal ideological themes continue to dominate our conceptions of doctors, patients, and national health insurance. When Republicans lock horns with Democrats on the roles of the private and public sectors, the public is not well served. The crisis in American medicine lies in our thinking as much as in our medical care arrangements.

What Can We Do?
Although the sense of crisis reflects political strategy as much as medical care reality, ignoring it would be a mistake, for two reasons. First, while most of the problems may not be truly critical, they are real. Second, once voters have been "sold" on the existence of crisis, the most appealing plan, politically, is a mixed one. By a mixed plan I mean a compromise, on both financing and administrative centralization, which would disperse regulatory and financial responsibility among citizens and patients, governments and private insurance companies, states and the federal government. CHIP is a good example; and the 1974 Kennedy-Mills proposal was very similar in financial, if not administrative, dispersion.

But, again, mixed compromises in medical-care financing bring out the worst of the private and public worlds. A mixed plan will institutionalize the inflation problem, as the Swedish and Canadian experiences suggest.[27] In fact, whenever insurance, public or private, is offered as a cure for medical inflation, it becomes (to borrow a medical phrase) iatrogenic, the disease of which it purports to be the cure. National health insurance will increase inflationary pressures under the best of circumstances.[28] Plans that mix private, state, and federal financing—and regulation—offer us the least hope for resisting this inflation while expanding access.

We need, instead, a plan that provides ample protection against disastrous medical costs, encourages worthwhile preventive care, offers incentives to efficient practice, and, for the sake of political feasibility, does not suddenly run $118 billion through the federal budget.

Catastrophic Insurance and Kiddie Care: A Staged Implementation Plan for NHI

What I propose is a staged implementation plan for national health insurance that finances the medical care of preschool children (zero to six) and all mothers (Kennedy-Corman for children and mothers) and insures all against financial disaster and ill health.

NHI advocates typically respond to fiscal constraints by varying the richness of the proposed benefit package, not be changing the beneficiaries. In Canada, incremental developments took place by type of service, first national hospital insurance in the late 1950s and then national medical insurance a decade later. But the American pattern thus far has been to phase programs in by age and income group, as with Medicare and Medicaid in the 1960s. A comprehensive health insurance program for all preschool children — combined with catastrophic protection for all — could be a sensible and traditionally American way to introduce national health insurance amidst current budgetary restraints.

Children should be singled out for a number of reasons. First, poor children have benefited less than poor adults from the redistribution of medical care services that took place during the 1960s.[29] Second, the care that children need most is readily producible, relatively cheap, and reasonably likely to improve the health of preschoolers. Immunization is an example of the inexpensive but effective preventive care that liberals and conservatives alike know is important. It is also an example of an area where the dispersion of responsibility has left glaring inadequacies, with one out of three children not fully immunized against dread diseases.[30] Preventive care here can help — individually, socially, and financially.

Take the case of infants with low birth weights. Of the approximately 240,000 such babies born in the United States annually, a fifth do not survive the first five months of life, and many of those who do survive sustain permanent developmental impairments. As former HEW Secretary Wilbur Cohen observed recently, "In addition to immeasurable personal suffering, the cost to society for medical care alone in the first year of life [totals] about $1 billion."[31] But research results show that we can reduce the problem through prenatal intervention programs, improved diagnostic techniques, methods to delay the onset of labor, and special attention to groups, such as teenage mothers, at high risk of having infants with low birth weights. Preventive care could do more for infants than for any other age group.

A comprehensive health insurance program for preschool children could be relatively cheap. The cost of medical care for children is less than for any other age group and, indeed, about one-sixth that for the elderly. In 1974, per capita expenditures were $183 for those under 19 years of age, $420 for those aged 19 to 64, and $1,218 for those aged 65 and over. Children account for a third of the population but for only about 15 percent of all health expenditures.[32] Thus, a comprehensive program for children is within our *fiscal grasp.* Per capita payments of $200 a year per child under 6 would total about $4 billion; and the annual cost of prenatal and postnatal care, for approximately 3.2 million births, would probably be around $3 billion. Approximately $7 billion annually, then, would pay for Kennedy-Corman benefits for preschool children and their mothers.[33]

Not only would the total initial cost be modest, but the chances of an unpredictable inflationary surge are less with young children than others. Most of the care needed for children is predictable, relating to prevention (immunization), well-baby checkups, and routine procedures for common illness. The expenses associated with pregnancy, while not modest on a per case basis, are relatively uniform and predictable and hence less susceptible to overuse under national health insurance.

A program for mothers and young children could be reimbursed through capitation—that is, by paying yearly lump-sum amounts for medical care—thus furthering a widely praised method of remunerating doctors. American doctors generally favor the traditional fee-for-service payment, but one can imagine far less medical objection to capitation if confined to obstetrical and pediatric care. We already have an existing pattern of prepaid lump-sum payments for obstetrical care, encouraged by the predictable character of the required medical services. Moreover, the familiar nature of the required care for mothers and infants obviates in large measure the possibility of capitation's discouraging needed care: It is assumed that capitation gives the provider economic incentives either to keep patients well or to deprive them of expensive care; deprivation is the (unethical) alternative to preventive and efficient services. But the widely understood and fairly clear standards for adequate mother and infant care will make it relatively easy to monitor the quality and cost of the care being delivered by a group of providers.

The routine nature of so much of pediatric care is another reason for using children's insurance to help reform our current system. Routine care can be delivered quite easily by medical assistants and nurse practitioners.[34] In other parts of the world, most such care is so delivered; and in many medical facilities in America, pediatric nurses are already serving as extensions of, and sometimes substitutes for, the doctor. Not only would the appropriate use of substitutes render the system more efficient, but per capita payments would make such substitution financially attractive to pediatricians and family physicians.

Critics might argue that, since the number of preschool children will ultimately decline over the next quarter century, substituting nondoctors in a dwindling market will raise strong medical objections. But this problem is manageable, for at least two reasons. First, the volume of unmet needs among preschoolers, particularly poor ones, is significant;[35] primary physicians and their assistants will be kept busy, even as the number of children declines. Further, family physicians, who now deliver more than half the care to children, will see the advantages of being able to adjust their practices among the different age groups; by hiring assistants to do their more routine work, they will be free to deal with other patients or other problems.

The nature of children's medical problems and care makes a "kiddie care" national health insurance plan a sensible first (or last) step toward improving financial access to medical care through government. Others have urged smaller benefits for the whole population as an initial step. My own view is that such schemes—whether of the CHIP or the Kennedy-Mills variety—are fiscally irresponsible: they will expand the demand for medical care for groups whose most pressing health problems do not call for conventional services and whose most serious medical concern is financial catastrophe. Those considerations raise two points with regard to a children's plan: (1) the nature of the benefits must meet children's real needs, and (2) a catastrophic protection plan (described below) must be offered to make sure that the adult population—especially the childless—do not regard children as their public policy nemesis.

Children's needs will not be met by a plan that requires substantial cost-sharing by their parents. The rationale for cost-sharing (that is, for coinsurance, copayments, or deductibles) hardly applies to children. The simple and largely preventive procedures of routine care should not be rationed via complex financial hurdles. Since the overall children's medical-care budget would be relatively low, cost-sharing to ease the governmental burden (the real rationale in the Kennedy-Mills and CHIP plans) would not be a political necessity.[36] Nor would cost sharing be justified as a means of reducing unnecessary utilization: compared to medical care for adults, care for children poses more limited risks of "overuse." To the extent that such risks exist (tonsillectomies, unnecessary hospitalization, drug prescriptions), they can be reduced by the capitation mode of payment. California's Kaiser plans and Group Health of Puget Sound illustrate the reduction of hospitalization and surgery rates in prepaid as compared to fee-for-service plans. It is worrisome that the "tonsillectomy rate for government-wide Blue Shield plans [was] over 2.5 times that of group practice plans,"[37] but a plan to pay for children's care need not encourage such questionable practice. Indeed, the concentration of financing in government hands for all children will increase the incentives to restrain harmful care.

In today's economic and political context, the form of national health insurance we choose must be administrable, less costly to the federal treasury than the complete Kennedy-Corman bill, and unlikely to worsen the inflation rate in health. A plan that starts with children, with catastrophic protection for all, is a compelling alternative to the muted versions of the universal proposals that have emerged so far. Children rightly have political appeal as promising recipients of our medical dollars, and the relatively limited costs of even a comprehensive "kiddie care" plan answer the demand for financial staging.

The great appeal of some other plans is their suggestion of ways to put a lid on health expenditures, a specific feature of the Kennedy-Corman proposal. Kennedy-Corman also eschews cost sharing and strongly supports capitation payments. All these features are maintained in a Kennedy-Corman program for preschoolers, although it is to preschoolers only that the expenditure lid applies. Kiddie care would not, in itself, restrain medical inflation across the board; other measures in connection with Medicare, health planning legislation, and facility control would have to be (and now are) employed. But kiddie care would assist this effort, not undercut it.

Those who seek the most far-reaching changes are saddled with the political burden of running much of the $118 billion health budget through federal government accounts. At a time of widespread concern over the size of the federal budget, a reform alternative with limited costs is appealing. Kiddie care meets that standard and can be undergirded by a catastrophic credit income tax scheme costing less than $3 billion. Gross federal expenditures of $8 to $9 billion would finance such a joint plan. Almost everything could be financed by the current tax expenditures for health—the $3.5 billion for medical care deductions from the taxable income of individuals who now spend more than 3 percent of family income on medical care, and the nearly equal amount that the federal government loses by subsidizing health insurance premiums. Through tax reform, in short, child health and universal catastrophic protection would not cost us much more than we are already spending through foregone tax revenues.[38]

I propose catastrophic protection not because it is politically fashionable—that is fortuitous—but because a responsible national health insurance program should respond to the widespread fears of financial ruin. If less than 1 percent of the population had expenses of more than $5,000 per year, and if the deductible were set high in relation to average expenditures and low in relation to economic ruin, the plan would be fiscally possible. As table 10.2 shows, the IRS could implement it with the great political appeal of benefiting everyone (through insurance protection) while actually paying few direct beneficiaries. Further, such tax reform would have the great substantive advantage of making the tax treatment of health care costs more equitable and efficacious.

The following sections sketch the features of a joint children's and catastrophic program.

TABLE 10.2. TAX CREDITS UNDER PROPOSED PLAN AND TAX SAVINGS UNDER CURRENT PERSONAL INCOME TAX MEDICAL DEDUCTIONS, FOR DIFFERENT MEDICAL-EXPENSE AND INCOME LEVELS

Adjusted Gross Income	Out-of-Pocket Medical Expenses			
	$500	$1,000	$2,000	$5,000
	Amount of Tax Credit under Proposed Plan			
$ 5,000	$0-500	$250	$750	$4,000
10,000	0	0	500	3,000
15,000	0	0	250	2,000
20,000	0	0	0	1,000
	Amount of Reduced Tax under Current Personal Income Tax Provisions*			
$ 5,000	$ 0	$ 0	$ 0	$ 0
10,000	55	150	334	806
15,000	33	141	361	957
20,000	38	123	373	1,093

*Based on a family with four exemptions. Assumes that families with less than $5,000 in income take the standard deduction. Assumes also that other families have itemized deductions of $1,500 plus medical expenses; and that $150 of the medical expenses are fully deductible as health insurance premiums, with the remainder subject to an exclusion of 3 percent of adjusted gross income. Calculations are based on the tax law in effect in 1974.

SOURCE: Karen Davis, "Tax Credits for Health Relief for the Working Class, Unemployed, and Disadvantaged" (revised version of a paper presented to the National Health Council Annual Forum, Orlando, Florida, 18 March 1975).

Comprehensive Health Insurance for Preschoolers and Pregnant Women

BENEFITS

The benefit package would be inclusive. It would be partly preventive in nature, including prenatal care for mothers, fertility benefits, *dental care,* such kinds of nutritional and well-baby care as seem to work, immunizations, the setting of broken bones, etc. Neonatal intensive care, renal dialysis, and heart surgery would be included, as would all conventional minor acute care.

PROVIDER REIMBURSEMENT

The only form of payment would be capitation. The federal government would offer, say, $200 per year per child (possibly adjusted for regional differences) to any qualified provider, individual or organization, capable of delivering the benefits. Providers would sign up children, just as GPs in Britain sign up families. Those wishing to buy care in the regular fee-for-service system would be free to do so but not with government subsidy. Pregnant women would be included and, in the case of teenagers, could enroll in their own names even though minors.

PATIENT COST SHARING
No cost sharing at the time of receiving care would be required, except perhaps for some nominal payment for drugs or other care where the serious possibility of overuse exists.

QUALITY REVIEW
A mechanism for monitoring quality would be established in order to reduce the likelihood of providers' giving too little care for the fixed per capita price.

FINANCING
There would be straight, general revenue financing, with the following tax adjustment: either reduction in the $750 exemption for children as partial payment for the benefit, or half the tax credit for children at the medium income as partial payment. Tax adjustments should provide approximately half the cost and be adjusted as costs increase.

COST
At $4 billion ($200 per child per year on the average) and $3 billion (prenatal and postnatal care for an estimated 3.2 million births), cost would be $7 billion per year.

ADMINISTRATION
The program would be administered by the local health boards specified in the Kennedy-Corman legislation. The setting of capitation rates and broad policy would fall to the National Health Security Board specified in the 1975 version of Kennedy-Corman. The catastrophic tax-credit program would be administered by the division of the Internal Revenue Service that implements the medical expense deductions under current tax law.

RESEARCH AND DEVELOPMENT
Some research should be done to reduce the need for the services covered by the children's program and to produce technology for delivering those services more efficiently. Among the possibilities: contraceptive research; demonstrations of better manpower utilization (e.g., pediatric assistants); further research on prenatal care and well-baby care, to determine effectiveness and to modify

program benefits accordingly; and a research and statistical effort comparable to Medicare's, so that we can learn from doing.

The Catastrophic Tax-Credit Program[39]

The covered services in a catastrophic program should be comprehensive. That is, practically all medical care expenses should be eligible for tax credits, although the amount of the deductible, coinsurance, and maximum out-of-pocket liability could vary. One promising schedule, whose distribution of benefits by income level is compared in table 10.2 with our current regressive tax deduction policy, has a deductible of 10 percent of taxable income and 50 percent coinsurance up to a maximum family expenditure of 20 percent of taxable income. Taxable income for this tax purpose would be more broadly defined than under current law. The point is to avoid incorporating loopholes into a plan whose very definition of catastrophe depends upon the relative burden of medical expenses on family wealth.

These benefits, it should be emphasized, would provide only minimal protection against burdensome medical expenses. The tax credit would work like a catastrophic health insurance plan that requires families to pay up to 10 percent of their taxable income before insurance benefits begin. By providing 50 cents for each dollar of further expense up to the maximum family liability, the plan shares expenses with those having high costs and places a ceiling on the family's medical liabilities short of financial disaster. Further, it does so progressively, so that at higher income levels, as table 10.2 shows, benefits decline gradually. And it is progressively financed, as Karen Davis of Brookings has emphasized, through foregone tax revenues (income tax revenues).[40]

Benefit payments would be integrated into the current tax cycle. That would mean annual adjustments for most, but quarterly adjustments for those who chose to so report their income and expenses. The schedule shown in table 10.2 illustrates how the tax credit for out-of-pocket expenses (including health insurance premiums) would affect families at different income levels. A family with an income of $5,000 and ruinous expenses at $5,000 would be entitled to a tax credit of $4,000. The credit would decline for families with the same expenses but higher incomes, as the fourth column illustrates. For a family earning $15,000, with the same $5,000 in medical expenses, the tax credit would be $2,000 for the year.

A credit against one's tax bill would work for those with incomes high enough for the IRS to tax. A credit in the form of a cash rebate would be paid in April for those (say, pensioners on social security) who have little or no taxable income. Some critics of this plan worry about the problems health providers might have in getting prompt payment of their bills by the poor and the old. The plan would not address that difficulty directly; it would provide protection for individuals, not protection against cash flow problems of hospitals, doctors, and nursing homes. On the other hand, the assurance that no patient could be made destitute by medical expenses would substantially underwrite the working poor and the medically impoverished and, in that sense, assist the providers. Moreover, the possibility of using quarterly declarations and year-end tax adjustments might go far toward allaying the critics' fears.

Staging

The children's program would be expanded, if thought desirable, on a manageable basis each year for the *first five years*. Adding two years annually to the eligibility age would mean that children under fifteen would be completely covered by the end of the program's first half decade. This would leave open the option, at that time, of extending the children's health insurance policy to the rest of the population. Over the first five-year period—extending into the 1980s—the rest of the population, and most particularly the unemployed, aged, and working poor, would be relieved of the worry of medical expenses' bankrupting them. Medicare and Medicaid would be left in place as further protection. Some 4 percent of the population spend more than a quarter of their incomes on medical care.[41] Up to 4 million alone are potential candidates for coronary bypass surgery, an expensive new procedure costing, according to government estimates, about $7,000 per operation. So catastrophic protection would relieve a burden that now falls most heavily on the sick, aged, unemployed, and poor.

Conclusion

A combination of children's and catastrophic insurance is not only politically appealing but fiscally and administratively feasible. The deductible provisions of the tax-credit plan limit its costs; and the introduction of a Kennedy-Corman plan for children is aimed at the very group that will not use enormous resources in the expensive hospital-surgical part of medicine.

The children's program, moreover, involves pediatricians and family practitioners, who are far easier to monitor than others and less likely to obstruct the capitation mode of payment. For those insistent on fee-for-service medicine, this plan would not apply. The financing for both plans would come largely from the current tax expenditures for medical care but would be far more progressive in effect than our tax treatment of illness. An additional source of funding would be some portion of the yearly child allowance now paid by the IRS in tax credits or deductions. A part of that allowance could be earmarked for children's health insurance, reminding parents everywhere that medical care is not free, even if the sick do not have to pay every time they use medical services.

At a time when the country doubts the capacity of government and the competence of the governors, a plan that is manageable but effective would do much for the health of the political order.

Postscript

This chapter is a slightly altered version of the testimony on national health insurance that I submitted to the Ways and Means Committee in December 1975 and presented orally to the Subcommittee on Health in Chicago on February 26, 1976.

The origins of the proposal were twofold. Working on the Harvard Child Health Project, financed by the Robert Wood Johnson Foundation, I became involved in the problems of children and in the politics of NHI options. An invitation to give a paper at the Sun Valley Forum on Health in August 1975 prompted me to think about the effects of national health insurance on children. Once the forum paper was written, I had a manuscript looking for other audiences.

Personal and political links explain why this testimony emerged before the Ways and Means Committee. One of my former students, a legislative assistant to Congressman James Corman, was aware of my interest in the issue of national health insurance. This led to an invitation through Corman to testify, even though my proposal did not wholly support the Kennedy-Corman bill. Moreover, I had testified in 1971 through a similar process and was known to members of the committee staff; in fact, one of the staff, Bill Fullerton, had also been a commentator at the Sun Valley Forum.

Translating my ideas into the actual form of the testimony was not easy, but I went through the trouble of testifying because (1) I had an unusual proposal that the political system could not be predicted to produce, (2) I had the fantasy that testimony just might turn the minds of the committee and prompt further congressional consideration; and (3) with my more sober side, I realized that copies of the testimony might, through a press release, attract some attention to a promising idea.

Effects of the Testimony

A press release on the testimony, from the University of Chicago's public information office, generated local news stories and was picked up by national newspapers. That resulted in the American Academy of Pediatrics' regarding the proposal as a serious contribution to the NHI debate — a recognition that probably would not have occurred through publication in academic journals — and in my being invited to address other groups interested in national health insurance. But what particularly increased my sense of involvement and reduced the feeling of impotence I had after testifying was the introduction of a bill for children's health insurance—the Maternal and Child Health Care Act of 1976—by Congressman James Scheuer; I was called to testify on that bill before the House Subcommittee on Health of the Interstate and Foreign Commerce Committee on June 16, 1976.

Effects of Testifying in Chicago
At least four effects are clear:

(1) I shaved my mustache in a no doubt inefficient effort to reduce extraneous barriers to committee discussion.

(2) A Hyde Park resident verbally assaulted both me and my mother for supporting that "catastrophic" plan of catastrophic insurance.

(3) I wasted a whole morning: no questions were asked, and the presentation had no visible effect on the subcommittee.

(4) But the subcommittee staff took notice. The Republican assistant counsel expressed interest in following up on the plan and subsequently arranged another meeting in Washington. The other members of the staff suggested that there would be later hearings more suited to serious questioning.

Overall, the effort has been moderately successful. The plan will now be in the congressional record, it will be familiar to the staff of one of the committees with NHI jurisdiction, and other occasions for presenting the proposal are now available. What is crucial—but unclear—is whether backers of the Kennedy-Corman proposal regard this plan as one of the compromises they could support if their bill remains stalemated.

NOTES

1. John K. Iglehart, "Health Report/Explosive Rise in Medical Costs Puts Government in Quandry," *National Journal,* 20 September 1975, pp. 1319-27.
2. See postscript at end of chapter.
3. With Nixon warning of a "massive crisis" that could soon lead to a "breakdown in our medical care system . . . affecting millions," and Kennedy writing a book on American health care entitled *In Critical Condition* (New York: Simon and Schuster, 1972), no wonder the AFL-CIO's George Meany could treat the "crisis" as "generally accepted." See Richard Nixon, "The Nation's Health Care System," *Weekly Compilation of Presidential Documents* 5, no. 28 (10 July 1969): 963; "Our Ailing Medical System," *Fortune,* January 1970; and George Meany's statement for the AFL-CIO in U.S. Congress, House, Committee on Ways and Means, *Hearings on National Health Insurance,* 11 vols., October-November 1971, p. 239.

4. In 1975, health care was ranked as a "very, very important" issue (5 on a 5-point scale) by 55 percent of the population, compared to 42 percent three years earlier. See remarks by Dorothy Lynch in National Health Council, *A Declaration of Interdependence: Developing America's Health Policy,* Proceedings of the Twenty-Fourth Annual National Health Forum, 16-17 March 1976, Philadelphia, Pennsylvania, p. 36.
5. Ronald Andersen et al., "The Public's View of the Crisis in Medical Care: An Impetus for Changing Delivery Systems?" *Economic and Business Bulletin* 24 (Fall 1971): 44-52. See also Aaron Wildavsky, "Doing Better and Feeling Worse," Working Paper #19 (Berkeley, Calif.: Graduate School of Public Policy, University of California, March 1975), p. 2.
6. Anthony Downs, "Up and Down with Ecology—The 'Issue Attention Cycle,' " *Public Interest,* no. 28 (Summer 1972).
7. Iglehart, "Health Report," p. 1320; Theodore Marmor, Thomas Heagy, and Donald Wittman, "The Politics of Medical Inflation," *Journal of Health Politics, Policy, and Law* 1, no. 1 (1976).
8. Fewer than 1 percent spend more than $5,000 a year on medical care. See Michael Meyer, *Catastrophic Illnesses and Catastrophic Health Insurance* (Washington, D.C.: Heritage Foundation, 1974), p. 4.
9. U.S. Department of Health, Education, and Welfare, Social Security Administration, Office of Research and Statistics, *Compendium of National Health Expenditures Data,* DHEW Publication No.(SSA) 76-11927 (Washington, D.C.: U.S. Government Printing Office, January 1976), p. 59.
10. American Medical Association, *Profiles of Medical Practice,* 1974 ref. ed. (Chicago, 1974), pp. 95, 100.
11. Barbara and John Ehrenreich, *The American Health Empire: Power, Profit and Politics* (New York: Random House, 1970).
12. See, for example, Rick Carlson, *The End of Medicine* (New York: Wiley, 1975).
13. S.3; H.R.23, 1975.
14. Saul Waldman, *National Health Insurance Proposals: Provisions of Bills Introduced in the 93rd Congress of July, 1974,* DHEW Publication No. (SSA) 75-11920 (Washington, D.C.: U.S. Government Printing Office, 1974), p. 189.
15. Martin Feldstein, "A New Approach to National Health Insurance," *Public Interest,* no. 23 (Spring 1971): 93-105. This is only one version of Feldstein's MRI. A variant has a lower deductible (5 percent of family income) followed by 50 percent coinsurance over a further 10 percent of family income. The advantage of this more complex scheme is to keep persons partly financially responsible over a wider band of medical expenditures. See Theodore R. Marmor and Robert Kudrle, "National Health Insurance Plans and Their Implications for Mental Health" (paper delivered at the Symposium on Political and Community Problems in Mental Health Care, Northern Illinois University, 22-23 April 1975), p. 12.
16. Waldman, *National Health Insurance Proposals,* pp. 194-95.
17. Ibid., pp. 16, 161; John Holahan, *Financing Health Care for the Poor* (Boston: Heath, 1975), pp. 86-90.

18. AMA Statement on National Health Insurance (by Dr. Max Parrot), *Hearings on National Health Insurance,* U.S. Congress, House, Committee on Ways and Means, October-November 1971, p. 1951.

19. This thesis is developed with respect to Canada in Theodore R. Marmor, Thomas Heagy, and Wayne Hoffman, "National Health Insurance: Some Lessons from the Canadian Experience," *Policy Sciences* 6, no. 4 (special issue on comparative policy research, December 1975): 447-66. The article is a revised version of the one by Marmor in *National Health Insurance: Can We Learn from Canada?* ed. Spyros Andreopoulos (New York: Wiley, 1975), chap. 4. More specifically on inflation controls, see Theodore Marmor, Donald Wittman, and Thomas Heagy, "Politics, Public Policy, and Medical Inflation, " in *Health: A Victim or Cause of Inflation,* ed. Michael Zubkoff (New York: Prodist, 1976).

20. See the discussion of financing modes and inflation in Zubkoff, *Health;* and Marmor, Heagy, and Hoffman, "National Health Insurance: Some Lessons," table 2.

21. Lynch, in *Declaration of Interdependence,* p. 35.

22. By concentration I mean a single unit of government paying the bill—the Health Security Board in the case of the Kennedy-Corman proposal. By contrast, our present medical financing is dispersed among patients, numerous insurance carriers, and federal, state, and local government agencies.

23. Interviews with HEW officials suggest that any effort to change the current tax advantages of health insurance meet with fierce resistance. This resistance has led Stuart Altman, deputy assistant secretary for health, Office of Planning and Evaluation, HEW, to conclude that more drastic constraints on insurance would have a near-zero probability of enactment.

24. See, for example, the comments by Michael Zubkoff in National Health Council, *Declaration of Interdependence,* p. 62.

25. See U.S. Congress, House, Committee on Ways and Means, Subcommittee on Health, *National Health Insurance, Panel Discussion,* 94th Cong., 1st sess., 10, 11, 17, 24 July and 12 September 1975.

26. But note that there is little evidence to support the general enthusiasm for preventive care. There are indications that prenatal care effectively prevents some maternal and infant problems, but there is evidence that mass screening programs and even annual physical checkups are wasteful and only occasionally detect conditions that are aided by early treatment. Economists Ralph Andreano and Burton Weisbrod conclude that preventive care can increase costs without significantly improving health. They attribute the apparent cost-savings in Kaiser-Permanente (often cited as a model of the medical and financial efficacy of prevention) to "various factors many of which are unrelated to preventive care." See their *American Health Policy: Perspectives and Choices* (Chicago: Rand McNally, 1974), p. 35.

27. This point is developed in Marmor, Wittman, and Heagy, "Politics, Public Policy, and Medical Inflation," and draws on the Canadian data presented in Marmor, Heagy, and Hoffman, "National Health Insurance: Some Lessons.

28. Joseph P. Newhouse, "Inflation and Health Insurance," in Zubkoff, ed. *Health: A Victim or Cause of Inflation,* pp. 210-24; and Joseph P. Newhouse, Charles E. Phelps, and William B. Schwartz, "Policy Options and the Impact of National Health Insurance," *New England Journal of Medicine* 290 (13 June 1970): 1345-59.

29. Karen Davis and Roger Reynolds, "The Impact of Medicare and Medicaid on Access to Medical Care" (Washington, D.C.: Brookings Institution, n.d.), p. 3; published also in *The Role of Insurance in the Health Service Sector,* ed. Richard Rosett (New York: National Bureau of Economic Research, 1976).

30. John A. Butler, "National Health Insurance and Primary Medical Care" (draft of Ph.D. diss., Harvard University, Graduate School of Education, 1976), p. 7.

31. Wilbur J. Cohen, "A Comprehensive Program for Children, Youth, and the Family," Statement to the Subcommittee on Oversight and Investigations of the House Committee on Interstate and Foreign Commerce (Washington, D.C., 7 October 1975), p. 9. Mimeographed.

32. Gerald Weber, "An Evaluation of an Expanded Public Role in the Health Care of Children" (paper presented to the Sun Valley Forum on National Health, Sun Valley, Idaho, 25-30 August 1975).

33. Compare this estimated outlay with the current national expenditures of approximately $7 billion through the tax system's medical expense deduction and favorable treatment of insurance as a fringe benefit. Consider, too, that the projected annual increase in Medicare and Medicaid for fiscal year 1977 is $5.2 billion. See Karen Davis, "Tax Credits for Health Relief for the Working Class, Unemployed, and Disadvantaged" (revised version of a paper presented to the National Health Council Annual Forum, Orlando, Florida, 18 March 1975); and Clifton Gaus, Testimony of the Social Security Administration before the President's Biomedical Research Panel (29 September 1975), p. 1. Mimeographed.

34. An illuminating example is the program for pediatric nurse practitioners at the University of Colorado's School of Medicine under Dr. Henry Silver, cited in Gerald I. Weber, "An Evaluation of an Expanded Public Role in the Financing of Health Care Services for Children: An Option" (San Francisco: University of California Medical School, n.d.), pp. 13-14. Mimeographed.

35. See Weber, "Evaluation of an Expanded Public Role in the Financing of Health Care Services for Children."

36. Davis, "Tax Credits, " p. 61.

37. U.S., Congress, House, Committee on Interstate and Foreign Commerce, *Cost and Quality of Health Care: Unnecessary Surgery,* Report by the Subcommittee on Oversight and Investigation, 94th Cong., 2d sess., January 1976, p. 12.

38. Bridger Mitchell and Ronald Vogel, "Health Taxes: An Assessment of the Medical Deduction," *Southern Economic Journal* 41, no. 4 (April 1975): 660-72.

39. See Davis, "Tax Credits," for an approach that is very similar to the one briefly described below.
40. Ibid.
41. Walter McClure, "The Medical Care System under National Health Insurance: Four Models" (Minneapolis: Interstudy, 23 January 1976), p. 6a (mimeographed); also published in the *Journal of Health Politics, Policy, and Law* 1, no. 1 (Spring 1976).

Lawrence M. Mead

11. HEALTH POLICY: THE NEED FOR GOVERNANCE

The American health care system is facing a serious cost crisis. In response, public policy is moving to assert control over providers and limit the share of national resources devoted to health. Other mechanisms which might have controlled costs, such as delegation of responsibility to the providers or the market, have failed to do so. Hence, explicit public control of the health system seems inevitable.

This chapter discusses the problem of governance implied by control. Health policy has drifted toward intervention while seeking to evade the dilemmas of governing the health system publicly. Unpleasant tensions must be resolved on a continuing basis. The providers must be controlled, yet allowed to function; the public must be given care, yet prevented from consuming more resources than it really wants or needs.

These problems have no simple solutions. American politics has typically sought to avoid them. The advantage of the alternative approaches to control is that they avoid the need to grapple with governance. But now that public control seems inevitable, success will depend importantly on our ability to deal with governance wisely.

Some qualifications should be stated. This interpretation looks at the health cost problem, not other health or policy issues. The problem is addressed from the viewpoint of political theory and political development. Other interpretations could be equally valid. Since the argument is general, there are no specific policy recommendations, though some implications for policy are clear.

The health system is treated as if it were undifferentiated. The cost crisis and the trend of policy are addressed from a federal, not a state or local, perspective. The problems of the various kinds of providers and the different third-party payment systems, public and private, are treated as broadly similar. At the general level of this argument, these assumptions are useful and defensible. However, it is recognized that actual public policies based on the analysis would have to be much more complicated, varying with the level of government, reimbursement system, or type of provider.

Crisis and Response

The attention of health policy makers is concentrated on the rapid rise in health costs. Spending has exploded since the enactment of Medicare and Medicaid in 1965. In fiscal 1950, the nation spent $12 billion on all health expenditures. In 1965, the figure was $38.9 billion. In 1976, the figure was $139.3 billion, or a growth of more than $100 billion in eleven years. In these same years, public spending for health grew from $3.1 billion, to $9.5 billion, to $58.8 billion. The lion's share of the last figure was federal and state government funding for Medicare and Medicaid. Most serious of all, the share of total national resources, or GNP, going to health almost doubled, from 4.5 percent in 1950 to 8.6 percent in 1976.[1] The enactment of national health insurance (NHI) — now on the political agenda — could raise the figure as high as 11 percent.[2]

The cost explosion has forced government to intervene increasingly in the health system. When Medicare and Medicaid were enacted, the federal government claimed only to act as paymaster for private health care expenditures, without controlling the providers or overall spending. At the insistence of health interests, the preamble of the Medicare law carefully stated that, "Nothing in this title shall be construed to authorize any Federal officer or employee to exercise any supervision or control over the practice of medicine or the manner in which medical services are provided. . . ."[3]

At the outset, both Medicare and Medicaid were conceived in expansive terms. Providers were usually reimbursed for services on the basis of their costs or usual charges. Federal funding was open-ended; that is, limited only by the number of patients claiming reimbursement. The range of services covered was wide.[4] Eligibility was broad, with Medicare covering most of the elderly, and Medicaid, at least potentially, most of the needy.[5]

As soon as spending soared, flaws in this basic design became apparent. Cost-based reimbursement encouraged providers to dispense unnecessary services and raise prices, since their income expanded in proportion to the costs claimed. The presence of public funding, like other third-party payment, encouraged patients to demand, and providers to prescribe, more health care than would be the case had the patient paid for services out-of-pocket. And open-ended funding allowed spending to increase without any overall limit.

Federal responses have tended toward greater regulation, but stopped short of outright cost controls. Medicare's cost-based reimbursement rules for hospitals and nursing homes and Medicaid's eligibility rules were tightened. In both programs, there were increasing requirements for peer review procedures to deny funding for care judged medically unnecessary. At the state level, Medicaid programs used their discretion over eligibility, benefits, and reimbursement to exclude many needy from coverage, cut back services provided, and, in many instances, replace cost-based reimbursement of doctors and nursing homes with fee schedules.[6]

The 1972 amendments to the Social Security Act added a number of innovations: denial of some reimbursement for new health facilities built in defiance of state health plans, a cut in reimbursement rates for long-term institutional care under Medicaid in states without approved utilization controls, vesting of utilization control responsibility in new peer review bodies (Professional Standards Review Organizations), and experiments with funding of services through prepaid group practices (Health Maintenance Organizations).

However, the cost spiral goes on. During fiscal 1974-76 alone, national health expenditures rose by over 30 percent and Medicare/Medicaid spending by more than 50 percent.[7] In response, HEW has combined Medicare and Medicaid in a single health financing agency with a stronger mandate for cost control, and it has proposed to limit hospitals' revenue increases to 9 percent per year. Politicians and health administrators increasingly say that national health insurance will be impossible without much firmer cost controls.

These developments show both a trend toward public control and an ambivalence about it. The underlying dynamic is clear. In this, as in other areas of policy, government intervention is driven by economic scarcity. As health expenditures grow, apparently without limit, they come up against resources increasingly limited by sluggish economic growth and other demands. Since other mechanisms have not limited health spending to what seems socially desirable, government has no choice but to seek control through authority.

Some officials and academics now recognize that the government should have exerted controls right from the inception of Medicare and Medicaid. The attempt to fund expanded services through the existing health system without reforming or reorganizing it was bound to fail. For in a system without strong market restraints on prices, much of the new funding was lost to inflation rather than going into increased supplies of services.[8]

Public debate, however, is couched in terms of more limited objectives. Most federal policy makers confine the government's role in health service provision to distributing benefits to the population and eliminating obvious abuses by the providers. Liberals want to provide insurance coverage for all Americans as a basic right, and for this cost control is necessary.[9] Others focus on the more egregious faults of the reimbursement systems, notably over generous rates and the high incidence of fraudulent reimbursement claims.[10] Legislative amendments have attempted to deal with these problems ad hoc without admitting any larger agenda. There has been no attempt to guide or restructure the health system in more general terms.

Governance

While doubts can be raised about public controls on several grounds, the main reason we shy away from it is probably fear of the political costs involved. Public control involves more than the imposition of curbs on the providers and the level of spending once and for all. It requires a process of governance to administer these controls on a continuing basis.

The Problem in General

Governance poses difficult political problems which, in their nature, have no self-evident solutions. Governance, like any form of social control, faces basically two challenges—order and rationality. The authorities must first control society and, second, do so in ways favoring the social good.

Difficulties arise because there is disagreement about how to achieve these goals. The questions central to politics are how much public control is necessary and what form it should take. Groups argue on practical, constitutional, or ideological grounds that they should be exempted from control, or that control should be exercised in their interests. In part, the differences arise from genuine disagreement about what serves the general interest; in part, they arise from partial interest. Groups are driven toward self-serving proposals, not only by self-interest but by incentives inherent in the collective nature of government. Since government and policy are "public goods" in the economist's sense, not market goods, how much every individual or group benefits from them has little connection to how much each pays for them in taxes or other costs. Therefore, each can gain by seeking to sway the common policy, with its common costs, in a self-serving direction.[11] There is little incentive to support policies serving the general interest, as the benefits of these will be available in any case.[12]

The labor of governance is the continual struggle to resolve these disagreements in ways favoring the public, to the degree that the public interest can be known. Sheldon Wolin has written: "This is the basic dilemma of political judgments: how to create a common rule in a context of differences? The dilemma cannot be overcome, but what is possible is to lessen the crudities of the judgment."[13] The struggle is shared by public officials who have to make choices and by the public, which must review its choices directly or indirectly. The effort is burdensome because it is never-ending and the stakes are high.

Worse, there are no clear criteria for success or failure. What serves the general good cannot be known separately from the political process. Every approach to allocation attempts to distribute resources optimally among social needs. An optimal solution is at least conceivable if market mechanisms are used. A market aggregates and ranks preferences that are openly and sincerely declared by individuals through their buying and selling decisions. But if choices are made by government, the competition to influence policy, just mentioned, inflates claims and conceals true preferences. Now needs cannot be accurately known, and an optimal allocation is impossible even in theory.[14] Although empirical projections of consequences can shed some light on the different options, the choice among them depends centrally on value judgments that for practical purposes are arbitrary.

This, in turn, leads to a moral problem. Choices must be made without clear guidance among values all of which imply moral imperatives. Should the policy maker spend more on health services for needy people or more on national defense so that the entire country will be secure? There can be no clearly best course of action. All options are both good and bad depending on the values they serve and deny.[15] Morally, the statesman's cross is the knowledge that he cannot be blameless whatever his choices.[16]

These intellectual and moral dilemmas are perhaps the deepest reasons why health policy has sought to avoid direct public control of the health system. American politics has great reluctance to impose ironclad control over groups or individuals through authority. However, the argument below is that governance must be faced. Order and rationality have not been achieved in the American health system, and there is no good prospect that nongovernmental mechanisms can attain them. The scarce commodity in health policy is not so much resources as governance and the political fortitude it requires.

The Problem of Order

From the viewpoint of order, one fact about the American health system cries out: The providers are not clearly accountable to society. Both the market (for reasons to be discussed below) and government leave them remarkably free to determine the price and supply of health services by themselves.

The reimbursement mechanisms give society no firm control over the incomes of providers or the share of national resources they consume. Cost-based reimbursement, which applies uniformly to hospitals and extensively to other providers, means that income rises in proportion to costs claimed. This gives providers an incentive to raise costs and ignore waste and inefficiency. Some third-party reimbursers, including Medicaid programs in some states, have imposed fee schedules on providers other than hospitals. However, the providers are always free to withdraw from these systems and take more patients who have more liberal reimbursement or pay out-of-pocket. Further, the fee schedules are often keyed to prevailing prices for health services in an area and are thus vulnerable to increases as the general health price level rises.

Our health system's freedom from public control is unusual compared to other advanced countries. Abroad, the health system is more often socialized. If reimbursement funds remain private, they are usually closely supervised by the government. The United States shows lower levels of management and organization in health than in other sectors of American society.[17] And what is most remarkable, the general public supports, to some extent, the idea that the medical profession's unusual autonomy is an essential freedom.[18]

In American political thinking, both the drive for control and the resistance to it are deeply rooted. On the one hand, the increasing regulation of health care responds to a gut feeling among politicians and the public that the extravagant privileges of doctors and hospitals must be curbed. "*Vox populi,* made strident by sky-rocketing rates for health care, is declaring, 'There ought to be a law!' And there will be—certainly at the state level—and perhaps also in the form of congressional enactment."[19]

But on the other hand, there is a fear of control stemming from the nation's deep-seated suspicion of governmental authority. There is intense uneasiness when government tries to regulate private interests in ways they view as authoritarian. Inevitably, compromises are made and firm control slips away. To obtain consensus is more important than to strictly achieve the public interest.

Some initiatives for control, such as the health planning movement, have been so vitiated by these fears that the planning agencies have never acquired real authority. The Comprehensive Health Planning (CHP) agencies set up in each state by federal statute in 1966 had very limited powers to limit the building of unneeded new hospitals and other expensive health facilities. The Health Services Agencies (HSAs) authorized in 1975 have somewhat greater but still minimal, authority. Some proposals for health planning seem, not to assert and justify public authority, but to argue against it and insist that health planning must remain in the hands of "voluntary" (i.e., private) or state agencies heavily influenced by provider interests.[20]

Even health academics, who understand the cost crisis, are reluctant to recommend statist solutions. There is a tendency to prefer the present evils of "continued inflation, frustration, and inequitable distribution" of health resources if the only alternative is an "inordinate concentration of power."[21] There is a preference for forms of government control which would preserve elements of the present, pluralist, semiprivate system, such as private health insurance companies.[22] And yet there is no denying that the problem of order must be solved. Somehow, the providers must be brought under control. Behind many of the frictions and inefficiences of the American health system is the fact that the medical profession resists unambiguous accountability.[23] Until this resistance is broken—probably by government—a moderation of the cost crisis will be difficult to imagine.

The Problem of Rationality

Control, however achieved, should be used to direct the health system rationally; that is, for the social good. The system behaves irrationally now chiefly in that the share of national resources going to health services is probably too great. The rapid rise in total spending for health, government health spending, and the percentage of GNP going to health has already been mentioned. It is not clear that increases on this scale have served the public well. The level of resources now devoted to health probably exceeds what is necessary, at least from a medical viewpoint.

The occupancy rate for hospital beds dropped from 82.3 percent in 1965 to 76.7 percent in 1975 because construction of new community hospitals boomed while the overall need for hospitalization dropped.[24] Liberal public financing for construction and service reimbursement promotes building of hospitals and expensive treatment facilities regardless of need. Federal policy has made half-hearted attempts to stop this through the health planning legislation mentioned above and the requirement that new facilities obtain "certificates-of-need" from state planning agencies before purchase or construction.

There may also be too many doctors. In the last ten years, the number of medical schools and medical graduates has increased sharply. There are now a third as many doctors in training (roughly 100,000) as in practice. Between 1960 and 1975, the number of doctors per 100,000 population rose from 148 to 174. By 1985, the number will probably be 210 or 218—higher than any other country except Israel and the USSR. Traditionally, federal policy has subsidized medical education in the belief that there was a shortage of doctors. Now that policy has been questioned, and in October 1976 Congress ended the practice of encouraging the immigration of foreign medical graduates.[25]

It is now recognized that the health resource problem is more one of distribution than quantity. There are too many doctors in suburban areas, too few in rural or inner-city locations. There are too many medical specialists, especially surgeons, and too few primary care physicians. The better-off receive too much health care; the needy, too little. Some needy have very poor access to care, while others, in states with generous Medicaid programs, have better access than some of the better-off.[26]

Most fundamentally, there is little evidence that health services have much to do with the health of society. Most other industrialized countries have lower morbidity and mortality rates than does the United States, even though their health systems are less affluent or technically advanced.[27] In the past, the health rates responded to better nutrition, the growth of income, and public health measures against infectious diseases. Today, when the chief threats to health are the degenerative diseases (heart disease, cancer, and stroke), health depends much more on the life style of the patient than on medical care.[28]

There is excessive spending, in part, because the problem of order discussed above has not been solved. Until control of costs is achieved, choice about spending is impossible. The public did not clearly desire or chose the present level of health spending. Even spending for Medicare and Medicaid has not been subject to public control. Both programs quickly exceeded the cost projections made at their inception.[29] Both have open-ended funding, so that aggregate spending levels are not set by governmental decision.

Further, in all reimbursement systems, third-party payment makes collective decision about spending difficult. Third-party mechanisms have the effect of depressing the marginal cost of care to the patient below its actual costs to the society. This motivates patients to consume resources with little concern for social costs. The total consumed probably exceeds what people would choose collectively, as citizens, if government set the overall level.[30]

However, even if society did take collective decisions on spending, the level of resources would probably still exceed what is necessary for adequate services. Third-party mechanisms have been set up on the supposition that the demand for care would be limited by levels of morbidity and mortality in the population, even if the marginal price of services was zero. In practice, the demand for care seems to be nearly inexhaustible when price is removed as a barrier. Once urgent health needs are met, people bring increasing numbers of minor, chronic, and psychosomatic problems to the attention of physicians.[31] It is mainly because of increased demand, not restricted supply, that the United States has seemed to have a shortage of physicians.[32]

This suggests that, at bottom, the population is asking for help in dealing with existential anxieties about death and the human condition which are not strictly speaking medical problems at all.[33] Need for health services per se may be limited, but the need for caring in a broader sense is unlimited. Society has an increasing tendency to delegate the caring function to doctors and other professionals.[34]

There are several reasons why the proportion of resources going to health must be limited, perhaps even to levels below what is spent now. One is that unlimited spending is inefficient. As health care becomes more expensive relative to the incremental health improvements achieved, diminishing marginal returns set in. After a point, the social gain of investing resources elsewhere than in health clearly become greater. Limits have to be imposed and tradeoffs struck, both among different health needs and between the health sector and the other needs of society.[35]

A more philosophic argument is that public policy should not encourage the public's increasing dependence on health services. The fact that Americans now commonly regard easy access to comprehensive health care as a necessity can be viewed, not as a fortunate thing, but as a species of unfreedom. The modern hospital bids fair to become, like the medieval cathedral, an institution in which society vests extravagant hopes for salvation and consolation. A rational health policy should disabuse the public of this illusion. The share of resources going to health should be stabilized or cut so that more of the burden of coping with illness and death can be returned to individuals.[36]

Why, then, do we resist placing firm limits on health resources? For the same reason we resist imposing control on the providers: We do not wish to govern people. Health policy makers never wish to be responsible for denying benefits to individuals, even if this were to the advantage of society. Democratic government can impose sacrifices on large groups of people much more easily than on small ones, where suffering would be visible in individuals.[37] We fear the impersonality of a solution to the allocation problem by either bureaucratic or market means. Once decisions are taken about funding on broad social grounds, there is no guarantee that any given individual will obtain care.[38]

But again, the need for governance is imperative. If nothing else, unlimited demand for health spending puts an intolerable strain on public discourse. Demands that grow out of biological need tend to be private and urgent. They take no account of the needs of others or competing claims to resources. Public demands for welfare, housing, employment, etc., are all of this kind. Health needs, which grow out of physical suffering, are the most coercive of all. Such needs, if expressed without limit, overburden public discourse with moral imperatives, even if the economic costs of meeting them can be borne. It becomes difficult to discuss compromise or other priorities openly. But some detachment from particular needs is essential to wise decisions in public. Hence, some limits on health demands are necessary, not only for economic or cultural reasons, but to preserve the civility of the political process.[39]

Approaches to Control

The order and rationality problems in health come down to the fact that there is no person or mechanism with the authority to limit health spending and force tradeoffs against other social priorities.

> There is for all practical purposes no one in the system of insured-fee-for-service health care who has and can consistently act on an incentive to conserve resources; neither patient, nor physician, nor institution, nor insurer, nor regulator, nor government faces in any true sense the cost of each procedure at a point where it can be effectively weighted against its benefit.[40]

The financing system is a web of transactions among patients, providers, and reimbursers all of which serve immediate, private interests. Control requires the construction of an Archimedian point somewhere within or outside the system, where the social interest in restraint will reliably be brought to bear and the necessary tradeoffs forced.

What mechanisms might be used? There are basically three: delegation to the health professionals, the market, and direct public control.[41] Until recently, public policy has chiefly relied on the first two. They have the advantage, so attractive to American politics, of avoiding the need for governance. But, in fact, the structure of the health system, as well as experience, suggests that these approaches cannot provide the firm control needed. If public control is inevitable, so are problems of governance. In this light, the attempt of the other approaches to avoid open control becomes, not a virtue, but a serious problem for public policy. The attempt perpetuates the belief that governance can be avoided just at the time when it must be faced.

The Professional Solution

The chief basis of current health policy is still the belief that the medical profession can be trusted to make decisions on health service provision for the public.[42] While some changes to Medicare and Medicaid have tightened cost-based reimbursement and placed other restrictions on the providers, others have given them more responsibility, notably the Professional Standards Review Organizations (PSROs) set up since 1972. The PSROs are peer review bodies of doctors supposed to uphold the quality of care and prevent unnecessary care for both Medicare and Medicaid within a region.

The basic problem with PSRO, and the whole idea of professional control, is that medical professionals are attuned to improving the quality and quantity of care, not to preventing unnecessary care or controlling costs. Order and rationality in the senses used here require that decisions be taken from a macro viewpoint that favors society as a whole. The medical ethic, however, stresses micro decisions, favoring the welfare of individual patients. Everything necessary is to be done for the patient at hand; aggregate costs or other social consequences get much less attention.[43] Philosophically, the medical ethic is nonpolitical and nongovernmental. It deals in private moral conceptions, such as the doctor's virtue and duty, not public ones, such as justice, utility, or the proper role of institutions.[44]

In terms of structure, as well as attitudes, the medical profession has difficulty governing the health system. Control would require an authority structure; that is, organization among health professionals that allowed leaders acting in the social interest to make decisions binding on all. Not surprisingly, peer review bodies like utilization review committees and PSROs control costs best when they are able to reverse individual doctors' care decisions and have authoritative standards to work from.[45] Similarly, the most efficient hospitals seem to be those where the doctors are most highly organized and, hence, accountable to an administrative structure.[46]

Typically, however, medical societies and health institutions impose little structure on providers. They have no clear goals or authority patterns to which physicians are accountable.[47] Poor organization is perhaps the basic reason why American health care is more expensive compared to that of other countries.[48] The failure of the system to govern itself in the public interest implies, of course, that restraint must be imposed from outside.

The Market Solution
One way to accomplish governance in the public interest could be the market. According to economic theory, if consumers had sufficient information and resources and providers were truly competitive (among other conditions) the market would allocate resources among health services and among health and other needs both optimally and automatically.

The advantage of the market is that explicit public governance is unnecessary. Government need only maintain the conditions for a free market. The providers are held accountable to social need by their need to offer services consumers are willing to buy. The consumers are prevented from spending more on health than is socially rational because, one way or another, they have to pay the full marginal cost of care. The tradeoff of benefit and cost is forced, as it must be, but the burden of it is dispersed to the individual patients and providers, rather than concentrated in public decisions. Order and rationality are achieved by the Smithian "invisible hand" rather than by the visible, and much more invidious, hand of government.

No one pretends that the health system is significantly subject to the market now. Providers are not competitive because entry into the field is limited by licensure or certificate-of-need and price competition is limited by medical societies and third-party reimbursers. The producers, not consumers, seem to control demand, because patients usually defer to providers' decisions about what care is needed.[49] Cost-based reimbursement frees both providers and recipients from the need to weigh true costs and benefits in their decisions about which health services to consume.

Market-oriented reformers say the market has failed to control health costs only because it has not been tried. If the restrictions just mentioned were broken down, the market could succeed. There should be expanded licensure of providers, and price competition—including advertising—should be fostered. Cost-based or retrospective (post-service) reimbursement, which gives providers no incentive to economize on services or expenses, should be replaced by prospective reimbursement. Hospitals would be reimbursed only for the average costs of all hospitals (the rates would be different for different regions or types of hospitals) and other providers would be paid capitation fees per patient served per year.[50] Since income is fixed in advance of costs or the number of services provided, providers have an incentive, not to inflate costs, but to restrain them, as they would under market conditions.

There would be heavy reliance on Health Maintenance Organizations (HMOs), group practices aimed at community care, which would economize on service provision because of prospective reimbursement (capitation fees per enrollee) and competition among themselves.[51] Heavier cost-sharing requirements would be imposed on health insurance, forcing patients to pay a greater proportion of cost out-of-pocket and hence be more conscious of cost-benefit tradeoffs.[52]

The more pessimistic view, adopted here, is that the market solution is implausible for practical and more fundamental reasons. Obviously, if medical and provider interests have used public regulation to shield themselves from the market, they probably have the influence to prevent the market from being forced upon them. To enforce the market would take, perhaps, a greater exertion of state power than public governance. Hence, the political attraction of the "invisible hand" would be lost.

More important, the market model assumes that consumers are able to economize for themselves; that is, know their own preferences and confine spending to care which is worth its cost. In health, however, the patient almost always knows less than the provider about what services he needs and how much he is likely to profit by them.[53]

For these reasons, no society has trusted health care primarily to the market. The market presumes that individuals are self-reliant and able to choose for themselves. In fact, health problems are so threatening and imponderable that people seek to give up their independence and make themselves dependent on some authoritative individual or institution which will make decisions for them.[54] The institutions on which they rely must be the health professions, government, or some combination. And since, as we have already seen, the professional model probably cannot achieve cost control, the weakness of the market solution leads directly to public control.

Public Control

In the above analysis, the health system is already based mainly on governance, not the market. The providers govern patients for their own good. Public control would simply extend this principle at a higher level, with government controlling the providers for the good of society. Control would basically involve firm limits on provider reimbursement and on overall spending for health.

The basic idea behind public control is that the political marketplace can allocate resources rationally, where the economic market and delegation to the providers have failed. The political process will aggregate, express, and rank public preferences more accurately than individual buying and selling decisions can do because of market imperfections.[55]

I. STRUGGLES OVER GOVERNANCE

Public control is no panacea. It makes governance possible, not inevitable. It casts an institutional structure around the health system which it cannot evade, so that cost control is at last conceivable. But this structure only provides an arena for the struggles over governance described theoretically above. The burden of dealing with the providers and the public's demand for care must still be faced. The economic problem of cost control is internalized and becomes a political problem.

Though order could now be enforced on the providers, they would seek to influence it from within. They would seek to capture the regulatory agencies and escape cost controls,[56] as they virtually captured the Social Security Administration in the early years of Medicare.[57] They might in fact dominate the political marketplace as they now do the economic one.[58]

Whether they succeeded would depend critically on whether politicians and the general public could sustain an interest in health questions after the publicity surrounding initial enactments had passed. Interest group pressures for higher spending arise because the groups' interest in more spending for themselves always outweighs their interest, as taxpayers, in reduced spending. Cost control depends on the mobilization of the general public, which, alone, is more conscious of the cost than the benefits of government.[59]

Similarly, to achieve rationality through public control would require dealing with contradictory public attitudes toward spending. No doubt, the level of the health spending necessary to limit the health share of resources in the long run would be lower than people wished to face in the short run. There would be the danger that too severe limitations would divert resources into uncontrolled sectors of the health system or (assuming all sectors were controlled) into a black market for illicit services.[60]

A solution depends on effective leadership by health policy makers and deference to that leadership. Rationality requires that people subordinate immediate interests to the longer-term social benefit. Leaders persuade them to, essentially, by a combination of appeals to long-term consequences and personal relationship. The voter's trust of the leader gives him short-run reassurance and makes him willing to sacrifice short-term interests for the larger good.[61]

Any realistic approach to public control must accept wrestling with governance and eschew unpolitical solutions. This requires that an uneasy balance be struck and maintained between provider interests and the public pressure for accountability.

2. THE PUBLIC-UTILITY APPROACH

At one extreme, one step removed from cost-based reimbursement, is the public-utility model of determining payment rates for providers. The idea is to use economic analysis to pay the provider, like other utilities, only the rate he needs to stay in business assuming efficient operation.[62] It is supposed that analysis can separate true costs from the unnecessary costs due, heretofore, to inefficient cost-based reimbursement. The result may be a reimbursement rate paid prospectively or an incentive rate, under which the provider keeps part of the saving if costs are kept below income.

However, such rates have not shown significant cost savings compared to standard cost-based methods.[63] The reason seems to be that the provider and his costs still set the agenda for payment rates. The public, not the provider, still bears the burden of economizing—of adjusting costs and income to each other. This puts the provider in a strong bargaining position. The regulators are dependent on him for cost information, and they have great difficulty telling necessary costs from unnecessary ones.[64] Further, they cannot compare him to other providers easily because there is no common accounting system and no agreed classification system for units and quality of care.[65]

The basic illusion is the idea that the cost problem can have a technical, rather than a political, solution. It is the attempt to set rates objectively that shifts discussion toward concrete costs, where the provider dominates. For effective cost control, government must play a more authoritative role. Reimbursement must respond not only to the provider's costs but government's needs, meaning other claims to resources. Rates must not only reflect provider costs, but *define* them, by setting an income exogenously, within which costs must live. Such rates will look arbitrary alongside rates calculated with reference to the provider alone. But then some of the provider's costs will look unjustified to government.[66] As in all governance, no uniquely right solution is possible. Rather, there is mutual adjustment between incommensurable perspectives. The outcome cannot be fully rationalized by either.

3. THE RADICAL POLITICAL APPROACH

At the other extreme are radical critics of the health system who would sacrifice the providers completely to public accountability. From this perspective, the cost crisis is only a symptom of a larger evil: a network of provider and other interests dedicated to profit and exploitation rather than the service of society.[67] Some critics also argue dialectically that fundamental contradictions, such as technology and dependence on public funding and regulation, are driving the system toward collapse.[68] The solution to control and allocation problems is to expropriate the providers. There should be complete public control of the

health system, not only at the level of government,[69] but through democratiza-
tion of provider institutions.[70] This will lead to a dispersal of the medical monopolies and the return of care to popular control.

Despite appearances, this solution is no less unpolitical than public utility
regulation. There the providers were insufficiently constrained; here, their independence is completely abrogated. The political problem is then supposed to
disappear. The provider interests are no longer distinct from society. They are
merged into a political marketplace—"the people"—as seamless as the ideal
economic market of the market reformers or the simulated market of the utility
regulators.

In fact, providers could not function without some autonomy. They have
to be able to make an income and invest for the future, even though these activities can appear to exploit the public in the short run. Rationality requires that
some separation be made between what seems immediately moral and what is
necessary for the longer-term social good. As a practical matter, the providers
have to be governed by an uneasy combination of regulation and incentives,
meaning freedom to operate in the market or make money from public reimbursement.[71]

Once this is admitted, simplicities disappear and moral and intellectual relativism returns. Control comes to mean a mix of fiat and freedom, not wholly
understandable from either a governmental or market perspective. Such anti-
monies are in the nature of governance. No approach to public control which
does not embrace them can hope to succeed.

4. TOP-END BUDGET CONTROL

Public control must provide an institutional structure within which issues of
governance can be wrestled with fruitfully and resolved in the public interest.
Control will very likely take the form of central control of spending, coupled
with decentralized administration and delivery of services. Most Western countries seem to be gravitating toward this kind of system, through gradual reform
of insurance funds and administrative arrangements.[72] The reason for the grav-
itation may be that this structure aids governance, or the political crafting of
solutions to the problems of order and rationality.

A fixed budget would be set for federal reimbursement programs by the
federal government, coupled with restrictions on the spending of private insurance systems, should any remain. Then, allocations from the budget would be
made downward through the administrative system on the basis of need or population—to states, local health agencies, and providers. In each locality, the
agency or local medical society would adjust reimbursement or capitation rates
to keep service provision within the budget, or some other means of rationing
services would be used.[73]

The essence of the system is to reverse the flow of spending decisions in the health system. With existing, largely retrospective reimbursement, providers and patients make the initial decisions, and the burden of matching costs with resources is borne by higher levels. With top-end budgeting, spending is first determined at the top level, and the burden of economizing—of reducing costs to income—is devolved to lower levels and the providers. The effect is to force cost-benefit tradeoffs at every level and improve the efficiency of service provision.[74]

Centralized budgeting facilitates a solution to the problem of rationality. The essential spending decisions are sited at the point in the system at which health costs are most salient politically and health benefits least so. At the center, the general public pressure for lower taxes is strong, while the specific groups and individuals who might be denied services may be less visible. Federal budget cutters can claim not to know how limited funding will affect particular sufferers, because the allocation of funds to services would be made at lower levels. This eases the moral problem democratic government has denying benefits to people.

At the same time, decentralized administration eases the problem of order by siting the regulatory authorities at the local level, where they are less distant and impersonal. The structure, of course, should be responsive to the local population as a whole, and not simply provider interests. This requires that health planning agencies be an integral part of state and local government and accountable to it, not separate corporations as they often are now.[75]

Decentralized administration also eases the considerable bureaucratic problems of a large public organization. Since public regulation is, by definition, outside the market, the agencies that enforce it face no automatic incentives to be efficient. The agencies that run Medicare and Medicaid have been notably ineffective at cost control.[76] Bureaucratic inefficiency is one of the strongest arguments against a nationalized health system and in favor of the present pluralist system.[77]

A decentralized structure diminishes the amount of information any one agency has to process—the major problem for any bureaucracy.[78] The attempt to administer an entire national health system centrally would create insufferable planning and coordination problems.[79] With decentralization, the organizations involved are smaller and more numerous, more akin to present arrangements.

Conclusion

This discussion has concentrated on the problem of governance inherent in public control of the health system. Only a limited attempt was made to argue an abstract case for public control, as against the other proposed strategies for cost control. Whether public control, taken in the round, is preferable to the other approaches is an important issue. The question may be unanswerable in the abstract.

It may also be irrelevant. Since other means of restraining costs have failed, there is no practicable alternative to some form of public control. The discussion of the alternatives in abstract terms eventually becomes, in itself, an evasion of governance. Government does not choose its actions as much as respond to necessity. Public control is the *last* option, whether or not it seems a good one. Commitment eventually drives out deliberation. Public officials ultimately say that public control must succeed, whether or not commentators say it will.

The more necessary public control seems, the more, in fact, it is likely to succeed. Control entails struggles over governance. Success requires that these struggles be resolved in the general interest. In the nature of governance, what serves the general good cannot be known in advance of the political process. However, a widespread sense of scarcity is necessary to support the social interest in economy against provider and patient pressures for more and more resources. From this vigilance, and ultimately from this alone, can come the political resolution to wrestle with health governance over the long haul.

NOTES

1. Robert M. Gibson and Marjorie Smith Mueller, "National Health Expenditures, Fiscal Year 1976," *Social Security Bulletin* 40, no. 4 (April 1977): 4.
2. Joseph P. Newhouse, Charles E. Phelps, and William B. Schwartz, "Policy Options and the Impact of National Health Insurance," *New England Journal of Medicine* 290, no. 24 (13 June 1974): 1354.
3. Social Security Act (as amended through 4 January 1975) and related laws, sec. 1801.
4. There were, and are, important restrictions. Medicare provides hospital care, but only limited long-term care and no prescription drugs. Medicaid covers hospital, nursing home, and physician care, but less essential services are at the discretion of state programs.
5. Medicare covers people drawing social security, old age, survivors, or disability benefits. Under Medicaid, welfare recipients are usually eligible, but states decide which of a number of other groups to cover. Eligibility thus varies widely but can extend to cover most of the needy.
6. Robert Stevens and Rosemary Stevens, *Welfare Medicine in America: A Case Study of Medicaid* (New York: Free Press, 1974), pts. 2-4.
7. Gibson and Mueller, "National Health Expenditures," pp. 4, 11, 13.
8. Howard N. Newman, "Medicare and Medicaid," *Annals of the American Academy of Political and Social Science* 399 (January 1972): 114-24; Rashi Fein, "On Achieving Access and Equity in Health Care," in *Economic Aspects of Health Care,* ed. John B. McKinlay (New York: Prodist, 1973), pp. 39-41.

9. Edward Kennedy, *In Critical Condition: The Crisis in America's Health Care* (New York: Simon and Schuster, 1972); Karen Davis, *National Health Insurance: Benefits, Costs, and Consequences* (Washington, D.C.: Brookings Institution, 1975), pp. 31-57, 68-69.

10. U.S. Congress, Senate, Committee on Finance, "Medicare and Medicaid: Problem, Issues, and Alternatives," 91st Cong., 1st sess., 1970.

11. Kenneth Arrow, *Social Choice and Individual Values* (New York: Wiley, 1951).

12. Mancur Olson, *The Logic of Collective Action: Public Goods and the Theory of Groups* (Cambridge, Mass.: Harvard University Press, 1971).

13. Sheldon S. Wolin, *Politics and Vision: Continuity and Innovation in Western Political Thought* (London: Allen and Unwin, 1961), p. 61.

14. Arrow, *Social Choice and Individual Values*.

15. Guido Calabresi, "Comment," in *Ethics of Health Care*, ed. Laurence R. Tancredi (Washington, D.C.: Institute of Medicine, National Academy of Sciences, 1974), pp. 48-55.

16. Max Weber, "Politics as a Vocation," in *From Max Weber: Essays in Sociology*, ed. and trans. H. H. Gerth and C. Wright Mills (New York: Oxford University Press, 1958), pp. 115-28.

17. John Fry, "The Agonies of Medicine in the USA," *International Journal of Health Services* 3, no. 3 (Summer 1973): 502-3.

18. Fein, "Achieving Access and Equity," pp. 41-49.

19. A. J. G. Priest, "Possible Adaptation of Public Utility Concepts in the Health Care Field," *Law and Contemporary Problems* 35, no. 4 (Autumn 1970): 841.

20. See, for example, Department of Health, Education, and Welfare, *Report of the Task Force on Medicaid and Related Programs* (Washington, D.C.: U.S. Government Printing Office, 1970), pp. 75-82; Lester Breslow, "Political Jurisdiction, Voluntarism, and Health Planning," *American Journal of Public Health* 58, no. 7 (July 1968): 1147-53.

21. Anne R. Somers, "The Nation's Health: Issues for the Future," *Annals of the American Academy of Political and Social Science* 399 (January 1972): 171-73.

22. Davis, *National Health Insurance*, chap. 8.

23. Nathan Glazer, "Perspectives on Health Care," *The Public Interest*, no. 31 (Spring 1973): 115-25.

24. *Hospital Statistics*, 1976 ed. (Chicago: American Hospital Association, 1976), p. vi.

25. Paul Starr, "Too Many Doctors?" *Washington Post* (13 March 1977), p. C3; Lawrence Myer, "New U.S. Problem: Too Many Doctors," *Washington Post* (6 July 1977), pp. A1, A12.

26. Nathan Glazer, "Paradoxes of Health Care," *The Public Interest*, no. 22 (Winter 1971): 67-69.

27. Robert Maxwell, *Health Care: The Growing Dilemma*, 2d ed. (New York: McKinsey, 1975), p. 14.

28. Victor R. Fuchs, *Who Shall Live? Health, Economics, and Social Choice* (New York: Basic, 1974), pp. 30-55; Ivan Illich, *Medical Nemesis: The Expropriation of Health* (New York: Random House, 1976), pp. 13-36.

29. Senate Committee on Finance, "Medicare and Medicaid," pp. 29-44.
30. Clark C. Havighurst and James F. Blumstein, "Coping with Quality/Cost Tradeoffs in Medical Care: The Role of PSROs," *Northwestern University Law Review* 70, no. 1 (March-April 1975): 9-20, 25, 25n.; Martin Feldstein, "The Welfare Loss of Excessive Health Insurance," *Journal of Political Economy* 81, no. 2, pt. 1 (March-April 1973): 251-80.
31. Maxwell, *Health Care,* p. 5.
32. Michael Lynch, "The Physician Shortage: The Economists' Mirror," *Annals of the American Academy of Political and Social Science* 399 (January 1972): 82-88.
33. Illich, *Medical Nemesis,* pp. 37-208.
34. Fuchs, *Who Shall Live?,* pp. 64-67, 144; George Teeling-Smith, "More Money into the Health Sector: Is This the Answer?" *International Journal of Health Services* 3, no. 3 (Summer 1973): 493-500.
35. Fuchs, *Who Shall Live?,* pp. 5-7, 17-29, 127-28; Maxwell, *Health Care,* pp. 7-13.
36. Illich, *Medical Nemesis,* pp. 209-75.
37. Havighurst and Blumstein, "Coping with Quality/Cost Tradeoffs," pp. 20-25.
38. David Mechanic, "Human Problems and the Organization of Health Care," *Annals of the American Academy of Political and Social Science* 399 (January 1972): 1-11; Clark C. Havighurst, "Health Maintenance Organizations and the Market for Health Services," *Law and Contemporary Problems* 35, no. 4 (Autumn 1970): 793.
39. Hannah Arendt, *The Human Condition* (Chicago: University of Chicago Press, 1958), chap. 2.
40. Havighurst and Blumstein, "Coping with Quality/Cost Tradeoffs," p. 19.
41. Paul M. Elwood, Jr., "Models for Organizing Health Services and Implications for Legislative Proposals," *Organizational Issues in the Delivery of Health Services,* ed. Irving K. Zola and John B. McKinlay (New York: Prodist, 1974), pp. 67-95.
42. Senate Committee on Finance, "Medicare and Medicaid," p. 2.
43. Havighurst and Blumstein, "Coping with Quality/Cost Tradeoffs," pp. 25-30, 38-60.
44. Albert R. Jonsen and Andre E. Hellegers, "Conceptual Foundations for an Ethics of Medical Care," in *Ethics of Health Care,* ed. Laurence R. Tancredi (Washington, D.C.: Institute of Medicine, National Academy of Science, 1974), pp. 3-20.
45. John Holahan and Bruce Stuart, *Controlling Medicaid Utilization Patterns* (Washington, D.C.: Urban Institute, 1977), pp. 29-114.
46. Milton I. Roemer and J. Friedman, *Doctors in Hospitals: Medical Staff Organization and Hospital Performance* (Baltimore: Johns Hopkins Press, 1971).
47. Richard W. Scott, "Some Implications of Organization Theory for Research on Health Services," in *Organizational Issues in the Delivery of Health Services,* ed. Irving K. Zola and John B. McKinlay (New York: Prodist, 1974), pp. 3-27.
48. Nathan Glazer, "Perspectives on Health Care," pp. 62-67, 71-73.

49. John Holahan, *Financing Health Care for the Poor: The Medicaid Experience* (Lexington, Mass.: Heath, 1975), pp. 5-6, 70, 111-12; John Holahan, *Physician Supply, Peer Review and Use of Health Services in Medicaid* (Washington, D.C.: Urban Institute, 1976), pp. 37-46.
50. Fuchs, *Who Shall Live?*, pp. 100-102.
51. Havighurst, "Health Maintenance Organizations."
52. Mark V. Pauly, *Medical Care at Public Expense: A Study in Applied Welfare Economics* (New York: Praeger, 1971).
53. Kenneth Arrow, "Government Decision Making and the Preciousness of Life," in *Ethics of Health Care,* ed. Laurence R. Tancredi (Washington, D.C.: Institute of Medicine, National Academy of Sciences, 1974), pp., 33-47.
54. Kenneth Arrow, "Uncertainty and the Welfare Economics of Medical Care," *American Economic Review* 53, no. 5 (December 1963): 941-73; Kenneth Boulding, "The Concept of Need for Health Services," in *Economic Aspects of Health Care,* ed. John B. McKinlay (New York: Prodist, 1973), pp. 17-19.
55. Vincente Navarro, "A Critique of the Present and Proposed Strategies for Redistributing Resources in the Health Sector and a Discussion of Alternatives," *Medical Care* 12, no. 9 (September 1974): 721-42.
56. Clark C. Havighurst, "Regulation of Health Facilities by 'Certificate of Need,' " *Virginia Law Review* 59, no. 7 (October 1973): 1178-1215.
57. Theodore R. Marmor, *The Politics of Medicare* (Chicago: Aldine, 1973), chap. 5.
58. Theodore R. Marmor, "Politics, Public Policy, and Medical Inflation" (unpublished paper, 1975).
59. Anthony Downs, "Why the Government Budget Is Too Small in a Democracy," *World Politics* 12 (1960): 541-63.
60. Somers, "The Nation's Health," pp. 168-71.
61. This was Jeremy Bentham's ultimate solution to the problem of rationality in representative democracy. See Lawrence M. Mead, "Bentham's Theory of Political Development" (Ph.D. diss., Harvard University, 1973), pp. 475-82.
62. Priest, "Possible Adaptation of Public Utility Concepts," pp. 844-47.
63. John Holahan, et al., *Altering Medicaid Provider Reimbursement Methods* (Washington, D.C.: Urban Institute, 1977), pp. 70-93.
64. James F. Blumstein and Michael Zubkoff, "Perspectives on Government Policy in the Health Sector," *Milbank Memorial Fund Quarterly* 51, no. 3 (Summer 1973): 415-18.
65. Priest, "Possible Adaptation of Public Utility Concepts," pp. 841-42; Sylvester E. Berki, "The Pricing of Hospital Services," in *Public Prices for Public Products,* ed. Selma Mushkin (Washington, D.C.: Urban Institute, 1972), pp. 351-70.
66. The effectiveness of "arbitrary" cost controls is shown by the sharp reduction of health sector inflation during fiscal 1972-74, when the health system, like other sectors, was subject to price controls. See Gibson and Mueller, "National Health Expenditures," p. 3.

67. Barbara Ehrenreich and John Ehrenreich, *The American Health Empire: Power, Profits, and Politics* (New York: Random House, 1970); Robert R. Alford, "The Political Economy of Health Care: Dynamics Without Change," *Politics and Society* 2, no. 2 (Winter 1972): 127-64; Howard S. Berliner, "The Origins of Health Insurance for the Aged," *International Journal of Health Services* 3, no. 3 (Summer 1973): 465-74.

68. Sander Kelman, "Toward a Political Economy of Medical Care," *Inquiry* 8, no. 3 (September 1971): 30-38; Eric H. Helt, "Economic Determinism: A Model of the Political Economy of Medical Care," *International Journal of Health Services* 3, no. 3 (Summer 1973): 475-85.

69. Illich, *Medical Nemesis,* pp. 221-75; Alford, "Political Economy of Health Care," p. 164.

70. Ehrenreich and Ehrenreich, *American Health Empire,* chaps. 10-19; Navarro, "Critique of Present and Proposed Strategies," pp. 737-40.

71. Anne R. Somers, *Hospital Regulation: The Dilemma of Public Policy* (Princeton, N.J.: Princeton University Industrial Relations Section, 1969).

72. Christa Altenstetter, "New Dimensions in Comparative Health Analysis: The Importance of Organizational Arrangements for Policy Performance" (paper presented to the International Conference on Changing National-Subnational Relations in Health: Opportunities and Constraints, National Institutes of Health, 24-26 May 1976); Anne R. Somers, "The Rationalization of Health Services: A Universal Priority," *Inquiry* 8, no. 1 (March 1971): 48-60.

73. Fry, "Agonies of Medicine," p. 504; Maxwell, *Health Care,* pp. 30, 35, 45-46; Milton I. Roemer, "Nationalized Medicare for America" *Trans-Action,* September 1971, pp. 31-36; David D. Rutstein, *Blueprint for Medical Care* (Cambridge, Mass.: MIT Press, 1974).

74. Maxwell, *Health Care,* pp. 30-31.

75. Navarro, "Critique of Present and Proposed Strategies," pp. 735-37.

76. Senate Committee on Finance, "Medicare and Medicaid," chaps. 14-15; Department of Health, Education, and Welfare, *Report of the Task Force,* pp. 53-70, 119-26; Sylvia A. Law, *Blue Cross: What Went Wrong?* (New Haven, Conn.: Yale University Press, 1974), chap. 4; Lawrence M. Mead, *Institutional Analysis: An Approach to Implementation Problems in Medicaid* (Washington, D.C.: Urban Institute, 1977), pp. 83-97, 114-34.

77. Harry Schwartz, "Health Care in America: A Heretical Diagnosis," *Saturday Review,* 14 August 1971, p. 35.

78. Anthony Downs, *Inside Bureaucracy* (Boston: Little, Brown, 1967), pp. 112-210.

79. Davis, *National Health Insurance,* p. 26.

John Ehrenreich

12. Toward a Healing Society

Viewing the nation's medical care system as a microcosm of the wider society, radical critics have repeatedly diagnosed the United States as a sick society. Most radical critiques have been concerned with the problem of access and distribution—who gets what kind of health services—but, more and more, radical criticism is questioning the nature of scientific medicine itself, doubting its efficacy and directing attention to the social relations it engenders.

The traditional political-economic critique concentrates on the inequitable distribution of health services: The main problem is that beneficial services are not available to those who can't pay for them.[1] The more recent cultural critique contends that modern medical care does not consist of essentially salutary techniques but is frequently either useless or harmful. The "scientific" knowledge of the doctors is sometimes not knowledge at all, but rather social messages wrapped up in technical language. Above all, both the doctor-patient relationship and the entire structure of medical services reproduce the exploitative relations of the larger society from which many of our social and institutional problems, medical and otherwise, derive.[2]

Both the political-economic critics and the cultural critics make compelling indictments of contemporary medical care. But a word on their limitations is in order.

The political-economic critique follows the conventional Marxist pattern of analysis: Medical care is treated as a commodity like any other; the important things about medical care can then be derived from the laws of production and distribution. (Of course, in the case of medical care and other services, production and distribution occur simultaneously.) The primary problems identified by the political-economic critque are distributional: Poor and working-class people in the United States and elsewhere do not have access to adequate care. By contrast, in a socialist society, health care would be socialized and everyone would have equal access to high quality treatment.

But medical care as we know it in a capitalist society is not just an unambiguously useful commodity like shoes or swimming lessons. Like many other more complex commodities, it is permeated with capitalist priorities and capitalist social relations. The distribution of medical services, the transaction between doctor and patient, and medical technology itself (which is based on certain assumptions about the nature of disease and its cure, and the relationship of individuals to their own bodies) embody the social values created by capitalist society. It is by no means clear that we want to pass these along to a socialist society; socialized medicine is not necessarily socialist medicine.

Medicine is not unique in this respect, of course. Apparently, objective technology is penetrated by and recreates the social relations in all facets of the society which developed it; the single family housing unit presupposes (and creates) a noncollective mode of living; individual automobiles imply an entire conception of energy, time, and space use; assembly line production assumes and reinforces the separation and antagonistic relationship between mental and manual labor; and so forth. In medicine this is not quite so obvious. For one thing, an unusual amount of mystery surrounds the technology (the result, in part, of doctors' efforts to keep their knowledge esoteric); for another, the presumably benevolent purposes of medicine mask the antagonistic social relations built into it.

The political-economic critique, overemphasizes the commodity nature of medical care. The healing relation is not simply a commercial transaction but is also a direct relationship between two people (usually of sharply differing class, sex, or race), unmediated by the commodity form. The doctor is actually in there, touching and penetrating your body, asking intimate personal questions, giving you orders to follow at your life's peril; he sympathizes and cares or scorns and disparages. The political-economic critic, to whom the personal interactions which go on in the doctor's office are "unmaterialist" or of no interest, gives an extraordinary example of what Marx called the "fetishism of commodities," in which relations between people can be understood only in the form of relations between the products of their labor.

To be sure, one aspect of the relationship between doctor and patient is a commodity relationship—the doctor as producer and seller of medical care, the patient as purchaser and consumer. But simultaneously, it is a direct relationship of personal support, of domination, and even, in some cases, of physical exploitation. It is hard to see how it could be much more "material." Marx and Engels' comment in *The German Ideology* reminds us that a "materialist" analysis involves more than "economic" activities:

> We must begin by stating the first premise of all human existence, and therefore of all history, the premise namely that men must be in a position to live in order to be able to "make history." But life involves before everything else eating and drinking, a habitation, clothing, and many other things [including, presumably, care of the sick or disabled]. . . . The production of life . . . appears as a double relationship: on the one hand as a natural, on the other hand as a social relationship.[3]

That medical technology and healing activities contain what Marx calls "natural" relationships is far from a matter of purely academic interest. Understanding those relationships is the key to understanding how medicine, as it has gained in technical mastery over people's bodily processes, has lost its ties to people's daily mode of life, to individual and social feelings about birth, death, suffering, pain, and dependency. This, in turn, helps in grasping such contemporary phenomena as the decline of faith in medicine, the continued popularity of premodern healing modalities, the investment with political content of supposedly technical medical questions such as the effectiveness of Laetrile, and the spread of "neurotic" dependency on the medical system with consequently soaring utilization and equally soaring expenditures.

The cultural critique thus has major political implications for health policy. The question increasingly raised by conservatives is why should money be poured into health care, producing high utilization of medical services without corresponding improvements in health. Within the narrow political-economic framework, this reasonable question is unanswerable. Conversely, the lack of mass popular support for national health insurance or other bureaucratic forms of socialized medicine reflects the unarticulated understanding that there is something very wrong with medicine as we have come to practice it.

The political-economic critique emerges out of a consciousness of scarcity and is less concerned about the nature of medical services than their existence at all. In contrast, the cultural critique emerges out of a consciousness of plenty. It should not be thought, however, that the cultural critique is thereby irrelevant to the poor nations of the world or to the needs of poor people in the rich countries. It may be true that it is only when we have the luxury of plenty that we can, for the first time, examine closely just what it is that we have plenty of. But the insights of the cultural critique about medical care, if not the conditions under which it has reached them, are highly significant for medical care in any society.

The cultural critique's concern for the overall efficacy, safety, and social impact of Western-style scientific medicine has wide application, to the poor as well as to the more affluent, to the industrialized socialist countries as well as to the industrialized capitalist countries, to the developing nations as well as to the developed. In fact, the cultural critique as it evolved in the affluent West drew in part on the parallel medical approaches of the decidedly nonaffluent Chinese. Especially during and since the Cultural Revolution of 1966-69, the Chinese health care system has embraced many of the policies advocated by cultural critics in the United States and England, such as the radical deprofessionalization of medical care (e.g., barefoot doctors, shortened academic training of doctors); promotion of egalitarian relations between doctors and patients and other health workers; integration of holistic, traditional modes of medicine with Western modes; involvement of patients as active participants in their own cures; and concern with the social and political roots of disease.[4]

Many aspects of these policies stem from broader social and political concerns rather than from an analysis of the problem of medical care per se. But, as I shall discuss, as soon as the assumption that medical care is a commodity is reached, the fusion of questions of health policy and of overall political and social values is exposed.

The various analyses of scientific medicine which I call the cultural critique are not uniformly applicable to nonaffluent situations. Parts of the cultural critique, in their extreme formulations at least, show clearly their origins in what the Chinese would call a "fat" country, and exhibit a serious lack of concern about the scarcity situation which characterizes medical care for most of the world (and for a considerable part of the United States as well). To take an obvious example, when Ivan Illich insists that "a world of optimal and widespread health is obviously a world of minimal and only occasional medical intervention,"[5] from the perspective of those who now have "minimal and only occasional medical intervention," he has "obviously" overstated the case against modern medicine to the point of vitiating the entire cultural critique.

A Failure of Health

Modern medicine does work in preventing death and reducing pain and suffering, even if less often and less effectively than its admirers have claimed. For example, in a 1968 National Academy of Sciences study of the impact of prenatal and postnatal care on infant birth weight and mortality, women were classified according to their ethnic group, to medical and social criteria indicating whether their babies were at high or low risk (e.g., a tubercular mother or a mother living in a slum area would be placed in the high-risk category), and to the adequacy of the medical care they received. In every ethnic and risk group, the more adequate the medical care, the more likely was the birth of a healthy baby. Among low-risk mothers, improvements in medical care above a certain fairly low level had relatively little effect; but among higher-risk mothers, every increment in medical care markedly improved the baby's chances of survival. Other studies have come to similar conclusions: statistically, at least, above a relatively modest level of medical care services, the marginal impact of additional medical services is low. But below that level of services, the reverse is true. Providing medical services, even in the absence of changes in environment, housing, nutrition, etc., produces significant improvements in health.[6] And, of course, numerous clinical trials and much clinical experience provide evidence for the beneficial impact of medical care in the case of particular diseases in individuals.

How, then, can we explain the overall failure of health to respond to additional inputs of medical care, as charged by Illich, Powles, and other cultural critics? We may, of course, simply be using inappropriate measures of health status. More likely, the losses to health resulting from the combination of incompetent medical practice, poor distribution and low accessibility of services, poor patient compliance with doctors' instructions, growing environmental hazards, and clinical iatrogenesis balance off the gains in health produced by medical intervention.

Cultural critics also have denounced medicine as a mode of extending bourgeois cultural and political hegemony. Medicine, they argue, produces dependency and reduces individual autonomy; it reinforces racism and sexism; it depoliticizes a variety of social (class, race, gender) issues making them seem like individual problems. In sum, it is a major instrument of bourgeois domination. All these criticisms seem to be relevant not only to our own situation but to those who presently lack care and are seeking access to medical services and desiring to construct new health systems.

Medicine does have these effects, among others, but legitimate concern can all too easily fall prey to a kind of snobbery. The complex dialectical interplay of both fundamental and manipulated needs for dependency and autonomy on the part of patients, of benevolence and of domination and greed on the part of doctors and health institutions, necessitates dissection, not mere denunciation. The dependency and passivity characteristic of modern medical care, are sought by patients as well as imposed by doctors; they reflect not only the interests of the doctors and of giant corporations but also the expectations of patients. Medicine as practiced in the United States may reinforce dependency and passivity in the face of bourgeois domination; it does not, however, create them.

Toward a Socialist Health Policy

These two styles of radical criticism are, in part, in opposition to each other. The incompatibility between the two seems especially evident when medical services are cut back. With assaults on social services of all kinds the order of the day in the industrialized countries, restoring the services available a few years ago seems highly desirable. In this context, the cultural critique, which stresses the limits of modern medicine, seems to play right into the hands of conservatives. To policy makers looking to justify cutbacks in health services or trying to resist popular pressures for expensive national health insurance programs, the cultural critique provides a certain "liberal" legitimacy. (It is, of course, that part of the cultural critique which insists upon the "uselessness" of medical care that is seized upon; fiscal conservatives have not, to my knowledge, argued that health services should be reduced because they are inherently racist and sexist, or because they help preserve and legitimate the status quo.)

Conversely, hard times have led many liberals and radicals to reject the cultural critique entirely. It seems evident to them that the perception of scarcity, not the dangers of plenty, is the grievance out of which a movement to demand the restoration and expansion of social services can come. Some go so far as to drop even the more radical versions of the political-economic critique as politically impractical, replacing, for instance, the demand for a national health service with a demand for a national health insurance system (i.e., a system to finance care which would remain privately delivered and controlled).[7] Other critics would preserve aspects of the cultural critique, but only nominally; they relegate changes in the nature of health care and the meaning of health to some far-off, postrevolutionary period, when the class control of health institutions has changed.[8]

But to limit the critique of medicine to complaints about its scarcity is to surrender the insights gained in the last few years. It is saying that despite the powerful critique of medical care of the last decade, we will take any crumbs given to us. This, of course, is precisely one of the purposes of cutbacks and recession in capitalist society: to make people satisfied with, even grateful for, much less than they had come to expect and demand.

The dilemma is a familiar one in the history of radical movements. On the one hand, a "cultural critique" of existing institutions seems irrelevant in the face of existing scarcity. The tendency is to put it off until some affluent, postrevolutionary, and "postscarcity" period. On the other hand, the struggle around the distribution of commodities, when the demand for these commodities and the commodities themselves have been hideously deformed by bourgeois social relations, risks falling into the narrowest, most limited reformism. "Reform or revolution"—upon the pole of this dichotomy, the left has been stuck for more than half a century.

How can we escape this dilemma? How do we build a movement that can go from what we have to what is implied by the full radical critique of medical care, considering that even what we have now is endangered? Much of the argument between proponents of the two schools of radical thought seems to me sterile and unable to provide insight into this question. To develop a socialist health policy we must create a dialectical understanding of the crisis in medical care which draws from and integrates both the political-economic and cultural concerns.

To begin, we must reject the belief that the two approaches to criticizing medical care are actually contradictory. It is only the stagnation of mass movements in the last few years that makes them seem incompatible. If there were a large-scale popular demand for improved health care, the two critiques would not appear to be in conflict. Conversely, it is only by connecting the two critiques that a base for such a popular movement is possible.

First, neither the demands growing out of the political-economic critique nor the demands growing out of the cultural critique can be realized except through a mass movement. The vested power of the doctors, drug companies, insurance companies, etc., can only be overcome through a massive popular upsurge. On the face of the matter, some of the demands growing out of the cultural critique—for example, a health system based on more self-help, less dependency on professional medical care, an approach to health emphasizing the importance of personal habits such as eating, exercise, smoking—do not appear to require such confrontations with economic and political power. However, they do require major changes in how people perceive themselves, their bodies, their relationships to others, and an unleashing of people's imaginations. It is only under conditions of massive involvement in a social movement that these changes are likely to occur on a wide scale.

Moreover, a mass popular movement could readily embrace the demands growing out of both critiques, as in the 1960s. The cultural critique grew in large measure, out of the radical community and feminist movements. This suggests that the idea that the political-economic demand for "more" grows out of scarcity and the cultural demand for "different" grows out of plenty is, perhaps, too simple and static. Mounting scarcity can produce passivity, as we have seen repeatedly in the last few years. It is in the perception that "more" is possible, even though it has not yet been achieved, that stimulates people to examine their own experience, to imagine how they would like services to be, and hence to experiment with alternatives. In the absence of a mass movement to demand better health care, the demands stemming from the two modes of criticism of medical care seem opposed. But the opposition is illusory and disappears in the context of a popular movement.

Finally, it seems hard to imagine that any large and effective movement could develop if it did not emphasize both the need for more services and the need for a different approach to health altogether. A movement will not develop if it does not offer people the hope of increasing services to meet perceived needs which now go unmet. But if people also perceive that there is something very wrong with the services they have, they will not join a movement that only offers them more of the same. The lack of mass enthusiasm (though not of vague, passive support) for national health insurance is instructive. Why should anyone get excited about another bureaucracy to help them pay for services which they know are inadequate? Would not a movement which held out the vision not of more hospital beds and clinics but of a caring society, not of paying for ever more medical care but of reducing dependency on medical institutions be more likely to capture people's imaginations?

What Is Socialist Medicine?

It is evident that a socialist health system would offer high-quality, dignified, readily available health services of all kinds on an equitable basis, regardless of geographic location, race or nationality, or ability to pay. Although it is beyond the scope of this chapter to argue the case fully, if such a system is not to become a bottomless pit devouring money and placing its institutional priorities ahead of its patients' needs, it must take the form of a decentralized, community and worker controlled, national health service, rather than either national health insurance or a uniform, bureaucratically centralized national health service.

In addition, a socialist health system would be compelled to deal with the social and environmental causes of bad health, eliminating poverty, and its ill-effects on housing, nutrition, and schools; eliminating or sharply reducing air and water pollution; as well as combating unhealthy life styles (e.g., smoking, lack of exercise).

To further examine a socialist health system, the mystification of medical care imposed by its complex technology and by its historical appearance as a commodity must be peeled away. Medicine is the mechanism by which a society deals with human biological interdependency—with death, birth, pain; with care of the young, the sick, the disabled, and the aged. It is fundamentally a social, not a technical or commercial relationship. It is embedded in the social relationships of the overall society and expresses the values of the broader society. To ask what kind of medical care we want is to ask some very basic questions about the kind of society we want. I should like to conclude this essay by exploring a few of the problems in medical care such a perspective suggests.

The Problem of Dependency

The cultural critique focuses attention on the way in which the medical system fosters and abuses dependency. To take an extreme case, Ivan Illich has argued that increasing access to medical care would merely increase what he considers socially debilitating individual dependency, and has called for a radical demedicalization of society in which people should learn to cope autonomously with pain, sickness, or disability. Illich's demand is echoed in the growing cries of many people for autonomous control over their own bodies, even in situations where doctors would consider major medical intervention. The number of home deliveries is rising rapidly; the self-help concept spreads; and a variety of health fads (e.g., herbal remedies and massage therapies) have become extremely popular. However, rejecting all medical technology is, at the very least, a self-destructive form of "autonomy," since some of it is useful, though inappropriate for untrained hands. In any case, the replacement of dependency on doctors with dependency on midwives and friends is not a rejection of dependency per se, but a redirecting of dependency.

How can the needs for autonomy and dependency be reconciled? The major problem of the medical system is not that it generates dependency, but the kind of dependency and its social impact. What we have to develop is a medical system which acknowledges our need for autonomous control over our bodies and which accepts our need for dependency. Such a system should enhance autonomy but, when we feel the necessity to be dependent, should deal with the need in a dignified and nurturing way.

More broadly, we might ask whether the medical system should be the major mechanism for dealing with biological dependency. In the last half century or so, the medical system has increasingly assumed this role, taking over from the disintegrating family and community. Any society needs institutions to deal with dependency. The existence of mutual dependency with regard to biological functions is virtually the defining characteristic of humans as social animals. It is natural, not morbid, that people sometimes need to depend on others for care.

But is the medical system the right institution to do this? If not, what alternatives are there? Do we imagine that the family, with appropriate social supporting mechanisms, can once again take over the care of the aged, or the disabled? How useful, in this context, are images of the family drawn from other times (the patriarchal, extended family of preindustrial Europe) or from other places (the contemporary Chinese family, embedded in small, stable communities)? In any case, do we want to concentrate healing and caring in one social institution or spread them throughout a variety of them?

The Problem of Professionalism

In order to evolve a health care system that is both a curing system and a caring system, we must confront the problem of professionalism. In our system, professionalism is primarily a defense of status and privilege. Although doctors and other health professionals have defended professsionalism as a bulwark of quality, it has functioned more effectively as a mechanism to protect the professionals from scrutiny, to limit access to the occupation and to medical knowledge, and to preserve doctors' control over the medical system. To change the health system at all, much less to create a medical system which maximally utilizes self-help and mutual help and which encourages an active rather than a passive role for the patient, will require radical deprofessionalization.

We will have to expand radically the use of community health aides, to spread medical knowledge to patients and to nonphysician health workers, and to minimize the social distance between doctors and patients. It should be emphasized that deprofessionalization has nothing to do with eliminating the skills of the doctors. Skills are essential and incompetent people should not perform medical services—we have too much of that as it is! It is the privileges, the power, and the monopolization of medical knowledge that should be removed in an effort toward deprofessionalization.

However, in another sense, we have to *reprofessionalize* medical care. One of the traditional components of professionalism is the idea that providing health care is a calling, attended by a strong ethic of service. But years of control of the medical system by doctors in their narrow self-interests has resulted in the spread of apathy, cynicism, even callousness among both physicians and non-physician health workers, who have seen the impossibility of delivering decent health care under our present health system.

It seems to me urgent to build a health system in which the idea of health care as a calling can be restored. In the context of a capitalist society, however, the idea of selfless caring is considered masochistic. Stating this reemphasizes the magnitude of the social transformation required to have a humane health system. If socialized medicine means health care delivered by callous bureaucracies, like so many of our public hospitals and clinics today, we can hardly wonder that it fails to arouse public enthusiasm.

The Problem of Technology

What part of the technology of modern medicine is salvageable? Recall that a significant proportion of medicine's proudest claims to effectiveness may be false, and that a significant part of modern medical practice may do more physical harm than good. In any case, much of what doctors do in actual practice is not based on scientifically validated knowledge. For instance, a National Academy of Sciences panel, studying the evidence of effectiveness of prescription drugs marketed in the United States in the mid-1960s, found that fully one half of these drugs were either completely ineffective, ineffective in the form normally prescribed or, at best, "possibly effective." Doctors, despite their claims to be people of science, widely disregard scientific evidence. In the case of the antibiotic, Chloramphenicol, for example, doctors go on prescribing the drug in situations where its use is not indicated, despite the availability of alternative drugs and despite its widely publicized and occasionally lethal side effects.

The question, then, is not one of throwing out scientific medicine; it is whether medicine can *become* a science. This, in turn, raises questions about science's basic assumptions (in the sense of physics, chemistry, biology). The traditional natural sciences objectify the things they study; they have no place for consciousness or subjectivity. But human beings are conscious creatures; as I have repeatedly emphasized, the healing relationship is not merely physiological but psychological and social. Do biology, chemistry and physics form an adequate, appropriate and complete basis for a science of healing human beings? If not, what is the basis (or the limitations) of scientific medicine? The conditions of medical practice in capitalist society have not permitted this question to be raised seriously.

Medicine as a Rational Social Endeavor

In repudiating our present dependency on institutionalized medicine for all aspects of health care, it would be easy to embrace the opposite extreme—medical anarchy. Notions of rationality in determining methods of care, of discipline in obtaining and using skills, of belief in medical authority would be discarded; what feels good, physically or psychologically, would become the arbiter of the kind of medical care one would seek. Already signs of such a revolt against medicine as a rational and social endeavor abound, evidenced for example in the booming demand for almost certainly useless drugs such as Laetrile, and the widespread reliance on home remedies for serious and readily treatable ailments. Ultimately, the critical question to be grappled with is how to reconcile notions of individual freedom and dignity with a rational and social approach to healing technology.

Questions such as these make it clear that the problems of health and medicine cannot be treated as problems of technique, of administration, or of distribution, separate from the overall problems of social values and nonmedical social institutions. Questions of health policy are not narrow questions of how to reform the health system; they are among the most profound questions we can ask about the society in which we live.

NOTES

1. For examples of the "political-economic" critique, see *Medical Care for the American People* (Chicago: University of Chicago Press, 1932); Barbara and John Ehrenreich, *The American Health Empire: Power, Profits and Politics* (New York: Random House, 1970); Ed Cray, *In Failing Health* (Indianapolis: Bobbs-Merrill, 1970); T. Bodenheimer et al., *Billions for Bandaids* (San Francisco: Medical Committee for Human Rights, 1972); David Kotelchuck, ed., *Prognosis Negative: Crisis in the Health Care System* (New York: Vintage, 1976); Vincente Navarro, *Medicine Under Capitalism* (New York: Prodist, 1976).

2. The "cultural critique" is exemplified, in whole or in part, by such diverse books and articles as Rene Dubos, *The Mirage of Health* (New York: Harper, 1959); Thomas Szasz, *The Myth of Mental Illness* (New York: Harper, 1961); Thomas McKeown, *Medicine in Modern Society* (London: Allen & Unwin, 1965); Barbara Seaman, *Free and Female* (Garden City, N.Y.: Doubleday, 1972); Barbara Ehrenreich and Deidre English, *Complaints and Disorders: The Sexual Politics of Sickness* (Old Westbury: Feminist Press, 1973); John Powles, "On the Limitations of Modern Medicine," *Science, Medicine and Man* 1 (1973); Barbara and John Ehrenreich, "Medicine and Social Control," *Social Policy,* May-June 1974; Howard Waitzkin and Barbara Waterman, *The Exploitation of Illness in Capitalist Society* (Indianapolis: Bobbs-Merrill, 1974); Ivan Illich, *Medical Nemesis: Expropriation of Health* (New York: Pantheon, 1976).

3. Karl Marx and Frederick Engels, *The German Ideology* (New York: International Publishers, 1947), p. 16 and 18.

4. Joshua Horn, *Away With All Pests* (New York: Monthly Review, 1971); Victor Sidel and Ruth Sidel, *Serve the People* (Boston: Beacon, 1974). Whether any of these policies stem from a Chinese analysis of Western medical experience (other than in its imperialistic form in pre-Liberation China) is questionable. Certainly Western concerns with the social impact of air pollution and of occupational health hazards do not appear to have found much echo in China. (Environmental concerns exist, but seem more aroused by problems of waste and efficiency than by potential health problems.

5. Ivan Illich, *Medical Nemesis: The Expropriation of Health* (New York: Pantheon, 1976), p. 74.

6. *Infant Death: An Analysis by Maternal Risk and Health Care* (Washington, D.C.: Institute of Medicine, National Academy of Science, 1973); also see Victor Fuchs, *Who Shall Live?* (New York: Basic, 1975), pp. 31-35.

7. See, for example, M. I. Roemer and S. J. Axelrod, "A National Health Service and Social Security," *American Journal of Public Health* 67 (1977): 462-65.

8. See, for example, Vincente Navarro, *Medicine Under Capitalism* (New York: Prodist, 1976), pp. 126-28.

PART FOUR

Regulatory Policy: The Visible Hand

Is government regulatory policy designed to protect the profits of industries subject to regulation, or is it a means by which consumers are guarded from exploitation? Beginning with the Progressive era, around the turn of the century, government regulation of railroads, trucking, airlines, television, and the like has been the U.S. policy fashioned to protect the interests of the American consumer from the overweaning power of big business. Recently, such revisionist historians as Gabriel Kolko have questioned this conventional interpretation of history and have argued that big business advocated regulatory agencies in order to protect their markets and profits from new competition (*The Triumph of Conservatism*, 1963).

Regardless of how this historical debate is resolved, modern policy analysts and politicians have lately taken a fresh look at the economic impact of government regulatory agencies. While deregulation has been an abiding principle of the Republican party, leading Democratic politicians have recently pointed to the anticompetitive effects of some governmental regulation, particularly regulation of the airline and the trucking industries. These leaders, former President Jimmy Carter included, have concluded that certain regulatory agencies have become too friendly toward the industries they are supposed to control. Political scientists frequently argue that these "family connections" manifest an unhealthy relationship in which former employees of regulatory agencies often find employment with those they previously regulated, and vice versa.

Peter Schuck's chapter examines the newly emergent role of public interest groups in the regulatory process, arguing that the insularity of these agencies in the pre-Nader period accounts for the close ties between them and regulated industries. Since Ralph Nader's exposé of the Federal Trade Commission in 1968, "public interest groups" have become involved in the administrative process. That is, someone other than special-interest groups has an input into the regulatory process. Public interest groups that speak for the consumer, or the general good, are hampered in their attempts to influence agency proceedings by several factors: (1) the high cost of participating in rule-making proceedings, (2) the fact that industry groups can swamp the agency with their comments, (3) the greater access to relevant data available to business interests, and (4) the lack of former and future agency officials in their organizations. Despite these handicaps, public interest groups have played a valuable role in overseeing procedures and exposing faulty practices to public scrutiny. They have altered the balance of forces exerted on the regulatory agencies.

Lilley and Miller examine the newer "social regulatory" agencies of the 1970s, which attempt to protect workers on the job (OSHA) and the environment in which we live (EPA). In their study, they employ a common tool of policy analysts: cost-benefit. Although they favor the objectives of these agencies, the authors conclude that in many cases the costs of certain regulations exceed the benefits and that more efficient means ought to be sought to achieve desired ends.

The *visible hand* of government seems to be more suspect today than at any time since Franklin Roosevelt's New Deal, but it has its articulate defenders, as Steven Kelman demonstrates. Kelman offers a ringing defense of regulation not on a cost-benefit analysis but on the basis of justice, fairness, and human dignity. New social regulatory agencies are defensible because, unlike the old coopted agencies (e.g., the Interstate Commerce Commission and the Civil Aeronautics Board), they benefit disadvantaged members of society. Even though regulation may be costly in monetary terms, Kelman contends that many benefits of social regulation cannot be judged on a cost-benefit criterion.

In a way, Tibor Machan agrees with Kelman that the issue cannot be decided simply in monetary terms but must be contested on the moral plane of justice or equity. However, Machan reaches a diametrically opposite conclusion from Kelman. Machan argues that deregulation is really an issue of rights, and the fight for deregulation cannot be won on purely economic grounds of efficiency. Although he thinks that the economic arguments support the case for deregulation, he does not think that economic arguments will be persuasive independent of moral values. For Machan, then, the moral issue of human rights takes precedence over efficiency considerations.

These chapters capture the essence of the debate on ideological influence on policy. For both Machan and Kelman, the criterion to be employed in decision making is a moral one. Yet, because their moral principles differ so dramatically, they reach incompatible solutions: Kelman favors regulation, and Machan endorses the free market. Interestingly enough, Lilley and Miller do not consider the problem as having a moral dimension at all, and attempt to formulate their policy by employing a pragmatic, cost-benefit criterion. Finally, Schuck looks to institutional change, mainly to greater input by public interest groups, as the vehicle by which regulatory agencies can be rendered more accountable to the consumer.

Peter H. Schuck

13. Public Interest Groups and the Policy Process

The heightened public consciousness of regulatory agencies is a political phenomenon of very recent vintage. At a time when cries of "regulatory reform" and "openness in government" regularly issue forth from the presidential hustings of both parties, and when routine decisions of the Food and Drug Administration elicit passionate insertions in the *Congressional Record* and angry denunciations in the daily press, it is easy to forget the noiseless obscurity and insularity in which even the most significant federal agencies labored as recently as a decade ago.

Their lack of visiblity was not so much the result of secrecy or design, although those were sometimes contributing factors. Indeed, had the agencies flung open their doors and welcomed the public inside, few citizens would have noticed, much less entered. Public administration, however political, lacks the theatricality, celebrities, and pace that make presidential and, occasionally, congressional politics major American spectator sports. Viewed from the outside, at least, public administration appears dull, bloodless, intensely rational, and plodding. The public agency, as a large bureaucratic organization, is accustomed to dealing only with other organizations—a congressional subcommittee, an industry group, a client organization. An occasional political scientist or wayward journalist may poke around a bit, but to the unorganized public, the administrative landscape has been *terra incognita*.

Many agency administrators have regarded this public indifference as a profound deficiency of the decision-making process. Former Federal Trade Commissioner Elman used to complain that one of his agency's main problems was that no one but the cognoscenti—those groups with a routine, focused economic stake in the FTC's actions (or inactions)—showed any interest in it. That lament was uttered before the task force organized by Ralph Nader in 1968 published its harsh indictment of the FTC, which led directly to a fundamental reorganization (some would say a renaissance) of the agency under new leadership.

The Nader report on the Federal Trade Commission emerged from what was perhaps the first visible effort by a "public interest group" to plumb the depths of a federal agency. It inaugurated what may be the most innovative challenge to public administration since the overthrow of the spoils system almost a century ago, one that overshadows such managerial innovations as PPBS, which received far more attention in the professional literature. The emergence of the "public interest group" and its more recent offspring, "public interest law," as important elements in the administrative process merits serious study.

Some Definitions and Distinctions

The term "public interest group," resonant with Platonic virtue, is often used, abused, exploited, and derided. In Washington parlance, however, it is a conventional term of art; so long as the arrogation of the phrase "public interest" is not taken too literally, it is a useful description of a limited universe of organizations sharing certain common characteristics. As used here, then, "public interest group" refers to an organizational entity that purports to represent very broad, diffuse, noncommercial interests which traditionally have received little explicit or direct representation in the processes by which agencies, courts, and legislatures make public policy.

Because public interest groups are almost invariably "liberal" and Democratic in political outlook — a fact of no small significance — it is useful to distinguish them from other politically active groups of a liberal persuasion, such as the NAACP, American Public Health Association, Americans for Democratic Action, and United Auto Workers. Unlike the public interest groups, these latter groups are usually organized around the common professional, occupational, or political ties of their members, and their political agendas will normally, though not always, reflect these rather well-defined interests. The public interest group, in contrast, is organized around a status or role which virtually all persons in the community are thought to share in common — the status of consumer, citizen, taxpayer, member of the biosphere. Examples are Public Citizen, Common Cause, and the Environmental Defense Fund. It is the extreme breadth and diffuseness of its appeal, then, that most clearly distinguishes the public interest group from its allies and adversaries in the political constellation.[1] And, as we shall see, it is this defining characteristic that largely accounts for the strengths and the weaknesses of such groups in the political and bureaucratic arenas.

Institutionalizing Innovation

Public interest groups have operated at the community level for many years, but their emergence as a force in national policy making is a phenomenon of the period since 1965 and coincides with several social developments—the evolution of the civil rights movement into an organizational pattern that largely excluded middleclass whites from leadership roles; the oppositional and protest Zeitgeist unleashed by the wars waged against poverty, discrimination, and Vietnam; and the meteoric and dramatic rise to national prominence of Ralph Nader. Less visible but perhaps equally important was the continuation of certain long-term trends in American society—the growth of a large, well-educated, prosperous urban and suburban population sympathetic to "good government" and "reform" principles; a growing commitment of foundations to financial support of broad-based social reform and institutional innovation; increasingly influential media always eager for new faces and issues; a growing cadre of investigative journalists freed from the routine of daily deadlines; and a deepening sensitivity and defensiveness of large institutions, public and private, to the new waves of public criticism.

In contrast to the local community action groups spawned by the poverty program, public interest groups have emerged exclusively from the private sector and are not publicly subsidized to any significant extent. Many of the most visible and influential groups are funded directly by Ralph Nader and his organization, Public Citizen, and operate solely in Washington. Others, such as Common Cause, are organized on a statewide basis but have a sizable national office as well. Consumers Union has created yet another variant; essentially a publishing and educational organization, it has established a small Washington office to engage in public interest advocacy on consumer issues. Finally, many groups are foundation-supported or university-supported and tend to focus on specific public policy issues from a broad, citizen perspective. Examples of this latter category are the Media Access Project, the Agribusiness Accountability Project, the National Organization for Reform of Marijuana Laws, the Women's Rights Project, the Freedom of Information Clearinghouse, the National Council for the Public Assessment of Technology, and the Privacy Project of the American Civil Liberties Union.

The profusion of these organizations and their intimate involvement in the highly technical legislative, judicial, and regulatory processes have spawned yet another innovation—the "public interest law firm." This is a group of lawyers (often assisted by law students), usually supported by a foundation, a university, or by fees from public interest groups, which furnishes formal legal representation to such groups as well as unorganized interests (such as mental patients) without fee in some or all of these forums. There are several in Washington, including the Center for Law and Social Policy, Public Citizen Litigation Group, and the Institute for Public Interest Representation at Georgetown Law School. The growing legitimacy of public interest law in the legal profession is evidenced by the formation of a special section in the American Bar Association on public interest practice, by the creation of the Council on Public Interest Law, a group funded by the ABA and several foundations for the purpose of seeking long-range financial and legislative support for public interest law, and by the sponsorship by several local bar associations of public interest law firms in their communities. Public interest groups, like so many other American institutions, are dominated by lawyers. This development, which would not have surprised de Tocqueville, has imparted a decidedly legalistic, litigation-oriented cast to public interest activity, often at the expense of economic and technical expertise.

Political Behavior

In most respects, public interest groups behave in the conventional political mode. They identify issues, mobilize political support, form alliances, bargain and accommodate, accumulate and expend political influence, perform and demand favors, and nurture their organizational base. To a very considerable extent, their behavior is determined by the political system of which they are a part and by whose rules they are constrained to play. Indeed, this is hardly surprising, for the *raison d'être* of the public interest group is to supplement and fill a void in the array of forces represented in the traditional pluralistic bargaining process.

Lobbying

Because public interest groups have been heavily dependent upon foundation funding, their ability to lobby has been severely hampered. Most foundations and wealthy contributors to public interest groups will make grants only to so-called 501(c)(3) organizations, which organizations (unlike their corporate and trade association adversaries) are required by federal income tax laws to refrain from seeking to influence the defeat or passage of legislation, except as an insubstantial part of its activities.[2]

Despite this legal disability, some groups with substantial membership revenue, such as Public Citizen's Congress Watch, the American Civil Liberties Union, Common Cause, and the Sierra Club, have managed to allocate program resources to lobbying, often by bifurcating their structures to create "501(c)(3)" foundations which receive tax-deductible contributions to perform their educational and research functions, while leaving the lobbying functions to the parent organization. Moreover, even "501(c)(3)" groups can (and do) testify at congressional hearings, write editorials, support other organizations that do lobby, communicate with congressional staff on legislative matters, and urge readers of their publications to contact members of Congress.

The lobbying achievements of public interest groups have sometimes been striking. Thus, for example, Common Cause played a critical role in the adoption of campaign finance legislation; Public Citizen's Congress Watch significantly influenced the natural gas deregulation legislation; Public Citizen's Tax Reform Research Group is credited with having produced the repeal of the oil depletion allowance; and environmental groups ended SST appropriations against the combined forces of industry, labor, and the federal bureaucracy.

Public interest groups possess certain characteristic strengths and weaknesses which largely determine their relative legislative influence. First, their lobbying budgets are extremely small, particularly when compared with those of their corporate adversaries. As a result, their lobbyists are relatively young and inexperienced; their research is heavily based upon existing sources of data, particularly government statistics; they must do without the assistance of staff economists, accountants, public relations experts, technicians, and speechwriters; and they must pick and choose among issues with great care.

Second, and more significant, they usually (some environmental groups are notable exceptions) lack a well-organized network capable of mobilizing the grassroots voter and media pressure or support to which members of Congress are most responsive, except on issues on which the labor unions are active allies. Unable to deliver votes or campaign contributions, public interest groups are obliged to concentrate on the supply of other important but often less dependable political resources—research, information, legitimacy, media attention, and symbolism. Unable to exert constituent pressure to sway (or, after the fact, punish) unsympathetic legislators, the role of the public interest lobbyist becomes one primarily of servicing, steadying, and supporting their natural allies.

This is not an insignificant task. Given the bargaining and accommodation norms which govern Congress, it is always difficult to hold even friendly members "in line," particularly when the issue is one such as energy legislation, which arrays many powerful economic interests against them and provides many natural "trading points." Congressional allies must be supplied with "early warning" systems, speech material, legal arguments, rebuttals, strategic options, quick head counts, expert witnesses and testimony at committee hearings, redrafts of bill provisions, and numerous other services if they are to stand fast and perhaps win over some of the uncommitted. If public interest groups, through their often excellent access to the liberal and urban media, can successfully identify their position in the public mind as "the consumer position" or "the environmental view," the issue may well take on a new political complexion (albeit perhaps a more simplistic one) and the terms upon which it will be resolved may be altered considerably. Such symbolism, more than any conventional "clout," probably accounts for their legislative successes, such as passage of a consumer protection agency bill in the 94th Congress in the face of widespread anti-Washington sentiment.[3] (The bill was permitted to die in conference in the face of a presidential veto threat and the nomination of a Democratic candidate committed to a strong consumer agency bill in the 95th Congress.)

Lack of widespread grass-roots influence, coupled with the inertia which characterizes the congressional system and the numerous veto points which line the road to final legislative approval, means that public interest groups are far better able to obstruct or modify a change which they oppose than to gain the adoption of some new measure which they have advanced. Their alliances, with some important and growing exceptions, are at the most liberal end of the political spectrum, and they are usually disabled, both by ideology and by political weakness, from bargaining effectively with centrist and conservative elements to forge a majority coalition.

Moreover, public interest groups tend to be interested less in the politics of bargaining and reelection than in the merits of particular public policy issues. This intensely policy-oriented approach to politics goes well beyond the imperatives of grass-roots weakness, for it is also highly characteristic of the type of liberal reformer who gravitates both to public interest groups and to the left wing of the Democratic party. This kind of orientation is an anathema to most elected politicians—it reduces their most precious asset, flexibility—but is highly congenial to many of their legislative aides. As a result, public interest groups tend to work closely with congressional staff whose ideological commitment to the goals of the groups is often quite profound, occasionally approaching in zeal their commitment to their employers. This symbiosis constitutes a strength for the public interest group and a weakness. It provides easy and sometimes even preferential access to important sources of power in an increasingly staff-dominated Congress, and an outlet for innovative ideas and legislative strategies. But it also adds to their existing political weakness an additional dependency, and places them at an additional remove from the bargaining table, where ultimate power in Congress is exercised. On balance, however, the ongoing devolution of power in Congress from individual members to committees and senior staff aides has worked to the benefit of the public interest groups, a process that is likely to continue.

Litigation

The judicial activism legitimized and encouraged by the Warren Court was approaching its high water mark in the mid-1960s when public interest groups arrived on the Washington scene and when the now familiar critique of the regulation process was first being popularized. Indeed, judicial recognition of the importance of such groups dates from 1966 when then Circuit Court Judge Warren Burger stated in the *United Church of Christ* case that:

> The theory that the Commission can always effectively represent listener interests in a renewal proceeding without the aid and participation of legitimate listener representatives fulfilling the role of private attorneys general is one of those assumptions we collectively try to work with so long as they are reasonably adequate. When it becomes clear, as it does to us now, that it is no longer a valid assumption which stands up under the realities of actual experience, neither we nor the Commission can continue to rely on it.[4]

Congress has enacted much legislation in recent years which sanctions and often encourages resort to the courts by public interest groups. Perhaps the two most notable statutes are the National Environmental Policy Act of 1969 and the Freedom of Information Act, adopted in 1966 and amended in important respects in 1974. NEPA's requirement of an environmental impact statement prior to any proposal for any "major Federal actions significantly affecting the human environment," has spawned literally hundreds of lawsuits. Its appeal to public interest groups derives from the vagueness of its provisions and the courts' willingness to construe them quite liberally, and from the fact that the very limited remedies that it provides—delay and further study of alternatives— are admirably suited for groups whose objectives are often met by simply stopping or (what often amounts to the same thing) delaying agency actions rather than instituting some affirmative program of their own, which may require more political influence than they possess.

The Freedom of Information Act likewise has generated scores of court suits, many of which have been occasioned by information requests by Ralph Nader's researchers, financed by the Nader organizations, and litigated by Nader lawyers. The relative simplicity, low cost, and high success rate of FOIA litigation has made its prosecution by such groups possible. The prospect of court-awarded counsel fees under the 1974 amendments to the FOIA will certainly encourage more such cases.

Some of the legal doctrines which would have posed obstacles to public interest litigation in the past—impediments such as standing, sovereign immunity, and jurisdictional amount—have been substantially eroded during the last decade, at least in cases brought against federal agencies.[5] Furthermore, the availability of court-awarded counsel fees to successful parties, either under statutory authority or under various common law doctrines, has been an inducement to public interest litigation (although the *Alyeska* decision in 1975 eliminated one of the major bases for such awards). Pending legislation, if enacted, will vastly expand the number of such awards in cases against federal agencies.

Public interest groups have won some significant court victories against federal agencies, primarily in environmental and FOIA cases. However, with some other important exceptions (such as a suit compelling FDA to enforce efficacy requirements against over-the-counter drugs, a spate of suits challenging Nixon administration impoundments of agency program funds, and numerous actions overturning USDA regulations on food stamps), public interest groups have not been notably successful in using the courts to influence directly federal agency policy. The reasons lie primarily in the unique nature of the judicial process and the extraordinary deference that courts pay to the actions of federal agencies, deference that is institutionalized in the principles of administrative law. The legal standards applicable to judicial review of most governmental action, federal or state, tend to be highly favorable to the government. For example, one must first exhaust administrative remedies, often a truly exhausting activity. Then, having done so, one must often demonstrate that a federal agency has engaged in "arbitrary or capricious" behavior before one can establish a violation of law. In considering that question, courts tend to indulge numerous presumptions which favor the agencies, such as the presumption in favor of agency interpretations of their governing statutes. Except where the agency has made a clear error of law, its decision can almost always be sustained in the courts, for there is almost always *some* evidence in the record to support its action. Thus, the critical point in the process is the administrative proceeding at which the record is compiled, not the court proceeding that follows. And it is at this point that public interest groups are at their most conspicuous disadvantage.

Agency Proceedings

Agency proceedings are where policy is refined and conflicting interests are ultimately resolved. Yet the most striking fact about public interest group participation in agency proceedings is how little of it there is at a *formal* level. The reasons are not difficult to perceive, and most of them revolve around limited resources and limited information. The cost of active participation in an FDA rule-making proceeding was estimated in 1972 (prior to double-digit inflation) to be in the range of $30,000-$40,000; an adjudicatory proceeding is likely to be considerably more expensive. Such sums exceed the *annual* budget of all but a few consumer and environmental organizations. The result is that most participation occurs, if at all, only in rule-making proceedings and primarily takes the form of submission of relatively brief written comments on proposed agency regulations. Such comments can often have a significant impact, particularly where the group can identify some agency illegality or gross error in the proposal. An example of this occurred in 1974 when Consumers Union and the Public Interest Research Group filed comments with the Federal Energy Administration pointing out three studies FEA had apparently overlooked which indicated that the agency had set the ceiling price of unleaded gasoline at a grossly excessive level. Threatened with a lawsuit and considerable embarrassment, FEA quickly reversed itself (although refusing to order refund of past overcharges).

More typically, however, the agency receives no comments from public interest groups. In general, the more complex the subject, the less likely that any but an industry group will file comments. Even when a public interest group manages to file a statement, however, it is swamped in a sea of submissions from the affected commercial interests, both individual firms and their trade associations. Agency officials deny making decisions on the basis of "a numbers game," and many presumably accord special weight to positions advocated by public interest groups as a way of attempting to redress the stark imbalance of representation which they often lament. Nevertheless, decision makers cannot help but be influenced by the lopsidedness of most submissions.

The nature of the submission by a public interest group is likely to differ from those filed by industry groups. While the regulated industry usually has access to the best and perhaps the only relevant data, the data base of public interest groups is relatively poor. Thus, they either must seek to discredit industry statistics, often without alternative data sources of high quality, or must take the industry data as given and seek to draw contrary inferences from it. The classic dilemma of this sort occurs in Federal Power Commission proceedings in which the cost of producing natural gas is often the central issue. Only the industry possesses the data from which those costs may be determined, the FPC has systematically failed to obtain it, and it is in any event exempt from public disclosure under the Freedom of Information Act.

Without the resources to hire expert specialists, without enough lawyers to endure incredibly protracted proceedings, without access to high quality information (or even good library resources), without the influence which comes from having former and future agency officials on one's payroll, compelled to rely upon the services of inexperienced generalists who will soon be forced by economic necessity to move on to other things, and faced with the reality that the agency will almost certainly reject its position, the public interest group finds that extensive participation in agency proceedings is possible only on a sporadic, almost ad hoc basis.

Under the circumstances, the wonder is that such groups participate at all. Yet for all of that, their contribution to the formal administrative decision-making process is often great indeed. Consider the testimony of William Ruckelshaus, former head of the Environmental Protection Agency:

I can remember in particular one major decision that I was faced with involving the extension of time of the automobile industry from emission standards. I remember the first hearing that was held on that matter in which a single piece of testimony from a public interest lawyer had more impact on my thinking than any of the testimony that occurred during those lengthy three-week hearings. He was able to sum up precisely what the broad issues were from the testimony of all of the vast array of automobile companies that appeared before me as the decision-maker in that proceeding. He did that in a way that contributed to the clarification of my own thought as to what direction should be taken in serving the public interest. That is only one example and many more could be cited.[6]

Other examples, each of which pitted a small public interest group or individual against some of the nation's most powerful industries, include the Health Research Group's four-year campaign to persuade the Food and Drug Administration to ban Red Dye No. 2, the Environmental Defense Fund's exhausting effort to induce EPA to terminate most uses of DDT, and activist John Banzhaf's solitary struggle to force the FCC to apply the "fairness doctrine" to cigarette commercials.

To focus solely upon the formal interventions by public interest groups in the administrative process (i.e., as a party in adjudications or rule making, or as a petitioner), however, is to miss an additional significant mode of influence. The informal monitoring of an agency vastly magnifies a group's impact upon the policy-making process.

This occurs in several ways. First, a public interest group that systematically "covers" an agency creates a persistent potential for embarrassing its officials and policies, even if it rarely becomes a formal party to agency proceedings. Every agency contains some officials at every level whose policy views are contrary to agency policy. Such persons may be motivated by personal pique or ambition, principled concern, ideological commitment, or simple boredom, but they have a common stake in taking their case outside the agency. The public interest group is a natural repository for confidences from such "whistleblowers" or "malcontents" (depending on one's point of view). FDA's 1969 ban on cyclamates, for example, resulted from a natural alliance of just this sort between an FDA scientist, whose research findings were suppressed by the agency, and several sympathetic outsiders, including a Nader attorney.

Second, public interest groups often have excellent access to the media, and their excoriations of agency officials or policies are sometimes considered highly newsworthy, particularly by Washington-based journalists who cover the agencies on a regular basis. Unfavorable publicity can make life difficult for officials by affecting their relationships with congressional committees, by disturbing power relationships within the agency, and by calling their own integrity, self-respect, and professional competence into public question. Again, FDA, which is monitored closely by the Health Research Group, furnishes a classic example. A combination of insider leaks and intense media pressure, with the Health Research Group constituting a crucial link between them, has triggered a congressional inquiry and the creation of a departmental commission of outside experts. Both these bodies are investigating FDA's alleged suppression of dissident agency researchers.

Finally, many agency officials report that the mere existence of public interest groups, the knowledge that the officials are "being watched," affects their behavior quite apart from any particular action that such groups may take. This *in terrorem* effect, of course, is in principle (if not in magnitude) identical to that frequently generated by the regulated industry. When public interest groups possess influential friends in Congress and a litigation capability, this effect can be considerable. Such an impact is apparent in the recent dramatic shift at the Civil Aeronautics Board toward more pro-competitive policies. To be sure, the CAB's new orientation reflects a number of factors, including the influence of Chairman John Robson. But an important influence on the CAB is the perceived "clout" of Nader lawyer Reuben Robertson III, who has peppered the agency with information requests, court actions, intense media criticism, and intensive hearings by a friendly Senate subcommittee resulting in far-reaching legislative proposals to reduce the CAB's regulatory authority.

These informal, "atmospheric" influences of public interest groups have reached their apogee in the recent willingness of the Senate Commerce Committee to defer to such groups in passing upon presidential nominees to the regulatory commissions under the Committee's jurisdiction. In recent years, the Committee has rejected and forced the withdrawal of several nominees opposed by public interest groups. Most recently, responding to opposition by several consumer organizations, it forced the nominee to the chairmanship of the Consumer Product Safety Commission to accept a short term, after nearly defeating the nomination altogether. By affecting the caliber of agency leadership in this manner, public interest groups are thus able to influence countless agency decisions and proceedings in which they could not hope to play a formal role.

These and other remarkable successes, however, should not obscure the fact that the vast majority of decisions and proceedings in all agencies are made and conducted without any participation, formal or informal, by public interest groups, and some agencies (such as the ICC and the Federal Maritime Commission) receive literally no attention from public interest groups. In some instances, of course, industrial interests will be present advocating positions that a public interest group would have taken had it been able to participate. For example, the importer associations will generally urge the free trade position before the International Trade Commission, and large corporate shippers often appear in ICC proceedings to urge lower rates. There are severe limits to the effectiveness of this indirect representation, however, and in any event, some other agencies regulate industries in which there is no "consumer proxy." Thus, in Federal Power Commission proceedings, neither the interstate pipelines nor the public utilities, both of which receive regulated rates of return, have any strong incentive to resist ever higher natural gas rates for producers. Yet consumer organizations rarely appear before the FPC.

There are some encouraging developments in this regard. First, Congress has begun to authorize agencies by statute to reimburse public interest groups and small businesses for the costs of their participation in agency proceedings under certain circumstances. The Federal Trade Commission has been operating such a program since 1975 in connection with its trade regulation rulemaking proceedings, and has expressed satisfaction with the results. Congress authorized a similar program for the Environmental Protection Agency under the recently enacted Toxic Substances Control Act.

Second, at least one agency — the Consumer Product Safety Commission — agreed in December 1976 to fund such a program even without explicit statutory direction. It did so in response to a petition filed by Consumers Union, which argued that agencies do not need explicit statutory authority to fund public participation, so long as such participation would assist the agency in performing its mission. Similar petitions have been filed with other agencies, with varying results. For example, FDA has solicited public comment on the proposal, while the Nuclear Regulatory Commission has decided not to institute this reform. In the Congress legislation to authorize such reimbursement by all agencies was reported favorably by the Senate Judiciary Committee in 1976 and will be reintroduced early in the 95th Congress.

If history is any guide, the money would be well spent. Public policy emerges best from a process in which the generation of relevant data is maximized, basic assumptions are questioned, expert witnesses are cross-examined, and a broad spectrum of values are advanced. Public interest groups are a necessary, if not always sufficient, condition of this process. If adequately funded, their activities should continue to improve, at least marginally, the quality of agency decision making, and should affect the direction of substantive agency policy.

NOTES

1. The distinction is more analytical than behavioral, and is certainly only one of degree. Both groups often agitate similar kinds of issues, use similar tactics, and appeal to similar constituencies.
2. This differential treatment under the Internal Revenue Code is under challenge in the courts. Legislation to relax the lobbying restrictions on certain "501(c)(3)" groups was enacted late in 1976.
3. Indeed, much of the consumer legislation of the 1960s apparently was enacted under such circumstances. See Mark V. Nadel, *The Politics of Consumer Protection* (Indianapolis: Bobbs-Merrill, 1971), pp. 101-54; James Q. Wilson, "The Politics of Regulation," in James W. McKie, ed., *Social Responsibility and the Business Predicament* (Washington, D.C.: Brookings Institution, 1974), pp. 144-45.
4. *Office of United Church of Christ v. FCC,* 359 F2d 994, 1003 (1966).
5. A recent decision of the Supreme Court, *Eastern Kentucky Welfare Rights Organization v. Simon,* 96 Sup. Ct. 1917 (1976), threatens to resuscitate the standing defense, even in suits against federal agencies, but the meaning of this decision remains unclear. Because standing is in part a doctrine of constitutional interpretation (the requirement in Article III that the federal courts may entertain only actual "case or controversies"), a legislative solution to this problem may be impossible.
6. Subcommittee on Administrative Practice and Procedure, Committee on the Judiciary, U.S. Senate, 94th Congress, 2d Session, *Hearings, Public Participation in Federal Agency Proceedings,* S. 2715, p. 119.

William Lilley III and
James C. Miller III

14. THE NEW "SOCIAL REGULATION"

The last few years have witnessed a quiet explosion in the scope and pervasiveness of federal regulation. Beyond a small group of experts and practitioners, however, little notice has been taken, even though this constitutes a significant change in the relationship between the federal government and the private sector, with highly significant economic and political implications.

As shown in table 14.1, the growth in federal regulatory activity has been dramatic. Over the period 1970 through 1975, the number of pages published annually in the *Federal Register* more than tripled, while the number of pages in the *Code of Federal Regulations* grew by 33 percent. Although the total budget of the major regulatory agencies (nearly $4.7 billion in fiscal year 1975) is small compared with the combined federal budget ($235 billion in fiscal year 1975), it does not reflect the costs incurred by private participants in the regulatory process nor the gargantuan costs—and, presumably, benefits—imposed on the private sector by agency decisions. For example, according to the Council on Environmental Quality, the regulations of the Environmental Protection Agency (EPA) will cost the economy an *additional* $40 billion per year by 1984.[1] In just one recent proceeding, a report commissioned by the Occupational Safety and Health Administration (OSHA) admitted that the OSHA proposal then under consideration could impose capital costs of $18.5 billion, and billions of dollars more in annual operating costs.[2]

Coping with the flow of Federal regulations has given rise to a sizable corps of regulatory professionals—private as well as public. In 1975 there appeared in the *Federal Register* 177 proposed new rules and 2,865 proposed amendments to existing rules. During the same period, the *Federal Register* published 309 final rules and 7,305 final rule amendments. This means that during 1975, agencies had under consideration over 10,000 regulations—and this represented a 14 percent increase over the previous year! As shown in table 14.1, between 1970 and 1975 seven major federal regulatory agencies were created—all with their own objectives, their own approaches, and their own styles of dealing with adversaries appearing before them. Equally important, as shown in table 14.2,

TABLE 14.1. INDICES OF GROWTH IN FEDERAL REGULATION, 1970-75

Year	Number of Major "Economic" Regulatory Agencies[a]	Number of Major "Social" Regulatory Agencies[b]	Expenditures of Major "Economic" Regulatory Agencies (in Millions)[c]	Expenditures of Major "Social" Regulatory Agencies (in Millions)[d]	Number of Pages in Federal Register	Number of Pages in Code of Federal Regulations
1970	8	12	$166.1	$1,449.3	20,036	54,105
1971	8	14	$196.8	$1,882.2	25,447	54,487
1972	8	14	$246.3	$2,247.5	28,924	61,035
1973	8	17	$198.7	$2,773.7	35,592	64,852
1974	9	17	$304.3	$3,860.1	42,422	69,270
1975	10	17	$427.6	$4,251.4	60,221	72,200
Percent Increase (1970-75)	25	42	157	193	201	33

[a]Agencies included Civil Aeronautics Board, Commodity Futures Trading Commission (1975), Federal Communications Commission, Federal Energy Administration (1974-75), Federal Maritime Commission, Federal Power Commission, Federal Trade Commission, International Trade Commission (1974-75), Interstate Commerce Commission, Securities and Exchange Commission, and the Tariff Commission (1970-73).

[b]Agencies included Agricultural Marketing Service (1972-75), Atomic Energy Commission (1970-74), Consumer and Marketing Service (1970-71), Coast Guard, Consumer Product Safety Commission (1973-75), Employment Standards Administration (1971-75), Environmental Protection Agency, Equal Employment Opportunity Commission, Federal Aviation Administration, Federal Highway Administration, Federal Railroad Administration, Food and Drug Administration, Mining Enforcement and Safety Administration (1973-75), National Highway Traffic Administration, National Labor Relations Board, National Transportation Safety Board (1971-75), Nuclear Regulatory Commission (1975), Occupational Safety and Health Administration (1973-75), Occupational Safety and Health Review Commission (1971-75), and Workplace Standards Administration.

SOURCE: *The Budget of the United States*, 1972 to 1977.

[c]Same as note c. Total expenditures of all agencies listed in note b above, except only health- and safety-related expenditures for the following agencies: Atomic Energy Commission (1970-74; "regulatory activities"), Coast Guard ("operating expenses": merchant marine safety and marine law enforcement/marine environmental protection), Federal Aviation Administration ("operations": flight standards program, medical standards program; "facilities": engineering and development; and "safety regulation"), Federal Highway Administration ("motor carrier and highway safety"), and Federal Railroad Administration ("Bureau of Railroad Safety").

over this period 30 important laws were enacted, making substantial changes in our regulatory framework.

This escalating flow of regulations and the proliferation of new agencies and laws have had a number of little-noticed yet important effects. One presumably unintended result is that since larger institutions can more easily participate successfully in the regulatory process, and since regulations tend to impose costs on institutions in less than direct proportion to their size, the current approach tends to penalize smaller institutions (e.g., highly competitive, small-scale entrepreneurs and loosely organized labor groups) and reward bigness. This could lead to more concentrated industries and larger and more powerful unions.

Another important effect results from the timing of regulation. While it is relatively easy in the short run for industry to adjust to a few regulatory changes, or in the long run to adjust to several, it is terribly difficult to adjust well to many regulations in a short period of time. Moreover, the political will to impose regulations may be increased because of the tendency for there to be a lag between the time when costs are imposed and when they are borne. For example, a politician may be able to please an advocate of regulation by favorable action, and when the costs are finally apparent no one associates them directly with his action.

The "New-Style" Regulation

The rising tide of regulation primarily reflects a growth in "social" regulation rather than the old-style "economic" regulation (see table 14.1). While all regulation is essentially "social" in that it affects human welfare, the economic/social distinction emphasizes some very significant differences. The old-style economic regulation typically focuses on markets, rates, and the obligation to serve. Thus an enterprise wishing to engage in interstate transportation must obtain from either the Civil Aeronautics Board (CAB) or the Interstate Commerce Commission (ICC) a "certificate of public convenience and necessity" (which specifies the markets to be served), must have its rates approved, and must open itself to all comers (i.e., meet its "common carrier obligation").

On the other hand, the new-style social regulation affects the conditions under which goods and services are produced and the physical characteristics of products that are manufactured. As an example of the former, the EPA sets constraints on the amounts of pollution a manufacturer may emit in the course of its operations. As an example of the latter, the Consumer Product Safety Commission (CPSC) specifies minimum safety standards for products that in its judgment are potentially "unsafe."

The new-style regulation also extends to far more industries and ultimately affects far more consumers than the old-style regulation, which tends to be con-

TABLE 14.2. IMPORTANT FEDERAL REGULATORY LEGISLATION, 1970-75

Year Enacted	Title of Statute
1970	Clean Air Amendments
	Occupational Safety and Health Act
	Poison Prevention Packaging Act
	Securities Investor Protection Act
1971	Economic Stabilization Act Amendments
	Federal Boat Safety Act
	Lead-Based Paint Elimination Act
1972	Consumer Product Safety Act
	Equal Employment Opportunity Act
	Federal Election Campaign Act
	Federal Environmental Pesticide Control Act
	Federal Water Pollution Control Act Amendments
	Noise Control Act
	Ports and Waterways Safety Act
1973	Agriculture and Consumer Protection Act
	Economic Stabilization Act Amendments
	Emergency Petroleum Allocation Act
	Flood Disaster Protection Act
1974	Atomic Energy Act
	Commodity Futures Trading Commission Act
	Council on Wage and Price Stability Act
	Employee Retirement Income Security Act
	Federal Energy Administration Act
	Hazardous Materials Transportation Act
	Housing and Community Devlopment Act
	Magnuson-Moss Warranty—Federal Trade Commission Improvement Act
	Pension Reform Act
	Privacy Act
	Safe Drinking Water Act
1975	Energy Policy and Conservation Act

fined to specific sectors. Whereas the effects of CAB regulation are largely limited to air carriers (including their stockholders and employees) and air passengers, the regulations of OSHA apply to every employer engaged in a business affecting commerce.

With the new-style regulation, the government often becomes involved with very detailed facets of the production process. As a result, the business manager has fewer "degrees of freedom." For instance, the approach of OSHA in recent cases has been to specify not performance standards but the precise engineering controls that must be adopted.[3] The CPSC does not merely require that products be safe but mandates (often in great detail) certain characteristics that products must have.[4] The Federal Trade Commission proposes that truthful advertising of over-the-counter drugs can only use certain words and not others. This kind of activity involves the government in many more details of business management, and consequently regulatory agencies have become a major factor in determining product and service costs as well as the choices available to consumers.

As should be apparent, the quality of regulatory statutes and the performance of regulatory agencies should be a matter of great public concern. Although most of us prefer a cleaner environment, freedom from occupational related accidents and diseases, safer automobiles, less discrimination in employment and education, and less risky market transactions, we must acknowledge the tremendous costs involved in achieving such worthwhile objectives and address the problem of maximizing the *net* benefits derived. In order to do this, we must confront the issue of benefits and costs squarely. Some of the benefits and costs of regulation are becoming evident and are being widely discussed, at least within professional circles. For example, many serious policy makers and analysts are examing the tradeoffs between improved health and safety and the costs thus imposed.[5] But this kind of evaluation has just begun; accelerating it to improve the performance of our regulatory institutions could mean enormous gains to society.

Our year's experience at the Council on Wage and Price Stability monitoring the regulatory activities of the federal government convinces us that the net benefits from regulation are lower than they should be; in short, the country is paying far too much for what it is getting.[6] In some important instances, the whole regulatory approach is at fault and thus the enabling legislation and those responsible for it should be blamed. But in all too many cases the problem is the poor performance of the regulatory agencies. We have observed that decision makers often approach issues with the wrong attitude, without necessary technical skills, and often without sufficient information.

The combination of escalating activity and poor performance by regulatory agencies is a matter that merits serious concern—over not just the conventional economic costs, but also some problems resulting from the present system that pose a danger to certain of our democratic processes.

Presidential Power and Public Faith

Two potential threats to our democratic processes that flow from the present scope and method of regulation are worth noting. First, the regulatory activity in the health, safety, and environmental areas concentrates enormous amounts of power in the Presidency. This new nucleus of power could prove irresistible in some future crisis, real or imagined: Some future President might be tempted to use *overtly* legal means to achieve *covertly* illegal ends.

As an instructive illustration, imagine a President today confronting the steel industry, as President John F. Kennedy did in 1962. It is striking how much more power a sitting President could exercise today in "jawboning" down price increases. President Kennedy was limited to harassing steel executives by ordering visits from agents of the Federal Bureau of Investigation and the Internal Revenue Service and threatening to sell off stockpile reserves, but a sitting President today could literally shut down the entire industry—by the simple expedient of sending OSHA and EPA inspectors to the major plants with orders to leave no stone unturned. Needless to say, it is almost impossible to ensure that any given plant will always be in full compliance with the thousands of OSHA and EPA regulations now on the books, many of which reach down into the most minute details of production. As a result of even an implied threat, industry executives might well choose to roll back prices on the wholly rational grounds that absorbing the losses would cost less than a forced shutdown.

A second danger is the possibility that imprudent and unnecessary "overstrengthening" of government through the accretion of new regulatory powers and controls could ultimately, and paradoxically, lead to an undermining of the public's "faith in government"—a backlash against *all* government because of an eventual negative reaction to the perceived regulatory "excesses" of the mid-1970s. In short, in the late 1970s there may be a replay of the attitudes concerning *domestic* issues of the late 1960s—which were dominated, in part, by a popular reaction to the legislative excesses of the Great Society and by a corresponding loss of public confidence in government.*

The Great Society programs were perceived to affect directly only a fraction of the society—the poor and the near-poor—and much of the public consternation concerned what the programs did *not* do rather than what they did. On the other hand, regulatory failures affect us all, and the potential reaction will arise concerning what regulations have done *to* us, as well as what they did not accomplish. And because it tends to be very easy to launch new programs and difficult or impossible to cast them off, the public may be "stuck" with the costs of an oversold program, just as we have found it difficult to alter those Great Society programs that proved to be unsuccessful. This "rachet effect" could intensify disgruntlement over perceived regulatory excesses, and the resulting backlash could inflict deep and lasting wounds on public trust in the competence and integrity of government.

*Indeed, this prediction has been manifested in part by such events as the Proposition 13 tax revolt, the partial deregulation of the airlines industry, the deregulation of the trucking industry, and the Reagan administration's promise to lift a broad array of regulations affecting the private sector. —Ed.

Why Regulation Costs More Than It Should

From our experience at the Council on Wage and Price Stability we have concluded that the regulatory decision-making process is inefficient, that it leads to costs much higher than would be necessary to secure the stated objectives. There are several reasons for this poor performance.

First, many decisions are reached on the basis of grossly inadequate information. While many people are under the illusion that regulatory decisions are made only after serious evaluation of a "full and complete record," often this is not the case. Sometimes information is available and could be analyzed, but decision makers do not bother to get it, and the adversary process, governed by the Administrative Procedures Act, does not supply it. On other occasions, it is simply unavailable or would be difficult to obtain—yet decisions are nonetheless reached as if evidence existed to substantiate them. In any event, opportunities are often missed for achieving regulatory goals at lower cost, or reaching higher goals at the same cost.

Even when information about the ramifications of a proposed regulation is available, decisions do not necessarily reflect rational judgment concerning costs and benefits. In some cases, only the most extreme and unrealistic assumptions could lead to the conclusion that a regulation is worth its costs and should be promulgated, or that its costs exceed its benefits and it should thus be rejected. In other cases, where regulatory agencies have discretion to make the regulation "stronger" or "weaker" (or "tighter" or "looser"), little attempt is made to trade off costs and benefits. As a result, a regulation is often promulgated whereby the final incremental improvement to achieve a stated objective yields small benefits relative to costs or great costs relative to benefits. In addition, regulators often do not evaluate the components of a comprehensive regulation. For example, there may be several ways of reducing worker exposure to an airborne carcinogen (e.g., exhaust fans; automatic, enclosed transport of the target substance; and more frequent cleaning of work areas), and the proposed regulation may require certain steps to be taken in all of these areas. Yet, it may ignore differences in the marginal costs of these methods compared with the marginal effects that they have. Such disregard invariably leads to excessive regulatory costs for a given level of benefits, or lower benefits for a given level of costs.

Finally, in all too many cases there is strong resistance to considering alternative and sometimes truly innovative approaches. In many cases OSHA refuses to entertain the use of personal protective devices (e.g., goggles or earplugs) even when they could secure a safe and healthy working environment at a small fraction of the cost of mandated engineering controls. As required by statute, EPA refuses to consider effluent-charge approaches to controlling pollution, and instead mandates standards for maximum effluents.

Since cases of the sort just described are found throughout the whole of regulatory activity, it would appear appropriate to ask, "Why?" Our own experience in serving as the federal government's "watchdog" over regulation has convinced us that there are two major reasons: (*a*) the constraints placed on regulators that *forbid* them to make rational decisions, and (*b*) the nature of the bureaucrat/decision maker and the incentives to which he responds.

Actually, the number of instances where statutes prohibit agencies from considering the costs and benefits of proposals is not all that large, although important cases are alleged to exist. For example, the Clean Air Act of 1970 specifically instructs EPA to establish air-quality standards based on considerations of public health, and this has been interpreted within the agency to mean that other considerations, such as economics, simply cannot be considered. Somewhat the same argument has been made regarding the enforcement by EPA of the Water Pollution Control Act, even though the act itself contains numerous provisions urging a cost-effective regulatory approach. In one case brought to our attention, pulp and paper producers in the Northwest are being required to install secondary liquid-waste treatment plants even though they empty into the Pacific Ocean, with little or no damage to the environment according to expert scientific opinion. Here is a case of regulation imposing sizable costs with little or no benefit to society.

To the extent that a statute forces an agency to promulgate regulations that are contrary to the public interest, or to the extent that an agency's decision making is guided by "political" pressures from Congress and the White House, then the blame for "bad" regulation must be shared by these parties. However, it has been our experience that much of the problem lies with agency decision makers, whose actions can be explained by the type of people agencies tend to attract and the economic incentives they respond to on the job.

"Quis custodiet ipsos custodes"?

Regulatory agencies tend to lure personnel who "believe" in regulation. It is not surprising, for example, that EPA has a reputation for having a staff composed largely of "environmentalists" (just as ICC is staffed principally by people who disagree strongly with those economists who argue that the transportation sector would be much more efficient without regulation). Moreover, abetted by the civil service system, regulatory agencies tend to be staffed by people who are risk-averse, very security-conscious about their jobs, and unwilling to take initiatives they fear may conflict with the agency's "mission." These tendencies are reinforced by actual on-the-job incentives to produce inefficient regulation.

It has been our experience that, particularly in the area of social regulation, many officials behave as though driven by a desire to "punish" a transgressor.

Understandably, kicking around some company because it has done something wrong can be fun. Treating all polluters as sinners is also much easier than making quantitative judgments about optimal levels of cleanliness in the air and water, but it leads to inefficient regulations, especially where governing statutes imply rigid, national, uniform standards. An example of this is the recent EPA regulation requiring that motorcycles emit no more pollution than automobiles, despite the fact that alternative approaches could reduce pollution at far less cost. A major reason for the regulation was the conviction of the EPA staff that letting motorcyle owners off "scot-free" would be "unjust." As another example, there is evidence that cleaning up the steel industry costs more marginally than cleaning up the paper industry. A cost-minimizing approach to effluent reduction would mean going "light" on steel and "heavy" on paper. But EPA is reluctant to do this, some say, because this would mean "letting big steel off," while "punishing" the paper industry for the transgressions of the steel industry.

The tendency toward a rigid framework can be very costly. For example, EPA recently established new water effluent guidelines for the $35-billion-per-year iron and steel industry. Compliance with these guidelines, EPA estimated, would cost the industry (and ultimately consumers) $2.5 billion in added capital costs, and $1.3 billion annually in added operating and maintenance costs. These costs are unnecessarily high, the Council on Wage and Price Stability has argued, because EPA treats *uniformly* all the five major processes in the industry involving heavy waste loads of total suspended solids. EPA does so even though the marginal costs of cleaning up each vary widely.[7] Obviously, there exists an opportunity for EPA to establish new standards calibrated to reduce water pollution by the same amount as originally proposed, but at a lower cost to society.

The risk-aversion and security-consciousness of government regulators cause them to try to avoid criticism, which in turn breeds rigidity and inflexibility. This explains a number of bureaucratic traits. First, once a regulation has been proposed (usually in the *Federal Register*), there is great resistance to having it withdrawn for fear that withdrawal would be looked upon as an admission of incompetence. Second, regulations are often proposed and promulgated prematurely, for fear that delay in meeting arbitrary deadlines would invite criticism from Congress. Third, regulations are often proposed or promulgated under the pretense that available information justifies them, for fear of protest from vocal constituencies. Fourth, there is even a tendency to propose or promulgate "extremist" and/or "nonsense" regulations, for fear that failing to leave any stone unturned would raise questions about the regulators' "commitment" to the social objective.

The tendency toward risk-aversion extends up as well as down the hierarchy. The bureaucratic "loop" that any regulation must clear before being published in the *Federal Register* is typically so extensive, and the "sign-offs" so numerous, that one cannot blame inefficiencies solely on low-level bureaucrats. Misguided and inexperienced GS-13s do not publish regulations in the *Federal Register*. While they might draft them, only very senior officials are authorized to approve them for publication, usually only after an extensive clearance process within the agency. For example, regulations proposed in 1974 and 1975 by the Department of Housing and Urban Development typically required the ratifying initials of thirteen individuals scattered among no fewer than four offices within the Department *before* the proposal was forwarded to the Secretary or the appropriate Assistant Secretary.

Notwithstanding this elaborate safety net, a growing number of highly questionable regulations are appearing. These often simply evoke laughter and ridicule, but they are sometimes quite serious in their repercussions. There are numerous recent examples: The Department of Health, Education, and Welfare once proscribed father-son/mother-daughter dinners; EPA has approved regulations forbidding steel companies to allow their plants to emit any visible emissions whatsover; OSHA informed businesses that their toilet seats cannot be round but must be horseshoe-shaped, and proposed that farmers and ranchers must provide enclosed toilet facilities within five minutes walking distance of any point where employees are at work.

Moving Toward Accountability

Our experience at the Council on Wage and Price Stability has convinced us of two things: Many regulatory laws are poorly drawn, and the agency decision-making process is not performing very well. The result is that the public is paying far more than necessary to achieve the legitimate goals of regulation.

With respect to traditional economic regulation, more and more questions are being asked and closer scrutiny is being undertaken. In the past year there have been rail-reform legislation, numerous proposals to reform airline regulation, at least one serious proposal to reform the regulation of the trucking industry, and various other proposals to minimize the anticompetitive and inefficient controls imposed by the traditional economic regulatory agencies.

But although the old-line agencies have their critics, government action has really shifted to the new-style social regulatory agencies, where fewer questions are being raised. It is easy to understand why these agencies are getting a freer ride. Most have been around only a short time, and many think it is too early to be very critical of them. Moreover, in the minds of most of the public, the regulatory objectives are within reach and the costs either will not materialize or will be borne by someone else. Sooner or later, however, the moment of truth will come and the public will hold government accountable for the performance of the new social regulators. That moment may be closer than many in government now realize.

NOTES

1. See Council on Environmental Quality, *Environmental Quality: Seventh Annual Report* (Washington, D.C.: U.S. Government Printing Office, 1976), p. 145. Other sources report higher costs. For example, a recently published staff report to the National Commission on Water Quality estimates that meeting 1983 standards for water pollution alone will require industry to spend $59.2 billion for capital equipment and another $12.6 billion annually for operation and maintenance. See *Staff Report to the National Commission on Water Quality* (Washington, D.C.: U.S. Government Printing Office, 1976), sec. 1, p. 34.

2. See Bolt, Beranek, and Newman, Inc., *Economic Impact Analysis of Proposed Noise Control Regulations* (Washington, D.C.: Occupational Safety and Health Administration, 1976). The study did not attempt to quantify the benefits of the proposal in monetary terms.

3. See the recent decision by OSHA in the case involving exposure to coke-oven emissions (41 *Federal Register* 46762). The former administrator of OSHA, Dr. Morton Corn, was reported as hinting that this approach would become formal policy toward worker health and safety (see the *Wall Street Journal*, 21 October 1976, p. 2). This policy was continued in a recent OSHA proposal applying primarily to the textile industry. See "OSHA Proposes Standard for Worker Exposure to Cotton Dust, Sets April 5 Hearing," U.S. Department of Labor Release 76-1528, 23 December 1976.

4. Cf. 16 CFR 1207 et seq. on non-full-sized baby cribs; and 16 CFR 1512 et. seq. on bicycles. Recent CPSC activity indicates that priority attention is being directed to such items as matches, contact adhesives, upholstered furniture, aerosols, household chemicals, Christmas tree lights, soft-drink bottles, ladders, and children's toys. See "CPSC Releases Product Profiles," Consumer Product Safety Commission Release 76-67, 17 October 1976.

5. A growing number of experts have begun to focus public attention on this issue. Among others are Allen V. Kneese and Charles L. Schultze, *Pollution, Prices, and Public Policy* (Washington, D.C.: Brookings Institution, 1975); Nina W. Cornell, Roger G. Noll, and Barry Weingast, "Safety Regulation," in *Setting National Priorities: The Next 10 Years*, ed. H. Owen and Charles L. Schultze (Washington, D.C.: Brookings Institution, 1976); and several of the recent "evaluative studies" prepared under the auspices of the American Enterprise Institute for Public Policy Research (e.g., Robert S. Smith, *The Occupational Safety and Health Act: Its Goals and Its Achievements*, 1976; Henry G. Grabowski, *Drug Regulation and Innovation: Empirical Evidence and Policy Options*, 1976; William M. Wardell and Louis Lasagna, *Regulation and Drug Development*, 1975; and Sam Peltzman, *Regulation of Automobile Safety*, 1975).

6. Under the Council on Wage and Price Stability Act, the council monitors activities of the federal agencies and intervenes in regulatory proceedings.

7. For example, the incremental annual costs per ton of total suspended solids removed by added controls range from about $1,957 for the "hot forming primary with scarfing" process, to about $18,000 per ton of total suspended solids removed by the "integrated seamless pipes and tubes" process. See "Comments of the Council on Wage and Price Stability on Effluent Guidelines and Standards for Existing and New Sources in the Iron and Steel Manufacturing Point Source Category," 24 June 1976.

Steven Kelman

15. REGULATION THAT WORKS

The last decade has seen dramatic restrictions in the freedom of action society chooses to allow to business firms. A series of laws in areas like environmental protection, occupational safety and health, consumer product safety, and equal opportunity has restricted the prerogatives of business firms to pursue production, hiring, and marketing practices that would have continued without these laws. Business and conservatives have now launched a counterattack against these changes. Cleverly exploiting various popular resentments, the counterattacking forces seek to lump "excessive government regulation" together with themes as diverse as high taxes and school busing to generate an all-embracing demand to "get the government out of our hair." To hear the critics of the new government regulatory programs tell it, nothing less fundamental than our very freedom is at stake in the battle against meddlesome bureaucrats. And now, with national concern over inflation growing, we are being told that the new regulatory programs are an important cause of the increased cost of living, and must be reduced for that reason as well.

One fact is important to get clear from the beginning: The alleged popular groundswell against government regulation of business does not exist. A recent Louis Harris survey asked Americans, "In the future, do you think there should be more government regulation of business, less government regulation, or the same amount there is now?" By 53 percent to 30 percent, those polled favored either more regulation or the same amount as now, over less regulation. In fact, almost as many respondents (24 percent) favored more regulation as favored less regulation (30 percent). Repeated polls have shown wide popular support for measures to make workplaces safe and clean up the environment.

This absence of any groundswell against the new regulatory thrust of the last decade is reassuring because the conservative and business counterattack is, I believe, largely wrong. New regulatory programs neither threaten freedom nor contribute significantly to inflation. On the whole, the new regulation is a good thing. Certainly there have been excesses by bureaucrats, but what is more impressive than these excesses is the unfinished work the new agencies still have before them to deal with the injustices that prompted their creation in the first place.

226

Two kinds of activities are often lumped together as "government regulation." When denouncing the "costs of government regulation," opponents of the new regulatory agencies tend to forget this distinction. An older generation of liberals, fond of asserting that regulatory agencies always get captured by those they regulate, also ignore this distinction.

Most of the regulatory agencies established before the last decade were set up to regulate prices and conditions of entry in various industries. The grandfather of such agencies was the Interstate Commerce Commission, established in 1887 to regulate railroads. There is a lively dispute among historians about whether the ICC, when it was established, was an attempt to tame a powerful and oppressive industry, or a government-sanctioned effort by the railroads themselves to set up a cartel to avoid price competition. It is much clearer that other agencies, regulating market conditions in various industries (e.g., the Civil Aeronautics Board and the Federal Communications Commission), were originally established at the behest of industries seeking to avoid "excessive" competition. These agencies, by maintaining artificially high prices in various industries, have been very costly to consumers and the economy as a whole. But you do not hear the voices of business complaining about them. Indeed, when proposals are made to deregulate surface transportation, airlines, or television, the main opponents of such proposals have been the industries being "regulated."

The situation is very different, both politically and conceptually, for the regulatory agencies that have blossomed during the last decade—intended to regulate nonmarket behavior by business firms. Usually they regulate acts that injure third parties. These "social" regulatory agencies include the Environmental Protection Agency, the Occupational Safety and Health Administration, the National Highway Transportation Safety Board, the Consumer Product Safety Commission, and the Equal Employment Opportunity Commission. These agencies generally came into being despite genuine business resistance. Business representatives certainly have ample opportunity to participate in developing the regulations these agencies promulgate, but other organized constituencies are interested in their work as well (e.g., environmentalists at EPA, trade unions at OSHA, civil rights and women's groups at EEOC). Few reasonable people believe the social regulatory agencies have been "captured" by business—least of all, as the current attacks demonstrate, business itself.

The conceptual basis for the social regulatory agencies also is different from that of agencies intended to limit or replace the free market. In any society, one of the basic tasks of government and the legal system is to decide which acts of individuals are so harmful to others that they cannot be freely permitted (and which harmful acts may rightfully be performed, even though others are indeed harmed). A common dictum has been that people may act freely as long as their actions concern only themselves: "My freedom to move my arm ends where your face begins." But clearly this dictum is unsatisfying. Virtually everything we do affects others. Even acts as trivial as appearing at work with a blue shirt, or consuming a bottle of Perrier water in a public place, injure the person who despises the color blue or who is offended to see people buy products from France. Anything we do that damages our own welfare hurts those who hold us dear. What the legal system must do is to determine which acts affecting others should be allowed, and which should be proscribed. The social regulatory agencies are engaged in this age-old task. There is nothing conceptually new about their activities. What is new is that they have redefined certain acts by business firms previously regarded as acceptable, and determined that they are henceforth unacceptable.

Government has never left businessmen "unregulated," as business spokesmen now wistfully but erroneously imagine. The voluminous case and statute law of property, contracts, and torts, along with large chunks of the criminal law, constitute an elaborate system far more complex and intricate than any OSHA standard regulating acts that injure property holders, as well as acts by property holders that injure others. A starving person does not have the freedom to injure a rich man by appropriating the rich man's money in order to buy food. People do not have the freedom to injure a landowner by trespassing on his land. (Richard Posner, a professor of law at the University of Chicago, argues that traditional common-law rules merely reproduce what would have occurred through market transactions, if the costs of negotiating such transactions were not too high, and that modern social regulations, by contrast, subvert expected market outcomes. Even if this statement were true, and it is subject to much debate, it is still not obvious why legal rules ought to mimic the outcomes of market transactions.) Furthermore, the process by which these older rules were elucidated and enforced through litigation was much more cumbersome and arbitrary than the rule making of today's regulatory agencies.

The plethora of regulations regarding property that has grown up over the centuries is not some sort of natural order, onto which new regulations of business behavior in areas like safety, health, environmental protection, consumer fraud, and discrimination represent an unnatural intrusion. As long as the regulations were restricting the freedom of nonproperty holders to injure them, businessmen raised no chorus of complaints about an oppressive government stifling freedom. The chorus of complaints from business has begun only as regulations have begun increasingly to restrict the freedom of business firms to injure others.

The harms that social regulations of the last decade were intended to curb were not insignificant. Urban air had become unhealthy as well as unpleasant to breathe. Rivers were catching on fire. Many working people were dying from exposure to chemicals on their jobs. Firms were selling products of whose hazards consumers were ignorant. And the nation faced a legacy of racial and sexual discrimination. Frequently the harm was borne disproportionately by the more disadvantaged members of society, while the more advantaged produced the harm. The social regulation of the past decade grew largely, then, out of a sense of fairness—a view that people, frequently disadvantaged people, were being victimized by others in unacceptable ways.

The impact of the new agencies in alleviating these injuries has begun to be felt. Racial and sexual discrimination have decreased, partly thanks to broader social trends, but partly thanks to government efforts. There has been a vast increase in the amount of information manufacturers are required to tell consumers about their products, and surveys indicate that many consumers use this information in making purchasing decisions.

Since the much-maligned OSHA and its sister agency regulating coal mining safety have come into existence, the number of accidental workplace deaths has been cut almost in half. Worker exposures to harmful amounts of coal dust and chemicals like vinyl chloride, asbestos and lead have been reduced, and this will reduce the toll of occupational sickness and death in the years to come. Improvements in emergency medical care and some changes in workforce composition since 1970 may be partially responsible for the dramatic reduction in workplace deaths. But today's figures don't even reflect the reduction in deaths due to occupational disease, which will be felt mainly in future years because of the frequently lengthy period separating exposure to harmful levels of a chemical and death or illness due to that exposure.

Environmental regulation has produced significant improvements in the quality of air in the United States. Without regulation the situation would have gotten worse because economic growth tends to increase the level of pollution. Carbon monoxide levels in eight representative cities declined 46 percent between 1972 and 1976. Carbon monoxide levels that had been found in urban air were enough to increase the incidence of heart attacks and of painful angina attacks among people with heart disease. There has been a major decline in heart attacks in the United States during the 1970s. No one yet knows why, but I predict that studies will show that improvement in air quality has played a role in this decline. Another common air pollutant, sulfur dioxide, which definitely causes respiratory illness and death and is suspected of causing cancer, has now declined to a point where almost every place in the country is in compliance with EPA standards.

Water pollution has been reduced as well. There are rivers and lakes around the country—from the Pemigewasset River in New Hampshire through the Mohawk River in New York to the Willamette River in Oregon—previously badly polluted, that are now opened in parts for fishing and swimming. Levels of various pesticides in streams and rivers, as well as of phenol—an organic waste considered a good indicator of the presence of toxic industrial wastes—have declined dramatically during the 1970s.

Lives have been saved by other regulatory actions. The introduction of childproof containers on household poisons appears to have reduced accidental poisoning significantly. Highway deaths declined by almost 15 percent between 1965 and 1972, even before the post-OPEC speed-limit reductions. Some of this decline may be due to factors other than new auto safety regulations, such as fewer teenagers on the roads. But the decline in traffic fatalities has occurred despite an enormous increase in the number of bicycle and motorcycle fatalities caused by the new popularity of these vehicles.

The critics ask: Have the benefits outweighed the costs? Are they feeding inflation, for example? Allegations that health, safety, environmental and anti-discrimination regulations are a major cause of inflation are little short of grotesque. Much of the business thunder about regulation begins by citing some overall figure for the "cost of regulation," and then goes on to zero-in on agencies like OSHA and EPA. These agencies are chosen, however, only because business dislikes them especially, not because they are major contributors to the "cost of regulation." Most of the cost of regulation is imposed by market-fixing agencies like the ICC, which the business world likes. Murray Weidenbaum, director of the Center for the Study of American Business and an adjunct scholar at the American Enterprise Institute, estimated that in 1976 federal regulation in the areas he examined cost $62.3 billion to comply with. But of this sum, approximately $26 billion, or 42 percent, was the estimated impact on consumer prices of tariff protection against imports and of price and entry regulations by the ICC, CAB, and FCC. (The largest figure in this category was the cost of ICC regulation of transportation.) Another $18 billion—29 percent of the estimated total cost—represented the alleged cost of federal paperwork. Certainly there are plenty of pointless federal paperwork requirements. But few of these relate to what would normally be thought of as "government regulation." Much federal paperwork takes the form of reports for statistical purposes and of requirements for federal contractors or other citizens receiving federal benefits.

Only 5 percent of Weidenbaum's estimated total $3.2 billion in 1976 was spent on complying with OSHA regulations. Another $7.8 billion allegedly was spent to comply with EPA regulations—less than 13 percent of the total. (Weidenbaum also estimated a $3.7 billion retail cost for auto safety and emissions requirements.)

Even these modest figures do not reflect the direct savings that result from some of these regulations. The actual monetary cost of pollution abatement measures, for example, is the cost to firms of capital equipment, energy, and maintenance, minus the savings in medical bills, damaged crops, premature corrosion of property, laundering expenses, and so forth, that would otherwise be borne by victims of pollution. Most accounts of the "inflationary impact" of government regulation do not calculate such savings.

More fundamentally, these estimates of the "cost" of regulation ignore widespread benefits that do not have a direct monetary value, but are real nonetheless. In the case of pollution control, for example, the air smells a bit better for 5 million people; 100,000 people get to see mountains in the distance which they would not have seen had the air not been as clean; and 50 lives are saved. There is no way of objectively determining whether these nonpriced benefits justify the net monetary costs. Economists have come up with different ways to assign dollar values to benefits like clean air that are not traded on markets, which would then allow us to weigh all the benefits against all the more concrete costs. But there are philosophical difficulties, as well as technical ones, with these efforts.

In deciding whether a given act that injures a third party should be allowed, one relevant factor is how much a third party suffers as a result of the behavior, as compared to the benefits the perpetrator gains from the behavior. The greater the benefit, and the more inconsequential the injury suffered by the third party, the stronger the case is to allow the behavior to be exercised freely.

But since the costs of injury are borne by its victims, while its benefits are reaped by its perpetrators, simple cost-benefit calculations may be less important than more abstract conceptions of justice, fairness, and human dignity. We would not condone a rape even if it could be demonstrated that the rapist derived enormous pleasure from his actions, while the victim suffered in only small ways. Behind the conception of "rights" is the notion that some concept of justice, fairness, or human dignity demands that individuals ought to be able to perform certain acts, despite the harm to others, and ought to be protected against certain acts, despite the loss this causes to the would-be perpetrators. Thus we undertake no cost-benefit analysis of the effects of freedom of speech or trial by jury before allowing them to continue. As the steelworkers union noted in commenting on an OSHA regulation of coke-oven emissions, no analysis of its inflationary impact was performed before the Emancipation Proclamation was issued. This notion of individual rights that supersedes a neutral cost-benefit analysis is ordinarily dear to the hearts of American conservatives. Yet, when it comes to the regulation of business activities that intrude on the lives of individual consumers or workers, they perversely see the government regulation itself as an intrusion on individual rights.

The costs and benefits of the business behavior now coming under regulation have not been distributed randomly. Much of the new social regulation benefits the more disadvantaged groups in society. To put it somewhat simply but not, in my view, unfairly—those who argue, say, that OSHA should "go soft" on its health regulations in order to spare the country the burden of additional costs, are saying that some workers should die so that consumers can pay a few bucks less for the products they purchase, and stockholders can make a somewhat higher return on their investments. It is hard to see why workers exposed to health hazards should be at the front line of the battle against inflation, however the overall costs and benefits tally up.

There are, to be sure, those sudden friends of the poor who allege that environmental regulation has significantly added to unemployment, or who point out that regulation induced price increases weigh most heavily on the poor. But studies have concluded, that, on balance, environmental legislation has probably created many more jobs than it has cost. And one must wonder whether there aren't more direct ways to help the poor than to eliminate the health, safety, and environmental regulations that slightly increase the cost of goods they buy.

Some economists argue that workers are compensated for working at risky jobs by receiving risk premiums (higher pay). To the extent this is true, occupational safety and health regulation amounts to in-kind benefits redistributed to workers, over and above what they are able to bargain for on the market. Some economists argue that workers themselves bear the primary cost of such regulations, in foregone wage increases in the long run. There is no real empirical evidence that safety regulations actually have this effect. But even if this were true, it would reduce the cost burden such regulations imposed on the economy, because the cost of the regulations would be counteracted by lower wages paid to workers.

There is a final reason to doubt the calls to subject everything to cost-benefit analyses. Many of the benefits of social regulation, as noted earlier, have no ready dollar value because they are not traded on markets. To economists this is an unfortunate obstacle to analysis, and economists are forever scurrying around, trying to come up with measures of people's "willingness to pay" for clean-smelling air, living in a quiet environment, recreational benefits, or reduced risks of premature death. But the very fact that there is no dollar value assigned to those benefits is one reason many people celebrate them in a special way. Most reasonable people agree that there is a place for markets in society, but most reasonable people also agree that market relationships have their costs as well. Dealings in the market promote certain undesirable personal attitudes and interpersonal relationships. Few are even the economists (although there are some!) who would wish market relationships to dominate within families, or among friends. An obsession with the calculative mindset of market relationships and cost-benefit analyses would itself remove something of what is special about the social regulatory agencies as expressions of a desire to keep market relationships in their place.

None of this means that every regulation promulgated by social regulatory agencies in the last few years is justified. In some instances, as with some affirmative action requirements, regulations may have gone beyond their conceptual justifications. Affirmative action requirements may be an example. In other instances the administrative burden, the paperwork requirements, or the monetary costs of regulating may be too great to justify the benefits, however real, received by those whom the regulations are intended to protect. Offhand, for example, it appears to me that the costs of retrofitting older urban subway systems to accommodate the handicapped, only a small number of whom could be expected to use these systems anyway, appear unjustified, even though failure to retrofit does indeed injure some disadvantaged people. Questions like this should be considered case by case, but with sympathy for those people injured by the failure to regulate.

The thrust of the current movement against social regulation in the United States is a wish by the strong to regain prerogatives whose disappearance, for the most part, is one of the most welcome events of the past decade. Individual regulations can and should be criticized. But the assault on the concept of regulation must be resisted if we are to continue to be a decent people living in a decent society.

Tibor R. Machan

16. DEREGULATION IS A MORAL ISSUE

There are now plenty of studies, economic analyses and investigations, and related work showing that government regulation is harmful, stifling, inefficient, and otherwise destructive. Despite this, the actual regulatory onslaught continues full force, and more is to be expected. Why is this so?

The research has shown that the regulation rarely achieves the goals set for it by Congress. Studies indicate that it has undermined productivity and competition and increased political favoritism and corruption. What used to be called market imperfections have not been eliminated by way of government regulation. Why do millions still continue to believe in the desirability of this discredited system?

Even those few prominent individuals who have come to doubt that regulation is useful consider it a proper function of government where it can achieve its goals. Many more believe that even where government regulation has proven to be ineffective and harmful, the task is simply to muster up greater effort, to "clean up" the agencies, to tighten regulatory specifications — never to abandon the task. In a recent article in *Commentary,* Paul H. Weaver points out that Americans overwhelmingly support "the full range of present-day public programs to which [the New Deal] has given birth. Indeed, something like half the population would like to see the government provide even more benefits and intervene in more areas of social life than it already does. . . . Yet by almost equally large margins, Americans also say that the institutions responsible for creating and running the New Deal state are currently in the hands of liars, cheats, frauds, and profligates." Never mind that economists and social scientists have produced an enormous body of evidence that discredits the very *activity* of regulating!

Why More Regulation?

Some solutions have been offered to the resulting puzzle about the persistent belief in regulation's desirability. Since it is mostly economists who study regulatory activity, they are also the ones interested in why their studies fail to alter policy. The explanation usually offered is that regulation has not been discontinued because the legislators and regulatory bureaucrats are like all other people—they work to benefit *themselves.* It's self-interest that accounts for the continuation of regulatory activities.

This explanation, however, is vacuous. We can't get anything from it, any more than we can from an explanation of animal behavior by reference to instincts. It doesn't explain anything. Why do cats swim in water? Well, they have the instinct to swim in water. What does that mean? It means simply that if you throw them in water they will swim. Why do regulators continue with regulation? Because they continue their regulatory schemes. This is not at all enlightening.

Of course, this misrepresents the complexity of the theory that underlies such explanations. But instead of dwelling on this here, let's consider an alternative explanation.

People often act as they do because they are guided by certain ideas and ideals. Ideas have consequences! And many of the central ideas guiding people in their personal conduct are moral or ethical ideas. Ralph Nader, for example, often makes reference to justice. He insists that it is *unjust* not to prevent product failures. He insists that certain people are being victimized. He argues that certain kinds of corporate activities are evil. Freely using these concepts to explain political and economic affairs, he reflects the views of many in our culture.

These kinds of ideas and ideals are powerful guidelines and motivators of human action. And there is something distinctive about moral or ethical ideals —as opposed to, say, scientific, technological, or legal ideas—as principles of human action.

A moral idea (and *idea* and *ideal* are interchangeable here) is one that provides guidelines to human beings simply as human beings. Why should I be honest? Because human beings *as such* ought to be honest. Why should I be just? Because human beings as such should be just; if an action, policy, or entire institution recommends itself on the grounds that it is just, *any* human being in the community should support it.

Moral Reasons

This is very different from offering an economic explanation for what I do. "It paid well" is not comparable to "It was the just thing to do." Nor is it the same as referring to my preferences. Why did I select that ice cream? Well, I prefer it. That I selected it or that I prefer it does not imply that everyone should do the same thing.

Why then is government regulatory activity continued? Because, despite what economists and many others have demonstrated, people believe that the goals that regulation aims to accomplish are *just* goals; they are morally justifiable goals to strive for. A person who believes that to defend his community or to educate his children is a matter of justice is not likely to be moved—and, if his belief is correct, he shouldn't be moved—by the fact that these will be very expensive. He will say: "I'm sorry. Those sacrifices are justified because this is a moral goal; it is one's duty to do it."

We can talk endlessly to Mr. Nader and Co. about how costly and inefficient government regulation is. If he believes that the goals are morally superior to the other goals that have to be sacrificed so as to pursue them, he will insist that economic concerns can be discounted. This view has been voiced by David Ferber, solicitor with the SEC, in a reply to free-market economist Henry Manne, both writing in the *Vanderbilt Law Review.* Commenting on the regulations imposed by the SEC, Ferber observed, "Since I believe Congress was attempting to improve the morality of the marketplace, I think that the economic effect is largely irrelevant." Edwin M. Zimmerman, assistant attorney general with the antitrust division of the Justice Department, made the same point in his essay in *Promoting Competition,* a Brookings Institution volume. He denies that economic efficiency was ever the impetus for regulatory laws.

Plainly put, many who support regulation believe this to be the correct way to try to achieve valued goals. They are dead-serious about this. And if they are right, they are also on target when they counter that objections based on inefficiency and high cost are trivial, if not outright callous.

So moral ideas are important in this area, so important that there are some who even feign moral reasons for supporting government regulation. When lobbyists and corporate executives appear before Congress and ask for handouts or subsidies or tariffs, often the bottom line is that these would be in the public interest, the public good, the national destiny—or for God and country, as the old saying goes. Those are usually ornaments for shortcuts on the marketplace. But unless people took such ideas seriously, those asking for favors would not bother even to mention them. These are crucial moral terms that count. There are enough people everywhere motivated by just such moral ideas.

Can anyone doubt, then, that *deregulatory* policies would also require moral support? It's not enough to say, "Well, regulation costs too much and it's inefficient." An alternative moral perspective is needed to conclusively establish the propriety of deregulation. Economic arguments alone do not suffice. But *is* there anything in the way of ethics that might support deregulation?

If we look at prominent and widely articulated beliefs about what is right and wrong, we find that altruism is pervasive. Altruism literally means "other-orientedness." This morality is a sort of grab bag for all the various moral systems the bottom line of which is that one's life must be led so as to secure the welfare of others, either today or tomorrow. It is the view that every person's *prime* purpose is to live for others—humanity, one's country, one's race. There are variations on this view, but they all come to this.

Just Helping Out

When made to apply to political policy, the altruist ethic implies that government must try at all costs to achieve the goal of helping people, however bungling, inefficient, or otherwise objectionable such efforts might be. In a debate in *Analog* magazine (April 1975), we find this attitude well illustrated in the words of Alan E. Nourse, a fervent defender of national health insurance. He tells us that it is "not a new concept nor is it a particularly efficient concept as far as health care delivery is concerned, because many many precious dollars will be dribbled away to administration."

Does this suffice to dissuade Mr. Nourse? Do such economic considerations lead to the conclusion that national health insurance is a bad idea? No, counters Nourse, because "it is a concept that might—repeat *might*—meet some of the desperate health care needs that exist today." If the primary responsibility of government is to engage in helping other people, then trying, even in the face of *evidence* that it will not do any good, is quite justifiable. People who share those values will simply continue in the face of disastrous performance records.

But we need to consider whether altruism is really the system that should guide us in our lives. The question is not whether certain of our virtues are other-oriented, nor whether in certain circumstances we are obligated to look out for others. The question is whether we are to live our lives *primarily* for other people.

In a few paragraphs, all the issues involved cannot be covered. There is one interesting point to be raised against altruism, however. Why is it that everyone deserves this prime consideration from others, but not from themselves? Why is it supposed to be this daisy chain of my doing benefit to you, your doing benefit to him, his doing benefit to her, etc.? It clearly engenders a meddlesomeness in human affairs. It invites more rigorous attention to other people's circumstances than to one's own; because if one is first morally obligated to benefit other people, then *their* circumstances, *their* needs, *their* aspirations, and *their* wishes must be known. One must obtain the maximum amount of information about those people, and one must do everything possible to find out what will indeed benefit them.

This explains why there is such widespread government information-intrusion in people's lives. Government, too, must know about others in order to help others. It must be able to walk into private homes, for example, to make sure that welfare recipients get the right care. It is its obligation, according to altruism.

Although altruism claims that individuals should live their lives so as to benefit others but not primarily to benefit themselves, they would, just on the face of it, seem to know much more about themselves to start with. So if people do deserve a lot, why is it that others should do it for them as opposed to their doing it for themselves? This *is* a puzzle, and it's worth considering. But let's leave aside the full criticism that could be offered against altruism and take up as an alternative moral theory that, not surprisingly, is going to be called ethical egoism.

Self-Help

Now *egoism* is not the same as *egotism*. Egotism is an excessive concern with your image or at least with your pleasures and desires. Ethical egoism, in contrast, is a rational concern with one's own happiness. It holds that every human being's prime moral purpose in living is to achieve happiness in life—the fulfillment, throughout one's life, of one's potential as a human being. Happiness is the result of excellence at being human. Here, a person's *primary* responsibility is not to do good for others, although it may still be true that on many occasions human beings should do good for others. The primary moral responsibility of individuals is to achieve their own happiness in life.

So we have an alternative ethics. Is it possible, in terms of this ethics, that in the process of regulating our commercial and many other activities, government is violating certain moral and political principles?

Government regulation usually involves the following. Some activity by some commercial agents, manufacturers, or industrialists might be of harm to someone who is going to buy their product. If it is possible—just barely possible —that these activities will produce some harm to others, the activity is prohibited or regulated. As Senator Javits once put it in a personal communication on the subject of vitamin C, the government must protect citizens against *potential possible hazard.*

Now watch those qualifiers. *Potential, possible* hazards. Even a hazard is only a possible harm. A hazard doesn't guarantee harm. A lot of people have hazardous jobs, meaning that the likelihood of getting hurt in those jobs is considerable. Now imagine a possible hazard. What then is a potentially possible hazard? To be safe in life from "potentially possible hazards," one must be protected in everything.

If, however, one's primary obligation in life is to achieve happiness, and if one shares this obligation with other people—so that *they* should achieve *their* happiness—then, what must first of all be protected and preserved in a social context are the conditions that make it possible for people to strive for or to pursue their happiness. For example, the Declaration of Independence refers to the protection and preservation of rights we have as human beings—the rights to life, liberty, and the pursuit of happiness.

If these are indeed rights that we have and that ought to be protected, then in the pursuit of our happiness, someone else's interference would be wrong, morally wrong. Not just inefficient and very costly, but morally wrong—wrong because human beings should not act that way. In most of the criminal law this point is observed carefully, even if not fully consistently. The burden of proof rests with the prosecution—those who believe they have reason to impose burdens on citizens. Unfortunately, the same principle goes by the wayside when it comes to administering government regulations. If members of an industry, profession, or trade engage in "potentially possible hazardous" activities, there are now legal grounds for placing heavy burdens upon them.

A Risky Business

The most persuasive argument in support of this practice involves what Ralph Nader never tires of citing—the famous thalidomide case. The drug was taken by many Europeans during pregnancy, but the FDA barred its distribution in the United States. It had tragic results in Europe; but in America, almost no one was hurt from the drug. This is constantly noted by Nader in his numerous talks and essays in support of federal regulation of the food and drug industry.

Now it is clear that if guaranteed safety is the highest value we should aim for in life, then Mr. Nader and Co. are on the right track. If it is our prime duty to make certain that other people are safe, then we should never profit from nor allow others to profit from selling them some goods or services that just might be hazardous. But if freedom to seek our own well-being, the political and economic liberty to make our own way in life, is the highest political good, then even the tragic events associated with the thalidomide case do not suffice to give support to government regulation.

Life is undoubtedly a risky business. Those who want to accept risks may not be prevented from doing so regardless of how convinced we are that they are foolish to take these risks. We may not prevent mountain climbers, auto racers, horseback riders, firefighters, and even plain, ordinary consumers of voluntarily acquired drugs and foods from doing what they have chosen to do. *Nor* may we gather into majorities and legislate these wise prohibitions for them.

We can, however, point out how life can be made safer! Hazards can be overcome in a free society, even when other people pose them by their sloppiness, negligence, greed, or stupidity. Government regulations preempt a crucial human virtue: the willingness of industrialists, manufacturers, professionals, to do well at what they have promised themselves to do well—their jobs. By usurping the field of morality, by forbidding the risky business of people's developing themselves and getting on in society through mutual self-development, government regulation is a gross denigration of human dignity itself.

Altruism is the main moral game in town. The only place it is not advocated very much is in psychotherapy sessions and books on self-help therapy, because in these areas people have come to face up to the debilitating consequences of living by such a moral point of view. Entire political institutions, however, are built on the doctrine of altruism. Among these, governmental regulation of people's productive, trading, or consuming activities is just one. Others include all the victimless crime laws, "blue laws," involuntary mental hospitalization statutes; and the list could go on.

But altruism is a view that does not prepare one for coping with life on earth. It stifles personal growth, ambition, self-development; and it encourages deceit. We must claim that everything we want to do will be good for others, just so we can "get away with doing it." And it also gives perfect excuses for our failures—"I did it for you. I lied, killed, maimed, stole, cheated, only because I meant well for you."

Stopping Meddling

Without affirming, with utmost confidence, the alternative moral position—so that each person can realize that the prime moral goal in life is to excel as a person, to become the best one can become in life, given one's human nature and one's personal potentials as an individual human being—the case for stopping all this meddling in people's lives cannot be made conclusively. Sure, governmental regulation is inefficient, devours our income, breeds corruption, centralizes enormous power, stifles production, leaves people overburdened with bureaucratic trivia; but if its goals are morally superior to others, so what? We must be heroic; we must sacrifice for the great good that we might—"repeat might"—achieve. We must toss aside this materialist concern for efficiency, thrift, and prudence. We must march on the noble trail of doing good for our fellow human beings, whether they want it or not.

If, however, we *should* aspire to our own happiness, if this is our primary moral task, then others should abstain from interfering with us; then regulation is not just uneconomic, but wrong. Government regulation violates our rights —period. And we have those rights because it is we, individually and in voluntary cooperation, who should strive to live, produce, trade, and consume. Only by realizing that this is a matter of profound moral truth—not merely of convenience, efficiency, cost, or pleasure (although not without rewards in these respects)—can we overcome the intellectual and basic moral force of tne case for regulation.

That will not lead to instant deregulation. But it will have robbed the meddlers of their most potent weapon—the appeal to people's frequent, even if not fully consistent, concern for doing what is right in personal and political matters.

PART FIVE

Equality and Social Justice: Affirmative Action

In recent years, the most divisive issue of equality and social justice has been the "affirmative action" policy of the federal government. Beginning with interpretations of Title VI of the Civil Rights Act of 1964 in the Nixon administration, universities and contractors who receive federal funds or operate under federal contracts must actively pursue minority-group members and women to demonstrate a good-faith effort to redress the effects of past discrimination.

Proponents of affirmative action maintain that it is not a sufficient interpretation of the idea of justice for an employer to treat all people without prejudice and hire only on the basis of merit. This approach neglects the historical effects of past discrimination. How, they argue, can a black and a white compete in a fair race when the black has to carry a 100-pound sack of flour on his back?

In the landmark *Bakke* case of 1978, the U.S. Supreme Court attempted to resolve this issue. Bakke, a white applicant for medical school, was denied admission even though his grades and test scores exceeded those of nonwhite students admitted under a program for minorities. Nathan Glazer analyzes the decision written by Justice Powell and concludes that while he personally opposes rigid goals or quotas, the *Bakke* decision was the best compromise that was politically feasible. This mode of analysis captures what we had in mind when we discussed "political feasibility" in chapter 1.

Both Thomas Sowell and Ernest van den Haag argue against reverse discrimination. Van den Haag evaluates the pragmatic and ethical arguments in support of and opposition to affirmative action and concludes that all the opposition arguments are severely flawed. Sowell contends that the standard of representation—how many minority members are employed in this business or university—is defective because it ignores the question of availability of potential employees with the requisite skills. He also attacks preferential admissions, hiring, and school busing. Sowell claims that all these policies are opposed by those they are intended to benefit, and benefit only the bureaucrats and liberal politicians who support them.

Hardy Jones analyzes this issue from a radical perspective. He believes that justice can be served only by what he terms a "fair counterfactual meritocracy." Under such a policy, an employer must consider whether a potential employee who is white has attained his superior qualifications as a result of previous injustices against minority groups. People, then, would deserve jobs based on what their qualifications would have been had they been neither victims nor beneficiaries of injustice. Jones concludes in an even more radical vein with the allegation that true justice will never be achieved until the private property system has been surmounted. Jones is a solid supporter of affirmative action policies.

The debate over social justice, that is, how goods in society will be distributed, has been limited by our basically free enterprise system, which operates under the principle that each person gets what he has earned or what other people are willing to give him. Advocates of affirmative action present a fundamental challenge to this conception of justice with their charge that justice cannot be realized—we cannot have a fair race—unless the system is corrected to recompense victims of past injustice.

Nathan Glazer

17. WHY *Bakke* WON'T END REVERSE DISCRIMINATION

If the long opinion written by Justice Powell in the *Bakke* case were truly "the judgment of the Court," then I believe there would be grounds for satisfaction among those of us concerned to protect individual rights and constrain the growing tendency of government and private institutions alike to act on the basis of a person's race and ethnicity. But how can we have any great confidence in the staying power of an opinion written by a single justice, and requiring, to become the judgment of the Court, four justices to uphold the first of its two key parts, and four other justices to uphold the second? To make matters worse, the four justices who upheld Bakke's right of admission stand on much narrower ground than the four who would have denied him admission, and who wish to go much further than Justice Powell in legitimating the use of race and ethnic criteria. And to make matters still worse, all the nine justices agree that deference is due to existing legislation, and the executive and administrative action that implements it—action which has already saddled us with many requirements to take race and ethnicity into account.

These, it seems to me, are the troubling problems that remain even after Justice Powell's opinion—an opinion that I would find consistent with the Constitution, with the broad and sound range of sentiment among the American people—both black and white—as to the kind of society they want, and with the common sense that should guide us in dealing with racial and ethnic diversity.

In reviewing the California Supreme Court's decision in the *Bakke* case, Justice Powell upheld that part of its judgment declaring the admissions program of the University of California Medical School at Davis to be unlawful. One group of four justices—Burger, Stewart, Rehnquist, and Stevens—concurred in this, but did not subscribe to Justice Powell's reasoning. On the other hand, Justice Powell reversed the California Supreme Court's ruling that race cannot be given "any consideration" in the admissions process. Another group of four—Brennan, White, Marshall, and Blackmun—concurred in this, but again their reasoning was very different from Justice Powell's. What weight therefore Justice Powell's opinion, standing as it does on this razor's edge, will have in the future, when similar and related cases must be decided, is uncertain.

Justice Powell begins with a review of the facts in the case. Neutral and straightforward though this account is, it nevertheless raises two questions, which unfortunately play no part in the opinion but have to be taken into account in a broader examination of the problem of the judicial role in our educational institutions, and the adequacy of those institutions themselves.

First, the admissions process of the University of California Medical School at Davis has been subjected to an examination so searching that in itself it seems—to a nonlegal mind—to constitute an excessive degree of interference in the operations of what should be an independent and autonomous institution. Undoubtedly educational institutions, and particularly those that take money in one form or another from the federal government (as almost all do), are not entitled to as much protection as we grant religious institutions, or purely private social institutions, or the family. Yet having personally been involved in admissions processes in different departments in two universities, I am made uneasy when a complex enterprise involving many factors must be dissected, explicated, and justified to a court. We live in a society in which all action, it seems, must be laid fully bare, legally defended. But with what effect on what should be subtle and balanced judgments?

I do not think government is improved when everything is done in the expectation that correspondence and conversations and notes will be subjected by hostile persons to strict and unsympathetic scrutiny. This undoubtedly leads to the practice of "defensive" government, in which actions that should have been taken are not, actions that should not be taken are, in which action is delayed, and in which the costs of action pile up. Similarly, we see the spread of "defensive" medicine to protect against possible malpractice suits. And now we must expect "defensive" admissions and appointments in higher education in anticipation of government intrusion and private litigation. In every field these developments drive out valuable people who will not subject themselves to unfair inquiry, attack, and litigation. I do not have a solution to this problem, and neither does the Supreme Court. Nevertheless I cannot let pass without comment the grotesquely expanded scale of the processes of determining publicly what is fair, and their effect on our institutions and our lives.

In the case of admissions, to be sure, there is an alternative that would obviate such effects: an exclusive reliance on examinations, numbers, scores. This is how it was done when I entered New York's City College in 1940—no interview, no judgment of my past contributions in high school, or of my future contribution to society; in short, to reverse Melbourne, no damn nonsense about anything but merit, as defined by grades. It is not a bad system; we see it in operation in many countries for the distribution of scarce places in institutions of higher education. And yet undoubtedly we gain something in this country from the fact that every school and every graduate department has its *own* admissions procedures in which other factors are considered in addition to grades and scores. Can this diversity and the benefits it provides survive rigorous and repeated judicial examination?

If the first question raised by Justice Powell's review of the facts of the *Bakke* case asks why the procedures of autonomous institutions should be subjected to such searching examination, the second question concerns the soundness of the criteria used by autonomous institutions. Here is what the Supreme Court tells us about the percentile scores on the Medical College Admissions Test (MCAT) of Bakke and the two groups of regular and special admittees in 1973 and 1974:

	Verbal	Quantitative	Science	General Information
1973: Bakke	96	94	97	72
Average of Regular Admittee	81	76	83	69
Average of Special Admittee	46	24	35	33
1974: Bakke	96	94	97	82
Average of Regular Admittee	69	67	82	72
Average of Special Admittee	34	30	37	18

One may put aside the verbal and general-information parts of the MCAT as perhaps not directly relevant to medical practice. But the enormous gap between the regular and special admittees in their quantitative and science scores certainly casts serious doubt on whether the special admittees could actually succeed in getting through medical school, and if they did, what their success could possibly mean.

My two concerns are of course in contradiction: I want the courts to keep out of this kind of business, but I want the institutions to act responsibly as educational institutions. (In an earlier case this year, a student at the University of Missouri-Kansas City Medical School was dismissed shortly before she was due to graduate, and the judgment of the Court was to allow the dismissal to stand. I approved the Court's deference to an autonomous educational institution, but at the same time I was bothered by the possibility of unfairness to the student in question.) But in any event, neither the issue of educational autonomy nor the issue of responsibility played any part in the *Bakke* opinions.

Part II of Justice Powell's argument considers whether the provisions of Title VI of the Civil Rights Act of 1964 are applicable: "No person in the United States, shall, on the ground of race, color, or national origin, be excluded from participation in, be denied the benefits of, or be subjected to discrimination under any program or activity receiving federal financial assistance." Is the Civil Rights Act more restrictive in the way it looks upon the use of racial classifications than the Equal Protection Clause of the Fourteenth Amendment ("No State shall . . . deny to any person within its jurisdiction the equal protection of the laws")? Examining the legislative history, Justice Powell concludes that "Title VI must be held to proscribe only those racial classifications that would violate the Equal Protection Clause. . . ."

Therefore, he engages, in Part II, in a lengthy analysis of the question of whether the Equal Protection Caluse protects only blacks or whether it protects everyone. Clearly this is a crucial point, affecting our judgment of the degree to which remedial action for blacks (or other minorities that we consider equivalent to them under the Fourteenth Amendment) may be permitted to harm individuals in other groups. Justice Powell says, first, that even the University of California admits that decisions based on race or ethnic origin do raise questions under the Fourteenth Amendment, and that, on the other side, even Bakke did not argue that "all racial or ethnic classifications are *per se* invalid." Interestingly enough, of the four cases that Justice Powell cites to shore up the position that government may under some circumstances take account of race, two came out of the deportation of Japanese-Americans from California in World War II and a third is the recent case unsuccessfully brought by the Hasidim of Williamsburg in Brooklyn against an action designed by the New York State legislature to increase the voting power of blacks and which reduced their own voting power. This is not a promising group of cases on which to ground a constitutional right to make racial and ethnic distinction.

Be that as it may, Justice Powell goes on to say that the use of racial and ethnic categories does require "strict scrutiny by courts." White males are protected by the Constitution, just as blacks are. We cannot set up a "two-class" view of the Fourteenth Amendment, in which persons in some groups are deserving of less protection than others. In the decades after the passage of the Fourteenth Amendment, Justice Powell writes, "the United States had become a nation of minorities. Each had to struggle — and to some extent struggles still — to overcome the prejudices not of a monolithic majority, but of a 'majority' composed of various minority groups. . . . As the nation filled with the stock of many lands, the reach of the Clause was gradually extended to all ethnic groups seeking protection against discrimination." Justice Powell refers to cases protecting Celtic Irishmen, Chinese, Austrian resident aliens, Japanese, Mexican Americans. "The guarantees of equal protection, the Court said in *Yick Wo* [1886], 'are universal in their application to all persons within the territorial jurisdiction, without regard to any differences of race, color, or nationality. . . .' "

Justice Powell takes a strong line in this section of his opinion. He rejects the argument of the University of California that "discrimination against members of the white 'majority' cannot be suspect if its purpose can be characterized as 'benign.' " And he attacks directly the view of the second group of four (Brennan, White, Marshall, and Blackmun) that only if there is a "stigma" on a group is it covered by the Equal Protection Clause:

> The Equal Protection Clause is not framed in terms of "stigma." . . . The word has no clearly defined constitutional meaning. It reflects a subjective judgment that is standardless. *All* state-imposed classifications that rearrange burdens and benefits on the basis of race are likely to be viewed with deep resentment by the individual burdened. The denial to innocent persons of equal rights and opportunities may outrage those so deprived and therefore may be perceived as invidious. These individuals are likely to find little comfort in the notion that the deprivation they are asked to endure is merely the price of membership in the dominant majority and that its imposition is inspired by the supposedly benign purpose of aiding others. One should not lightly dismiss the inherent unfairness of, and the perception of mistreatment that accompanies, a system of allocating benefits and privileges on the basis of skin color and ethnic origin.

In attacking the "two-class" theory of the Fourteenth Amendment, Justice Powell takes up a more sophisticated and complex position on the ethnic character of the United States than I have seen before in any opinion of the Supreme Court:

> . . . The difficulties entailed in varying the level of judicial review according to a perceived "preferred" status of a particular racial and ethnic minority are intractable. The concepts of "majority" and "minority" necessarily reflect temporary arrangements and political judgments. As observed above, the white "majority" itself is composed of various minority goups, most of which can lay claim to a history of prior discrimination at the hands of the state and private individuals. Not all of these groups can receive preferential treatment and corresponding judicial tolerance of distinctions drawn in terms of race and nationality, for then the only "majority" left would be a new minority of White Anglo-Saxon Protestants. There is no principled basis for deciding which groups would merit "heightened judicial solicitude" and which would not. Courts would be asked to evaluate the extent of prejudice and consequent harm suffered by various minority goups. Those whose societal injury is thought to exceed some arbitrary level of tolerability would be entitled to preferential classifications. . . . As these preferences began to have their desired effect, and the consequences of past discrimination were undone, new judicial rankings would be necessary. The kind of variable sociological and political analysis necessary to produce such rankings simply does not lie within the judicial competence — even if they otherwise were politically feasible and socially desirable.

And Justice Powell goes on to quote at length Justice Douglas's ringing dissent in *DeFunis* against the use of racial and ethnic categories.

It is of particular importance, I believe, that Justice Powell has attacked the theory that only stigmatized groups, groups thought inferior, deserve the protection of the Constitution. This theory—recently put forth by Ronald Dworkin in an article on the *Bakke* case, and also embraced by the second group of four—is remarkably dangerous in a world in which economically and educationally successful minorities have met, in many countries, the fiercest discrimination, going as far as the confiscation of their property and the loss of their lives. Are we to believe that discrimination against such minorities—Jews, for example, or Chinese—is lawful under our Constitution? Have these groups overcome their historic "stigma" just by becoming prosperous? And are minorities alone in bearing a stigma? In many of our colleges and universities in the past decade, not a few whites may well have felt burdened by a "stigma," and it may have affected them in not inconsequential ways. One can recognize that there is a considerable range in the stigmas borne by various groups, and yet still applaud Justice Powell's contention that all racial and ethnic discrimination is deserving of "strict scrutiny."

Having concluded that the Constitution protects all individuals from discrimination on grounds of race and ethnicity, Justice Powell examines the arguments that might justify, even under "strict scrutiny," the Davis admission program. The language of the Court as to what might justify a "suspect classification"—race—is that "a state must show that its use of the classification is 'necessary . . . to the accomplishment' of its purpose or the safeguarding of its interest." This language, from earlier cases, is not very helpful, but it is all there is. With its guidance Justice Powell considers four arguments for the use of racial classifications in medical admissions.

The first is "to reduce the historic deficit of traditionally disfavored minorities in medical schools and the medical profession." While this may seem an adequate basis for racial classification to some, Justice Powell dismisses it out of hand. The second is to counter the effects of past discrimination. He rejects this too. The state certainly has an interest in overcoming the effects of past discrimination, but in order to use racial classification to do this, there must be "judicial, legislative, or administrative findings of constitutional or statutory violations." There are none in this case. The third is to increase the number of physicians in underserved communities. Justice Powell here supports the view of the Supreme Court of California that race is no index of where a physician will serve. Finally, there is the argument that racial classification is necessary to attain a diverse student body. This to Justice Powell is a legitimate objective of academic freedom, which apparently is protected in our well-interpreted Constitution under the First Amendment.

But racial classification of the rigid sort practiced by the Davis Medical School, he says, is not the only road to a diverse student body. The state interest involved is not simply in a racially or ethnically diverse student body: "The diversity that furthers a compelling state interest encompasses a far broader array of qualifications and characteristics of which racial or ethnic origin is but a single though important element. [Davis's] special-admissions program, focused *solely* on ethnic diversity, would hinder rather than further attainment of genuine diversity." Justice Powell then goes on to commend the Harvard College admissions program, in which factors like geographical distribution and academic interests are taken into account in choosing students, as well as race.

The troubling problem of the competence of judicial intervention into educational programs is illustrated by the fact that a *college* admissions program — which inevitably must concern itself with such questions as whether there are enough students to fill the labs, the orchestra, and the athletic teams — is used by Justice Powell as an example of the kind of admissions program that might guide a highly selective professional school. Without going into the questions that might be raised by this distinction, Justice Powell commends the looser Harvard College approach as against the more rigid Davis Medical School quota. He recognizes — as the Brennan group argues — that this is only a more subtle and sophisticated way of taking race into account. But there is a key difference to him between making race *the* factor and "an admission program where race and ethnic background is simply one element — to be weighed fairly against other elements — in the selection process."

The Stevens four, who joined with Powell to make possible Bakke's admission, had no need for such refined analysis. To them, Title VI of the Civil Rights Act of 1964, banning discrimination on grounds of race in governmentally supported programs, was sufficient. It was unnecessary to go into the Constitution, or into issues of when and how race could be used.

It is the distinction, made by Justice Powell alone, between the legitimate and illegitimate use of race in admissions, that dismays those who hoped that the *Bakke* decision might give a decisive answer to the problem of affirmative discrimination. If race may be "a" factor, may it not covertly be "the" factor? Will not the Davis approach in other guises — e.g., the commended Harvard approach — in effect creep back into the admissions process? Will not a rigid statistical standard, not announced in so many words and numbers, boldly, but held covertly in the minds of an admissions committee, prevail?

Concerned as I am to erect a wall against the use of racial and ethnic categories by government and public institutions, I am nevertheless content with Justice Powell's position. The argument that it only drives the Davis type of program underground would remain even if Justice Powell had upheld the California Supreme Court in its denial of any role to race or ethnicity. The fact is that in any system that goes beyond test scores and grades it is impossible for racial and ethnic considerations not to play a role in admissions, whatever the Supreme

Court may say. These considerations played a role before the rise of statistically based affirmative action, at a time when it was still illegal in many places even to seek information as to race and ethnic background. Colleges and professional schools sought diversity, or sought for members of given minority groups. This was not the only criterion, of course, but it was often a factor in making up a class.

And, indeed, how could it not be? If one took as relevant to the composition of a class geographical representation, representation from small undergraduate schools and large ones, a range of interests in the sub-parts of the field, how could one totally rule out racial and ethnic background in a country in which these are dominant social forces? To exclude constitutionally any consideration of these factors would inevitably lead to their being considered covertly.

There are two arguments for the position taken by the Supreme Court of California that considerations of race and ethnicity must be totally excluded. One is the constitutional and statutory argument: This is what the Constitution says we must do; this is what the law, as passed by Congress, says we must do. It is the position I myself would like to hold. Certainly it is the way I read the Constitution, and the way I read the Civil Rights Act of 1964. Unfortunately it is not the way a majority of the Supreme Court reads the Constitution, at least for the moment.

But even more damaging to this position, it is not the way the Congress is willing to read its own legislation. Congress had the opportunity, in 1972, when revising sections of the Civil Rights Act of 1964, to make it absolutely clear that the original legislation meant what it said when it prohibited racial preferences because of a statistical "imbalance" in employment. Congress refused to take this opportunity. Since Justice Powell leans heavily on statutes, on the intention of Congress—as do the Stevens four which supported him on Bakke's right to admission—it is particularly damaging to the future stability of their position that Congress has been pusillanimous in asserting that it would not stand for racial and ethnic tests in federally funded programs. Quite the contrary, as the Brennan four point out, Congress has mandated them in at least one important program. In 1977, it required that 10 percent of grants for local public-works projects should be spent for "minority business enterprises," defined as businesses 50 percent of which are owned by "Negroes, Spanish-speaking, Orientals, Indians, Eskimos, and Aleuts."

The Brennan four write of this act of Congress (a challenge to which, incidentally, the Supreme Court refused to review a few days after the *Bakke* decision):

> What is most significant about the congressional consideration of this measure is that although the use of a racial quota or "set-aside" by a recipient of

federal funds would constitute a direct violation of Title VI if that statute were read to prohibit race-conscious action, no mention was made during the debates in either the House or the Senate of even the possibility that the quota provisions for minority contractors might in any way conflict with or modify Title VI. It is inconceivable that such a purported conflict would have escaped congressional attention through inadvertent failure to recognize the relevance of Title VI.

Even worse, in another section of the public-works act with its minority set-aside there is a provision barring discrimination on the basis of sex which provides that it should be enforced "through agency provisions and rules similar to those already established, with respect to racial and other discrimination under Title VI of the Civil Rights Act of 1964."

That Congress in 1977 passed this ill-advised legislation does not tell us what congressional intent in 1964 was. But if this intent must be reaffirmed by new congressional action, in the face of administrative determination to impose racial and ethnic goals and quotas, and in order to guide wavering courts who will give deference to congressional statute, then can we expect such reaffirmation from a Congress capable of passing a bill prescribing racial quotas?

To doubt the viability of the strict line taken by the California Supreme Court is, I realize, tantamount to saying that we are unlikely to get anything better than Justice Powell's position in the fight against these new benign Nuremberg laws either from the Supreme Court or from Congress. I would hope that the continued exploration and demonstration of the evils of reverse Nurembergism would eventually persuade Congress and the courts—as, according to all the survey data, they have persuaded a huge majority of the American people—that we want no governmentally imposed racial and ethnic classifications, and that state judgment, and the judgment of institutions that carry a state interest, must be based on individual, not racial and ethnic, grounds. Thus, an exploration of how the 10 percent set-aside has been administered—the fact that businessmen have to show their minority credentials to be "accredited," that corruption and deception are fostered, that waste is encouraged, that successful minority businesses are not in fact made this way, and that those which are set up by protected government contracts will be blown away in any light wind—might dissuade Congress from trying to deal any further with ethnic and racial problems by means of such crude requirements.

There is a second, more substantial argument in favor of the Supreme Court of California's total prohibition on the use of race. If we want a society in which individuals are treated as individuals by public bodies, and as far as possible in private life, without regard to race and ethnicity, then we cannot get there by allowing or prescribing public action in the opposite direction, even on a temporary basis. These measures will not be temporary, as the Brennan four hope, since those who profit from racial and ethnic distinction will not easily give up their benefits. And there will always be some statistic to point to that will justify continued preferential treatment.

The difficulty of determining a standard for ending affirmative discrimination is well illustrated in a section of the Brennan opinion which points out that the Davis 16 percent quota is lower than the proportion of blacks and Chicanos in California (22 percent). The Brennan opinion did not bother to look into the distribution of these groups by age (how many are in the 22-26-year range which typically encompasses medical school?), or by percentage of college graduates, or by percentage of college graduates with minimal science and math, all of which might demonstrate, in direct opposition to the Brennan group's reasoning, that the 16 percent quota is much too high, and leads to the admission of students with the lamentably low scores that Justice Powell reported.

The statistical standard also leaves in silence the fate of groups, like the Japanese and Chinese, who are simultaneously "overrepresented" in relation to their proportion of the state population, and are eligible for quota admission. Thus, Asians, 4 percent of the population of California, were 9.5 percent of those admitted under the regular program to Davis in 1971, 13 percent in 1972, and 15.5 percent in 1973, and yet were eligible under the special admissions program (just as "Orientals" are included in the 10 percent set-aside). If "proportionateness" is the standard, even a rough proportionateness, then groups like the Jews, drawn to medicine, adept at science and math, motivated to become doctors, will suffer, while others less suited by training or motivation will become doctors because quotas make it easier for them.

Despite these and other powerful substantive arguments against "any consideration" of race and ethnicity, I believe we must accept Justice Powell's position. In a multiethnic society, while we would not want government to prescribe the degree of such considerations by imposing quotas and goals, we would want individuals and institutions to take these factors into account voluntarily and by their own lights. In a typical example, we would not want government to require a balanced ticket, but we would want the good sense of political leaders to operate so that all groups get political representation. In other fields, we all accept programs with the same objective. Our various work programs address themselves not only to the poor and the unemployed but to blacks, Mexican-Americans, Puerto Ricans. Our various minority recruiting, tutoring, and assistance programs address themselves not only to those outside the normal channels of recruitment and the underprepared as such but to specific racial and ethnic groups.

By not drawing a "fence around the law," Justice Powell left open many difficult decisions. How will institutions and individuals differentiate between race as "the" factor and race as "a" factor? He recognizes this problem and quotes Justice Frankfurter: "A boundary line is none the worse for being narrow." Alas, the problem is more difficult than mere narrowness. Thus, critics of Justice Powell's distinction assert it will encourage litigation. It will. But the only decision that would have discouraged litigation is one which simply accepted racial quotas. Ruling out race entirely would not have discouraged litigation, for many would have claimed—and I am sure justly—that it had been a factor.

Justice Powell ends with a plea that is surprising—that we have more trust in the good faith of institutions: ". . . a court would not assume that a university, professing to employ a facially nondiscriminatory admissions policy, would operate it as a cover for the functional equivalent of a quota system. In short, good faith would be presumed in the absence of a showing to the contrary in the manner permitted by our cases." And here he refers to a case in which the Supreme Court has accepted the good faith of a suburban community in denying permission to build a low-income housing project (*Arlington Heights* v. *Metropolitan Development Corp.*), and a case in which a test that selected low proportions of blacks for the police force was accepted as legal (*Washington* v. *Davis*). Whether we can hope for trust in "good faith" in a society in which so many people do not believe in the good faith of government, so many government administrators do not believe in the good faith of our educational institutions and businessmen, and so many patients do not believe in the good faith of doctors, is doubtful. Litigation there will be. Still, the distinction Justice Powell draws is a fair one, and if litigation is needed to refine it further, so be it.

Yet one looks forward with some trepidation to *how* the Court will refine it. Four members would accept quotas, with no safeguards. The four who voted to admit Bakke were not overly articulate in developing their position. But all three parties—Justice Powell, who wrote for himself alone, the Stevens group, and the Brennan group—told us clearly that congressional statutes, and executive and administrative findings and regulations, would receive their deference and play a major role in how they interpreted the legality of quotas and goals. Is this not the key signal that the Court has given us? Those of us who oppose rigid goals and quotas as a travesty of what America is supposed to be and wishes to be have nothing to hope for from the Carter administration and its bureaucratic appointees. But there is still the Congress, still responsive to public opinion, and capable of being troubled by the use of racial and ethnic categories to govern state action.

It is there, in the Congress, that we should seek for a sharper and clearer statement, spelled out so that administrators and courts will have no alternative but to follow it, that no American may be discriminated against on grounds of race and ethnicity.

Ernest van den Haag

18. Reverse Discrimination: A Brief Against It

How am I, as Secretary of HEW, ever going to find first-class black doctors, first-class black lawyers, first-class black scientists, first-class women scientists, if these people don't have the chance to get into the best [schools] in the country?

—Joseph A. Califano, Jr.,
New York Times, 18 March 1977

I

On April Fool's Day Mr. Califano wisely fudged these words he had spoken two weeks earlier. However, he still does not understand that reversing discrimination is inconsistent with enforcing equality of opportunity. Preferential admissions to colleges and professional schools are now widely practiced. So is "affirmative action," which is basically analogous to preferential admissions: it applies to hiring, promotion, and employment in general. Persons belonging to selected minorities or underrepresented groups (such as women, or blacks) are admitted or hired if they meet scholastic standards which are specially lowered for them. Or, they are given preference over others who have performed as well or better in meeting requirements. This practice, which Secretary Califano endorses, discriminates, in effect, against those who are being displaced in favor of those who displace them. Its legality has been attacked with respect to state institutions. But the Supreme Court, although it heard the *DeFunis* case (*DeFunis v. Odegaard,* 1974), avoided deciding it because DeFunis, who had sued the university, had by that time been admitted and graduated.

Both preferential admissions and affirmative action are meant to discriminate against discrimination, to reduce discrimination by favoring those discriminated against in the past, or elsewhere. Is this reversal morally justifiable? Can it be effective in achieving its purpose?

In the past Oxford and Cambridge gave preference to the sons of great English families even when their qualifications did not justify it. They were preferred because they would exercise power and influence whether admitted or not. It was thought that society would benefit more by educating these students than by educating others who, even if more meritorious, would be likely to exercise less influence on the course of social affairs. The advantage to the universities was expected to be greater as well—a matter that probably did not escape the attention of the admitting authorities. For similar reasons, American universities in the past gave preference to students likely to inherit great wealth. Is a reversal of this pattern required by justice, or is it socially useful, as the old pattern was thought to be? Let me consider the social usefulness before turning to the justice of reversal.

Could society benefit from the preferential admission of the disadvantaged as it might have benefited from the preferential admission of the privileged? Scarcely. There is no reason to believe that members of groups previously discriminated against will exercise disproportionate social power or influence, regardless of higher education denied or received. Hence their preferential admission cannot be justified by reasoning that their education deserves preference because it would be socially more useful than that of the more meritorious.

Preferential admissions might be useful in other respects. If one assumes that society consists of separate communities, each wanting indigenous leaders, preferential admissions (even quotas) might help provide higher education for the requisite number of members of each group. (This was the justification English universities advanced for giving some preference to potential Indian and African leaders.) But women, or even blacks, do not form segregated political or cultural communities. Where they do, our present policy is to integrate or at least to desegregate them. Although the "melting pot" image of America simplifies and exaggerates, the Swiss paradigm of full geographical and cultural separation is neither feasible nor desirable in the United States. (Anyway, those who desire it can avail themselves of the private colleges exclusively attended by the groups of their choice.) Preferential admission of the previously disadvantaged cannot rest, then, on the social benefit to be gained by educating the independently powerful, or on the need for indigenous leadership.

Another argument for preferential admissions conceives of institutions of higher learning and of other nonpolitical institutions as representative bodies, in which all classes, races, sexes, and religions—however well integrated—ought to be represented in proportion to their share of the population, even if admission standards have to differ for each group to secure its proportional representation. Yet educational or business, unlike political, institutions are not meant to be representative. In politics, representativeness, rightly or wrongly, plays a major role, although it is often hard to see who, and what, is represented: The occupational, class, age, and sex ratios of our representative bodies scarcely reflect those of the population. Still, it would be hard for a white man to be elected in Harlem; and political tickets wisely tend to represent important ethnic, religious, or geographical groupings of voters.

However, institutions of higher learning are not political bodies and cannot represent the voters without defeating their function, which is to teach and do research, not to make political decisions. So too with business enterprises; to require representativeness in faculties, or student bodies, is no more justified than to require representativeness in Chinese restaurants, prisons, hospitals, or opera houses. These institutions have nonrepresentative functions which require admission (or confinement) criteria relevant to those functions, regardless of representativeness. So too with graduate or professional schools. We want the most able and gifted to be prepared for the tasks at hand by the most able and gifted, regardless of sex or race. To demand representativeness would be contrary to the social interest which requires the best surgeon, or the best singer, to be educated for his task, not the racially or sexually most representative.

I can find no utilitarian justification, then, for preferential admission of previously underrepresented national, racial, or sexual groups. On the contrary, it would be dysfunctional, favoring persons less able to learn and teach than those rejected, and thus causing society to be served by the less able in the professions education prepares for. *Mutatis mutandis,* this applies to noneducational institutions as well. Let me turn now to nonutilitarian justifications.

II

Should the preference given the powerful in the past be reversed for the sake of justice? Surely, to do so would shift rather than repair injustice. Injustice would not be reduced, but merely inflicted on a different group. If the preference given the powerful was wrong because it violated equality of individual opportunity and the rule of admission by relevant qualification only, then violation of that rule in favor of a different group, the powerless, would be no less wrong, however generous the reparative intent.

Individual reparations can be justified if the victim of discrimination and the victimizer are individually identifiable. Thus, qualified persons who were not hired because they were discriminated against may be compensated for their loss. There is a case even for collective compensation, if losses are tangible (e.g., racial firings, confiscations, or delicensings as in Nazi Germany), and if victimizers and victims, though not individually identifiable, are roughly contemporary as groups. Matters become murky, however, if one considers granting compensation to persons not allowed to acquire the qualifications they might have acquired had they been admitted and which might have led to higher incomes than they actually did earn. Unjust losses certainly were suffered, but we cannot know their incidence and size.

Matters become even more murky if the discriminatory rules were imposed over a long period in the distant past. The incidence of the unjustly achieved advantages and of the unjustly imposed disadvantages becomes diffuse and uncertain, as does the liability for both. Moreover, current generations can bear no responsibility for discrimination imposed by generations past, other than to discontinue it. Can today's Italians be held liable for Caesar's invasion of Gaul, or today's Frenchmen for Napoleon's invasion of Germany? Can Polish or Italian workers be held liable for the fate inflicted on American Indians by the colonists? or Jewish teachers and students for disabilities imposed on blacks in the past? or contemporary males for past discrimination against women? We are told (Deut. 24:16): "The fathers shall not be put to death for the children, neither shall the children be put to death for the fathers: every man shall be put to death for his own sin." It is a good rule. Those not responsible for it cannot be asked to compensate for the damage. They can only be restrained from causing further losses.

Justice, then, requires the cessation of discriminatory activites, including discrimination in admissions or hiring, but no reversal. Preferential admissions to repair past injustice might "discriminate for" persons who themselves suffered no "discrimination against," at the expense of persons not responsible for past "discrimination against."

The problem of compensation for the present consequences of past injustice cannot be met, then, by preferential admissions. Still, efforts to solve it are demanded by generosity, if not by justice. Some members of the formerly "discriminated against" groups have native abilities which would justify admission to the schools or hiring by the enterprises to which they have applied, had these abilities not remained undeveloped because of unfavorable circumstances co-produced by past discrimination. Colleges and universities may play a role in helping such applicants to overcome hardships, in order to prepare them for (nonpreferential) admission. Pre-admission tutoring may be a reasonable effort to offset the present effects of past injustices in which colleges participated, and thus to make amends.

III

Occasionally it is argued that preferential admissions are needed to offset unfairness inherent in the tests which universities and professional schools use to decide on admissions. These tests are thought to discriminate against qualified persons who belong to disadvantaged groups. Actually, they are quite reliable in predicting the likely degree of success in the professional and graduate schools which use them. They measure relevant abilities, regardless of sex or race. Their value is limited; the tests do not measure nonacademic abilities or human characteristics, nor predict the degree of success in activities for which they are not designed. However, though less than perfect, the tests serve well the limited purpose for which they are used. Preferential admissions, far from offsetting unfairness, instead would introduce it by setting aside the objective measurement the tests permit, in favor of racial or sexual privileges.

IV

Sexes and races are not proportionally represented among students admitted to professional and graduate schools, nor among faculties, nor in the ranks of corporations. This has been regarded as evidence of discrimination against the underrepresented. Radicals insist that disproportionate representation is unfair even when it does reflect actual differences in abilities, qualifications, or motivations. Others, philosophically more moderate, believe that equal treatment necessarily would lead to proportional representation of all groups. Thus, disproportionate representation *eo ipso* demonstrates "discrimination against" the underrepresented, even if it cannot be verified independently, and preferential admission may become an appropriate remedy.

If one assumes that all relevant aptitudes, talents, and motivations are equally distributed among classes, sexes, nationalities, and races, then over- or underrepresentation of any one group in desirable activities necessarily indicates unequal treatment. Such an assumption has never been shown to be true. Widespread abilities (e.g., the ability to be a farmer, a janitor, or a clerk) seem to be distributed fairly equally among groups. But the ability to study mathematics or teach it, or to run a major enterprise, is not that widespread. Universities and corporations cannot draw on a number of talented people in each group proportional to the size of the group. And if the members of different groups are not necessarily equally qualified *ab initio,* objective tests need not lead to proportional representation. Over- or underrepresentation does not indicate bias any more than proportional representation of groups among admitted candidates indicates unbiased admissions standards. Racist theories notwithstanding, the overrepresentation of Jews in important professions in Germany, and the consequent underrepresentation of non-Jewish Germans, did not indicate a discriminatory policy to place the latter at a disadvantage in favor of the former.

V

Is preferential admission of students, or affirmative action in hiring faculty or executives, a suitable remedy for actual or suspected discrimination? Both policies set numerical goals which, when achieved, would make faculties and student bodies, or executive units, reflect the proportions in which women or various racial goups occur, either in the general population, or among candidates with appropriate prior degrees and specializations.

Outside academic institutions, the advantages of using affirmative action to establish equality of opportunity may at times outweigh the disadvantages, when a licensing or admissions board, or an employer, currently discriminates against a group. There is a *prima facie* indication of discrimination if all those admitted, employed, or licensed are white, or male, even though others wish to be, and if (1) no distinctive qualifications are needed for the job or license; or (2) the distinctive qualifications needed can be shown to be possessed by the rejected candidates in substantially the same degree as by the accepted ones; or (3) the relevant qualifications can be tested, yet no suitable tests are used (or the tests used discriminate irrelevantly). In such cases numerical goals help to attain equality of opportunity. Yet they should be abandoned as soon as improper discriminatory practices cease, for numerical goals necessarily reduce the appropriate discriminations in hiring, promotion, firing, or licensing in terms of actual skill, reliability, diligence, etc.

Numerical goals *ipso facto* disregard the distinctive individual qualifications of candidates, or reduce the decisive weight they should have in most cases. They certainly cannot be appropriate for educational institutions, where these distinctive qualifications must be paramount. Further, academic institutions can (and do) properly test individual qualifications for admission. Therefore, numerical goals, far from reducing irrelevant discrimination, perpetuate or introduce it into academic institutions by placing more qualified persons at a disadvantage relative to less qualified or equally qualified ones who belong to an underrepresented race or sex. (Where individual qualifications, although of decisive importance, are not always objectively testable — e.g., in hiring or promotions — universities and professional schools usually are willing to submit disputes to arbitrators.)

VI

Consider now the effects on persons, rather than institutions. The effect of academic affirmative action, or of preferential admissions, on those discriminated for is likely to be unhelpful. There are three possibilities. First, there is the unqualified law student who was preferentially admitted. He will drop out because of low grades which were predictable from his entrance test. He may be worse off than before.

Second, some preferentially admitted students graduate by dint of preferential grading or undemanding curricula specially fashioned for them. They profit from the credentials obtained. But the group which was to be favored pays a high price: The black college graduate, Ph.D., or lawyer who graduated because lower standards were applied to him than to his white counterparts is not as competent as they are and will reinforce the prejudice which maintains that blacks are necessarily less competent than whites.

Third, there is the preferentially admitted black student who, despite low entrance scores, actually catches up and does well without preferential grading. Yet he may never know whether he graduated because he was black or because he deserved to. If he does know, others will not; he will suffer from the image perpetuated by his fellow student whose preferential admission was complemented by preferential grading. Similarly, female or black professors hired or promoted because of affirmative action will not know whether they were hired because they were qualified or because they were female or black; nor will others. Those hired because they belong to an underrepresented group though they are not the most qualified persons also will perpetuate the image of low competence of the underrepresented group — the image that contributed to discrimination against it in the first place.

The persons excluded because of preferential admissions or affirmative action naturally are no less bitter than those who in the past were excluded by discrimination. Since "discrimination for" merely reverses "discrimination against," it cannot but perpetuate the group hostilities of the past. This applies as well to all enterprises which practice reverse discrimination.

There is also an unattractive arbitrariness about the whole procedure. Unless inclusion into the groups discriminated for is determined by sex, it often must be capricious. Puerto Ricans, Spaniards, Argentinians, and Mexicans are all "Spanish surnamed." It is hard to see what else they have in common, or why they should receive different treatment than Portuguese, Brazilians, or Arabs. And it is not obvious that various white "ethnics" suffered less from discrimination than females did. Yet they are not preferentially admitted, or hired, by affirmative action. These remedies, then, are not only counterproductive and unjust most of the time, but also arbitrarily selective. Perhaps this is a minor defect compared to those already mentioned: If an idea is bad, arbitrary application does not make it much worse. Nonetheless the inherent capriciousness of the scheme and the unavoidable arbitrariness in execution are psychologically repulsive.

VII

Affirmative action and preferential admissions were aided and abetted by persons who felt guilty enough about past discrimination to make amends, even at the expense of innocent third persons. Groups which, rightly or wrongly, felt discriminated against in the past also have supported affirmative action and preferential admissions. But in the main these are creatures of the federal bureaucracy and judiciary. The bureaucracy actually gave birth to the illegitimate child; the judiciary adopted and legalized it.

Fears that a bureaucratic monstrosity would be foisted on the country were voiced in Congress during the debate on the Civil Rights Act of 1964. Such fears were laid to rest when the managers of the bill, Senators Joseph Clark and Clifford Case, submitted a memorandum stating:

> There is no requirement in Title VII that an employer maintain a racial balance in his work force. On the contrary, any deliberate attempt to maintain a racial balance, whatever such balance may be, would involve a violation of Title VII because maintaining such a balance would require an employer to hire or refuse to hire on the basis of race. It must be emphasized that discrimination is prohibited as to any individual . . . the question in each case would be whether that individual was discriminated against. (110 *Congressional Record* 7213, 8 April 1964)

Further, at the behest of the bill's sponsors, the Department of Justice submitted a memorandum stating:

> Finally, it has been asserted that Title VII would impose a requirement for "racial balance." This is incorrect. There is no provision, either in Title VII or in any other part of this bill, that requires or authorizes any federal agency or federal court to require preferential treatment for any individual group for the purpose of achieving racial balance.
>
> No employer is required to hire an individual because that individual is a Negro. No employer is required to maintain any ratio of Negroes to whites, Jews to gentiles, Italians to English, or women to men. (110 *Congressional Record* 7207, 8 April 1964)

Despite the clear language of these memoranda, the bureaucracy has perverted the intent of the legislation. Racial balance and the group preferences needed to attain it are prescribed and enforced. The courts have found constitutional arguments to help administrative agencies override the intent of Congress. Bureaucracy has replaced both democracy and common sense. They can be reinstated only when the citizens push Congress and the courts into disciplining and limiting the bureaucracy.

Thomas Sowell

19. Are Quotas Good for Blacks?

Race has never been an area noted for rationality of thought or action. Almost every conceivable form of nonsense has been believed about racial or ethnic groups at one time or another. Theologians used to debate whether black people had souls (today's terminology might suggest that *only* black people have souls). As late as the 1920s, a leading authority on mental tests claimed that test results disproved the popular belief that Jews are intelligent. Since then, Jewish IQs have risen above the national average and more than one fourth of all American Nobel Prize winners have been Jewish.

Today's grand fallacy about race and ethnicity is that the statistical "representation" of a group—in jobs, schools, etc.—shows and measures *discrimination*. This notion is at the center of such controversial policies as affirmative action hiring, preferential admissions to college, and public school busing. But despite the fact that far-reaching judicial rulings, political crusades, and bureaucratic empires owe their existence to that belief, it remains an unexamined assumption. Tons of statistics have been collected, but only to be interpreted in the light of that assumption, never to test the assumption itself. Glaring facts to the contrary are routinely ignored. Questioning the "representation" theory is stigmatized as not only inexpedient but immoral. It is the noble lie of our time.

Affirmative Action Hiring

"Representation" or "underrepresentation" is based on comparisons of a given group's percentage in the population with its percentage in some occupation, institution, or activity. This might make sense if the various ethnic groups were even approximately similar in age distribution, education, and other crucial variables. But they are not.

Some ethnic groups are a whole decade younger than others. Some are two decades younger. The average age of Mexican-Americans and Puerto Ricans is under twenty, while the average age of Irish-Americans or Italian-Americans is over thirty—and the average age of Jewish-Americans is over forty. This is because of large differences in the number of children per family from one group to another. Some ethnic groups have more than twice as many children per family as others. Over half of the Mexican-American and Puerto Rican population consists of teenagers, children, and infants. These two groups are likely to be underrepresented in any adult activity, whether work or recreation, whether controlled by others or entirely by themselves, and whether there is discrimination or not.

Educational contrasts are also great. More than half of all Americans over thirty-five of German, Irish, Jewish, or Oriental ancestry have completed at least four years of high school. Less than 20 percent of all Mexican-Americans in the same age bracket have done so. The disparities become even greater when you consider quality of school, field of specialization, postgraduate study, and other factors that are important in the kind of high-level jobs on which special attention is focused by those emphasizing representation. Those goups with the most education—Jews and Orientals—also have the highest-quality education, as measured by the rankings of the institutions from which they receive their college degrees, and specialize in the more difficult and remunerative fields, such as science and medicine. Orientals in the United States are so heavily concentrated in the scientific area that there are more Oriental scientists than there are black scientists in absolute numbers, even though the black population of the United States is more than twenty times the size of the Oriental population.

Attention has been focused most on high-level positions—the kind of jobs people reach after years of experience or education, or both. There is no way to get the experience or education without also growing older in the process, so when we are talking about top-level jobs, we are talking about the kind of positions people reach in their forties and fifties rather than in their teens and twenties. Representation in such jobs cannot be compared to representation in a population that includes many five-year-olds—yet it is.

The general ethnic differences in age become extreme in some of the older age brackets. Half of the Jewish population of the United States is forty-five years old or older, but only 12 percent of the Puerto Rican population is that old. Even if Jews and Puerto Ricans were identical in every other respect, and even if no employer ever had a speck of prejudice, there would still be huge disparities between the two groups in top-level positions, just from age differences alone.

Virtually every underrepresented racial or ethnic group in the United States has a lower than average age and consists disproportionately of children and inexperienced young adults. Almost invariably these groups also have less education, both quantitatively and qualitatively. The point here is not that we should "blame the victim" or "blame society." The point is that we should, first of all, *talk sense*! "Representation" talk is cheap, easy, and misleading; discrimination and opportunity are too serious to be discussed in gobbledy-gook.

The idea that preferential treatment is going to "compensate" people for past wrongs flies in the face of two hard facts:

(1) Public-opinion polls have repeatedly shown most blacks opposed to preferential treatment either in jobs or college admissions. A Gallup poll in March 1977, for example, found only 27 percent of nonwhites favoring "preferential treatment" over "ability as determined by test scores," while 64 percent preferred the latter and 9 percent were undecided. (The Gallup breakdown of the U.S. population by race, sex, income, education, etc., found that "not a single population group supports affirmative action."[1])

How can you compensate people by giving them something they have explicitly rejected?

(2) The income of blacks relative to whites reached its peak *before* affirmative action hiring and has *declined* since. The median income of blacks reached a peak of 60.9 percent of the median income of whites in 1970 — the year before "goals" and "timetables" became part of the affirmative action concept. "In only one year of the last six years," writes Andrew Brimmer, "has the proportion been as high as 60 percent."[2]

Before something can be a "compensation," it must first be a benefit.

The repudiation of the numerical or preferential approach by the very people it is supposed to benefit points out the large gap between illusion and reality that is characteristic of affirmative action. So does the cold fact that there are few, if any, benefits to offset all the bitterness generated by this heavy-handed program. The bitterness is largely a result of a deeply resented principle, galling bureaucratic processes, and individual horror stories. Overall, the program has changed little for minorities or women. Supporters of the program try to cover up its ineffectiveness by comparing the position of minorities today with their position many years ago. This ignores all the progress that took place under straight equal-treatment laws in the 1960s — progress that has not continued at anywhere near the same pace under affirmative action.

Among the reasons for such disappointing results is that hiring someone to fill a quota gets the government off the employer's back for the moment, but buys more trouble down the road whenever a disgruntled employee chooses to go to an administrative agency or a court with a complaint based on nothing but numbers. Regardless of the merits, or the end result, a very costly process for the employer must be endured, and the threat of this is an incentive *not* to hire from the groups designated as special by the government. The affirmative action program has meant mutually canceling incentives to hire and not to hire — and great bitterness and cost from the process, either way.

If blacks are opposed to preferential treatment and whites are opposed to it, who then is in favor of it, and how does it go on? The implications of these questions are even more far-reaching and more disturbing than the policy itself. They show how vulnerable our democratic and constitutional safeguards are to a relative handful of determined people. Some of those people promoting preferential treatment and numerical goals are so convinced of the rightness of what they are doing that they are prepared to sacrifice whatever needs to be sacrificed — whether it be other people, the law, or simple honesty in discussing what they are doing (note "goals," "desegregation," and similar euphemisms). Other supporters of numerical policies have the powerful drive of self-interest as well as self-righteousness. Bureaucratic empires have grown up to administer these programs, reaching into virtually every business, school, hospital, or other organization. The rulers and agents of this empire can order employers around, make college presidents bow and scrape, assign schoolteachers by race, or otherwise gain power, publicity, and career advancement — regardless of whether minorities are benefited or not.

While self-righteousness and self-interest are powerful drives for those who have them, they can succeed only insofar as other people can be persuaded, swept along by feelings, or neutralized. Rhetoric has accomplished this with images of historic wrongs, visions of social atonement, and a horror of being classed with bigots. These tactics have worked best with those most affected by words and least required to pay a price personally: nonelected judges, the media, and the intellectual establishment.

The "color-blind" words of the Civil Rights Act of 1964, or even the protections of the Constitution, mean little when judges can creatively reinterpret them out of existence. It is hard to achieve the goal of an informed public when the mass media show only selective indignation about power grabs and a sense of pious virtue in covering up the failures of school integration. Even civil libertarians — who insist that the Fifth Amendment protection against self-incrimination is a sacred right that cannot be denied Nazis, communists, or criminals — show no concern when the government routinely forces employers to confess "deficiencies" in their hiring processes, without a speck of evidence other than a numerical pattern different from the government's preconception.

Preferential Admissions

Preferential admissions to colleges and universities are "justified" by similar rhetoric and the similar assumption that statistical underrepresentation means institutional exclusion. Sometimes this assumption is buttressed by notions of "compensation" and a theory that (1) black communities need more black practitioners in various fields, and (2) black students will ultimately supply that need. The idea that the black community's doctors, lawyers, etc., should be black is an idea held by white liberals, but no such demand has come from the black community, which has rejected preferential admissions in poll after poll. Moreover, the idea that an admissions committee can predict what a youth is going to do with his life years later is even more incredible – even if the youth is one's own son or daughter, much less someone from a wholly different background.

These moral or ideological reasons for special minority programs are by no means the whole story. The public image of a college or university is often its chief financial asset. Bending a few rules here and there to get the right body count of minority students seems a small price to pay for maintaining an image that will keep money coming in from the government and the foundations. When a few thousand dollars in financial aid to students can keep millions of tax dollars rolling in, it is clearly a profitable investment for the institution. For the young people brought in under false pretense, it can turn out to be a disastrous and permanently scarring experience.

The most urgent concern over image and over government subsidies, foundation grants, and other donations is at those institutions which have the most of all these things to maintain – that is, at prestigious colleges and universities at the top of the academic pecking order. The Ivy League schools and the leading state and private institutions have the scholarship money and the brand-name visibility to draw in enough minority youngsters to look good statistically. The extremely high admissions standards of these institutions usually cannot be met by the minority students – just as most students in general cannot meet them. But in order to have a certain minority body count, the schools bend (or disregard) their usual standards. The net result is that thousands of minority students who would normally qualify for good, nonprestigious colleges where they could succeed, are instead enrolled in famous institutions where they fail. For example, at Cornell during the guns-on-campus crisis, fully half of the black students were on academic probation, despite easier grading standards for them in many courses. Yet these students were by no means unqualified. Their average test scores put them in the top quarter of all American college students – but the other Cornell students ranked in the top 1 *percent*. In other words, minority students with every prospect of success in a normal college environment were artificially turned into failures by being mismatched with an institution with standards too severe for them.

When the top institutions reach further down to get minority students, then academic institutions at the next level are forced to reach still further down, so that they too will end up with a minority body count high enough to escape criticism and avoid trouble with the government and other donors. Each academic level, therefore, ends up with minority students underqualified for that level, though usually perfectly qualified for some other level. The end result is a systematic mismatching of minority students and the institutions they attend, even though the wide range of American colleges and universities is easily capable of accommodating those same students under their normal standards.

Proponents of "special" (lower) admissions standards argue that without such standards no increase in minority enrollment would have been possible. But this blithely disregards the fact that when more *money* is available to finance college, more low-income people go to college. The GI Bill after World War II caused an even more dramatic increase in the number of people going to college who could never have gone otherwise—and without lowering admissions standards. The growth of special minority programs in recent times has meant both a greater availability of money and lower admissions standards for black and other designated students. It is as ridiculous to ignore the role of money in increasing the numbers of minority students in the system as a whole as it is to ignore the effect of double standards on their maldistribution among institutions. It is the double standards that are the problem, and they can be ended without driving minority students out of the system. Of course, many academic hustlers who administer special programs might lose their jobs, but that would hardly be a loss to anyone else.

As long as admission to colleges and universities is not unlimited, someone's opportunity to attend has to be sacrificed as the price of preferential admission for others. No amount of verbal sleight-of-hand can get around this fact. None of those sacrificed is old enough to have had anything to do with historic injustices that are supposedly being compensated. Moreover, it is not the offspring of the privileged who are likely to pay the price. It is not a Rockefeller or a Kennedy who will be dropped to make room for quotas; it is a DeFunis or a Bakke. Even aside from personal influence on admissions decisions, the rich can give their children the kind of private schooling that will virtually assure them test scores far about the cutoff level at which sacrifices are made.

Just as the students who are sacrificed are likely to come from the bottom of the white distribution, so the minority students chosen are likely to be from the top of the minority distribution. In short, it is a forced transfer of benefits from those least able to afford it to those least in need of it. In some cases, the loose term "minority" is used to include individuals who are personally from more fortunate backgrounds than the average American. Sometimes it includes whole groups, such as Chinese- or Japanese-Americans, who have higher incomes than whites. One fourth of all employed Chinese in this country are in professional occupations—nearly double the national average. No amount of favoritism to the son or daughter of a Chinese doctor or mathematician today is going to compensate some Chinese of the past who was excluded from virtually every kind of work except washing clothes or washing dishes.

The past is a great unchangeable fact. *Nothing* is going to undo its sufferings and injustices, whatever their magnitude. Statistical categories and historic labels may seem real to those inspired by words, but only living flesh-and-blood people can feel joy or pain. Neither the sins nor the sufferings of those now dead are within our power to change. Being honest and honorable with the people living in our own time is more than enough moral challenge, without indulging in illusions about rewriting moral history with numbers and categories.

School Busing

It is chilling to hear parents say that the worst racists they know are their own children. Yet such statements have been made by black and white parents, liberals and conservatives, and without regard to geographical location. It is commonplace to hear of integrated schools where no child of either race would dare to enter a toilet alone. The fears and hatreds of these schoolchildren are going to be part of the American psyche long after the passing of an older generation of crusading social experimenters. It is quite a legacy to leave.

The ringing principles of equal rights announced in the 1954 Supreme Court decision in *Brown* v. *Board of Education* have been transformed by twenty years of political and judicial jockeying into a nightmare pursuit of elusive statistical "balance." The original idea that the government should not classify children by race was turned around completely to mean that the government must classify children by race. The fact that the racial integration of youngsters from similar backgrounds has worked under voluntary conditions was seized upon as a reason for forcing statistical integration of schoolchildren, without regard to vast contrasts of income, way of life, or cultural values. Considerations of cost, time, feelings, or education all give way before the almighty numbers. As more and more evidence of negative consequences to the children has piled up, the original notion that this was going to benefit somebody has given way to the idea that "the law of the land" has to be carried out, even if the skies fall. Less grandly, it means that judges cannot back off from the can of worms they have opened, without admitting that they have made asses of themselves.

The civil rights establishment has a similar investment of ego and self-interest to protect. The NAACP Legal Defense Fund now insists that the issue is not "educational" but "constitutional." This might be an understandable position for an academic association of legal theorists, but not for an organization claiming to speak in the name of flesh-and-blood black people—people who reject busing in nationwide polls and who reject it by large majorities in cities where it has been tried. The head of the NAACP Legal Defense Fund brushes this aside by saying that that they cannot ask "each and every black person" his opinion before proceeding, but the real question is whether they can consistently go counter to the majority opinions of the very people in whose name they presume to speak.

The tragic Boston busing case shows all these institutional ego forces at work. Local black organizations urged Judge Garrity *not* to bus their children to South Boston, where educational standards were notoriously low and racial hostility notoriously high. Both the NAACP and the judge proceeded full-speed-ahead anyway. Black children were forced to run a gauntlet of violence and insults for the greater glory of institutional grand designs. In Detroit, Atlanta, and San Francisco the NAACP also opposed local blacks on busing—including local chapters of its own organization in the last two cities. The supreme irony is that Linda Brown, of *Brown* v. *Board of Education*, has now gone into court to try to keep her children from being bused.

That "a small band of willful men" could inflict this on two races opposed to it is a sobering commentary on the fragility of democracy. Moreover, what is involved is not merely mistaken zealotry. What is involved is an organization fueled by money from affluent liberals whose own children are safely tucked away in private schools, and a crusade begun by men like Thurgood Marshall and Kenneth B. Clark whose own children were also in private schools away from the storms they created for others. The very real educational problems of black children, and the early hopes that desegregation would solve them, provided the impetus and the suport for a crusade that has now degenerated into a numerical fetish and a judicial unwillingness to lose face. What actually happens to black children, or white children, has been openly relegated to a secondary consideration in principle, and less than that in practice.

The 1954 *Brown* decision did not limit itself to ruling that it is unconstitutional for a state to segregate by race. It brought in sociological speculation that separate schools are inherently inferior. Yet within walking distance of the Supreme Court was an all-black high school whose eighty-year history would have refuted that assumption—if anyone had been interested in facts. As far back as 1939, the average IQ at Dunbar High School was 11 percent above the national average—fifteen years before the Court declared this impossible. The counsel for the NAACP in that very case came from a similar quality all-black school in Baltimore. There are, and have been, other schools around the country where black children learned quite well without white children (or teachers) around, as well as other schools where each race failed to learn, with or without the presence of the other. The most cursory look at the history of all-Jewish or all-Oriental schools would have reduced the separate-is-inferior doctrine to a laughingstock instead of the revered "law of the land."

The Court's excursion into sociology came back to haunt it. When the end of state-enforced segregation did not produce any dramatic change in the racial makeup of neighborhood schools, or any of the educational benefits antici-pated, the civil rights establishment pushed on for more desegregation—now stretched to mean statistical balance, opposition to ability grouping, and even the hiring and assignment of teachers by race. If the magic policy of integration had not worked, it could only be because there had not yet been enough of it! Meanwhile, the real problems of educating real children were lost in the shuffle.

However futile the various numerical approaches have been in their avowed goal of advancing minorities, their impact has been strongly felt in other ways. The message that comes through loud and clear is that minorities are losers who will never have anything unless someone gives it to them. The destructiveness of this message—on society in general and minority youth in particular—out-weighs any trivial gains that may occur here and there. The falseness of the mes-sage is shown by the great economic achievements of minorities during the peri-od of equal-rights legislation before numerical goals and timetables muddied the waters. By and large, the numerical approach has achieved nothing, and has achieved it at great cost.

Underlying the attempt to move people around and treat them like chess pieces on a board is a profound contempt for other human beings. To ignore or resent people's resistance—on behalf of their children or their livelihoods—is to deny our common humanity. To persist dogmatically in pursuit of some ab-stract goal, without regard to how it is reached, is to despise freedom and re-duce three-dimensional life to cardboard pictures of numerical results. The false practicality of results-oriented people ignores the fact that the ultimate re-sults are in the minds and hearts of human beings. Once personal choice be-comes a mere inconvenience to be brushed aside by bureaucrats or judges, something precious will have been lost by all people from all backgrounds.

A multiethnic society like the United States can ill-afford continually to build up stores of intergroup resentments about such powerful concerns as one's livelihood and one's children. It is a special madness when tensions are es-calated between groups who are basically in accord in their opposition to num-bers games, but whose legal establishments and "spokesmen" keep the fires fueled. We must never think that the disintegration and disaster that has hit other multiethnic societies "can't happen here." The mass internment of Japa-nese-Americans just a generation ago is a sobering reminder of the tragic idiocy that stress can bring on. We are not made of different clay from the Germans, who were historically more enlightened and humane toward Jews than many other Europeans—until the generation of Hitler and the Holocaust.

The situation in America today is, of course, not like that of the Pearl Harbor period, nor of the Weimar Republic. History does not literally repeat, but it can warn us of what people are capable of, when the stage has been set for tragedy. We certainly do not need to let emotionally combustible materials accumulate from ill-conceived social experiments.

NOTES

1. Gallup Opinion Index, June 1977, Report 143, p. 23.
2. *Black Enterprise,* April 1978, p. 62. A newly released RAND study similarly concludes that very little credit should be given to government affirmative-action programs for any narrowing of the income gap between white and black workers. The RAND researchers write, "Our results suggest that the effect of government on the aggregate black-white wage ratio is quite small and that the popular notion that . . . recent changes are being driven by government pressure has little empirical support" (*New York Times,* 8 May 1978).

Hardy Jones

20. Fairness, Meritocracy, and Reverse Discrimination

Is reverse discrimination ever justified? In recent years this question has received careful attention and the proposed answers are, predictably, quite varied. I will defend a "counterfactual meritocracy theory" for the justification of reverse discrimination. I argue that, subject to certain qualifications and under certain conditions, preferential treatment for members of certain groups is both permitted and required by justice. I assume that discrimination against females and blacks is unjust. The issue is whether employment discrimination against white males in favor of less qualified persons of another sex or color is ever morally justifiable. Another assumption is that employers can use objective standards for determining actual job qualifications — that they have access to, and can follow, nonsexist and nonracist criteria. This assumption may often fail in practice, but that should not affect the moral issue of concern here.

The position I advance differs from much of what is often urged in favor of reverse discrimination. There are several goals of this practice that, while worthy, are not sufficient to justify preferential treatment. Here I present them briefly so as to characterize my view more sharply.

To ensure that discrimination against blacks and females does not continue. Apparently our society is taking a long time to eradicate patterns of injustice that have prevailed for generations. Legislative acts and constitutional amendments appear insufficient. A program of reverse discrimination in employment would surely help to bring certain continuing injustices to a halt. To be assured that they are not being discriminated against, blacks and females may have to be favored.

To present a symbolic denunciation of the racist and sexist past. A well-publicized practice of preferential treatment could have the salutary effect of encouraging victims of unfair discrimination to work hard to overcome unfortunate consequences of injustice. And this gesture might represent a confession of past wrong and a resolution to be fair.

To provide role models for victimized blacks and females. A good way to throw off the shackles of past injustice is to become aware of relevantly similar persons who have good jobs. Noting the success of others in respectable positions, persons may be encouraged vigorously to pursue satisfying careers. This in turn will brighten the prospects of others. And so on.[1] All of these appear to be eminently good reasons for instituting programs of reverse discrimination. None of them, however, carries us very far into the serious complexities of the issue; and, even taken collectively, they aren't strong enough to provide an adequate defense of preferential treatment. What is?

1

Reverse discrimination is an important way of compensating victims by preferring them over beneficiaries of injustice. It seems fair to give extra benefits to those who have been treated unjustly and thus to make an effort toward "evening the score." Those benefiting directly from preferential treatment may not have been discriminated against, but they have suffered from injustices done to their ancestors. The effects of such injustices may involve their having been deprived of the wealth, education, health, or employment essential to equal opportunity competition. The white males to be discriminated against may not be responsible for unfair treatment, but many have greatly benefited from it. So it seems not improper for them now to be deprived, for the sake of fair compensation, of further benefits (in the form of jobs) of past acts of unjust discrimination.[2]

It is important to consider how persons have come to have their actual qualifications for positions. Many better-qualified white males would have been far less qualified had they not reaped the benefits of an unjust system favoring them at virtually every turn. And certain now-worse-qualified blacks and females would have been much better qualified if they and their ancestors had received fair, equal treatment from the start and all along the way. One meritocratic view holds that persons deserve jobs solely on the basis of present merit or ability—whatever their actual qualifications now happen to be. Here I reject this "meritocracy of present qualifications." What is also relevant is how applicants have obtained their qualifications and what these would have been if certain crucial features of their histories had been different.

The notion employed here is "counterfactual meritocracy." Persons are deserving, within the limits specified, of jobs on the basis of what their qualifications would have been if they had been neither victims nor beneficiaries of injustice. There are no insurmountable objections to the practice of a fair meritocracy.[3] What makes the usual meritocracy pernicious is that it allows past injustice to flow into the present by failing to factor-out unjust causes of present job qualifications. Whatever its own defects, fair counterfactual meritocracy attempts to provide a certain sort of corrective. In hiring contexts, the familiar distinction between positive action and negative action often breaks down. Not to practice reverse discrimination is not always merely a failure to rectify injustice. It often also involves, if unwittingly, the active perpetuation of injustice—a positive contribution to the furtherance of injustice. The point applies with special force in cases in which a male and female applicant have approximately equal actual qualifications. It might be urged that here we must invoke a rule of "treating like cases alike." One should give them equally good jobs, or give neither a job, or flip a coin. But their actual merit is not the decisive consideration. In view of the history of injustice, counterfactual factors become quite important. It is not unreasonable to suppose that the male benefited and that the female suffered. If so, they are really not "equally deserving"; their cases are not alike. So treating them equally now would be unfair, and an employer would further injustice by treating unlike cases alike.

It might seem that I am committed to the view that "the sins of the fathers be visited on the sons." Now I do not think that sons should be punished for their fathers' sins or even that they should be required to make restitution for them. It is *not* unreasonable, though, that sons sometimes be deprived of certain benefits that rather naturally derive from injustices done by their ancestors. Such deprivation is especially appropriate when they are competing for jobs with persons who have suffered from sins like those generating the benefits. Such benefits are not "due" them. They do not have a "right" to these good things even if they have themselves violated no one's rights. A son who has inherited stolen property should not be jailed for the theft; but he has no right to the goods and may reasonably be expected to give them up.[4] It seems entirely appropriate that they be transferred to the daughter or son of the thief's deceased victim. The analogy with reverse discrimination is imperfect, but it illustrates a guiding intuition underlying the fair counterfactual meritocracy.

I have stressed the conditions affecting the acquisition of job qualifications. But what if members of certain groups "start out" at levels different from those of other groups? I do not think it necessary to worry whether blacks or females are equal to white males in native or unlearned abilities. I know of no convincing evidence to establish that they are not, and I suspect that differences one way or another are rather minimal and probably negligible. Any relevant variance of this sort could, of course, affect the degree to which we should practice reverse discrimination. Relevant differences in unlearned abilities, however, are those among individual job applicants. Even if it were known that, as a race and as a sex, blacks and females have lesser abilities than white males, that would not be decisive for determining who should be hired. At most, this would be a factor in determining the degree to which lesser or greater actual qualifications are traceable to past injustice. For any given pool of applicants there is likely to be a large variety of differences in unlearned abilities. Some members of each sex/race category will be superior to some other members of each such category. Some white females will be better than certain blacks and certain males; some black males will be better than certain whites and certain females; and so on. It is unlikely that employers will obtain anything like knowledge or reasonable belief as to how who compares with whom with regard to native abilities. It is probably best in practice simply to discount this sort of factor.

But suppose that one knows that A is better qualified than B and that A has inherited superior biological abilities. Even here it is not obviously fair for A to receive the job, for the poor inheritance may be a product of injustice. Suppose B's inferior intelligence is due to his race's most intelligent members having been, for hundreds of years, systematically denied opportunities to reproduce. Then there is injustice in B having low intelligence. Perhaps this is not an injustice to *him* or a violation of *his* rights, since he would not have existed had justice been done. But it is injustice even so. Perhaps, then, he should be given preferential treatment. The failure to do so might not involve treating *him* injustly, but it would further injustice by allowing the products of former injustice to flourish. Good jobs for such persons might reduce these effects. I will not deal further with this sort of case, but it is important to note how injustice affects native abilities as well as acquired qualities.[5]

2

I wish to discuss certain standard objections to reverse discrimination. I will try to show that, subject to certain qualifications, the counterfactual meritocracy theory can withstand this critical scrutiny. And it is natural here to develop and refine the position by considering criticisms.

Insufficient Knowledge?
A scheme based on the notion of counterfactual meritocracy appears to require more knowledge about particular cases than one is likely to obtain. If one does not know that the white male to be passed over, in favor of a lesser qualified black or female, has benefited from injustice in acquiring his qualifications, then one runs a risk of unfairly discriminating against him. There is a strong, and widely shared, intuition that "two wrongs do not make a right" — that we cannot rightly rectify old injustices by committing new ones. It is difficult to evaluate counterfactual claims about what a white male's qualifications would have been without the benefits of injustice or what a black person's qualifications would have been without the liabilities of injustice. How can one tell? Recognizing no special favors and facing tougher competition, the white person might have worked harder to obtain high qualifications. Confronted with less

formidable obstacles, the black person might have felt less challenged to acquire good qualifications. And without injustice numerous factors could have worked very differently in the lives of both. So how could one ever know how good either would have been when they applied for jobs? The smooth operation of a counterfactual meritocracy appears to require an ideal social observer who knows how everyone has been affected by injustice and how things would have been in a just world. Never having such a God's-eye view of human society, we seem destined to be too ignorant to implement a fair program of preferential treatment.

This is a powerful objection, but it can be shown to be not at all devastating. The risk of unfair treatment of white males can be sharply reduced by establishing minimal differentials between better and lesser (yet acceptable) qualifications. A black female would perhaps receive the job if she were slightly less qualified than a white male who happens to be the very best qualified. If the difference is now very small it seems reasonable to suppose that but for unfair, past discrimination the black female would be better. Only a superficial knowledge of racist and sexist injustice in our history is required to show that unfair treatment has been widespread and has touched the lives of almost every person. Though lacking the knowledge of a godlike observer, we are not wholly ignorant of the effects of injustice. It is surely possible to increase our knowledge through interviews and other inquiries into the social backgrounds of job applicants. In many cases there will be sufficient information at least to be reasonably confident that preferential treatment is not unjust. In cases in which a small fraction of the needed knowledge is available, the job might standardly be given to the actually best qualified. A program of reverse discrimination need not be scrapped simply for lack of complete knowledge in all cases likely to arise.

It is also important to be realistic about the quality of available information bearing on present, actual qualifications. Experienced hiring officers have learned that it is quite difficult, and often impossible, to come to know the details of applicants' qualifications. It is not as though one ever has perfect knowledge of this and of how well a person who "looks good on paper (and in person)" will do once he starts the job. We must often acknowledge later that B, who appeared to be less qualified, would have done much better than A, who had seemed to be ideally suited. In such a case, there is a sort of injustice in A having been hired instead of B. This degree of uncertainty does not lead us to conclude that information about actual qualifications is irrelevant to employment decisions. And the, albeit greater, uncertainty of judgments about counterfactual qualifications is not a sufficient reason for ignoring *them* either.

It is useful to reflect on epistemically unavoidable risks in other areas of the social system. It is often difficult to get enough evidence to know whether a defendant is guilty or not guilty. The criminal trial system and the schedule of punishments present serious risks. Some innocent people will be found guilty and punished for crimes they did not commit; some guilty persons will be found not guilty and escape the punishment they deserve. Realistic about such pitfalls, we continue to support the system of indictments, trials, and punishments. We regard the risks of injustice as worth taking. If we are reasonable about this, then surely we are not unreasonable to implement a program of reverse discrimination with *its* attendant risks of unfair treatment. And an injustice of rejecting a deserving white male applicant seems far less serious than that of punishing an innocent person. With the latter we countenance a kind of tragedy. But with generally better opportunities now prevailing for white males, it does not seem tragic to unfairly prefer a female or a black.

There is often the objection that reverse discrimination will involve "punishing" white males in a way that is not fair. This sense of "punishment" is different from that used in discussion of the criminal law, but perhaps there is no harm in an extended use of the term. It would be a mistake, though, to conclude that undeserved "punishment" is as bad in one domain as in the other. Whatever injustices are involved in unfairly preferring blacks or females, punishing a person for a crime he did not commit is almost always much worse. In view of the lesser seriousness of the injustice in reverse discrimination, it seems appropriate to adopt an evidentiary standard rather less stringent than the "beyond a reasonable doubt" criterion for criminal trials. Other things equal, the lesser the *chances* of injustice and the lesser the *gravity* of the injustices the weaker the standard of evidence designed to avoid injustice. I have assumed that something like this principle is intuitively acceptable and that white male job applicants do not need to be "protected" as heavily as criminal defendants.

Furthermore, greater injustice may result from *not* practicing reverse discrimination than from doing so. If persons are hired solely on the basis of present qualifications, then many counterfactually deserving but actually less qualified females and blacks will be rejected. Not having a program for reverse discrimination runs a risk of more extensively victimizing persons already unfairly treated. This risk is more serious than that of unfairly preferring a black or a female to a white male who has not been badly victimized by injustice. It should be clear that I am not endorsing the weaker view that reverse discrimination is always unjust but sometimes overridden by other moral considerations. This part of the discussion can be summarized as follows: (1) Many cases of reverse discrimination will not be unjust and will be required by justice, because the counterfactual factors make the actually less qualified more deserving. (2) When a program of preferential hiring yields cases of injustice to white males, it is justified provided that not having it would involve even more, and more serious, injustices.

Individuals or Groups?

There are problems in preferring persons because they are members of a group most of whose members are victims of injustice and in rejecting persons because they are members of a group most of whose members are beneficiaries of injustice. One difficulty is simply that not everyone deserving compensation will receive it. A preferential hiring scheme cannot accommodate all.[6] One must, I think, acknowledge that reverse discrimination is *only one* method for compensating *some* victimized persons for *some* of the wrongs from which they suffer. It is out of the question to expect it to rectify all injustice. There are many other ways to provide compensation, and these could surely supplement a scheme of preferential treatment in employment. Perhaps a more comprehensive social program could compensate victims more fairly, thoroughly, and efficiently than a limited system of preferential hiring. In the absence of this, it is important to compensate whom one can within the unfortunate limitations. The fact that not every injustice can be rectified should not make us feel justified in compensating no one. The civil law system of compensating the negligently injured does not work perfectly to insure that every victim receives his due. But in the absence of a better one, that system is surely worth keeping. I regard a well-designed scheme of reverse discrimination as analogous.

But there is a more troubling problem. The counterfactual meritocracy would presumably allow market criteria to determine which members of victimized groups get jobs. These persons must still compete among themselves for positions, and the best qualified will obtain them. One result is that those who have suffered most lose out to persons who have suffered less. The better qualified are the ones likely to have suffered less from previous injustices, and those more greatly victimized will be lesser qualified. So the less deserving receive compensation at the expense of those who deserve it more. Compensatory benefits are not distributed in fair proportion to the degree of injustice-engendered liabilities.[7]

"Best qualified" and "better qualified" here refer to actual qualifications of members of the disadvantaged groups. One first groups those who have suffered from acts of unjust treatment. One then ranks these persons in terms of their actual qualifications. The "market criteria" approach would favor the best qualified (from this group) being hired over the actually best qualified of the group of beneficiaries of injustice. But an alternative approach would, if feasible, be more desirable. First, one groups victims of injustice. Next, one ranks them on a scale of actual qualifications. The third step would be to rank them on a scale of "degrees of victimization." Lastly, one adds scores from the second and third steps. The person with the highest score would then be hired, provided that the difference between his actual qualifications and those of the best qualified (of the beneficiaries) is within an acceptable range. If the difference is too large, one could revert to the first approach and select the actually best qualified of the victims. If the difference is still too large, then one would not have any preferential treatment.

A more extreme but not obviously unreasonable alternative would be to select the worst victimized, provided that his actual merit is above a minimal level. The "degrees of injustice" considerations are also relevant here. Reliance on market competition for selection *within* victimized groups would seem less unjust than hiring the actually best qualified and compensating no one. As knowledge of victimization grows, one can gradually incorporate new information so as to award jobs in better proportion to counterfactual merit.

Efficiency?

It is arguable that, even with adequate knowledge as to who deserves how much compensation, the program of reverse discrimination would be socially undesirable. A counterfactual meritocracy, comprehensively administered, could drastically reduce efficiency and productivity. To maintain these at high levels, jobs must be allocated according to actual merit rather than hypothetical "what would have been" qualifications. Everyone will suffer if many of the lesser qualified are preferred over best qualified applicants. And those who are already victims will probably suffer more than the rest. Poor or disadvantaged black students, for example, have a great need for the very best instructors in their schools.[8]

This point suggests a distinction between two kinds of efficiency. A system might be so inefficient that, in view of the serious waste of social resources, it becomes unjust or much less just than it otherwise could be. If this sort of inefficiency is caused by the system of preferential treatment, one must invoke the "degrees of injustice" considerations. There is no way to avoid weighing the inefficiency-engendered injustices against the injustices of allowing past unfairness to flow into the present. And I cannot suggest here just how to strike the balance. What of the other type of efficiency — that whose absence does not involve injustice? Here the problem is less serious, for surely any society must place a higher priority on justice than on efficiency.[9] At the least, *our* society can afford to tolerate some reductions in efficiency in order to rectify injustice and to keep old wrongs from continuing to affect the present.

Also, there are simple methods of minimizing the inefficiency of the scheme. One way is to establish a "threshold of minimal qualifications" variable from job to job. Anyone who is hired should have a degree of actual merit requisite for minimal competence. A person without training in music should not get a job as an opera singer even if it is injustice that has deprived him of the necessary background. Counterfactual merit, even in large amounts, is not a sufficient condition for being hired. No applicant could fall below the minimal standard and still be hired; no one could be hired if he were clearly unqualified. But the very best qualified might be rejected without unacceptable losses of efficiency. Another efficiency-conserving device is a "maximum differential of qualifications," again varying from job to job. This could insure that a lesser qualified applicant would not be hired if he were too far less qualified than someone else. Ideally, the differential would be small enough to minimize inefficiency, yet large enough that some victimized persons are given preference.

Unfairness to White Males?

A consequence of reverse discrimination is that white male applicants, new candidates for newly available positions, bear the major burden of compensation. They are the ones to suffer from this rectification of injustice. But why? Though most young white males have probably benefited from discrimination, they are surely not the only ones. Though some of them have perpetrated injustices against blacks and females, other persons are more largely responsible for unfair treatment. And though white males have tolerated injustices, so has virtually everyone else. Indeed, some victims have, perhaps unwittingly, tolerated injustices against themselves and others in cases in which they could have succeeded in preventing them. So why must white males be the ones to make the heavy sacrifices imposed by demands of compensatory justice? The costs of rectification appear to be unevenly shared among a large group of beneficiaries of injustice.[10]

Again, one must compare the degree of injustice caused by reverse discrimination with that rectified by it. Employment on the model of actual meritocracy brooks injustice by allowing the effects of past unfairness to penetrate into the future. The failure to give compensatory treatment is a failure to rectify injustices, but it also permits them to prevail and to remain infused in our society. All things considered, the amount of injustice tolerated without reverse discrimination may exceed that involved in making young white males bear the burden.

It has been suggested to me that the counterfactual assessments apply to everyone, minorities and majorities alike. I have argued that it is important that people not now be deprived because of injustice toward their ancestors. One critic has conjectured that the plausibility of this idea derives from a broader principle that conditions for which persons have no responsibility should not deprive them of what they would otherwise deserve to have.[11] This principle of responsibility, however, applies to almost every job candidate since so many have been affected by conditions for which they lack responsibility. Isn't such extensive counterfactual assessment impossible? And isn't it unfair to deprive white males by giving great weight to the counterfactual merits of blacks and females?

As earlier arguments suggest, there are reasons for questioning the responsibility principle. Other principles compete with and often seemingly override it. The considerations of justice on which I have relied have an appeal that is quite independent of the broader principle. I have argued that individuals do not deserve to be deprived of what they could otherwise obtain in "straight merit" competition, because of conditions of injustice. And I have claimed that often it is largely past injustice that prevents blacks and females from having better qualifications—ones good enough for them to do well in merit competition. Such persons have suffered, in historically traceable ways, from conditions of injustice; and those conditions have deleterious effects on their ability to compete favorably in a meritocracy of actual qualifications.

But there is another facet to the "white male objection." The case for reverse discrimination appears to rest not merely on blacks and females having suffered from injustice, but also on white males having benefited from it. But what if the latter is not the case? Suppose that even without a history of unfair discrimination, certain white males would have developed qualifications as good as or better than those they now have. Is preferential treatment justified under *these* conditions? I believe that it is, though perhaps the case for giving it is weaker. But why is there here any reason at all for preferring blacks or females with lesser qualifications? My answer is that there is surely a sense in which the white males have been benefited or advantaged *relative to the victimized.* Since the black females' qualifications are lesser than they would have been without injustice, it is injustice which now places the white males in a more favorable position (from the perspective of actual merit). Even if they have never before benefited from unfair treatment, to prefer them over all those who have suffered would allow them now to benefit from debilitating consequences of injustice to others. It is difficult to see why one should think they have a claim or right to such benefits.

So even if the qualifications of white males are invariant across factually unjust and counterfactually just worlds, it is not now unjust to reject them in favor of black females whose unjust world qualifications are somewhat lower. This is true even though the white males suffer so as to rectify injustices that they have neither caused nor exploited. Their suffering is not good, but it is not as bad as making blacks and females *continue* to suffer.

Still another dimension of the problem is that the white males to suffer are mostly young and thus new to the job market. Others who already have jobs have probably benefited more from injustice than new applicants for newly available positions. Older white males have in many cases had secure, satisfying, lucrative, and long careers. Their positions were acquired during times when there was not even the pretense of fair treatment and equal opportunity for blacks and females. And many well-entrenched individuals have been perpetrators, not mere beneficiaries, of injustice. They are much more "guilty" than the young who confront dismal job markets for the first time. It seems only fair that the former be required to share the burden of rectification.

What can be done about this problem? Realistically, probably not very much. But if the society were to choose to pursue compensation in a very thorough way, ways of doing so could be devised. One extreme and presently alarming strategy would be to subject all positions to "reconsideration" and proceed to "hire" again from scratch. Everyone—formerly secure veterans as well as hopeful new candidates—would have to apply.[12] Positions would be filled, within the constraints of knowledge and efficiency, in accordance with some combination of the criteria of actual merit and counterfactual desert. This proposal is interesting, but there is virtually no chance of its being even seriously considered.

There are other ways to lessen the burdens for the young. One sound reason for forced early retirement is that, in view of their roles as perpetrators and heavy beneficiaries of injustice, certain older white males are less deserving than those who would take their places. Here, as elsewhere, the way to do justice is not obvious, and a complicated variety of considerations are relevant. How is one to balance the conflicting factors? The heretofore well-entrenched employees have earned credit for past service that cannot simply be ignored or dismissed. Also, in many jobs long experience is quite valuable for maintaining a high level of efficiency. In all of the professions there are persons whose talents and accomplishments are *so* outstanding that, whatever their "records" as beneficiaries, their early retirement would involve significant social losses. And there is clearly something inhumane about forcing a person to leave a position intimately tied to his self-esteem.

But this combination of factors is not so important that it invariably outweighs the considerations favoring interesting, rewarding careers for younger persons—people with better records as regards discrimination. As matters currently stand, failure to obtain a job now means, for many persons, never having much of a chance to use and benefit from years of conscientious preparation. This also is not a very humane way to run a society's employment system. From this perspective, cutting off a few years at the ends of lengthy careers is often very sensible. Sufferings that result from this practice could be mitigated by early notification of termination and by safeguards designed to protect constitutional rights (and, in colleges and universities, academic freedom). Similar considerations apply to possible curtailments of seniority and tenure advantages. I do not pretend to provide here (or elsewhere!) an ideal or wise scheme for weighing the relevant factors. Reflection on the problem of reverse discrimination soon reveals that the larger issue of "the morality of employment" is very complicated. I have tried to illustrate the richness of the issues and to suggest that the quick defense of the status quo must be seriously questioned.

It should be noted that the need for preferential treatment varies with the degree of victimization of applicants. In some occupations, none of them may have suffered the sorts of injustice that adversely affect the development of job qualifications. I am not proposing reverse discrimination as a general compensatory tool for rectifying all forms of injustice. Perhaps the greatest need is in the professions which require highly specialized training. It is unquestionable that years of racism and sexism have hindered blacks and females in efforts to acquire good qualifications. And a large number have been discouraged from even trying in a serious way. Unfair treatment is pervasive and often affects motivation as well as actual success in getting a job or getting in to a school. The important point here is that the need for reverse discrimination varies not merely with the histories of unfair treatment in the fields but also (and more importantly) with the histories of injustice in the lives of the applicants.

Self-Respect?

If blacks and females know that they have been chosen over better-qualified persons, they may suffer losses of self-respect. But if someone believes he deserves his job because of his merit, ability, and prospects for success, then he can have a strong feeling of dignity or self-worth. Furthermore, wouldn't reverse discrimination be counterproductive with regard to the purposes of being employed? One strong motivation for having a good position is surely enhancement of self-esteem. This aim may be frustrated if persons are not hired solely because they possess the best qualifications.[13]

The criticism can, I think, be met rather easily. First, there are considerations of self-respect that cut in a different direction. There is hardly much rational self-respect on the part of persons whose good qualifications derive heavily from discrimination against others. One cannot expect to enhance reasonable self-esteem by holding a job solely on the basis of actual merit. A useful way for white males to increase self-respect might be to resign and then compete under fair conditions. It would, of course, be unreasonable for individuals to do this unilaterally, but a social system aimed at maximizing self-esteem might try it. White males should suffer no serious losses (as regards respect) if they are rejected in favor of very well qualified persons who have been hurt by injustice.

There would appear to be a stronger sense of self-esteem in foregoing benefits of injustice and in wishing not to profit from unfairness to others.[14]

Should a victimized lesser-qualified person who has been hired lose self-respect? It is surely desirable that employees and prospective employees not be deceived about why they are hired, and it would not be right to tell them that the best qualified are chosen. (Being lied to is still another source of diminished self-respect.) Assuming they should know the truth, how should it be presented to them? I believe that persons given preferential treatment should be told that their lesser qualifications are seen as being due to injustice. If this is correct and if the main claims of this paper are sound, then those who are hired can have the appropriately secure feeling that, whatever detractors may insinuate, they are getting what they deserve.

3

The counterfactual meritocracy theory may be viewed as a natural extension of an intuitive notion of equal opportunity.[15] It compensates for the lack of actual equal opportunity by considering what things would have been like with it. So far as this is determinable, jobs are awarded in accordance with counterfactual merit. One treats persons now so that what they receive is more closely approximate to what they would have naturally obtained in a just world. Such treatment is one good way of lessening the harmful consequences of injustice, but it is not sufficient to assure justice in hiring and working. My view is compatible with the sort of Marxist perspective from which it is claimed that complete justice requires far more drastic alterations in work arrangements. Providing equal opportunity and rectifying violations of equal opportunity are not enough. Social conditions may be such that all workers are exploited and thus treated unjustly even if the hiring processes are untainted by unfair discrimination and invidious selection. The sources of injustice run far deeper than failure to accord equal treatment.[16]

I have not wished to deny or deemphasize any of this. My suggestions regarding counterfactual meritocracy as an extension of equal opportunity are proposals for making social systems less unjust. Hiring in accord with certain counterfactual qualifications provides some increases in justice—or at least curtails further injustices. In a perfectly just counterfactual meritocracy all employees may be exploited by work arrangements, but none are additionally wronged by unfair discrimination. Appropriately cynical, we may view the justice engendered by reverse discrimination as taking place within a wider institutional setting, which is itself unjust.

NOTES

I am indebted to the referees for *Social Theory and Practice* for their criticisms and suggestions. Some ideas contained herein were much less thoroughly developed in my "On the Justifiability of Reverse Discrimination," in *Reverse Discrimination,* ed. Barry R. Gross (Buffalo: Prometheus, 1977), pp. 348-57. A version of that paper was presented at the American Philosophical Association (Western Division) meeting in 1976. I am grateful to Gertrude Ezorsky and Virginia Held for comments on that occasion.

1. Cf. Judith Jarvis Thomson, "Preferential Hiring," *Philosophy and Public Affairs* 2 (Summer 1973): 366-69.
2. Here I am indebted to Louis Katzner, "Is the Favoring of Women and Blacks in Employment and Educational Opportunities Justified?" in *Philosophy of Law,* ed. Joel Feinberg and Hyman Gross (Encino, Ca.: Dickinson, 1975), pp. 291-96.

   On compensation, see also Michael Bayles, "Compensatory Reverse Discrimination in Hiring," *Social Theory and Practice* 2 (Fall 1972): 301-12; James W. Nickel, "Preferential Policies in Hiring and Admissions: A Jurisprudential Approach," *Columbia Law Review* 75 (April 1975): 537-44; and George Sher, "Justifying Reverse Discrimination in Employment," *Philosophy and Public Affairs* 4 (Winter 1975): 160-67.
3. On meritocracy, see John Rawls, *A Theory of Justice* (Cambridge, Mass: Harvard University Press, 1971), pp. 100-108. For a view which questions the practice of "rewarding by desert," see Thomas Nagel, "Equal Treatment and Compensatory Discrimination," *Philosophy and Public Affairs* 2 (Summer 1973): 348-63.
4. For discussion of way in which current holding can be tainted by past injustice, see Robert Nozick, *Anarchy, State, and Utopia* (New York: Basic Books, 1974), pp. 149-55.
5. I am indebted to Gertrude Ezorsky for discussion on these points.
6. Objections like this are offered by Robert Simon, "Preferential Hiring," *Philosophy and Public Affairs* 3 (Spring 1974): 314-17.
7. An excellent discussion of this problem is provided by Alan H. Goldman, "Reparation to Individuals or Groups?" *Analysis* 35 (April 1975): 168-70.
8. Cf. Thomson and Nickel (notes 1 and 2).
9. On justice as the "first virtue" of social institutions, see Rawls, *Theory of Justice,* pp. 3-6.
10. Cf. Thomas, "Preferential Hiring," pp. 382-84. See also Nickel, "Preferential Policies," pp. 21-27.
11. Such considerations were suggested by Ezorsky.
12. For an interesting discussion of similar and alterantive proposals, see Virginia Held, "Reasonable Progress and Self-Respect," *The Monist* 57 (January 1973): 23-27.
13. Cf. Nickel, "Preferential Policies," pp. 553-55.
14. I am indebted here to Held, "Reasonable Progress," pp. 21-27.

15. On equality and equal opportunity, see Ronald Dworkin, "The DeFunis Case: The Right to Go to Law School," *New York Review of Books* 23 (5 February 1976): 29-33.
16. Joel Feinberg has noted interesting complications in the concept of justice. He has shown that acts of injustice are not confined to cases in which persons are unfairly treated in relation to and by comparison with others. See "Noncomparative Justice," *Philosophical Review* 83 (July 1974): 297-338.

PART SIX

Politics of Planning

When President Nixon, in an attempt to justify huge budget deficits, announced that "we are all Keynesians now," he sounded the death knell of Keynesian economics. The economic policies of Lord Keynes, which had gained currency in the United States during the New Deal and became the orthodoxy of liberal politicians, were being embraced by the Republican Nixon. How could liberals remain wedded to Keynesian budget deficits to stimulate the economy during recessions if this was the policy of Richard Nixon?

Perhaps, then, it would be appropriate to say that we are living now in a post-Keynesian era. Chronic inflation, enormous deficits, and burdensome taxation have forced liberals and conservatives, politicians and economists, to search for new policies. Paul Craig Roberts, in a March 1979 article in the *Wall Street Journal,* captured this new spirit:

> Dissatisfaction with the Keynesian management of economic policy reached new heights . . . with the appearance of the 1978 Annual Report of the Joint Economic Committee of Congress. When Senators Kennedy and McGovern [liberals] sign off on a report that disavows more government spending to stimulate the economy and call, instead, for a reduction of the tax wedge on production, chances are it's a new era for economic policy. . . . Gone altogether are the Keynesian ideas that investment is inflationary, that saving is a drag on the economy, and that spending will lead to economic growth regardless of the level of tax rates.

As the three chapters in this part illustrate, there is no universal agreement on what the post-Keynesian solution to our economic problems ought to be.

Abba Lerner contends that the problem of stagflation—that is, the simultaneous manifestation of inflation and high unemployment in an economy—is the principal challenge for a post-Keynesian economic analyst. For Lerner, solving the problem of inflation is critical. Inflation is similar to pollution, Lerner argues, because individual actions such as wage increases impose social costs on others, namely inflation. What he proposes is an incomes policy, a "wage-increase permit scheme," in which businesses would be allocated coupons permitting them to raise wages by a specified percentage. These coupons would be tradeable on the open market, thus allowing for flexibility. Realizing that such a policy might seem too novel for people to accept, he also endorses another incomes scheme, the Tax Incentive Incomes Policy, which would impose additional taxes on any corporation that raised wages above a national norm established by the government.

Several leading analysts have taken a more comprehensive approach to the problems exhibited by our economy. They believe that the failure of Keynesianism is not the failure of interventionism in general, but rather an indication that governmental involvement in the marketplace has not been extensive enough. In fact, this is precisely the position advanced by the Initiative Committee for National Economic Planning, headed by such luminaries as the socialist economist Wassily Leontief, the former president of the United Automobile Workers Union Leonard Woodcock, and the liberal economists John Kenneth Galbraith and Robert Heilbroner. This group contends that America's economic problems can be resolved only by a pronounced step in the direction of socialism; that is, by more governmental control over the marketplace. An office of national economic planning is required in order to establish production goals for all industries, allocate scarce resources, and establish a national economic plan. The group does not recommend complete socialism — the ownership of all the means of production by the state; nominal ownership of industries would be left in private hands but with guidelines provided by the government.

F. A. Hayek, the Nobel Prize-winning economist, has contested the planned economy for decades. In his book *The Road to Serfdom,* he argued that a government-controlled economy would inevitably lead to the destruction of individual liberty. Thus, for libertarian Hayek, economic freedom and personal freedom are inextricably connected. Hayek's post-Keynesian prescription for U.S. economic policy would consist of a return to a free-market economy, balanced budgets, and lower levels of taxation; it would mean an end to government inflation of the money supply and a return to a gold backing for our currency. Economic planning, instead of being a panacea for economic difficulties, would create further dislocations and a decrease in production. On grounds of economic efficiency and individual liberty, Hayek disputes those who advocate more planning by government.

Abba P. Lerner

21. STAGFLATION—ITS CAUSE AND CURE

To be able to deal effectively with stagflation—the combination of inflation with depression—we must first understand it. For this we have to move from a pre-Keynesian overconcentration on microeconomics through a Keynesian overconcentration on macroeconomics to a post-Keynesian integration of macroeconomics with microeconomics.

Pre- to Post-Keynesianism

The pre-Keynesians took prices seriously only as relative prices—as the rate of exchange of goods for goods in the "real" economy. The quantity of money was considered relevant only for the absolute price level. Involuntary unemployment was an excess supply of labor. It would cause the price of labor to fall relatively to the prices of the products. At the lower real wage the market would be cleared, and full employment automatically restored.

Keynes pointed out that this microeconomic argument, while good enough for a single firm or industry, would not do for a general reduction of wages. Costs, and prices, would also fall. There might not be any reduction in real wages, and so no reason why employers would want to increase the number of workers they employed. Depression and unemployment being due to a deficiency in overall spending, what is required is an increase in overall spending. Keynes turned to macroeconomics—to expansionary governmental monetary and fiscal measures—to increase the overall rate of spending in the economy.

Keynes admitted that if wages (and costs and prices) fell far enough, the existing volume of money spending would be able to buy enough at the lower prices to restore full employment; he argued most convincingly, however, that the resistance to falling wages rendered this route of no practical significance. For *upward* movements in wages and prices, however, Keynes remained perfectly classical. The laws of supply and demand did not work for a general deficiency of demand, but the law of excess demand lost none of its power to cause wages to rise in response to excess demand—that is, to an increase in total spending when there already was full employment. This asymmetry—wage flexibility upward but inflexibility downward—indicates that something was missing in the Keynesian revolution.

Wage Administration

Missing was a microanalysis of why the market laws of supply and demand did not work in the downward direction. The answer is that wages are determined not by the market, but by wage administrators—by wage negotiators, representing workers and employers, who have the power to command wages to stay up even when the market is telling them that they should be going down because supply is greater than demand.

Keynesian economic policy to avoid severe depression was beginning to be applied with some success in the 1950s and 1960s, and then the wage administrators discovered that their power to defy the market was not limited to keeping money wages from falling in the face of depression. They discovered that they could also use their power in the upward direction and get money wages to rise even in the absence of any excess demand.

By the early 1970s, extraneous events had brought about a rate of inflation in the United States of about 6 percent per annum, which was generally expected to continue. It was kept going by the wages rising to keep up with the prices, and the prices rising to keep up with costs. The same wage administrators who, with stable prices, had prevented wages from *falling,* now did exactly the same thing, in real terms, by preventing wages from *falling behind* the expected 6 percent rise in prices. And so the inflation could continue. But the law of excess demand—that excess demand always caused inflation—was read backward by the government. They read it as saying that inflation is always caused by excess demand (by too much money chasing too few goods) and their response was to try to check the inflation by holding down the level of spending. This did not stop the inflation (which was not being caused by excess spending) but it did reduce the level of employment and of economic activity and so we had stagflation—inflation with depression.

Keynesians, seeing wages and prices rising even though there was much less than full employment, realized that Keynesianism was not enough. Their response was to turn again to governmental macroeconmic policy (which had been so successful in dealing with depression) for a solution to the new problem of "premature inflation"—inflation setting in before increased spending had brought about full employment.

I was one of those Keynesians. In the middle 1940s I suggested that prices could be kept stable by certain regulations to stop wages from rising more rapidly than productivity. Many others suggested such regulations.

The regulations had two objectives: (1) to stabilize the price level by limiting the wage increases, on the average, to the expected average rate of increase of productivity in the economy; and (2) to bring about appropriate relative movements of wages by awarding higher wage increases in sectors where there was a less-than-average oversupply of labor (unemployment relatively low) and lower wage increases (or no wage increases) where there was a more-than-average oversupply of labor (unemployment relatively high). These ideas also surfaced later in theoretical discussions of "incomes policy" and in practical policies of "wages-price guideposts" under Kennedy and "wage-price guidelines" under Nixon.

Why Incomes Policy Has Failed

The incomes policies were unsuccessful. There are a number of obvious reasons for this. The incomes policies were applied unimaginatively and reluctantly by administrators who did not believe in them and who had consistently declared that they could not work. So much emphasis was put on objective (1), the desired *average* increase in wages, that this came to be regarded as the universally legitimate, fair, and just rate of increase to which everyone was entitled. Objective (2), the adjustments in *relative* wages, was lost sight of. When a severe shortage of some special skill called for an above-average increase in a wage, this was resisted. The regulation, instead of working as a (crude) substitute for the price mechanism, became a price control—an interference with the price mechanism. It interfered with the mobilization of the scarce skills. When the resistance was finally overcome by a bureaucratic recognition of the necessity for an "exception" (or was evaded by the development of a black market), workers everywhere else demanded equal treatment. The regulation then broke down and incomes policy was abandoned.

But there is a more fundamental reason underlying the breakdown of incomes policy. This was the Keynesian neglect of microeconomic or market analysis in favor of macroeconomic policy—governmental regulations—to solve the new problem of stagflation.

The macroeconomic task of adjusting the overall level of spending can be taken over by government because that does not interfere with the market determination of wages and prices. But incomes policy does. Uniform adjustment of all wages freezes relative wages and prices, and the market mechanism is immobilized. Continually changing conditions generate shortages and surpluses, which remain uncorrected, and the regulation must break down. Differential wage adjustments for different levels of unemployment in different sectors do tend to correct the shortages and surpluses. But such regulation is still an incomparably crude artificial substitute for the market. It mobilizes neither the specialized knowledge, nor the personal interest, of the man on the spot. The rules inevitably become much too complicated for general use long before they become sophisticated enough to be able to deal with all the different conditions which are effectively handled, in a market system, by the decentralized decision makers—by the men on the various spots.

The Market to the Rescue

The need for mobilizing the incentives and the initiatives of the decision makers throughout the economy in the operations of an incomes policy was recognized by Sidney Weintraub and Henry Wallich in their "Tax Incentive Incomes Policy" (TIP). This would mobilize the market micro-mechanism by imposing a progressive surtax on corporation incomes, based on the degree to which the corporation granted wage increases greater, on the average, than a national norm established by the government.

The great merit of the scheme is its flexibility. Wage increases above the norm are not prohibited and do not require bureaucratic authorization as justified exceptions. A bigger wage increase has only to overcome the resistance of the bigger tax liability it entails.

To prevent the surtax from being simply added to prices as wage-increase costs, and thus only intensifying the inflation, TIP proposes a completely offsetting reduction in the basic corporation income tax for all corporations. This would protect the average profits of the corporations in the country so that unless there is a change in the average degree of monopoly, any remaining inflation would be due to the average wage increase remaining above the norm, indicating that a heavier surtax is required (and a correspondingly larger reduction in the basic corporation tax rate). The effect of reducing the basic corporation income tax by the amount of the surtax is to cancel the inflation effect of the wage changes while leaving the necessary relative price effect.

However, TIP discourages a wage increase only if it is greater than the norm. But if the *average* wage increase is excessive, social efficiency requires that *all* wage increases be equally discouraged.

A supplement to TIP, suggested by Lawrence S. Seidman, would provide for progressive rebates on the payroll tax—*greater* rebates the more the average wage rate increase is *below* the norm. This would increase the efficiency of TIP by discouraging *all* wage increases, since it provides that the smaller the wage increase, the greater the rebate when the wage increase is below the norm. It still does not give equal discouragement to all wage increases, however.

Inflation as a Pollution

But I find myself much more deeply indebted to Seidman for another contribution. He threw a sudden bright light on the whole issue by pointing out that *raising wages by more than the average increase in productivity is a pollution-like activity (Challenge,* July/August 1976). Inflation pollution is thus comparable to oil-spill pollution or noise pollution, but much more serious. We can apply to the cure of stagflation some recent developments of the theory of environmental protection.

Economists, faced with the popular notion that pollution should simply be prohibited, have pointed out that there is an *appropriate degree of discouragement* of pollution that would result in an *optimum quantity of pollution.* This is where the marginal social benefit from the activities which result in pollution is just equal to the marginal social harm from the pollution. Further restriction of pollution would do more harm than good. The optimum degree of discouragement would be achieved by the optimum charge per unit of pollution committed. The optimum charge is one that is just equal to the social damage done by an additional unit of pollution.

As in the case of other forms of pollution, the government must step in and provide the appropriate discouragement of the inflation-generating acts of raising average wages by more than some norm—such as the average increase in productivity—in order to stabilize average costs and prices.

It is very difficult, if not impossible, to figure the marginal social damage from a unit of inflation-generating wage increases. But this problem too has been solved by the environmental protectionists. If it is hard to figure the marginal damage, which must determine the optimum charge, the total quantity of pollution to be permitted may be set instead. But the optimum allocation of the pollution is still a problem. This problem is solved by issuing a limited number of "pollution permits" and allowing the different polluters to bid for the permits. The result is that the pollution is concentrated in the firms where it makes possible the greatest saving of other factors of production or the greatest increase in valuable output. That is why those firms are able to outbid the others for the permits.

This device is directly applicable to our inflation problem. It is very easy to determine the optimum quantity or degree of inflation. By far the most common view is that the optimum degree of inflation is no inflation.

Wage-Increase Permits

The government can achieve this price-level stability by issuing wage-increase permits equal to 3 percent of the annual wage bill, distributing them to the employers in proportion to their wage bills, and requiring every employer to hold a number of permits equal to the wage increase he pays. The permits would have to be legally tradable or hirable on a free market. Those employers who want to raise wages by more than 3 percent would have to hold the corresponding additional permits. They would be able to get them only by buying them or renting them from employers who raise wages by less than 3 percent and are left with surplus permits. (Any employer who *lowered* wages would be entitled to corresponding additional wage-increase permits, which he would sell or rent out.) The result would be that while wages could rise only 3 percent per annum overall, the freely operating market in the permits would enable the man on the spot to decide how much to increase particular money wages in accordance with the infinite complications of demand and supply on the different markets. Furthermore, no other *direct* government intervention is called for — no surtaxes or tax rebates.

The wage-increase permit plan would, of course, be unacceptable if it led to an increase in the ratio of mark-ups over costs (which would increase profits relatively to wages). But there is little reason to expect this, even though it might appear unfair to have an incomes policy which held down wage increases without a similar mechanism for holding down profit increases. But the latter would be unnecessary because the mark-up is a *ratio* which automatically keeps profits in line with wages. The actual degree of competition, with all its imperfections, has succeeded in keeping the secular share of profits remarkably constant. Any stepping up of the measures against monopoly and restraint of trade would have the effect of *diminishing* the profit share and increasing labor's share of the national product. But much more effective in increasing labor's share would be the intensification of business competition when the cure of both inflation and depression made business enterprise much less risky and a smaller profit per unit would be needed to make enterprise rewarding. The government would therefore be able to leave the problem of depressionary inflation to be solved automatically by the extended market mechanism — including the market in wage-increase permits — and concentrate on the correction of other social inefficiencies.

An Acceptable Cure for Inflation

Although an additional 1 percent of unemployment is incomparably more damaging than an additional 1 percent of inflation, there is nevertheless an important sense in which inflation is our number-one problem. This is because we are not in a position to choose between the evils. As long as inflation continues, governments will continue to treat it as due to excess demand and they will hold down the rate of spending in the economy. This medicine will not cure the inflation but it will continue to give us high unemployment and the "paradox" of stagflation. We must therefore cure the inflation first.

In this article I have attempted to indicate the most logical and most efficient means for offsetting the excessive pressure for rising wages (and thus prices). But the wage-increase permit scheme is too rational, too simple, and too obvious, and therefore too suspect a device. It helps us to understand the issues, but there will have to be decades of debate before the practical problems of its application even begin to be seriously considered. The urgency of the problem therefore calls for an acceptable, if cruder, device that will fit in with our habitual procedures. The Weintraub-Wallich-Seidman TIP proposal is such a device. It would yield a large part of the benefits to be derived from a wage-increase permit scheme. Limited to, say, the thousand largest corporations, its administration would cost a few million dollars, while the gain in national product would run in the tens of billions of dollars.

Any suggestion for improvement does more harm than good if it unduly prolongs debate before action is taken; but I believe the following two modifications of TIP contain that modicum of rationality which would make the proposal more acceptable.

(1) I would consolidate Seidman's diminishing tax rebate (for wage restraint below a norm) with Weintraub-Wallich's increasing tax penalty (for wage increases above a norm). The diminishing tax benefit (like all "subsidies to combat pollution") consists of a lump-sum grant plus a tax per unit of wage increase (pollution). Consolidation means giving each of the corporations included in the plan a lump sum (which may take the form of a tax reduction) and imposing a charge on its average wage increase whether this is above or below "the norm." This means of course that there is no norm for the firm's wage increase. The intention would still be to achieve the *social norm* of wages rising in proportion to productivity and to make the sum of the grants equal to the sum of the charges.

(2) I would base the grant, or tax relief, as well as the charge, not on the profit of the firm but (as in Seidman's addendum) on a previous wage bill. The charge paid by the firm would then be proportional to its average wage rate increase times the base figure. This would prevent unjustified differences in the charge per unit of wage increase because of differences in the profitability of firms or because of the differences in the wage share of a firm's total costs.

Such a modified TIP, unlike the wage-increase permit scheme, would have no market indication of how high the charge would have to be to offset the excess pressure for wage increases. The charge, as well as the grants, would have to be set by trial and error; there would be no room for possible fine adjustment of the number of permits so as to try for a *gradual* reduction of the rate of inflation, if that should be considered desirable. To many it will seem an advantage of the modified TIP over the wage-increase permit scheme that the government could set the charge for wage increases for, say, a year at a time. This would make it easier for firms and labor unions to bargain about wage rates, having to worry only about what the charge would be next year.

However, the differences between the benefits from the "ideal" wage-increase permit scheme, the modified TIP, and the original TIP, even without the Seidman supplement, are minuscule compared with the benefits from any one of them as compared with allowing the stagflation to continue. A suggested improvement that has the effect of delaying rather than expediting some form of incomes policy will constitute a classic instance of the better as the enemy of the good.

Initiative Committee for
National Economic Planning*

22. FOR A NATIONAL ECONOMIC
PLANNING SYSTEM

Few Americans are satisfied with the way in which the economy is now operating. Unemployment is increasing; prices are rising. Inflation in the United States has become a source of instability in the world at large. No reliable mechanism in the modern economy relates needs to available manpower, plant, and materials. In consequence we have shortages of housing, medical care, municipal services, transportation, energy, and numerous other requirements of pressing importance.

We have not made it our business to foresee these critical problems and to take steps to forestall them. We do not plan. But in a modern economy planning is not a matter of preference or ideololgy. It is one of immediate need. In its absence we will all suffer. This suffering is avoidable.

We therefore urge that provision be made for planning at the highest level of the U.S. government and through regional, state, and local units of administration. This effort must be backed by education, by the widest public discussion of the methods and objectives of planning, and by full public participation in the planning process.

National Economic Planning

We believe that economic leadership must be exercised in a new way through an

---

*The Initiative Committee for National Economic Planning was formed on October 14, 1974, for the purpose of promoting the widest possible public discussion on the need for economic and social planning in the United States, and the drafting of legislation to put such planning into effect. The members of the Initiative Committee are Wassily Leontief and Leonard Woodcock (co-chairmen), Anne Carter, Abram Chayes, John Kenneth Galbraith, Robert Heilbroner, Robert Lekachman, Robert R. Nathan, Robert V. Roosa, Myron E. Sharpe, and Nat Weinberg. The following statement was sent to an initial group for reactions and support. Among those who endorsed the statement are the committee members and Clifford L. Alexander, Jr., Lee Benson, Peter L. Bernstein, Hans A. Bethe, Chester A. Bowles, Kenneth Clark, Carl Djerassi, Frances T. Farenthold, Betty Furness, Edmund Gordon, Ray Marshall, J. Irwin Miller, Gerard Piel, Ronald G. Ridker, Arthur Schlesinger, Jr., Melville J. Ulmer, Victor F. Weisskopf, and Willard Wirtz.

Office of National Economic Planning. This office must be in a position to perceive our country's economic and social needs now and for many years to come and to provide the public, Congress and the executive branch with alternative plans of action, not only to enable us to avert hardship and disaster, but to guide the economy in a direction consistent with our national values and goals.

Planning is neither strange nor unfamiliar. Every individual and business plans for the years ahead. Our space program is a good example of planning in its most sophisticated and successful form. It also illustrates the magnitude of the effort that must go into national economic planning. Nevertheless, the principles are simple. First, from a set of feasible alternatives, a definite and realizable goal was decided upon: to carry a man to the moon and bring him back to earth. This required setting up a long-range program to fulfill the mission. All the necessary information had to be gathered together in a consistent and useful form. Then, step by step, the program had to be carried out in the required sequence, the results monitored, and corrections made whenever necessary.

Just as it would have been impossible for a man to go to the moon and back by accident, it is impossible for us to achieve our economic objectives by accident.

But the most striking fact about the way we organize our economic life is that we leave so much to chance. We give little thought to the direction in which we would like to go. We make no consistent effort to balance different parts of the economy. We do not attempt to ensure that resources are allocated to meet our most urgent national needs. In fact, we know that they are not so allocated.

Instead of systematically trying to foresee the needs of the nation in years ahead, we have dozens of separate, uncoordinated agencies making policy in this area and that, without any thought of how it all fits together. We have over fifty federal offices collecting economic data, in most instances insufficiently detailed, frequently obsolete, often contradictory and incompatible. No single office is responsible for setting appropriate standards and bringing these data together so that they can be used to pursue coherent national objectives. We make economic policy from quarter to quarter or year to year without any perspective on where the economy is going or where we want it to go.

How Planning Could Work

The mere cataloguing of these problems reveals the inadequacy of our present economic techniques. We therefore recommend that an Office of National Economic Planning, described below, be established with

> Plenary power to accumulate, collate, and analyze detailed economic information from all sources

A mandate to examine major economic trends and work out realistic alternative long-term economic programs for periods of fifteen to twenty-five years, to be submitted to the President and Congress

A mandate to work out alternative plans of intermediate length, such as five or six years, to be submitted to the President and Congress, designed to carry us toward our long-range objectives

Responsibility to specify the labor, resources, financing, and other economic measures needed to realize these programs and plans

Needless to say, all programs and plans must be periodically reviewed and revised as changing circumstances require.

Let us examine how the Planning Office would go about its work. Its function would be to develop programs in specific areas where there are discernible national needs. Energy, transportation, and housing are obvious examples. But it is clear that a Planning Office cannot look at energy alone, transportation alone, housing alone, or at any other sector of the economy in isolation. All these sectors interact, draw on scarce resources, require definite numbers of workers with specific training, and require financing. Above all, planning is a way of looking at economic problems as a whole, providing the information needed to set explicit priorities in the use of resources, and guiding all sectors of the economy toward the attainment of our chosen goals. A planning system must balance resources with needs, set goals that can be realized, and inform the public what the choices really are.

Plan and Market

The heart of planning is to go from information to action. Most of the action in the U.S. economy takes place in the private sector. Democratic planning is not a substitute for a decentralized economy nor does it replace the millions of private decisions that are made in the market every day. Rather, to reach democratically chosen objectives, it influences those decisions with a consistent set of economic techniques. The means of influencing those decisions are already familiar to us. Some, such as tax incentives and disincentives, and traditional monetary and fiscal policies, influence individual actions indirectly. Others, such as selective credit controls, guidance of basic capital flows, limits to the use of air, water, and land, and mandatory resource allocation, affect individual actions directly. All these measures have been used at one time or another by the federal government, but—save in World War II—in a haphazard fashion, with no view to their overall effect. The purpose of planning is to provide that view.

It should be clear that the Planning Office would not set specific goals for General Motors, General Electric, General Foods, or any other individual firm.

But it would indicate the number of cars, the number of generators, and the quantity of frozen foods we are likely to require in, say, five years, and it would try to induce the relevant industries to act accordingly.

One of the best persuaders available to the Planning Office is information. The flow of goods, services, and money from one industry to another can be grasped in great detail through the use of input-output and other programming techniques. The Planning Office can provide a continuous stream of detailed information about how various sectors of the economy mesh — and are expected to mesh in the future — enabling individual firms, as well as federal, state, and local governments, to make enlightened and coherent decisions about production and consumption.

Organization

In order to be effective and useful, an Office of National Economic Planning must be set up at the center of our economic and political life as one of our most influential institutions. To provide leadership at the highest level, we propose the establishment of such an office within the Executive Office of the President, provided with sufficient funding and supported by a professional staff large enough to carry out the many functions discussed here. The Director of the Office of National Economic Planning should be designated as the chief adviser to the President for economic affairs. The office should oversee the implementation of the national economic plan within the executive branch of government. Accordingly, the membership of the board of this office should be composed of high administration officials and be supported by an advisory group representing the best talent of business, labor, farmers, consumers, minorities, and other sections of society.

We also propose that the Council of Economic Advisers be made a part of the Planning Office and continue to concentrate on short-run problems of full employment and stabilization, usefully supplementing the long-run concerns of the office.

Planning and Democracy

It goes without saying that the final choice among all feasible alternative planning objectives and programs belongs to Congress; and the execution of all laws embodying planning policy is the responsibility of the Administration. Congress and the executive branch must be equal partners in planning. We therefore recommend that a Joint Congressional Planning Committee, supported by a Congressional Office of Planning, with the necessary funding and technical assistance, be established to oversee all planning activities of the executive branch, and to initiate and review legislation related to planning.

But to be successful, planning has to be undertaken with the full understanding, acceptance, and support of the public. The participation of representatives of all important economic and social interests in every phase of planning is essential. Regional, state, and local units of government must fully share in the planning process. Every national forum—the press, Congress, and the executive branch—should be used for a continuous airing of opinion on planning goals and methods. A network of committees representing every area of economic life should be available for mutual consultation with members of the Planning Office.

No one can possibly argue that planning will solve all our problems. Nor will it reconcile conflicting interests between different sections of our society. These will continue to be contested in the political arena as before. But planning can spare all of us the sense of helplessness we feel as the economy drifts from crisis to crisis and replace frustration with a sense of hope, with the conviction that we can, in fact, exert some control over our affairs.

Nor is planning an easy task. It is one of the most difficult enterprises that any society can undertake. But the technical capability and know-how exist to do the job. We believe that the hard thinking, work, and experimentation required by planning effort will be repaid many times over. We are convinced that the American people will respond to the challenge.

F. A. Hayek

23. The New Confusion About "Planning"

I

It is a regrettable but undeniable fact that economics, more than other scientific disciplines, is liable to recurrent fashions and fads, the periodic reintrusion into professional discussion of popular superstitions which earlier generations of economists had successfully driven back into the circles of cranks and demagogues. Inflationism is one of these irrepressible themes which again and again attract some half-trained economists, and the advocacy of collectivist economic planning has become another since it first became popular under this name through its use by the Russian communists. The conception, originally developed by some of the organizers of the German war economy during World War I, was thoroughly discussed by economists in the 1920s and 1930s; and all those familiar with that discussion will agree that it greatly contributed to the clarification of concepts and that one ought today to be entitled to assume that no competent economist who lived through that discussion would ever again talk about the issue in terms of the vague and confused concepts initially bandied about.

Nobody is of course bound to accept what seemed then the conclusions of those discussions, which were very unfavorable to central planning; in any scientific discipline the discovery of new facts or new considerations may lead to the revision of conclusions arrived at in the past. But what one must expect from a professional economist of recognized standing is that he not talk as if those past discussions had never taken place, and that he not use expressions in the ambiguous and misleading senses which had been painfully eliminated in the course of the earlier discussion.

It is in this respect that the pronouncements of Professor Wassily Leontief, recently of Harvard University, in the course of the reopened debate on the subject are so bitterly disappointing. That a senior economist of international reputation should again use the term "planning" in all the ambiguity in which one would expect it to be used these days only by less responsible persons as a propaganda catchword, and that he should simply disregard the essential, if perhaps provisional, conclusions that emerged first from the discussion of central economic planning in the 1920s and 1930s and then from the no less intensive discussion of "indicative planning" more recently is wholly inexcusable. Although the statements with which I shall deal in this paper have been issued mostly on behalf of an "Initiative Committee for National Economic Planning," it would seem that for the economic argument embodied in those statements Professor Leontief must bear the principal responsibility. He is the visible prime mover of the committee and he clearly is the economist among its spokesmen who has the most relevant background of professional work. His co-chairman, Leonard Woodcock, president of the United Automobile Workers, is not, of course, a professional economist and has publicly acknowledged that he did not start to think seriously about economic planning on the part of government until the oil embargo. Indeed, some of the comments he has made rather suggest that he has not thought much about it even now.

II

The worst confusion by which the new American agitation for "planning" is permeated, not excluding the various statements by Professor Leontief himself, was most naively expressed in the first sentence of a lead editorial in the February 23, 1975 issue of the *New York Times*. It asked "Why is planning considered a good thing for individuals and business but a bad thing for the national economy?"

It is almost unbelievable that at this date an honest seeker after truth should innocently become the victim of the equivocal use of the word planning and believe that the discussion about economic planning refers to the question of whether people should plan their affairs and not to the question of *who* should plan their affairs. In reply to this I can only repeat what more than thirty years ago I had, as I even then believed at unnecesary length, explained in a popular book:[1]

> "Planning" owes its popularity largely to the fact that everybody desires, of course, that we should handle our common problems as rationally as possible and that, in so doing, we should use as much foresight as we can command. In this sense everybody who is not a complete fatalist is a planner, every political act is (or ought to be) an act of planning, and there can be differences only between good and bad, between wise and foresighted and foolish and shortsighted planning. An economist, whose whole task is the study of how men actually do and how they might plan their affairs, is the last person who could object to planning in this general sense. But it is not in this sense that our enthusiasts for a planned society now employ this term, nor merely in this sense that we must plan if we want the distribution of income or wealth to conform to some particular standard. According to

the modern planners, and for their purposes, it is not sufficient to design the most rational permanent framework within which the various activities would be conducted by different persons according to their individual plans. This liberal plan, according to them, is no plan—and it is, indeed, not a plan designed to satisfy particular views about who should have what. What our planners demand is a central direction of all economic activity according to a single plan, laying down how the resources of society should be "consciously directed" to serve particular ends in a definite way.

The dispute between the modern planners and their opponents is, therefore, *not* a dispute on whether we ought to choose intelligently between the various possible organizations of society; it is not a dispute on whether we ought to employ foresight and systematic thinking in planning our common affairs. It is a dispute about what is the best way of so doing. The question is whether for this purpose it is better that the holder of coercive power should confine himself in general to creating conditions under which the knowledge and initiative of individuals are given the best scope so that *they* can plan most successfully; or whether a rational utilization of our resources requires *central* direction and organization of all our activities according to some consciously constructed "blueprint." The socialists of all parties have appropriated the term "planning" for planning of the latter type, and it is now generally accepted in this sense. But though this is meant to suggest that this is the only rational way of handling our affairs, it does not, of course, prove this. It remains the point on which the planners and the liberals disagree.

The term "liberal" is of course used here and also in an earlier part of the quote in the classical English, not in the modern American, sense.

I should, perhaps, explain that this was written in a book concerned with the moral and political consequences of economic planning, written ten years after the great discussion of the question of its economic efficiency or inefficiency to which I shall now have to turn. And I might, perhaps, also add that J. A. Schumpeter then accused me with respect to that book of "politeness to a fault" because I "hardly ever attributed to opponents anything beyond intellectual error."[2] I mention this as an apology in case that, on encountering the same empty phrases more than thirty years later, I should not be able to command quite the same patience and forbearance.

III

The great debate of the 1920s and 1930s turned mainly on the question of the justification of the socialist hopes of increasing productivity by substituting central planning for marketplace competition as the instrument for guiding economic activity. I don't think it can now be gainsaid by anybody who has studied these discussions that those hopes were shattered and that it came to be recognized that an attempt at centralized collectivist planning of a large economic system was on the contrary bound greatly to decrease productivity. Even the communist countries have to various degrees felt compelled to reintroduce competition in order to provide both incentives and a set of meaningful prices to guide resource use. We can deal with those older ideals of centralized planning fairly briefly since even the proponents of the schemes under discussion today disclaim that they aim at a system of planning of the kind in which a central authority commands what the individual enterprise is to do—although it must remain doubtful whether what they aim at can be achieved without this sort of regimentation.

We shall therefore content ourselves, so far as the efficiency argument for central direction is concerned, with stating very briefly why such an argument is erroneous.

The chief reason why we cannot hope by central direction to achieve anything like the efficiency in the use of resources which the market makes possible is that the economic order of any large society rests on a utilization of the knowledge of particular circumstances widely dispersed among thousands or millions of individuals. Of course, there always are many facts which the individual conductor of a business ought to know in order to be able to make the right decisions but which he can never know directly. But among the alternative possibilities for coping with these difficulties—either conveying to a central directing authority all the relevant information possessed by the different individuals, or communicating to the separate individuals as much as possible of the information relevant for their decisions—we have discovered a solution for the second task only: the market and the competitive determination of prices have provided a procedure by which it is possible to convey to the individual managers of productive units as much information in condensed form as they need in order to fit their plans into the order of the rest of the system. The alternative of having all the individual managers of businesses convey to a central planning authority the knowledge of particular facts which they possess is clearly impossible—simply because they never can know beforehand which of the many concrete circumstances about which they have knowledge or could find out might be of importance to the central planning authority.

We have come to understand that the market and the price mechanism provide in this sense a sort of discovery procedure which both makes the utilization of more facts possible than any other known system, and which provides the incentive for constant discovery of new facts which improve adaptation to the ever-changing circumstances of the world in which we live. Of course this adaptation is never as perfect as the mathematical models of market equilibrium suggest; but it is certainly much better than any which we know how to bring about by any other means. I believe there is substantive agreement on these points among serious students of these matters.

IV

But, curiously, one recently has begun to hear more and more frequently a new argument which inverts the historical role that the market and the price mechanism have played in maximizing order and efficiency in individual economies and in the world economy at large. It is contended that the market may have been an adequate mechanism of coordination under earlier, simpler conditions, but that in modern times economic systems have become so complex that we no longer can rely on the spontaneous forces of the market for the ordering of economic priorities but must resort instead to central planning or direction. Such an argument carries some superficial plausibility, but, on examination, turns out to be particularly silly. In fact, of course, the very complexity which the structure of modern economic systems has assumed provides the strongest argument against central planning. It is becoming progressively less and less imaginable that any one mind or planning authority could picture or survey the millions of connections between the ever more numerous interlocking separate activities which have become indispensable for the efficient use of modern technology and even the maintenance of the standard of life Western man has achieved.

That we have been able to achieve a reasonably high degree of order in our economic lives despite modern complexities is *only* because our affairs have been guided, not by central direction, but by the operations of the market and competition in securing the mutual adjustment of separate efforts. The market system functions because it is able to take account of millions of separate facts and desires, because it reaches with thousands of sensitive feelers into every nook and cranny of the economic world and feeds back the information acquired in coded form to a "public information board." What the marketplace and its prices give most particularly is a continuing updating of the ever changing relative scarcities of different commodities and services. In other words, the complexity of the structure required to produce the real income we are now able to provide for the masses of the Western world—which exceeds anything we can survey or picture in detail—could develop *only* because we did *not* attempt to plan it or subject it to any central direction, but left it to be guided by a spontaneous ordering mechanism, or a self-generating order, as modern cybernetics calls it.

V

Apart from such occasional flare-ups of old misunderstandings in lay circles, the efficiency argument for central economic planning has almost universally been abandoned. If central direction of all economic activity is still sometimes demanded by serious students, this is on the different and logical argument that only in this manner could the distribution of income and wealth between individuals and groups be made to conform to some preconceived moral standard. Apparently a good many idealist socialists would be prepared to tolerate a substantial sacrifice of material welfare if thereby what they regard as greater distributive or social justice could be achieved.

The objections to this demand for greater social justice, of course, must be and are of an entirely different character from those against the presumed greater efficiency of a planned system. There are two different fundamental objections to these demands, each of which seems to me to be decisive. The first is that no agreement exists (or appears even conceivable) about the kind of distribution that is desirable or morally demanded; the second is that whatever particular distributive scheme were to be aimed at could in fact be realized only in a strictly totalitarian order in which individuals would not be allowed to use their own knowledge for their own purposes but would have to work under orders on jobs assigned to them for purposes determined by government authority.

Freedom in the choice of activity as we know it is possible only if the reward to be expected from any job undertaken corresponds to the value the products will have to those fellow men to whom they actually are supplied. But this value often will unavoidably bear no relation whatever to the deserts, needs, or other claims of the producer. The belief in a society in which the remuneration of individuals is made to correspond to something called "social justice" is a chimera which is threatening to seduce modern democracy to accept a system that would involve a disastrous loss of personal freedom. George Orwell and others ought by now to have taught even the layman what to expect from a system of such kind.

VI

The new American advocates of planning will claim, however, that they know all this and that they never have advocated a system of central direction of individual economic activities and even have said so. Yet it is very doubtful whether what they do advocate would not in fact lead that way. They leave a great deal obscure and it is precisely this state of muddle which is the sure way to hell. To be sure, the statement of the Initiative Committee for National Economic Planning (*The Case for Planning*) says that: It should be clear that the Planning Office would not set specific goals for General Motors, General Electric, General Foods, or any other individual firm. But it would indicate the number of cars, the number of generators, and the quantity of frozen foods we are likely to require in, say, five years, and it would try to induce the relevant industries to act accordingly." But one cannot help wondering how that "inducement" of an "industry" would work if, as the Initiative Committee's statement at another point makes clear, the "means of influencing" the decisions of industry would include "selective credit controls, guidance of basic capital flows, limits to the use of air, water and land, and *mandatory resource allocation* [italics added]."

Indeed, as one reads on, it becomes increasingly difficult to find out what precisely the authors of the statement mean by National Economic Planning. Nor, in spite of its magniloquent language, is the text of the proposed Balanced Growth and Economic Planning Act of 1975, inspired by the Committee and introduced in the Senate by Senators Humphrey, Jackson, Javits, McGovern, and others, in this respect more revealing. While the bill is loquacious on the organization of a proposed Economic Planning Board, it is remarkably reticent on the methods and powers by which this body is to secure the execution of the "balanced economic growth plan" which it is to draw up. About the elaborateness of the proposed machinery there can be no doubt. But what it is to do, and even more important, what good it is to do, is difficult to discover.

Underlying some of these arguments for central economic planning appears to be the curious conception that it would be an advantage, enhancing orderliness and predictability, if the gross outline, a sort of skeleton, of the future distribution of resources between industries and firms could be laid down for a fairly long period. In other words, what is today one of the chief tasks of business, namely to guess as correctly as possible future developments in its particular concerns, would be handled in advance by government decisions; only the details within this general framework would be handled by business. The hope apparently is thereby to increase the opportunity for managers of individual firms to make correct forecasts concerning the facts which will directly affect their activities. But the exact opposite would be the result of such planning; the uncertainty for managers would be greatly increased since the opportunity they would have to adapt to changes in their immediate environments (i.e., the quantities they would have to buy or sell and the prices at which they could do so) would depend on the "mandatory resource allocation," the "guidance of basic capital flows," etc., of the government planning office. For the manager of an individual firm, that halfway house between a completely planned system and a free market would indeed be the worst of all possible worlds, since his ability to make changes would become critically dependent on the red tape, delay, and unpredictability that are characteristic of bureaucratic decisions.

Implied in the argument for government planning of industrial and commercial activity is the belief that government (with an appropriately increased bureaucracy, of course) would be in a better position to predict the future needs of consumer goods, materials, and productive equipment than the individual firms. But is it really seriously contended that some government office (or, worse, some politically sensitive plan-making committee) would be more likely to foresee correctly the effects of future changes in tastes, the success of some new device or other technical innovation, changes in the scarcity of different raw materials, etc., on the amounts of some commodity that ought to be produced some years hence, than the producers or professional dealers of those things? Is it really likely that a National Planning Office would have a better judgment of "the number of cars, the numbers of generators, and the quantities of frozen foods we are likely to require in, say five years," than Ford or General Motors, etc., and, even more important, would it even be desirable that various companies in an industry all act on the same guess? Is it not the very rationale of the method of competition that we allow those who have shown the greatest skill in forecasting to make preparations for the future?

VII

In some sections of the statements made by the new advocates of "planning" it becomes clear, however, that they are thinking mainly of another kind of planning, one which also has been thoroughly examined in the past in a discussion of which its present protagonists show as little awareness as of any other of the earlier scientific examinations of the problem. They show indeed a curious tendency to reject with disdain any suggestion that other peoples' experiences are relevant and insist, in Professor Leontief's words, that "America cannot import a planning system from abroad. Countries differ in their planning methods because the countries themselves differ. We should want and expect a distinctive American style."[3]

The earlier extensive discussion of these problems, from which the American proponents of that other sort of planning ought to have profited, took place chiefly in France in the early 1960s under the heading of "indicative planning." This conception had for a short while attracted much attention until it was decently buried after a thorough discussion at the Congress of French Speaking Economists in 1964 had revealed all the confusion and contradictions involved in it.[4] There is no excuse whatever for ignorance of the upshot of these discussions which are clearly expounded in an excellent book in English by Dr. Vera Lutz.[5]

The whole idea of "indicative planning," it turned out, rests on a curious combination, or rather confusion, of actions — making a prediction and setting a target. It was conceived that somehow a forecast of the quantities of the different commodities and services that will be produced would assist in determining the respective quantities which ought to be produced. The plan is conceived as a forecast by government at the achievement of which industry is to aim.

This sort of self-fulfilling prophecy may at first appear plausible, but on reflection it turns out, at least so far as a market economy based on competition is concerned, to be an absurdity. There is absolutely no reason at all to assume that announcement of a target will make it likely that the aggregates of output named in it will actually be realized by the efforts of a number of producers acting in competition. Nor is there any reason to think that the government, or anybody else, is in a better position than are individual managers acting as they now do to determine beforehand appropriate quantities of different outputs of different industries so that supplies and demands will match.

It is at this point that it becomes clear that the present revival of the planning idea in the United States is inspired by the input-output representations developed by Professor Leontief, and rests entirely, I am sorry to say, on a colossal overestimation by its author of what this technique can achieve. Before the Joint Economic Committee,[6] Professor Leontief is reported to have explained that: "First of all, getting information is a passive activity. It does not tell anybody what to do. Presenting a picture of how good a situation could be if everything is geared nicely is not a dictation."

What Professor Leontief has in mind is clearly the technique of input-output tables which he himself has developed and which show in an instructive manner how, during some period in the past, various quantities of the products of different main branches of productive activity were used up by other branches. How the production of the tens of thousands of different things which are needed to produce a much smaller but still very large number of final products is determined by the market process is a matter of infinite complexity; and how order is brought about by a spontaneous mechanism which we do not fully understand is best illustrated by the very fact that we needed a Professor Leontief to give us even a very rough outline of the gross categories of commodities that in the past have passed from certain main groups of industries to others. One can understand that Professor Leontief wishes to refine and extend that technique and to construct input-output tables not for a few dozen but for a few thousand main classes of products. But the idea that such broad-outline information about what has happened in the past should be of significant help in deciding what ought to happen in the future is absurd. Even if we could get and organize information about the tens of thousands of different commodities actually produced in a specific past period, it would tell us about just one of an infinite number of possible input combinations that could produce a particular array of final products. It would tell us nothing at all about whether that specific combination of inputs or any other combinations would be economical under changed conditions.

The source of belief in the value of input-output representations is the wholly wrong idea that the efficient use of resources is determined mainly by technological and not by economic considerations. That belief is evident in the fact that the advocates of planning visualize a team of a few hundred technical experts (perhaps 500 of them, as we learn from one of their spokesmen, at the cost of $50 million a year[7]) — most of them scientists and engineers rather than economists — working on planning for either the White House or Congress.[8]

VIII

This, I am afraid, betrays a complete lack of understanding of how in the complex order of a great society the efficient use of resources can alone be determined. There is no need, to take a very simple example, for a particular quantity of a particular raw material in order to make a particular quantity of tarpaulins. In a situation in which the buyers of tarpaulins are indifferent to the raw material from which they are made, output can be maximized by choosing among hemp, flax, jute, cotton, nylon, etc., that material which costs least — that is, that which we can obtain for this purpose at the least sacrifice of other desirable products. That we can substitute one material for another in this and thousands of other cases (most of which in practice involve much greater complexities) is due to the circumstances that in a competitive market the relative prices of materials will enable us to determine readily how much more of one material than of another can be acquired at any given expenditure level.

There is, therefore, without a knowledge of prices, no possibility for determining from statistics of the past how much of different materials will be wanted in the future. And statistics of the past help us little to predict what prices will be and therefore what quantities will be needed of different commodities. It is therefore difficult to see what possible purpose would be served if it were announced beforehand what quantities of the different main classes of goods ought to be produced during a certain period of the future.

Even if it were possible, however, to say beforehand for every kind of commodity (or variety of a commodity) how much of it ought to be produced some years hence, it is difficult to see how this should lead the individual enterprises to produce just those amounts which together correspond to the desired quota — except, indeed, on the assumption that it is desired that the different firms should conspire together to produce an output of a certain size (presumably that must be profitable to them). This, in fact, is the ideal which clearly guided the French advocates of "indicative planning." And one cannot help feeling sometimes that the new American advocates of planning have become the innocent dupes of some aspiring cartelists.

The whole idea of "guiding" private industry by announcing beforehand what quantities of different goods firms ought to produce over a long period of the future is a muddle from beginning to end, wholly ineffective and misleading if left without sanctions constraining industry to do what it is predicted that it will do, destructive of the competitive market and free enterprise, and leading by its inherent logic straight to a socialist system. It seems to have attracted all those who since the era of the New Deal have hankered for a revival of President Franklin D. Roosevelt's National Resources Planning Board. Indeed, Professor Leontief has specifically couched his proposal in that way,[9] thereby apparently hoping to give it an aura of progressiveness. Yet, to the economist aware of the serious discussions of these problems during the last forty years these, far from being progressive, are antiquated ideas, completely out of date and in conflict with all that we have learned about the problems involved.

IX

There is, however, yet another undercurrent discernible in the present demands for planning which indeed expresses a very legitimate dissatisfaction with prominent features of our economic life. This involves the hope for a kind of planning which would be highly desirable but which is not only wholly impossible politically in present conditions but also in direct conflict with the other demands for planning. The hope is for government to plan its own activities ahead for long periods, announce and commit itself to the execution of these plans, and thereby make government action more predictable. It would indeed be a great boon for industry if it could know a few years in advance what the government is likely to do. But this is, of course, wholly irreconcilable with the established use of economic measures for vote-catching purposes. Such an idea is even more irreconcilable with demands that government interfere with the activities of private enterprise to make them conform more closely to some plan government has made. The current agitation in the United States for a broad new planning initiative explicitly includes, in most of its variants, an indictment of government for its failure to think out its policies for the longer future. But the legitimacy of that indictment is not a justification for the demand that the same government which so notoriously fails to plan its own affairs should be entrusted with the planning of business.

X

The Balanced Growth and Economic Planning Act of 1975—popularly known after its chief sponsors as the Humphrey-Javits bill—is a decidedly curious product, both as to parentage and other matters. The so-called Coordinator of the Initiative Committee for National Economic Planning—Myron Sharpe, editor of *Challenge*—claims that the bill was originally drafted by members of the Initiative Committee and that the final draft is the "joint product of the Initiative Committee and the original Senate sponsors."[10] Senator Javits, however, is on record as wanting to make it clear that the sponsors of the bill "aren't an instrument for the Committee for National Economic Planning" and that the Committee's definitive statement "isn't applicable to our bill."[11] Senator Humphrey, for his part has offered reassurance that no coerciveness would be involved.* "I can categorically state," he has said, "that it is not the intent of the authors of this bill or of the bill itself, and there is not a single word or phrase in this bill which could be used to expand the government's control over the economy."[12] Indeed the much touted National Planning Bill turns out to be an instrument for an undisclosed purpose. It proposes to create an enormous bureaucratic machinery for planning, but its chief sponsor, while constantly using the magic word planning, admittedly has no idea of what he means by it: Senator Humphrey explained the purpose of the Joint Economic Committee's Hearings on the bill last June by saying: "This is advisory and consultative, and hopefully out of this dialogue and discussion . . . we will come down to a much more clear and precise understanding of exactly what we are talking about and what we mean."[13]

It is difficult for an outsider to understand how, after introducing so ill-considered and irresponsible a piece of legislation—which promises merely an empty machinery with no stated purpose, which will perhaps give us input-output tables for a few hundred commodities that will be of no conceivable use to anybody except some future economic historian, but which may incidentally be used to enforce the disclosure of various sorts of information that would be exceedingly useful to a future authoritarian government—Senator Humphrey should be able to boast that it is his "single most important piece of legislation."[14] Somebody as innocent of American politics as this writer might suspect that the Senator from Minnesota is the unwitting tool of some other, presumably collectivist, wire pullers who want to use the machinery thus created for aims they prefer not to disclose. But when one rereads the accounts of how the campaign for national planning has evolved in the articles of the editor of the magazine *Challenge,* whose hand one seems to recognize also in several of the other statements supporting the plan, one feels reassured that nothing more sinister than sheer intellectual muddle is at work.

---

*In 1978, shortly after this article was published, Senator Hubert Humphrey died. —*Ed.*

NOTES

1. In chapter 3 of *The Road to Serfdom,* The University of Chicago Press, pp. 34ff.
2. J. A. Schumpeter, *Journal of Political Economy* 54 (1946): 269.
3. Quoted by Jack Friedman in the *New York Times,* 18 May 1975.
4. See particularly the contributions of Daniel Villey and Maurice Allais to the *Congrès des économistes de langue Francaise,* May 1964.
5. Vera Lutz, *Central Planning for the Market Economy: An Analysis of the French Theory and Experience* (London, 1969). There is also a briefer earlier statement by Dr. Lutz, *French Planning* (Washington, 1965).
6. *Notes from the Joint Economic Committee,* Congress of the United States, 1, no. 19 (1 July 1975): 10.
7. *Challenge,* May-June 1975, p. 6.
8. *New York Times,* 28 February 1975, "Diverse Group Advocates Economic Planning for U.S."
9. W. Leontief, "For a National Economic Planning Board," *New York Times,* 14 March 1974. Indeed the most familiar figures among the signatories of the statement of the Initiative Committee for National Economic Planning — Chester Bowles, John K. Galbraith, L.H. Keyserling, Gunnar Myrdal, Robert R. Nathan, and Arthur Schlesinger, Jr. — seem to be men who long for a new NRA and who in any other country would be called socialists, but in the United States call themselves liberals.
10. *Challenge,* May-June 1975, p. 3.
11. *Daily Report for Executives,* published by The Bureau of National Affairs, Inc., 11 June 1975, p. A11.
12. *Notes from the Joint Economic Committee,* U.S. Congress, 1, no. 19, p. 19.
13. Ibid., p. 2.
14. "Planning Economic Policy," *Challenge,* March-April 1975, p. 21.

About the Contributors

William U. Chandler is a consultant to the Institute for Energy Analysis, Oak Ridge Associated Universities, Oak Ridge, Tennessee.

John Ehrenreich teaches American Studies at the State University of New York, College at Old Westbury.

John H. Gibbons is a professor of physics at the University of Tennessee.

Nathan Glazer is professor of education and sociology at Harvard University.

F. A. Hayek received the Nobel Prize in economics in 1974 and has taught at leading universities in Austria, Germany, England, and the United States.

Hardy Jones is an associate professor of philosophy at the University of Nebraska.

Steven Kelman is on the faculty at the John F. Kennedy School of Government, Harvard University.

John V. Krutilla is director of the Natural Environments Program at Resources for the Future.

Abba P. Lerner is professor of economics at Queens College of the City University of New York and at Florida State University.

William Lilley III was formerly acting director of the Council on Wage and Price Stability and is now visiting professor of government at the University of Virginia.

Laurence E. Lynn, Jr. is professor of public policy and chairman of the Public Policy Program at the John F. Kennedy School of Government, Harvard University.

Samuel McCracken is assistant to the president of Boston University.

Tibor R. Machan teaches philosophy at the State University of New York, College at Fredonia.

Theodore R. Marmor is professor of political science and public health and chairman of the Center for Health Studies at Yale University.

Lawrence M. Mead was formerly a research associate of The Urban Institute and is currently assistant professor of politics at New York University.

James C. Miller III was formerly assistant director for government operations and research of the Council on Wage and Price Stability and is now a resident scholar at the American Enterprise Institute for Public Policy Research.

R. Talbot Page is conducting research in humanities at the California Institute of Technology.

Ellen Frankel Paul is an associate professor of political science at Bowling Green State University and research director of the Institute for Social Philosophy and Policy. She is also a national fellow at the Hoover Institution of Stanford University.

Murray N. Rothbard is teaching economics at New York Polytechnic Institute.

Philip A. Russo, Jr. is an assistant professor of political science at Miami University in Oxford, Ohio.

Peter H. Schuck was formerly director of Consumers Union, and is currently associate professor of law at the Yale Law School.

Thomas Sowell is a senior fellow of the Hoover Institution at Stanford University.

John E. Tropman is at the School of Social Work at the University of Michigan.

Ernest van den Haag is currently a lecturer on law at the New York Law School.

Bruce L. Welch is president of the Environmental Biomedicine Research Institute, Baltimore, and holds appointments in the schools of medicine at Johns Hopkins and Yale Universities.

Mark D. Worthington is an economist with the Office of Income Security Policy, Office of the Assistant Secretary for Planning and Evaluation, U.S. Department of Health and Human Services.